Finding, Reading, and Using the Law

The West Legal Studies Series

Your options keep growing with West Legal Studies
Each year our list continues to offer you more options for every area of the law to meet your course or on-the-job reference requirements. We now have over 140 titles from which to choose in the following areas:

Administrative Law	Family Law
Alternative Dispute Resolution	Federal Taxation
Bankruptcy	Intellectual Property
Business Organizations/Corporations	Introduction to Law
Civil Litigation and Procedure	Introduction to Paralegalism
CLA Exam Preparation	Law Office Management
Client Accounting	Law Office Procedures
Computer in the Law Office	Legal Research, Writing, and Analysis
Constitutional Law	Legal Terminology
Contract Law	Paralegal Employment
Criminal Law and Procedure	Real Estate Law
Document Preparation	Reference Materials
Environmental Law	Torts and Personal Injury Law
Ethics	Will, Trusts, and Estate Administration

You will find unparalleled, practical support
Each book is augmented by instructor and student supplements to ensure the best learning experience possible. We also offer custom publishing and other benefits such as West's Student Achievement Award. In addition, our sales representatives are ready to provide you with dependable service.

We want to hear from you
Our best contributions for improving the quality of our books and instructional materials is feedback from the people who use them. If you have a question, concern, or observation about any of our materials, or you have a product proposal or manuscript, we want to hear from you. Please contact your local representative or write us at the following address:

West Legal Studies, 3 Columbia Circle, P.O. Box 15015,
Albany, NY 12212-5015

For additional information point your browser at
www.westlegalstudies.com

Finding, Reading, and Using the Law

Anne M. Stevens

WEST

™

THOMSON LEARNING

Australia Canada Mexico Singapore Spain United Kingdom United States

WEST
THOMSON LEARNING™

Finding, Reading, and Using the Law
by Anne M. Stevens

Business Unit Director: Susan L. Simpfenderfer **Executive Editor:** Marlene McHugh Pratt **Acquisitions Editor:** Joan M. Gill **Developmental Editor:** Rhonda Dearborn	**Editorial Assistant:** Lisa Flatley **Executive Production Manager:** Wendy A. Troeger **Production Manager:** Carolyn Miller	**Executive Marketing Manager:** Donna J. Lewis **Channel Manager:** Nigar Hale

Library of Congress Cataloging-in-Publication Data
Stevens, Anne M.
   Finding, reading, and using the law / Anne M. Stevens
      p. cm.
   Includes bibliographical references and index.
   ISBN 0-314-12578-7
      1. Legal research—United States. 2. Legal composition. 3. Legal assistants—United States—Handbooks, manuals, etc. I. Title.
KF240.S784 2001
340'.07'2073—dc21

                                    2001045491

NOTICE TO THE READER

Contents

Preface

Introduction

For too long the law has been the exclusive province of lawyers and judges. If, indeed, law is the set of rules by which a society agrees to be bound, then the idea that "society" needs explainers or interpreters of those rules is anathema. Indeed, a society that cannot understand those rules defeats the major purpose of the law, which is to regulate human behavior and prevent wrongdoing. Because law must be understood by society is the major reason I have spent a large portion of my adult life teaching law to non-lawyers. Teaching access, understanding, and application of the law is essential to returning the law to its rightful owners—society and its members. This book is a vehicle to realize that desire. Although intended primarily as a text in legal research, analysis, and writing for paralegals, it is equally useful (and indeed has been used) to introduce law undergraduates in many disciplines.

At some point, all students must leave their teachers. Above all else, my goal in education is to foster independence and capability in students.

Why I Wrote This Book

This text is truly a labor of love. Soon after I began teaching computer-assisted legal research to paralegal students at the Paralegal Institute at the Elms College in Chicopee, MA, Katherine Currier (the Institute's director) asked if I would be interested in teaching an introductory course in legal research and writing. I said, "Yes." I had spent most of my legal career—first as a law clerk for the Massachusetts Superior Court, later as a staff attorney for the Massachusetts Appeals Courts and United States District Courts in legal research, analysis, and writing. I had been fortunate in my career to have the luxury of pure legal research—working for courts conducting legal research and analysis from an impartial decision-maker's position rather than from an advocacy position. I was fortunate also to begin teaching legal research, analysis, and writing from a syllabus and materials developed by a master educator: Katherine Currier. It is from this knowledge base that many of my teaching ideas and techniques evolved.

I write this book from a love of teaching legal research, analysis, and writing and because of a dearth of undergraduate texts that cover all three of those "elements" of the legal analytical process, legal research (finding the law), analysis (reading the law), and writing (using the law), together. Although law school legal research and writing courses routinely cover these three elements, few books geared to the undergraduate student cover all three of those elements. It is into that void that *Finding, Reading, and Using the Law* steps. I have found it makes little sense to teach legal research without teaching legal analysis (for what then is the point of legal research?), legal analysis without teaching legal writing (for what then is the point of legal analysis?), and legal writing without both legal research and analysis (for what then is there to write?). I therefore cover all three of these "elements" in my courses and in this text.

When I begin teaching, I routinely tell my students to forget whatever they've learned about researching, reading, thinking, and writing, for they are embarking on a new process of research, reading, thinking, and writing. And indeed, these processes are different in law than elsewhere. One of the largest hurdles for students taking legal research and writing is to shed their preconceptions (pre-knowledge) and open themselves up to the rigor of these activities in law. Once open to new ideas, students readily embrace, indeed enjoy, their new skills. Contrary to popular opinion, legal research, analysis and writing are no harder than other new skills—indeed, the interesting subject matter that is the law keeps the process from becoming rote.

To these ends, I dedicate *Finding, Reading, and Using the Law*.

Organization of the Text

I have organized *Finding, Reading, and Using the Law* as legal research, analysis, and writing is organized. Introductory chapters cover how legal professionals organize legal problems and introduce the student to the sources of law. These chapters contain sample and exercise problems used throughout the remainder of the text. Following chapters cover legal research (Finding the Law), analysis (Reading the Law), and writing (Using the Law). The final four chapters introduce various forms of legal writing (in increasing order of rigor): letters, intra-office/research memoranda, advocacy memoranda, and finally, appellate briefs.

Text Features

Each chapter includes a number of useful features:

- ✳ *Textbook Sample Problems:* Examples of concepts are introduced based on the sample exercise introduced in Chapter One: the problem of Vincent McCall, a fourteen-year-old middle school student caught up in a plan to sell pipe bombs.
- ✳ Many *illustrations, forms,* and *sample documents*
- ✳ chapter outlines
- ✳ learning objectives to help focus the student on key concepts

✷ *key terms* and a *running glossary* to help reinforce important terminology
✷ *Review Questions* to test retention of chapter concepts
✷ Exercises derived from a number of sources, including an exercise sample in the first chapter: the case of Kitty Barbour denied employment rights by poor legal advice.

Supplement Package

The text contains a supplement package to aid the student and instructor. The text supplements include:

✷ **Instructor's Manual.** A comprehensive Instructor's Manual offering suggested syllabi, teaching suggestions, transparency masters highlighting text concepts, and answers to the text review questions and exercises
✷ **Web Page.** Come visit us at our Web site at www.westlegalstudies.com, where you will find valuable information specific to this book, such as hot links and sample materials to download, as well as other West Legal Studies products.
✷ **WESTLAW®.** West Group's on-line computerized legal-research system offers students "hands-on" experience with a system commonly used in law offices. Qualified adopters can receive ten free hours of Westlaw®. Westlaw® can be accessed with Macintosh and IBM Pcs and compatibles. A modem is required.
✷ **Citation-At-A-Glance.** This handy reference card provides a quick, portable reference to the basic rules of citation for the most commonly cited legal sources, including judicial opinions, statues, and secondary sources. *Citation-At-A-Glance* uses the rules set forth in *The Bluebook: A Uniform System of Citation.* A free copy of this valuable supplement is included with every student text.
✷ **Strategies and Tips for Paralegal Educators.** *Strategies and Tips for Paralegal Educators,* a pamphlet by Anita Tebbe of Johnson County Community College, provides teaching strategies specifically designed for paralegal educators. A copy of this pamphlet is available to each adopter. Quantities for distribution to adjunct instructors are available for purchase at a minimal price. A coupon in the pamphlet provides ordering information.
✷ **Survival Guide for Paralegal Students.** This pamphlet by Kathleen Mercer Reed and Bradene Moore covers practical and basic information to help students make the most of their paralegal courses. Topics covered include choosing courses of study and note-taking skills.
✷ **Court TV Videos.** Available for purchase:

  ✷ **New York v. Ferguson** — Murder on the 5:33: Trial of Colin Ferguson
  ✷ **Ohio v. Alfieri** — Road Rage
  ✷ **Flynn v. Goldman Sachs** — Fired on Wall Street: A Case of Sex Discrimination?

✳ **Dodd v. Dodd** — Religion and Child Custody in Conflict
✳ **Fentress v. Eli Lilly & Co., et al.** — Prozac Trial
✳ *In re* **Custody of Baby Girl Clausen** — Child of Mine: The Fight for Baby Jessica

Acknowledgements

No text is the work of a single author and *Finding, Reading, and Using the Law* is no exception. I would like to thank the following folks, without whom *Finding, Reading, and Using the Law* would never have happened.

✳ Becky Crommett, dear friend, who managed to make sense of my squiggles and arrows when I couldn't
✳ Doug Danforth and Paul Cohen for their encouragement and support
✳ Liz Hannon, Rhonda Dearborn, . . . and the other kind folks at West Legal Studies who helped me put this text together and whose encouragement kept me going when I would much rather have quit
✳ Katherine Currier, director of the Paralegal Institute at the Elms College; Tony Butterfield and Linda Smirchech, leaders and teachers at the University of Massachusetts School of Management; and Ellen Erzen, Sandra Clawson, and Jules Tryk from Cuyahoga Community College for their example and encouragement
✳ My students at the American Institute for Paralegal Studies — Dolores Kelley, for their willingness to let me use their very fine work in this book
✳ The members of the American Association for Paralegal Education for their continual guidance and example
✳ The reviewers of my book, for their thoughtful advice and suggestions, including the following:

Laura Barnard, Lakeland Community College, OH
Jim Block, J.D. Davenport College, MI
Penny Sherburne Cierzan, MN
Nancy Cooper, Edison Community College, OH
Vickie Brown, Carl Sandburg College, IL
Wendy Edson, Hilbert College, NY
Marcy Fawcett, North Harris County College, TX
Richard Martin, Washburn University, KS
William D. Moyer Jr., Main Line Paralegal Institute, PA
Hamilton Peterson, Georgetown American University, MD
Joy Smucker, Highline Community College, WA

Avenue for Feedback

Just as no teacher (or student) is perfect, no text is without opportunity for improvement. I welcome your comments, corrections, and suggestions for improving *Finding, Reading, and Using the Law*. Those comments, corrections, and suggestions may be directed to:

www.westlegalstudies.com

Dedication

For Yurii, Justin, and Hester with great love and admiration and for Peter . . .

CHAPTER 1

Introduction

Chapter Outline
Textbook Exercise Problem
About this Book and Course
"Thinking Like a Lawyer"
Textbook Sample Problem

Learning Objectives
Upon completing this chapter, the student should be able to

* Identify some legal research materials
* Understand how lawyers analyze and recognize factual information
* Understand how legal research materials are organized
* Recognize the difference between federal and state law
* Recognize the difference between criminal and civil law
* Recognize the difference between procedural and substantive law
* Understand certain legal terms
* Understand the role paralegals play in the general practice law firm
* Look forward to studying how to find, read, and use the law

TEXTBOOK EXERCISE PROBLEM

It was a gray February day in Amherst. The snow, which had been so pristine and picturesque in December, lay piled and filthy in the street. Cars continued to darken it as they splashed by in the drizzle. It was cold, barely 35°, and had rained steadily all morning. I turned up the thermostat in my Main Street law office, unable to shake the bone-deep chill. Amherst is a funny place. Tracy Kidder, a local author, described it quite accurately as "a typical small college and university town that has a fine public school system and a foreign policy."[1]

Shivering, I watched local Quakers across the street holding "Peace" signs in their daily noontime vigil. I wished I were anywhere other than in my office slogging through the financial statements of a local restaurant that had filed for bankruptcy; at least I could be dressed in sweats, bulky socks, and slippers for the work. As I glanced back at the piles of paper on my desk, the rain picked up, beating hard against the office windows. The phone rang. Charlie, our office "guy-Friday," picked it up. I could barely hear him chant, "Stevens and Newport. How can we help you?" through the wall that separated my office from his. I heard no more as I picked up my client's three-month-old bank statement.

Suddenly, Charlie was in my doorway. "Anne, there's a lady on the phone who's quite upset. I barely got her name out of her, Kitty something. I thought you might be willing to talk to her. Paul's still at that deposition."

"Sure, Charlie, anything to distract me from these financial statements," I said. As I started to pick up the phone, Charlie interrupted, "By the way, Kim Hadley, the new paralegal, has completed the chef's tour and is getting used to our filing and word processing systems. She seems really good — is already banging out a draft of the Bentley wills."

"OK," I said, "I'll be out to see her in a few. . . "

I picked up the phone. All I heard was soft sniffling. "Hi," I said, "this is Anne Stevens. How can I help?"

A soft voice sobbed through the telephone. "I - I - I'm so upset — I can't believe he did this to me," the voice answered. "I trusted him."

"Whoa," I said, "Who's 'him'?"

"Mal, my lawyer. Oh, and the chief and Harry. I can't believe it. If Sybil hadn't told me, I never would have known . . . ," the voice choked.

"OK, let's start from the beginning." I said. "What's your name?"

"K-K-Kitty B-B-Barbour," the voice answered.

I jotted down the name on a nearby yellow "sticky" pad. "Where do you live?"

"H-h-here in Amherst. On Cottage Street."

"Well, then, neighbor, what's the address on Cottage?" I asked. I jotted down the number as she told me. "What's your phone number?" Again, I wrote it down as she rattled it off. "Now, what seems to be the problem?" Another torrent of tears, then a word or two I couldn't understand. "What did you say? I can barely hear you," I said. Another silence punctuated by sobs. "I'll tell you what," I said, "how about if you take some time to pull yourself together and come by my office this afternoon? Maybe it'll be easier to talk in person."

"O-O-O K," the muffled voice answered.

"Four o'clock all right with you? Our office is right on Main Street, next to the beadshop... I'll see you then and we can chat over tea, OK?"

"OK."

"Good then, I'll see you at four. You know, I'll bet we've seen each other around town and around the neighborhood a million times. Just never knew who we were." We said our good-byes and I hung up. I got up from my desk, walked out to Charlie's office, and asked where Kim was.

"In the back," he said, motioning with his head.

I wandered back to the office our paralegal uses. I found Kim hunched over the computer typing furiously. "Hi, Kim. Why don't you come into my office? I may have something for you to do already." Kim was a former student of mine at a local college. I was amazed when she agreed to come work for us. She was one of my top students, and I was sure she'd have a million offers after she graduated. We're a small, general practice firm, only Paul, me, Charlie, and a paralegal. We can't pay very well, but our practice is varied enough to make the work interesting ... except for bankruptcies.

"Gosh, I'm glad you're working here. You have no idea how wonderful it is to have a known quantity here. Are you all set? Do you have any questions or problems? Like most law firms, we like written legal analysis to be in certain stylized forms. Everyone here has their own personal computer loaded with word processing and legal software. We all do our own documents. Here is the firm's complete file in the Vincent McCall case, a school expulsion case we handled recently. The file includes interview and research notes, as well as intra-office and court documents in the case. Since the case involved issues of first impression that wound up in federal district court, the file is quite complete; the materials should help you with firm document format, with legal research, and court documents."

"I'd like you to sit in on an interview with the firm's newest client, Kitty Barbour. Although I don't know any of the details of Kitty's case, she'll be coming in this afternoon at 4:00. We'll work together on the case. I suspect her case may need some legal research and analysis. I'd like you to help with that.

You can do your research at the courthouse, which has a fairly complete federal and state legal research collection. You may want to run over there before we meet Kitty this afternoon, if only to get the 'lay of the land.' Also, take a look at the Leah A. file before our meeting to familiarize yourself with the firm's forms. Of course, should you have any questions, I'll be here, as will Paul and Charlie. Anything I can help with right off the bat?"

"No, I think I'm all set. Oh, by the way, do you have any standard form wills, or wills I can use as examples for the Bentley wills?" Kim asked.

"Sure, ask Charlie to pull the Brown file, and you can use the bar association will-making software on the computers. That should help. Anything else?" I asked.

"Nope, guess that's about it. I'm going to grab some lunch and head over to the library — see you a little before 4:00," Kim said. I sighed as I realized I had run out of excuses to avoid the financial statements on my desk . . .

Kim spent much of the afternoon in the local law library. The library staff was helpful, giving her a short tour. Kim noticed the following books in the library:

Black's Law Dictionary
Corpus Juris Secundum
American Jurisprudence Second
U.S. Reports
U.S. Supreme Court Reports
Federal Supplement (first and second)
Federal Reporter (first, second, and third)
Federal Digests
U.S. Code
U.S. Code Annotated
Code of Federal Regulations
North Eastern Reporter (first and second)
Atlantic Reporter (first and second)
South Eastern Reporter (first and second)
Southern Reporter (first and second)
South Western Reporter (first and second)
North Western Reporter (first and second)
New York Reporter (first, second, and third)
State Reporters
State Statutes
State Digests
State Encyclopedias
State Practice Books
Various Treatises
Various Law Reviews
Shepard's Citations for all jurisdictions represented

Later that afternoon, Kim and I interviewed Kitty Barbour.

Anne: Well, here we are. Won't you take a seat here, Ms. Barbour?

Kitty Barbour: Thank you very much.

Anne: May I offer you some refreshments, coffee perhaps?

Kitty: No, thank you. I find I'm drinking too much coffee lately.

Anne: To tell the truth, so am I. Actually, I've stopped having any after my cup at lunch because I find it's keeping me awake at night.

Kitty: Thankfully, I haven't had that problem. But I'm sure it can't be doing me much good.

Anne: Along with too many other things we used to enjoy, I understand. Now, to get some basic information: I have your name, address, and phone number. Are you currently employed?

Kitty: Yes. I work for the local office of the Wall Street Journal, *writing articles about banking.*

Kim: Sounds like a fascinating job.

Kitty: It is, though recently it has become a bit of a headache.

Anne: Your job must force you to keep on top of current economic conditions, both nationally and locally.

Kitty: Yes, it does. Actually, it's easier to understand the national picture, what with all the data in the general news as well as the trade journals. The local picture is much more difficult to read, to predict changes in employment patterns, how local consumers are reacting, and how the business community responds to shifting conditions and the like.

Anne: I assume — and here I'm just guessing — that the articles you write can have a significant effect on the local business scene.

Kitty: Although we like to think that's the case, I'm not sure that's true, at least in today's economy. I have the sense the banking community is simply reacting to rapidly changing conditions rather than setting policies or truly planning. On the one hand, if we don't make capital available, the local businesses will dry up, inventory won't be restocked, building and expansion will be nonexistent. On the other hand, it's risky to make loans; it's harder and harder to predict who's going to be in good condition down the line.

Kim: How does the Journal *decide what to write about? Is it a board decision or does everything rest with you?*

Kitty: Oh no, no. It's never one person. It involves the input of many, many people: Journal *reporters, its administration, its readers, and technical consultants who the* Journal *hires. So, you can see I'm just one tiny cog in a much larger wheel.*

Anne: Do you have any family?

Kitty: Oh yes, the lights of my life: my husband John, my son Johnny, who is now 11, and my daughters Emily, 9, and Hannah, 6.

Anne: And are they well?

Kitty: Oh my, yes, thank heaven. Johnny's a bit of a scamp and Em and Hannah both love ballet; they're so cute. In a funny sort of way, it was my kids, particularly Johnny, who began the events that bring me here.

Anne: Well, that's intriguing. I understand you've had some difficulties. Could you tell me what happened?

Kitty: Well, about twelve years ago, two years after I started working as a police officer for the local police department, John and I were expecting our first child, Johnny. We were quite excited, John and I. However, when I told Police Chief Beamish our happy news, he growled: "Lot of good a knocked-up cop is — Congratulations!"

Anne: That must have been very upsetting. What a cruel thing to say to someone looking forward to the birth of her first child.

Kitty: It really was. But that was just the beginning!

A month later, while I was working the juvenile session of local district court, Tessa Benson, a fourteen-year-old juvenile delinquent, bit me on the ankle as I tried to get her into court. Remembering my police academy training on humane "take-downs," I quickly subdued Tessa and "escorted" her to the juvenile lock-up.

Tessa apparently told her story to her Department of Social Services (DSS) social worker, a young woman I don't think had ever seen — or been — a fourteen-year-old girl. After searching her conscience (and the DSS regulations), the worker decided that, as a mandated reporter, she had to report me for abusing Tessa.

DSS investigated and branded me a child abuser. In the meantime, Tessa's long-absent father, Harry Benson, heard what happened. No doubt Harry thought his ship (Tessa) had finally come in. Claiming that he had searched high and low for his beloved daughter (whom he hadn't seen in thirteen years), Harry filed a multi-million dollar tort action against me and the police department. Chief Beamish fired me.

Kim: My word!

Kitty: On the advice of my union steward, who thought MaI Braithwaite was the best lawyer since Clarence Darrow, I went to see Attorney Braithwaite. He agreed to represent me and said he thought I should be able to get reinstated with back pay. I thought about it and checked around to see if it was typical, and then decided to go with him. He filed a grievance and then there were some, what do you call them, where the lawyers ask you questions in front of a reporter?

Kim: Depositions?

Kitty: Yes, depositions. Anyhow, the police deposed me, and I deposed the chief about the discharge. Soon after that, Braithwaite called me to his office. He said he had an offer from the chief to correct my record but would not reinstate me. Braithwaite thought that was not unreasonable. Well, I did. From what he had told me and from what I'd been able to learn from other people in discharge cases, I thought I could get reinstated with back pay. I told him I wanted at least that to settle. He said he'd go back to the chief, but that I could expect to litigate the case.

I didn't hear from him then for about another six weeks, when I got another call to come in. He said he had done some more negotiating but the chief was adamant. He urged me to settle; after the strain and bother of arbitration, I might end up with nothing, he said. He did, however, offer me $10,000 for what he called the case's nuisance value.

At first, I rejected the offer, but Braithwaite kept pressing me and I finally concluded, reluctantly, that I should take the money and run.

Anne: What happened next?

Kitty: Not much, let me tell you. Naturally nobody, either police departments or private detective agencies, were interested in hiring me. As well, my journalistic and creative writing interests waned. I just couldn't concentrate. After five years of unemployment, I returned to school to take some courses, and with the school's help was able to land my job with the Journal.

Two months ago, I ran into a friend who is a paralegal, I mentioned the case to her at a party. When my friend, Sybil Creasey, heard the story, she thought it sounded like Chief Beamish wanted to get rid of me even before the Tessa incident. She asked me if I'd filed pregnancy discrimination charges against the police department. When I said, "No, I had no idea I could do that," Sybil said: "Lady, you got bad legal advice. Braithwaite should have thought of that." Sybil suggested I come here for advice about suing Braithwaite. Well, I almost hit the ceiling. I would never have settled had I known then about a pregnancy discrimination claim. But Braithwaite never said anything at all about it. I felt hoodwinked.

Anne: You feel Mr. Braithwaite betrayed you. You're angry about it, and want to do something to correct matters.

Kitty: Exactly.

Anne: Let me get some more information about the events before we talk about Mr. Braithwaite. Can you describe exactly what the chief said when you told him you were pregnant?

Kitty: Well, it went pretty much the way I said. He just blurted it out: "Lot of good a knocked-up cop is — Congratulations!"

Anne: Tell us a bit more about your dealings with Attorney Braithwaite. Did you tell him about the Beamish incident when you announced your pregnancy?

Kitty: Of course. I had to go into everything that happened while I worked for the police department: all my citations, any warnings I'd been issued, all interactions with the chief.

Anne: Could you now describe just what Braithwaite told you when you discussed the chief's offer?

Kitty: He said he had spent a lot of time negotiating with the chief, who had a lot of experience in these kinds of cases. Beamish said that I would likely end up at trial and therefore he wouldn't budge from his offer. Braithwaite said I stood about a 50-50 chance of losing and getting nothing. He thought I might have difficulty proving some of my damages. Plus, he said there were advantages to having the cash in hand. Of course, he didn't remind me that after I paid him his $3000 fee and his expenses and the depositions, I would only be left with a little over $3000. Had I figured that out at the time, that alone would have dissuaded me from settling. That hardly seems worth the effort I put into the case.

Anne: You feel you were in the right, have suffered a lot, and deserve compensation accordingly. You resent the fact you didn't get a more appropriate settlement. The experience left you depressed and I imagine that just going through that kind of trauma had an unsettling effect.

Kitty: Yes, very much so. My job at the Journal requires intense concentration and creativity. I'm getting along, but I just don't feel I'm giving the newspaper 100 percent. I've not been able to produce either the journalistic or creative writing that I did before all this happened. I sort of feel like my writing, which had always meant a lot to me, has been on hold and will be into the foreseeable future.

It's also especially galling that Braithwaite got a pretty nice fee, for what he did, out of my suffering. And then when I learned about my possible pregnancy disability claim, I just couldn't believe it. I don't understand how he could do that to me. I mean, I trusted this guy, and then he turns around and does that to me. No offense, but I'm not very high on lawyers at this point. I don't want to get stung again.

Anne: You feel betrayed; you put your faith in Braithwaite as your advocate and he let you down. That hurts. And now you're much more cautious. That sense of suspicion is frustrating; it may reinforce your nervousness, which then, in turn, makes working more difficult.

Kitty: Yes, I believe you're right. It is a vicious cycle.

Kim: That seems fair to say.

Anne: Do you recall what your out-of-pocket losses were?

Kitty: Well, let's see. I lost over $150,000 income in the five years I was out of work. I've had to undergo psychotherapy to the tune of $10,000. What's more, my job with the Journal pays me less — $6,000 less — annually than my police job did.

Anne: I see. To summarize, then, you've gone through a lot; you've experienced stress, suffered emotional difficulties, and were not able to obtain a satisfactory compensation for your injuries. And now you feel your lawyer betrayed your trust in him. From what you've told me, I think the facts warrant going forward, at least for some additional investigation and research. I cannot, at this time, give you any advice on what your alternatives or your chances are. I can tell you that I can see some problem spots: I can't be confident, without further digging, that Braithwaite gave you bad advice, or that his failure to disclose the information about the pregnancy discrimination claim are grounds for recovery. I must also research inadequate counseling as a basis for malpractice before I can properly advise you. I can only tell you now there is cause for proceeding to those next steps, and I would like to help you if you want me to.

Once Kitty left the office, I turned to Kim: "There's a lot of stuff here, a lot of questions. Let me give you the file. Could you spend the next couple of days in the library coming up with a list of issues Kitty's case raises, and do enough preliminary research so we know whether there's any kind of case here? Let me know if you need anything or if you need any help. If I don't hear from you sooner, let's get together first thing Monday morning and see what you've found out. Any questions?"

About this Book and Course

Welcome to the study of law. Much of what lawyers do in advising clients, including legal research, analysis, writing, and advocacy, is like solving a mystery. Like a mystery, the case begins with a legal problem, a question, or a series of questions. It is the lawyer's job to investigate the problem to find out what law bears on the problem, to make sense of many legal materials, and present them in a way that is logical, concise, and compelling. During the advice process, lawyers must always keep the "other side" in mind. Legal advice is only as good as the "other guy's" argument. If a lawyer overlooks a key argument for the other side, or downplays that argument, the client will most certainly be unhappy; unhappy clients rarely pay legal bills happily.

In this course, you will learn that most important, interesting, and challenging part of any legal career: how to find, read, and use the law. This subject is both interesting and tedious, practical and theoretical, challenging and rote. The book begins, in this chapter, with an introduction to thinking about and organizing legal problems. Kitty undoubtedly felt overwhelmed and angry about all the awful things that happened to her. She hardly knew where to start relating her story. All the things that happened to her seemed equally important and equally awful. It is the lawyer's objectivity, her "distance" from the events, that allows her to make sense of those events, to sort out what is legally important from what is unimportant; to sort the hopeless jumble of events into legally significant events and classify those events in a way useful to her investigation.

The book then presents an overview of the American legal system, where law comes from, its various forms, and some of its reasons. This background is helpful to the legal professional during her "legal investigation" and in sorting out the different kinds of legal materials available and their importance to "solving" the mystery, and it helps answer the irate person who says "What do you mean it's not illegal? Well, it should be."

The book continues with a description of the "investigatory (legal research) materials" available to the legal professional and continues with a "game plan" for investigation. Legal research is NOT hard. In ten years of teaching college students (from 17- to 60-year-olds), I never encountered a student incapable of clear, simple, thorough legal research, analysis, and writing. Although occasionally students complain that legal research and analysis are difficult because the subject is new or that legal writing is difficult because their backgrounds are weak in grammar, spelling, and writing skills, by the end of the course, they all know what I always knew: that they can stand tall in their legal communities, for their skills are no less than those of many legal scholars, judges, professionals, and teachers. As a matter of fact, attention to detail often wins the day.

The book continues with a description of how to read the law, how to make sense of the (sometimes) confusing array of materials that seem to bear on the client's problem, and how to apply those materials to the client's problem. Once the harder research and analysis is done, it remains for the legal professional to use what she has learned or present it in a form that is useful to the various legal decision-makers. The book concludes with various forms of written legal presentation; it describes usual, intra-office communications, and communication to courts and other "outside" decision-makers.

Legal research, analysis, and use are all easy (indeed, after a while they become second nature) and fun after the first trips through them. For those first frustrating trips, it may help to approach legal research, analysis, and use as a mystery or puzzle to solve. Beginning with the mystery (the legal issue(s) posed by the client's story), legal research and use includes the investigation into and clarification of the mystery's players, materials, and statements. The mystery-solving process can be competently and simply accomplished through straightforward steps. Individual style and refinements follow experience. Students complaining of the "difficulty" of legal research, analysis, and use are usually those bright, eager beavers so anxious to solve the mystery that they try to shortcut the process and wind up thoroughly baffled and unable to retrace their steps. All legal professionals develop shortcuts; they are, after all, a busy and efficient group. At least initially, however, it is important to resist that "shortcut" urge. Follow the steps to clarify the process enough to recognize "benign" from "professional throat-cutting" short-cuts. This book and your instructor will provide safe shortcuts as you progress through the course. You will soon enough be developing your own shortcuts.

"Thinking Like a Lawyer"

John Houseman proclaimed to his law school contracts class, before each episode of the 1970's television show *The Paper Chase*, "You come here with a skull full of mush. You leave, thinking like a lawyer."

Lawyers do many things, including the following:

✳ they try cases
✳ they write letters
✳ they research legal issues
✳ they interview clients, witnesses, and jurors
✳ they keep time records and collect fees
✳ they supervise other staffers
✳ they negotiate settlements
✳ they prepare and file legal documents in court
✳ they read
✳ they argue
✳ they represent clients in and out of court

The list is long. However, the main thing lawyers provide (the main reason clients seek legal help) is legal advice; although some (very few) lawyers may hire themselves out as "hired guns" — will fight anyone, any time, over any issue (win or lose) — few clients truly want a long exhausting fight (followed by a hefty bill for attorney's fees) over the "principle of the thing." What clients hire lawyers for is advice — to assess their legal problems fairly and advise them whether to fight, give up, or settle.

Interestingly, everything lawyers do (save keeping time records and collecting fees) relates to advising clients. How does a lawyer best advise her client? By finding what the law is, by reading it, by applying the law to the facts of the client's case, by explaining the law and its application to the client, the opponent, and the court. It is no wonder, then, that legal research, analysis, and writing are so fundamental to the legal profession.

As a result of the need to research and to advise clients, legal professionals are always categorizing information. They do it for several reasons: it simplifies the information and issues; it simplifies legal research because legal research materials are arranged categorically; and it simplifies legal analysis and communication of that analysis.

Typically, legal professionals categorize facts and information by whether it involves federal or state law; civil or criminal law; and substantive or procedural law.

1. **Federal law** or **state law.** Either the information raises questions involving the United States Constitution, federal laws, or federal decisions or it raises other, non-federal issues.

2. **Civil case** or **criminal case.** A case brought by an individual against another for relief from the other's wrongs is a civil lawsuit. The plaintiff must prove the elements of her civil case (the **prima facie case** which can be found in statute or in court decisions) by a **preponderance of evidence**; that is, to recover, the plaintiff must prove that all elements of her action more likely than not occurred. If she successfully proves that her version of events was more likely than that of the defendant, she may be entitled to money damages or orders against the defendants to do or to stop doing something (an **injunction**).

By contrast, a criminal action is brought against a defendant for harm so serious (i.e., murder, rape, etc.) that society as a whole has decided to outlaw that behavior. In a criminal case, the government (through a district attorney or other government prosecutor) brings a lawsuit against the criminal defendant. In that suit, the government must prove each element of the crime (detailed in statute) **beyond a reasonable doubt**, that is, to a moral certainty, before the defendant may be convicted. The result of the successful criminal prosecution is a fine or jail sentence.

The differences between criminal and civil lawsuits are summarized in Figure 1–1.

Unfortunately, the differences between civil and criminal actions are not always as clear as Figure 1–1 indicates. A single criminal act may result in both criminal and civil liability. For instance, recall the Pamela Smart case: in that case, Pam Smart, a New Hampshire school teacher, convinced two of her high school students (with whom she was romantically involved) to kill her husband. When the deed was done and after an investigation, New Hampshire brought criminal murder charges against Pam and her students. Pam was eventually convicted of murdering her husband and remains in jail for that crime.

Soon after Pam's conviction, her former in-laws (the victim's parents) launched a civil "wrongful death" action against Pam seeking to recover damages for the loss of their son's companionship and support.

Issue	Civil	Criminal
Harm	Individual(s)	Societal
Parties	Plaintiff v. Defendant	State/United States v. Defendant
Applicable law	Statutes or common law	Statutes
Burden of proof	Preponderance of evidence	Beyond a reasonable doubt
Result	Damages; injunction	Fine or jail

Figure 1–1 Summary of differences between civil and criminal cases.

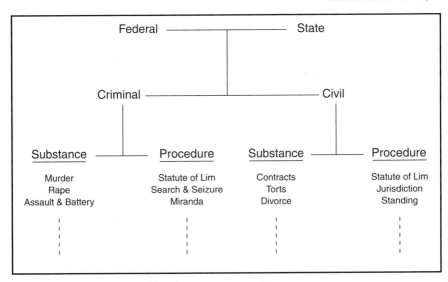

Figure 1–2 Categories of legal issues.

3. **Substantive issues**, that is, issues involving the merits of the dispute, or **procedural issues**, involving how the legal system operates.
This categorization might be diagrammed as shown in Figure 1–2.
The Textbook Sample Problem involving Vincent McCall provides explanations and examples of legal categories.

TEXTBOOK SAMPLE PROBLEM

Summary of interview with Vincent McCall and his parents

Vincent's difficulties began when he was a 14- year-old student at the Cuyahoga Public Middle School. One day, a friend called Vincent over to his locker and showed him a number of metal "tubes" that the friend explained were some really fine fireworks. The friend asked if Vincent was interested in buying a couple. Vincent asked their price and agreed to buy three later that afternoon. In the meantime, the boys selling these "super fireworks" sawed the lock off a nearby locker and stowed their "fireworks" in the other locker — locked, of course with the boys' lock. When the owner of the storage locker came by to get the books he needed for class, he couldn't open the lock anymore. He went to the school administrative office to ask for help. Help came in the form of a janitor who "snipped" the lock off with wire-cutters. When the janitor saw what looked like (and indeed, were) pipe bombs, he called the local bomb squad, who quietly removed the devices for testing and re-locked the locker with yet a third lock. The police then simply staked out the locker corridor until a number of youngsters (including Vincent) gathered around the locker. When they were unable to unlock the lock, the police moved in and took the boys, including our client Vincent, into custody. They were later released to their parents' custody pending the initiation of criminal charges. The school was evacuated for the remainder of the day so that the bomb specialists could ensure that there were no other bombs or incendiary devices on the premises (there were not). An emergency school committee meeting was held that night; the school committee summarily expelled the boys indefinitely.

As the story unraveled, it seems that three boys had learned to make pipe bombs over the Internet and as a lark had made up about ten of the bombs and had taken them to school intending to sell them to some of their friends. As it turned out, of course, no sales were completed and all the bombs were confiscated.

The Problem

Our client, Vincent McCall, and his parents had come to our law firm seeking help. Although Vincent was not one of the original three boys manufacturing the pipe bombs, the McCalls (all of them, including Vincent) agree that Vincent's involvement in the deal was at least stupid. Nevertheless, given Vincent's relatively minor involvement in the deal, they are horrified at the effect the expulsion will have on his chances for college.

Potential Issues

After the interview with the McCalls, I mused: "Hmmm. It sounds to me like the McCalls have more than their share of obstacles to meet. There may be both federal and state claims here in the matter of the expulsion — I wonder if the Individuals with Disabilities Education Act or the Ohio education law have any bearing on the issue of expulsion — and, of course, municipal laws and regulations may bear on the issue. There is also the issue of criminal charges. So far Ohio hasn't brought any charges, but Ohio has one of the stiffest gun control laws in the country. I wouldn't be surprised if some charges were brought. Then, too, there's the law that permits the juvenile court to bind a mature juvenile over for criminal trial as an adult if the crime committed is a serious one..." I needed to talk to Courtney, my legal assistant.

"Hi, Courtney. Could you do me a favor? I've just interviewed the McCalls, our new clients. They're in quite a fix. Seems their son Vincent was involved in buying some pipe bombs that three guys at school made and has been expelled from school. There may also be criminal charges filed against the boy.

"In the next couple of days, see what you can find out about local, state, and federal laws about purchasing pipe bombs or other incendiary devices. Also, look into whether possession of those devices on school property is cause for indefinite expulsion. If, as I suspect, it is grounds for expulsion, see if Vincent

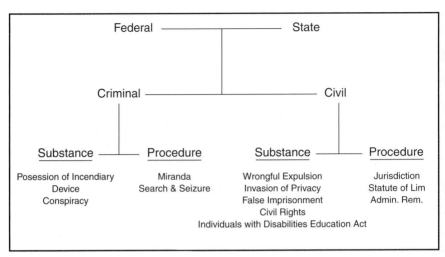

Figure 1–3 Categories of Vincent's case

has any right to appeal the expulsion, what that process is, and the school's obligation to educate him while he is expelled. Once you've narrowed down the list of possible issues, see if you can find any statutes, regulations, agency rulings, decisions, or court cases permitting alternative education under these circumstances. If you think of any other issues in Vincent's case, let me know.

"Once you've done your preliminary research, let's get back together and you can tell me what you've found. If things look promising, I'll tell the McCalls we'll take the case and you can do some more detailed research."

In that five-minute "thinking aloud" process, I noted that Vincent's story raised questions of both federal and state law, civil and criminal issues, and substantive (can a child be expelled under these circumstances?) and procedural (did the school have the right to search the locker without permission?) issues. My analysis might thus be pictured as shown in Figure 1–3.

Review Questions

1. Identify some legal research materials.
2. Explain how lawyers analyze and recognize factual information.
3. Explain how legal research materials are organized.
4. What are the differences between federal and state law?
5. What are the differences between criminal and civil law?
6. Explain the differences between procedural and substantive law.

7. Explain the following legal terms:
   Jurisdiction
   Federal courts
   Civil action
   Injunction
   Prima facie case
8. Explain the role paralegals play in the general practice law firm.

Exercise

Based on Kitty's interview with Anne, analyze Kitty's case under the categorization chart in Figure 1–2. What issues did you find?

Glossary

Beyond a reasonable doubt: The government's very high standard of proof in a criminal prosecution. The *beyond a reasonable doubt* standard reflects society's belief that it is better that ten criminals go free than that a single innocent person be jailed.

Civil case: A case brought between individuals (plaintiff and defendant) for damages or other wrongs allegedly caused by the defendant.

Criminal case: A case brought by the government to redress societal harms; a criminal case is always brought under an applicable criminal statute; the penalties are most often fines, jail, and/or community service.

Federal law: Any case involving the United States Constitution, federal laws, or federal decisions.

Injunction: Court orders against defendants to do or stop doing something or to undo some wrong or injury.

Preponderance of evidence: The standard of proof in a civil case. To prove a case by the preponderance of evidence, a civil litigant need only prove that her version of events more likely occurred than her opponent's.

Prima facie case: The minimum case a plaintiff (or the state) must prove to sustain its burden of proof; the elements of a cause of action.

Procedural issues: An issue involving how the legal system operates: Did police violate the criminal defendant's constitutional right against unreasonable search and seizure? Has the plaintiff waited too long to bring her lawsuit?

State law: Laws of a state or ordinances of a city or town (compare to federal law).

Substantive issues: An issue involving the merits of a law suit: Is the criminal defendant guilty? Did the defendant breach his contract with the plaintiff?

Notes

[1] *T. Kidder, House* 3 (Hougton Mifflin 1999)

Sources of Law

Chapter Outline

Learning Objectives

Upon completing this chapter, the student should be able to

* Understand and explain where American law originates
* Understand constitutional law as a provider of substantive law and a creator of American lawmaking bodies
* Understand the structure and operation of the Constitution
* Explain how a bill becomes law
* Understand congressional authority
* Understand the process of regulation promulgation
* Understand the limits of the judiciary

American Law: What it is and Where it Comes From

To find, read, and use the law, it is necessary to understand the law's forms and sources. The United States is a country of two legal systems: the federal legal system and fifty state legal systems. Fortunately, with few exceptions, state and federal legal systems are similarly structured and used.

Federal Law

When the first immigrants from Europe arrived in America, they arrived from places which still were monarchies. Many of them had felt the tyranny of a strong central government which ruled with an iron fist and made no allowances for individual desires, beliefs, or rights. It is not surprising then that when the colonists came together to forge a new government, uppermost in their desires was protecting the citizens against a powerful central government. That is why, as we'll see, the United States government is a government of expressly limited powers, and why states and individuals hold the bulk of authority in the United States.

Federal Jurisdiction

In this country, the federal government, unlike state governments, is a government of limited **jurisdiction** or power. This means the federal government can act only in certain prescribed and limited subject areas. Those areas include areas listed in Article III of the United States Constitution and cases arising under the United States Constitution, federal laws, and federal executive actions.

Primary limitations on the United States federal government are contained in the United States Constitution. The Constitution was written over 200 years ago, yet has been "**amended**" very little (fewer than thirty times). In many ways the United States Constitution is the source of all federal law: the Constitution is a source of substantive law and rights, many of which are found in its **Bill of Rights** and other amendments, and provides the structure of other federal lawmaking bodies, the three branches of federal government: the federal executive, legislature, and judiciary. The sources of federal law might thus be pictured as shown in Figure 2–1.

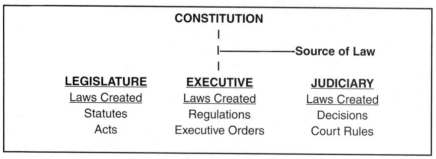

CONSTITUTION

|——————————Source of Law

LEGISLATURE	EXECUTIVE	JUDICIARY
Laws Created	Laws Created	Laws Created
Statutes	Regulations	Decisions
Acts	Executive Orders	Court Rules

Figure 2–1 Sources of Federal Law.

The Constitution: Source of Substantive Law

The United States Constitution is itself a source of substantive federal law. While the main constitutional articles set up and limit the power of the federal government to those matters that must be handled on behalf of all the states (i.e., dealings with foreign governments, waging war, federal taxation, immigration, and naturalization) or must be uniform among the states (i.e., interstate travel), much familiar substantive constitutional law is contained in amendments to the Constitution. For instance, the federal Bill of Rights (the first ten amendments to the United States Constitution) contains many substantive rights, including those shown in Figure 2–2.

Additionally, federal substantive law is contained in other Constitutional provisions and its later amendments. For instance, most federal civil rights legislation is based on the Constitution's interstate commerce clause and post-Civil War Amendments 13 and 14 shown in Figure 2–3.

The Constitution: Creator of Federal Lawmaking Bodies

Article II of the Constitution vests all legislative authority in the Congress to make all laws necessary to federal government operations, as it vests in the president the power to execute those laws, and in the judiciary the power to hear cases and controversies arising under those laws. In vesting those powers, the Constitution both authorizes and limits the powers of each government branch; only rarely and under well-controlled circumstances can one branch of government execute the powers of another. This **separation of powers** in the three government branches requires that each branch exercise its powers exclusively and not grant its authority to, or share its authority with, another branch.

The Congress: Creator of Law

Federal Congressional Authority.   The United States Constitution grants to **Congress**, the federal legislature, "all legislative power" necessary to make "all Laws which shall be necessary and proper for carrying into Execution" specific federal powers.

Congressional Structure and Operation.   The Constitution creates a **bicameral** (two-house) body of elected officials to enact federal law: (1) the **Senate**, with two elected senators from each state, each serving six-year terms, and (2) the **House of Representatives**, with its varying numbers (based on population) of state-elected representatives each serving two-year terms. The Senate and the House of Representatives, while performing similar tasks, perform those tasks differently. The Senate, because of its size, its members' longer terms, and broader constituency, is the legislative "generalist." Because its members' powers are more evenly distributed across the country's population than those of the House of Representatives, the Senate's legislative process is usually more cautious and deliberate than that of the House of Representatives. The House of Representatives, on the other hand, because

AMENDMENT 1: Religious and political freedom, freedom of speech.

Congress shall make no law respecting an establishment of religion, or prohibiting the free exercise thereof; or abridging the freedom of speech, or of the press; or the right of the people peaceably to assemble, and to petition the Government for a redress of grievances.

AMENDMENT 2: Right to bear arms.

A well-regulated Militia, being necessary to the security of a free State, the right of the people to keep and bear Arms, shall not be infringed.

AMENDMENT 4: Right against unreasonable searches and seizures.

The right of the people to be secure in their persons, houses, papers, and effects, against unreasonable searches and seizures, shall not be violated, and no Warrants shall issue, but upon probable cause, supported by Oath or affirmation, and particularly describing the place to be searched, and the persons or things to be seized.

AMENDMENT 5: Due process of law and just compensation clauses.

No person shall be held to answer for a capital, or otherwise infamous crime, unless on a presentment or indictment of a Grand Jury, except in cases arising in the land or naval forces, or in the Militia, when in actual service in time of War or public danger; nor shall any person be subject for the same offense to be twice put in jeopardy of life or limb; nor shall be compelled in any criminal case to be a witness against himself, nor be deprived of life, liberty, or property, without due process of law; nor shall private property be taken for public use, without just compensation.

AMENDMENT 6: Rights of the accused.

In all criminal prosecutions, the accused shall enjoy the right to a speedy and public trial, by an impartial jury of the State and district wherein the crime shall have been committed, which district shall have been previously ascertained by law, and to be informed of the nature and cause of the accusation; to be confronted with the witnesses against him; to have compulsory process for obtaining witnesses in his favor, and to have the Assistance of Counsel for his defense.

AMENDMENT 7: Trial by jury in civil cases.

In Suits at common law, where the value in controversy shall exceed twenty dollars, the right of trial by jury shall be preserved, and no fact tried by a jury shall be otherwise re-examined in any Court of the United States, than according to the rules of the common law.

AMENDMENT 8: No excessive bail.

Excessive bail shall not be required, nor excessive fines imposed, nor cruel and unusual punishments inflicted.

AMENDMENT 10: Powers reserved to states or people.

The powers not delegated to the United States by the Constitution, nor prohibited by it to the States, are reserved to the States respectively, or to the people. . . . .

Figure 2–2 Selected Substantive Amendments to the United States Constitution.

AMENDMENT 13: Abolishment of slavery

Neither slavery nor involuntary servitude, except as a punishment for crime whereof the party shall have been duly convicted shall exist within the United States, or any place subject to their jurisdiction.

AMENDMENT 14: Due process of law/equal protection.

All persons born or naturalized in the United States, and subject to the jurisdiction thereof, are citizens of the United States and of the State wherein they reside. No State shall make or enforce any law which shall abridge the privileges or immunities of citizens of the United States; nor shall any State deprive any person of life, liberty, or Property, without due Process of law; nor deny to any person within its jurisdiction the equal Protection of the laws.

Figure 2–3 Constitutional amendments 13 and 14.

of its larger membership (435), its members' shorter service (i.e., two years), and their narrower constituency, decides more quickly — at times, tumultuously.

How a Bill Becomes Law. Legislation is the process by which government (and those governed) present and encourage policy. It is therefore an **educative process** and a **deliberative process** (rather than an executive or dispute resolution process)[1]. Despite their differences, both federal congressional houses follow similar legislative steps.

1. Introduction of proposed legislation (a **bill**)
2. Referral to committee
3. Committee hearings, debates, amendment, and report to the full house
4. Full house debate, modification, and amendment
5. Referral to conference committee to resolve House and Senate differences; followed by full house debate and passage
6. Transmission of the **act** or **public law** to the President for signature
7. If the President rejects the act (a **veto**) or fails to approve the act within ten days (a **pocket veto**), Congress may override the President's veto by two-thirds vote in each house.

Figure 2–4 illustrates passage of a law by the federal government.

Legislation not passed during a two-year legislative session must be reintroduced in a later legislative session.

Codification. Once a law is enacted, it is published as a **slip law**. Depending on the length and complexity of the enacted law, a slip law may be a single page or a several-page "brochure." Slip laws are published by public law number. At the end of a legislative session, slip laws are gathered and published chronologically as

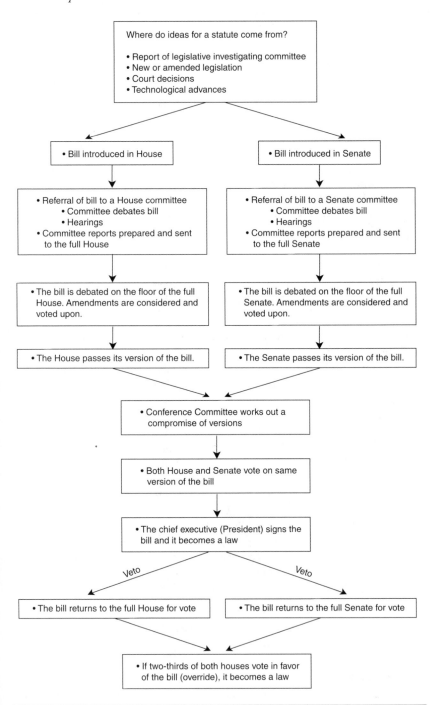

Figure 2–4 How a bill becomes law. Courtesy of Cohen Prac. Adm. Law

"session laws" in hardbound volumes like the **United States Statutes at Large** by public law number. From the statutes at large, publishers like the Government Printing Office, West Group®, and Reed Elsevier, **codify** those statutes, that is, update topically arranged and indexed compilations with "slip law" amendments.

An Example of Federal Legislation: Excerpt from the Gun Free Schools Act of 1994.
Figure 2–5 is an example of a section of the federal Gun Free Schools Act.

The Executive: Implementer of Law

Federal Executive Authority. United States Constitution Art. II vests "[t]he executive Power . . . in a President of the United States [which has the] Power [to] appoint . . . all other Officers of the United States."

Executive Structure and Operation: Executive Departments and Agencies.
Passed legislation, which represents the compromise of many political positions, is usually broad, "plain-vanilla," and non-controversial. To help implement those broad policy statements, Congress may create or empower a federal **executive department** or "officer" (a federal executive agency) to create the detailed implementing rules (also called **regulations**). The Gun Free School Act is typical: 20 U.S.C. § 8921 (1994) requires the United States Secretary of Education to promulgate such regulations as are necessary to carry out the act's requirements. These rules are one source of federal executive law.

To be enforceable, agencies must follow specific procedures in passing or **promulgating** regulations. There are a number of different rule-making procedures followed by the federal government, but by far the most common federal rule-making procedure is informal or "notice and comment" rule making. In informal rule making, an agency must follow the requirements shown in Figure 2–6.

---

20 U.S.C. § 8921 (1994)

(1) In general

Except as provided in paragraph (3), each State receiving Federal funds under this chapter shall have in effect a State law requiring local educational agencies to expel from school for a period of not less than one year a student who is determined to have brought a weapon to a school under the jurisdiction of local educational agencies in that State, except that such State law shall allow the chief administering officer of such local educational agency to modify such expulsion requirement for a student on a case-by-case basis.

Figure 2–5 Excerpt from the federal gun free school act.

U.S.C.§ 553. Rule making

(a) This section applies, according to the provisions thereof, except to the extent that there is involved– . . .

(b) General notice of proposed rule making shall be published in the Federal Register, unless persons subject thereto are named and either personally served or otherwise have actual notice thereof in accordance with law. The notice shall include—

(1) a statement of the time, place, and nature of public rule making proceedings;

(2) reference to the legal authority under which the rule is proposed; and

(3) either the terms or substance of the proposed rule or a description of the subjects and issues involved.

Except when notice or hearing is required by statute, this subsection does not apply—

(A) to interpretative rules, general statements of policy, or rules of agency organization, procedure, or practice; or

(B) when the agency for good cause finds (and incorporates the finding and a brief statement of reasons therefor in the rules issued) that notice and public procedure thereon are impracticable, unnecessary, or contrary to the public interest.

(c) After notice required by this section, the agency shall give interested persons an opportunity to participate in the rule making through submission of written data, views, or arguments with or without opportunity for oral presentation. After consideration of the relevant matter presented, the agency shall incorporate in the rules adopted a concise general statement of their basis and purpose. When rules are required by statute to be made on the record after opportunity for an agency hearing, sections 556 and 557 of this title apply instead of this subsection.

(d) The required publication or service of a substantive rule shall be made not less than 30 days before its effective date, except—

(1) a substantive rule which grants or recognizes an exemption or relieves a restriction;

(2) interpretative rules and statements of policy; or

(3) as otherwise provided by the agency for good cause found and published with the rule.

(e) Each agency shall give an interested person the right to petition for the issuance, amendment, or repeal of a rule.

Figure 2–6 Requirements for "notice and comment" rule making.

In informal rule making, an agency need not base its final rules on information received during the notice and comment period but must consider those comments and, thirty days before the rules become final, publish (in the Federal Register) "a concise general statement of [the rules'] basis and purpose." That statement of basis and purpose — the "rule-making history" — enables a reviewing court "to see [the] major issues of policy [that] were ventilated by the informal proceedings and why the agency reacted to them as it did."[2]

As well, the President occasionally issues **executive orders** binding all executive branch employees. Figure 2–7 shows an example of the executive order desegregating the Alabama public schools.

Executive Order 11118

PROVIDING ASSISTANCE FOR REMOVAL OF UNLAWFUL
OBSTRUCTIONS OF JUSTICE IN
THE STATE OF ALABAMA

September 10, 1963

WHEREAS, on September 10, 1963, I issued a proclamation entitled 'Obstructions of Justice in the State of Alabama' pursuant in part to the provisions of Section 334 of Title 10 of the United States Code; and

WHEREAS the commands contained in that proclamation have not been obeyed, and the unlawful obstructions of justice, assemblies, combinations, and conspiracies referred to therein continue:

NOW, THEREFORE, by virtue of the authority vested in me by the Constitution and laws of the United States, including Chapter 15 of Title 10 of the United States Code, particularly Sections 332, 333 and 334 thereof, and Section 301 of Title 3 of the United States Code, it is hereby ordered as follows:

SECTION 1. The Secretary of Defense is authorized and directed to take all appropriate steps to remove obstructions of justice in the State of Alabama, to enforce the laws of the United States within that State, including any orders of United States Courts relating to the enrollment and attendance of students in public schools in the State of Alabama, and to suppress unlawful assemblies, combinations, conspiracies, and domestic violence which oppose, obstruct, or hinder the execution of the law or impede the course of justice under the law within that State.

SEC. 2. In furtherance of the authorization and direction contained in Section 1 hereof, the Secretary of Defense is authorized to use such of the Armed Forces of the United States as he may deem necessary.

SEC. 3. I hereby authorize and direct the Secretary of Defense to call into the active military service of the United States, as he may deem appropriate to carry out the purposes of this order, any or all of the units of the Army National Guard and of the Air National Guard of the State of Alabama to serve in the active military service of the United States for an indefinite period and until relieved by appropriate orders. In carrying out the provisions of Section 1, the Secretary of Defense is authorized to use the units, and members thereof, of the Army National Guard and of the Air National Guard of the State of Alabama called into the active military service of the United States pursuant to this section or otherwise.

SEC. 4. The Secretary of Defense is authorized to delegate to the Secretary of the Army or the Secretary of the Air Force, or both, any of the authority conferred upon him by this order.

JOHN F. KENNEDY
THE WHITE HOUSE,
September 10, 1963.

Exec. Order No. 11118, 28 FR 9863, 1963 WL 8187 (Pres.)

Figure 2–7 Executive Order. From Westlaw®; reprinted with the permission of West Group.

The Judiciary: Interpreter of Law

Article III of the United States Constitution vests "in one Supreme Court, and in such inferior Courts as the Congress may from time to time ordain and establish [authority to determine] Cases, in Law and Equity, arising under this Constitution, the Laws of the United States . . . [and] Controversies to which the United States shall be a Party."

Federal Court Structure and Operation. Although the United States Constitution mentions only the **United States Supreme Court**, over the years, the job of the federal judiciary has grown so large that the Congress has "from time to time ordain[ed] and establish[ed]" inferior courts to hear and decide "Cases, in Law and Equity, arising under this Constitution, the Laws of the United States . . . [and] Controversies to which the United States shall be a Party." As presently constituted, the federal judiciary is a three-tiered system which may be pictured as shown in Figure 2–8.

United States District Courts. The **United States District Courts** are the federal trial courts. Numbering more than ninety, the federal district courts try federal criminal and civil cases involving federal questions, cases between states, cases between the United States and foreign countries, and cases of diversity jurisdiction or between parties from different states (where more than $75,000 is at issue).

The federal district courts are trial courts, which are where trials take place. Always presided over by a judge, and if requested, a jury, the district court is where parties and their attorneys question witnesses, introduce exhibits, and conduct tri-

---

U.S. SUPREME COURT
(Single, highest federal court; hears cases involving federal questions as well as cases involving conflicting circuit court decisions)

|
|

U.S. CIRCUIT COURTS OF APPEAL
(Thirteen regional intermediate appellate courts; hear appeals from district courts in their circuit)

|
|

U.S. DISTRICT COURTS
(Over ninety federal trial courts located throughout the United States, the District of Columbia, and U.S. protectorates; hears cases raising issues of federal constitutional, legislative, and executive issues)

Figure 2–8 Structure of the federal courts.

als. Although varying somewhat from case to case, the procedure typically followed in the trial of a case is shown in Figure 2–9.

Circuit Courts of Appeal. **United States Circuit Courts of Appeal** are the intermediate appellate court for the federal government. Each of the thirteen circuit courts hears appeals from federal district courts in its geographical circuit. Figure 2–10 shows a map of the thirteen federal circuits.

---

1. Complaint is filed by the plaintiff (the complaining party) or the government (in a criminal case)

2. The defendant (defending party) answers the complaint.

3. Parties may seek discovery of each other's witnesses, exhibits, and cases.

4. Parties may seek pre-trial dismissal of case on legal (non-factual) issues.

5. Trial:

   (a) Jury is selected unless parties wish to have judge decide the case.

   (b) Parties make opening statements explaining their theory of the case, and outlining their trial strategy.

   (c) Plaintiff (or government) presents witnesses and evidence supporting their case theory. Defendant may cross-examine (i.e., challenge) plaintiff's witnesses as each testify.

   (d) Defendant presents witnesses and evidence supporting their case theory. Plaintiff may cross-examine defendant's witnesses as each testify.

   (e) Parties make closing arguments summarizing their case and theory and rebutting the case and theories of the other side.

   (f) Parties make post-trial arguments to judge on dispositive legal issues.

   (g) Judge explains the jury's responsibilities to determine the case facts (the who did what to whom, when, and where of the case) based on the evidence they have heard and their determinations of the truth and believability of that evidence, what and how the law applies to the facts of the case.

   (h) Jury discusses the case until it agrees to the facts of the case and then applies the law to the case to reach a final decision (the verdict).

   (i) The verdict is announced in open court, the judge enters a final decision (judgment) in the case, and the parties bring various post-trial motions for judgment other than that entered or for reconsideration.

6. Appeal

Figure 2–9 Steps in Civil Litigation.

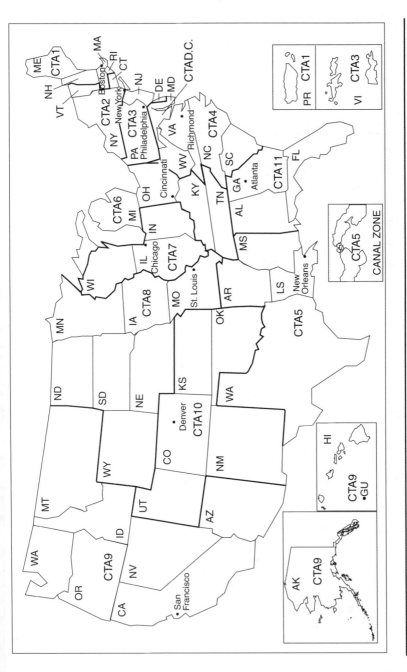

Figure 2–10 Map of federal circuit courts of appeal. From *Federal Reporter*, reprinted with the permission of West Group.

Court Abbreviations to Use in CTA Search	Coverage
first	The First Circuit covering Maine, Massachusetts, New Hampshire, Puerto Rico and Rhode Island
second	The Second Circuit covering Connecticut, New York and Vermont
third	The Third Circuit covering Delaware, New Jersey, Pennsylvania and the Virgin Islands
fourth	The Fourth Circuit covering Maryland, North Carolina, South Carolina, Virginia and West Virginia
fifth	The Fifth Circuit covering Louisiana, Mississippi, and Texas
sixth	The Sixth Circuit covering Kentucky, Michigan, Ohio and Tennessee
seventh	The Seventh Circuit covering Illinois, Indiana and Wisconsin
eighth	The Eighth Circuit covering Arkansas, Iowa, Minnesota, Missouri, Nebraska, North Dakota and South Dakota
ninth	The Ninth Circuit covering Alaska, Arizona, California, Guam, Hawaii, Idaho, Montana, Nevada, the Northern Mariana Islands, Oregon and Washington
tenth	The Tenth Circuit covering Colorado, Kansas, New Mexico, Oklahoma, Utah and Wyoming
eleventh	The Eleventh Circuit covering Alabama, Florida and Georgia
cadc	The District of Columbia Circuit
cafed	The Federal Circuit

Note: To retrieve courts of appeals cases from a particular circuit, access the database for that circuit. Restrict your search to the court field (co) when you want to retrieve cases from more than one circuit, but not all circuits. For example, to retrieve cases from the Second, Tenth and Federal Circuits, type **co(second tenth cafed)** in the CTA database.

Figure 2–10 (continued)

Unlike trial courts, neither witnesses nor evidence are presented in appellate courts. Rather, based on the trial court record (including a transcript of testimony, evidence, and decisions) and the parties' arguments, an appellate panel (usually three judges) reviews the trial record and will **affirm** (confirm, enforce) the trial court decision unless the appellate court finds legal or procedural error harming the losing party. If, based on the facts found at trial,[3] the appellate court finds such prejudicial error, it may **reverse** (overturn) the trial court decision and either enter a proper decision, or, if more evidence is necessary, **remand** (return) the case to the trial court for further action. Figure 2–11 shows the typical steps followed by an appellate court in hearing an appeal.

United States Supreme Court. The United States Supreme Court is the highest federal court. The court's nine justices hear appeals from the thirteen federal circuit courts of appeal in cases involving constitutional, statutory, and other federal questions. Unlike the intermediate circuit courts of appeal, the Supreme Court (or other highest tier appellate court in a three-tiered judiciary) is not obliged to hear and

---

1. Losing party files a Notice of Appeal in the trial court within thirty days of entry of judgment.

2. The trial court prepares its record.

3. The parties determine the issues they wish addressed by the appellate court.

4. The parties agree on the portions of the record they wish to include on appeal and prepare an appellate appendix containing those portions. (Although the appellate court is free to order the complete record from the trial court, it typically relies on the material in the parties' appendix in reviewing what happened at trial).

5. The appellant (appealing party) prepares an appellate brief setting out the case factual and procedural background and making legal arguments for reversing the trial court decision.

6. The appellee (the winner at trial) prepares her appellate brief.

7. If necessary, the appellant may file a reply brief responding to new issues or arguments raised in the appellee's brief.

8. The case can be argued by the attorneys to a panel of appellate justices (court's discretion).

9. The court issues a written decision in the case (can be for publication or a memorandum decision).

10. Parties may seek post-decision reconsideration or further appeal.

Figure 2–11 Steps in the Appellate Process.

decide every appeal filed. Rather, most appeals to appellate courts of last resort are heard only by permission of the court based on a party request called a **writ of certiorari.** Typically, certiorari courts decide the cases they will hear based on the importance and generality of its issues by vote of the justices; usually a vote by one less than a majority of justices (e.g., four justices of the nine United States Supreme Court justices) is required before the court will agree to hear a case. Once the case is to be heard, the appellate process usually proceeds as in any appellate court.

    Federal Court Law: Court Decisions, Rules of Court. Figure 2–12 shows an example of federal court decision on public school expulsion.

    As well, courts issue rules governing local or judiciary-wide practice. Figure 2–13 shows an example of a federal **court rule** governing documents, which must be filed when an appeal is taken.

State Law

As mentioned earlier, it is the states and the people who hold unlimited power in the United States; in fact, any power not specifically granted to the federal government (in the Constitution) resides in the States. This is so much the case that in fact state courts are permitted, indeed encouraged, to decide questions of federal law, including Constitutional law, subject only to the possible (though unlikely) oversight of the United States Supreme Court.

State Jurisdiction

Unlike the federal government, state governments are governments of "general" or "unlimited" jurisdictions. Indeed, the United States Constitution guarantees in Amendment X: "The powers not delegated to the United States by the Constitution, nor prohibited by it to the States, are reserved to the States respectively, or to the people." This means that no subject is off limits to the state governments, though states may not contradict or unreasonably restrict rights protected by the United States Constitution. Thus, while the United States Supreme court has reaffirmed the 1973 case of *Roe v. Wade,* 410 U.S. 113 (1973), which guarantees a woman's right to an abortion as a matter of United States Constitutional law and has ruled that states may not wholly deny or unreasonably restrict a woman's right to an abortion, the court has upheld state imposition of lesser restrictions on abortion, including: requiring parental notice or approval or judicial approval before a minor may have an abortion; requiring notification of a woman's husband before she may have an abortion; and restricting use of public funds to finance abortions.

State Government Structure

Most state governments are structured remarkably like the federal government. Most have constitutions setting up three branches of state government: its executive (the governor, executive agencies), its legislature (often bicameral, through its

(Text continues on page 39).

Jerrie TURNER, et al., Plaintiffs,

v.

SOUTH-WESTERN CITY SCHOOL DISTRICT, et al., Defendants.

82 F.Supp.2d 757 (S.D. Ohio 1999)

High school student, expelled for bringing look-alike gun to school and for disruptive conduct, sued school district seeking preliminary injunction compelling reinstatement, to allow him to graduate on schedule. The District Court, Marbley, J., held that: (1) procedural due process requirements associated with suspension and expulsion of student were complied with; (2) handbook provision barring look-alike weapons was not unconstitutionally overbroad or vague; (3) student failed to show irreparable injury; and (4) student failed to show that public interest would be furthered through reinstatement.

Injunction denied.

. . . .

[2] Constitutional Law k278.5(7)

92k278.5(7)

Procedural due process requirements for suspension of student lasting ten days or less include oral or written notice of charges against him, and if he denies them, explanation of evidence authorities have an opportunity to present his side of story. U.S.C.A. Const.Amend. 14.

[3] Constitutional Law k278.5(7)

92k278.5(7)

[3] Schools k177

345k177

Constitutional and statutory due process requirements for suspending student were followed in case of student who had toy replica of weapon in car and acted disruptively when confronted with it; student was presented with charges when first detained and given opportunity to explain, and parent was given notice of intent to suspend, together with counseling regarding procedural steps available to her. U.S.C.A. Const.Amend. 14; Ohio R.C. § 3313.66(A)(1, 2), (D, E). . . .

[5] Constitutional Law k278.5(7)

92k278.5(7)

[5] Schools k177

345k177

Constitutional and statutory due process requirements for expelling student were observed in case of student who had toy replica of weapon in car and acted disruptively when confronted with it; student was presented with charges when first detained and given opportunity to explain, and parent was given notice of intent to suspend, together with counseling regarding procedural steps available to her, there was pre-expulsion hearing before impartial official and detailed state statutory requirements for expulsion procedural were followed. U.S.C.A. Const.Amend. 14; Ohio R.C. § 3313.66(B). . . .

[9] Constitutional Law k90.1(1.4)

92k90.1(1.4)

Publications.

Figure 2–12 Edited United States District Court Decision. From *Federal Supplement 2d, Supreme Court*; reprinted with the permission of West Group.

[9] Schools k172

345k172

School handbook prohibition on bringing of weapons or objects that could reasonably be considered weapons to school was not overbroad, on grounds that it would chill permissible speech by deterring persons from bringing pictures of guns or props for school dramatic productions. U.S.C.A. Const.Amend. 1. . . .

[13] Schools k172

345k172

Provision of student handbook prohibiting bringing of weapon to school, with term further defined to include "look-alike gun," was not unconstitutionally vague; student of ordinary intelligence would know what was meant, and there was no question of interpretation delegated to enforcement official. U.S.C.A. Const.Amends. 5, 14. . . .

    *759 Jack L. Moser, Adams, Rosenberg & Associates, Columbus, Ohio, Danny W. Bank, Columbus, Ohio, for plaintiffs.

    Richard Wayne Ross, Means, Bichimer, Burkholder & Baker, Columbus, Ohio, for defendants.

    MARBLEY, District Judge.

    This case was originally brought before the Franklin County Court of Common Pleas by Stephen E. Koser, a high school student, and his mother Jerrie Turner, after Koser was expelled from Westland High School for bringing a look-alike gun to school and for disruptive behavior. . . .

    The Plaintiff, Stephen E. Koser, is a seventeen year old student at Westland High School ("Westland"), in Galloway, Ohio. On September 23, 1999, Deputy Cooper, of the Franklin County Sheriff's Department, was patrolling Westland's student parking lot checking cars for parking permits. Cooper approached Koser's car to issue him a parking violation for not having a parking permit. After placing the citation on Koser's windshield, he saw a partially concealed gun protruding from under the front driver's side seat of Koser's car. The gun looked like a Smith & Wesson 9mm gun; it was silver in color and appeared to have a wood grain grip. The Deputy contacted the Assistant Principal's office to inform him that he had found the gun.

    Assistant Principals Grube and McLaughlin, and Deputy Cooper located Koser in the high school library. The three officials escorted Koser to the principal's office, where Deputy Cooper conducted a pat-down of Koser. Deputy Cooper found a box of cigarettes and a pager on Koser's person. Deputy Cooper asked Koser for permission to search his car, which Koser granted. All four individuals, Grube, McLaughlin, Cooper and Koser, went to the high school parking lot where Koser's car was parked. Cooper opened Koser's car and examined the gun. The gun turned out to be a plastic toy gun that had a bright orange tip. The orange tip had been concealed from view.

    When Koser was asked to return to the Assistant Principal's office, he became belligerent and hostile, and refused to return to school. Eventually, he was persuaded to return to the building, but on the walk back, he began to use profanity, was disruptive and started to make veiled threats. Upon returning to the principal's office, Koser sat in front of Assistant Principal Grube's desk with clenched fists and pounded on the arms of his chair. Koser also leaned on the desk, toward Grube.

    During the time he spent in the office, Koser made threatening statements such as: "this is how I solve my problems," "if I wanted to bring a real gun to school, I would have brought a gun and blown holes in this mother," "you're my problem and I get rid

Figure 2–12 (continued)

of my problems," and "every dog has his day and you'll get yours." To Deputy Cooper, Koser said, "if you take your gun and badge off, you want to get froggy, leap," which Cooper took as a direct threat and an attempt by Koser to instigate a fight.

At the informal hearing on September 23, 1999, Koser was given the opportunity to explain his side of what happened. Koser said that the car was his mother's and that the toy gun had been left in the back seat of her car by a neighborhood child. Koser said that the first time he saw the toy gun was when he was escorted to the car by Deputy Cooper and the Assistant Principals.

At the same hearing, Koser was given a "Notice of Intent to Suspend," which indicated that he was being suspended for: "look-a-like gun in students car," "student used profanity repeatedly and refused to calm down after repeated requests," "threats directed at school officials," and "student also had cigarettes and a pager in his possession." The notice also stated:

You are hereby suspended 10 school days beginning 9/23/99 for the above- stated violation(s) of the adopted Code of Conduct and School Board Policy. You should return to school on 10/7/99. You have the right to appeal this suspension to the principal, to be granted a hearing on appeal, and to be represented in all appeal proceedings. If you wish to exercise the right of appeal, contact the principal's office immediately. If you fail to file an appeal within ten (10) days, you forfeit your right to appeal.

Koser refused to sign the notice.

Koser was also given a "Notice of Intended Expulsion" at the September 23, 1999, meeting. The reasons checked for Koser's potential expulsion were: "Disruption of Schools," and "Weapons/Dangerous Instruments." The notice also stated:

You and your parents, guardian, custodian, or representative will have the opportunity to appear in person for a hearing to be held at 2:00 p.m. on 9/29/9 [9] at Westland High School. You are not required to attend this meeting; however, it offers you the opportunity to challenge the reason(s) for the expulsion or explain your actions.

Koser also refused to sign this notice. Assistant Principal Grube contacted Jerrie Turner, Koser's mother, and she came to pick him up from school. Turner was given a copy of both notices at that time.

On September 24, 1999, Turner delivered a notice to school officials indicating that she was going to appeal her son's suspension. The suspension appeal hearing was held on September 29, 1999. Principal Voyles, Deputy Sheriff Cooper, and Assistants Principals McLaughlin and Grube attended the appeal. Turner stated that the car was hers and that the toy gun was left in the car by a child who lived in the neighborhood. Following the hearing, Principal Voyles upheld the suspension.

On September 30, 1999, Turner attended her son's pre-expulsion hearing. Also in attendance were Assistant Principals Grube and McLaughlin, and Shawn Koser, Stephen's older brother. Following the hearing, it was recommended that Koser be expelled. On October 4, 1999, Superintendent Hamilton issued Koser's Expulsion Notice. By letter dated October 5, 1999, and received by the Superintendent's office on October 6, 1999, Turner filed a request to appeal the expulsion.

Dr. Rinehart sent Turner a letter, dated October 12, 1999, scheduling a hearing for October 18, 1999, to appeal Koser's expulsion. [FN2] The hearing was held by Robert B. St. Clair, an independent hearing officer, on October 26, 1999.

The hearing included cross-examination and arguments by counsel. By report dated October 29, 1999, St. Clair recommended to the South-Western City School Board that

Figure 2–12 (continued)

Koser be expelled. On November 8, 1999, the school board met by regular meeting and adopted St. Clair's recommendation to expel Koser.

On October 14, 1999, Defendant's counsel sent a letter to Turner outlining the terms for readmitting Koser to class. Koser would have to attend alternative school until January 18, 1999. Starting on January 18, 1999, Koser would have to attend Westland High School from approximately 9:00 a.m. to 3:00 p.m., then attend alternative high school from 3:00 p.m. until 5:00 p.m. Koser would also have to complete a one-half credit class in anger management. After talking to Koser's psychologist, Turner rejected the terms. Turner was concerned that Koser would have to attend classes from 9:00 a.m. to 5:15 p.m. starting on January 18, 2000. Turner did not think that Koser could have handled that type of school schedule. Since his expulsion, Koser has been working thirty-five hours per week at Kohl's Department Store.

Koser is prohibited from returning to class and from being on South-Western City School property until January 18, 2000. . . . .

A. Procedural Due Process

The first issue is whether Koser is likely to succeed on his claim that his suspension and expulsion violated his right to procedural due process under the Fourteenth Amendment to the United States Constitution. Koser's suspension will be addressed separately from his expulsion as there are ***762** different procedural due process requirements for each action that the high school took. . . .

2. Expulsion.

Goss did not directly address what process is due for suspension of more than ten days. The Court, however, did recognize that suspensions longer than ten days require "more formal procedures," Goss, 419 U.S. at 584, 95 S.Ct. 729. In Newsome v. Batavia Local Sch. Dist., 842 F.2d 920, 921 (6th Cir.1988), where the Plaintiff was expelled from school for the remainder of the fall semester for allegedly possessing and attempting to sell marijuana, the Court noted in dicta that "[a] student faced with expulsion has the right to a pre-expulsion hearing before an impartial trier-of-fact—he does not have the right to a full-blown administrative appellate process." Id. at 927 (citing Brewer v. Austin Indep. Sch. Dist., 779 F.2d 260 (5th Cir.1985)); see also Hall v. Medical College of Ohio at Toledo, 742 F.2d 299, 309 (6th Cir.1984) (citing with favor Dixon v. Alabama State Bd. of Educ., 294 F.2d 150, 158-59 (5th Cir.1961), which held that a hearing which gives school authorities an opportunity to hear both sides is required in expulsion cases, but that a full-dress judicial hearing is not required).

[4] Following Goss and Newsome, the Sixth Circuit held in Ashiegbu v. Williams, No. 97-3173, 1997 WL 720477 at *1 (6th Cir. Nov. 12, 1997), that a student faced with expulsion for disciplinary reasons must be given the procedural requirements established by Goss, and in addition, "[t]he right to a pre-expulsion hearing before an impartial trier of fact." Id. at *3 (citing Newsome, 842 F.2d at 927).

[5] Section 3313.66(B) of the Ohio Revised Code establishes the procedures to be used in student expulsions, which are:

(4) No pupil shall be expelled under division (B)(1), (2), or (3) of this section unless, prior to his expulsion, the superintendent does both of the following:

(a) Gives the pupil and his parent, guardian, or custodian written notice of the intention to expel the pupil;

(b) Provides the pupil and his parent ... an opportunity to appear in person before the superintendent or his designee ... to challenge the reason for the intended expulsion or otherwise to explain the pupil's actions.

Figure 2–12 (continued)

The notice required in this division shall include the reasons for the expulsion, notification of the opportunity of the pupil and his parent ... to appear before the superintendent or his designee to challenge the reasons for the intended expulsion or otherwise to explain the pupil's actions, and notification of the time and place to appear. The time to appear shall not be earlier than three nor later than five school days after the notice is given, unless the superintendent grants an extension of time at the request of pupil or parent....

   Ohio Rev.Code § 3313.66(B)(4)(a)-(b) (emphasis added).[3]

[3]In addition, Ohio Revised Code § 3313.66(D)-(E) apply to expulsions.

   In this case, Westland High School officials gave Koser the process that was due prior to expelling him. First, as established, the requirements of Goss were met when Koser was suspended from school, and therefore, since the expulsion was based on the same conduct, those requirements were also met when Koser was expelled. Koser was given an opportunity to be heard and to explain his version of the events. Koser was also given written "Notice of Intended Expulsion." That notice indicated that Koser would have the opportunity for a hearing on September 29, 1999, at Westland High School. The notice gave the reasons for Koser's possible expulsion which included: "Disruption of Schools," and "Weapons/Dangerous Instruments."

   The next issue is whether Koser's expulsion satisfied the additional due process requirements as established by Newsome and Ashiegbu which include a pre-expulsion hearing before an independent trier of fact. Koser's expulsion hearing was held on September 30, 1999, at Westland High School. Present at the hearing were Assistant Principals Grube and McLaughlin, Shawn Koser, Stephen's older brother, and Koser's mother. Assistant Principal McLaughlin presided over the pre-expulsion hearing. Koser's pre-expulsion hearing satisfied Newsome's requirement, that there should be a hearing and that it should be held in front of an independent trier of fact. Under the circumstances of this case, the Court finds that Koser was accorded his due process rights pursuant to the United States Constitution prior to his expulsion from Westland High School.

   Koser's expulsion also met the more stringent requirements of the Ohio Revised Code. First, Koser was given written notice of the school's intent to expel him. See Ohio Rev.Code § 3313.66(B)(4)(a). Second, Koser and his mother had an opportunity to appear before Assistant Principal McLaughlin to challenge the reasons for his expulsion. See Ohio Rev.Code § 3313.66(B)(4)(b). Koser was given notice of the reasons for his potential expulsion, and the notice indicated that Turner and/or Koser could appear before the superintendent's designee to challenge the reasons for Koser's expulsion. See Ohio Rev.Code § 3313.66(B)(4)(b). The time set for the hearing also met the requirements established by the Code. The pre-expulsion hearing "shall not be earlier than three nor later than five school days after the notice is given...." Ohio Rev.Code § 3313.66(B)(4)(b). Here, Koser was given notice on September 23, 1999. The hearing was originally set for September 29, 1999, but was rescheduled for September 30, 1999 to accommodate the Plaintiff's appeal of his suspension. Three school days after Thursday, September 23, 1999, would have been September 28, 1999; five days after notice was given would have been September 30, 1999. Koser's pre-expulsion hearing, which was held on September 30, 1999, fell within the time requirement established by section 3313.66(B)(4)(b) of the Ohio Revised Code.

   Westland High School officials also met the requirements of section 3313.66(D) of the Ohio Revised Code. Following the pre-expulsion hearing, on Thursday, September

Figure 2–12 (continued)

30, 1999, it was recommended that Koser be expelled. Ohio statutes require parental notice within one school day after the pupil's pre-expulsion hearing. See Ohio Rev.Code § 3313.66(D). On Monday October 4, 1999, Superintendent Hamilton issued an expulsion notice and mailed it to Turner. Although the notice may have been one day late, this fact, in itself, is not a violation of the statute. See Stuble v. Board of Educ. of the Cuyahoga Valley Joint Vocational Sch. Dist., No. 44412, 1982 WL 5953 at *5 (Ohio Ct.App. Oct. 7, 1982) (finding that "[w]here delay by a public official with respect to the precise time in which a statutory act is performed does not affect the rights of the parties involved, that technical defect does not invalidate the officials subsequent action.") (citations omitted); The State v. Board of Educ. of Hamilton City Sch. Dist., 20 Ohio App.2d 154, 252 N.E.2d 318 (1969). In addition, as required by the Code, the notice gave the reasons for the expulsion: "[d]isruption and being in possession of a weapon/look-alike." See Ohio Rev.Code § 3313.66(D). The notice also stated, "I wish to advise you that according to the law the parent has the right to appeal this action within ten (10) days from the date of this letter. If you wish to do this, contact Dr. Rinehart in this office." See Ohio Rev.Code § 3313.66(D).

By letter dated October 5, 1999, Turner and her attorney informed Dr. Rinehart that she wished to appeal Koser's suspension. By letter dated October 12, 1999, Dr. Rinehart set an expulsion appeal hearing for October 18, 1999. See Ohio Rev.Code § 3313.66(E). The hearing was held by the board's designee, Robert B. St. Clair, an independent hearing officer, on October 26, 1999. The hearing included cross-examination and arguments by counsel. By report dated October 29, 1999, St. Clair recommended to the South-Western City School Board that Koser be expelled. On November 8, 1999, the School Board met by regular meeting and adopted St. Clair's recommendation. See Ohio Rev.Code § 3313.66(E).

The Court finds that Westland High School officials met the detailed requirements of the Ohio Revised Code when they expelled Koser from school until January 18, 2000. Based on the Court's finding that Koser was given the process due in both his suspension and expulsion and that the applicable Ohio Revised Code provisions were met, the Court finds that there is little likelihood of success on the merits on the Plaintiffs' claim that his right to procedural due process under the Fourteenth Amendment of the United States Constitution was violated when he was suspended and expelled from school. . . .

[16] The second element the Court needs to address is whether the Plaintiffs have demonstrated irreparable injury. In their Complaint, the Plaintiffs allege that Koser's irreparable injuries are that he cannot graduate in the spring, that he cannot further his academic career, and that he cannot attend a secondary institution next year. However, the Court find that Koser's injuries were not irreparable.

At the time of his suspension, Koser was given an opportunity to further his academic career, graduate in the spring and possibly attend a secondary institution next year. The plan provided by the school would have had Koser attending an alternative school for two hours a day until January 18, 2000. On January 18, 2000, Koser would have attended Westland High School from approximately 9:00 a.m. to 3:00 p.m. and then would have attended an alternative high school from 3:00 p.m. until 5:00 p.m. Koser would have also had to have completed a one-half credit class in anger management. This plan would have allowed Koser to graduate on time.

Turner rejected these terms after talking to Koser's psychologist; however, Koser's psychologist did not testify in this case. The Court must rely on Turner's assertion that Koser could not have handled *768 attending classes from 9:00 a.m. to 5:15 p.m. The Court views

Figure 2–12 (continued)

this assertion inconsistent with the fact that Koser has been working thirty-five hours a week for Kohl's Department Store since he was expelled. Given that Koser had an alternative to not graduating in the spring, the Court finds that he did not suffer irreparable injury. . . .

The third and fourth factors the Court must consider involve balancing the harm to others against the public interest in issuing an injunction. The Plaintiffs argue that the issuance of a preliminary injunction would not cause substantial harm to others in that it would allow the school to abide by compulsory attendance laws, provide education to children in the South-Western City School district, and allow the rules and regulations of Ohio schools to be followed. The Plaintiffs also argue that the public interest will be served in that the issuance of a preliminary injunction will avoid willful, unreasonable, and malicious expulsions within the school systems of Ohio, and will prevent the bad faith expulsions of students.

The Plaintiffs' arguments are not well taken. The Court finds the contrary to be the case. The public interest will be served if our children are allowed to attend safe schools—free from guns, disruption and profanity. The public interest will be served if school officials are permitted to regulate conduct which relates to school safety and discipline; to ensure the safety of the student body. It is in the interest of all students that weapons not be allowed to be brought into school. School officials should not be required to perform a detailed analysis to determine if a student's gun is real or fake. Furthermore, school officials should be allowed to complete their duties free from abusive behavior and from threats of violence from students.

The Court concludes that the public interest will not be served in issuing an injunction. The public interest is served by maintaining safe schools, by ensuring discipline and by the abeyance of abusive student behavior.

VII. CONCLUSION

The Court finds that there is no basis for the issuance of a preliminary injunction. The Plaintiffs' Motion for a Preliminary Injunction is DENIED.

IT IS SO ORDERED.

Figure 2–12 (continued)

FRAP ["Federal Rule of Appellate Procedure"] **10: THE RECORD ON APPEAL**

(a) Composition of the Record on Appeal. The original papers and exhibits filed in the district court, the transcript of proceedings, if any, and a certified copy of the docket entries prepared by the clerk of the district court shall constitute the record on appeal in all cases.

Figure 2–13 Federal Rule of Appellate Procedure 10. From *Federal Civil Judicial Procedure and Rules*; reprinted with the permission of West Group.

houses may not be called the "House of Representatives" and "Senate"), and its judiciary (which may be two- or three-tiered and bear odd-sounding names, like Massachusetts' Supreme Judicial Court, or New York's Supreme Court (New York's trial court), its Appellate Division of the Supreme Court (the intermediate appellate court), and its Supreme Court of Errors (its highest appellate court)).

Unlike federal courts, which deal exclusively with federal constitutional and statutory issues, some areas of law, particularly contracts, torts, and property law, may not be governed by statutes. Rather, those legal areas developed and were handed down from the English **common law** (judge-created law). Those common-law areas often continue to evolve, not by legislative or executive action, but by court decision. Figure 2–14 shows an amusing Massachusetts Appeals Court decision applying common law to a patent-infringement case involving a secret chocolate chip cookie recipe.

PEGGY LAWTON KITCHENS, INC.
v.
Terence M. HOGAN et al.
466 N.E.2d 138, 18 Mass.App.Ct. 937 (1984).

Before ARMSTRONG, CUTTER and KASS, JJ.

Nothing is sacred. We have before us a case of theft of a recipe for baking chocolate chip cookies. The issue is whether the plaintiff, Peggy Lawton Kitchens, Inc. (Kitchens), possessed a protected trade secret.

A Superior Court judge found that Kitchens first added chocolate chip cookies to its line of prepackaged bakery products in 1960. They were an indifferent success. In 1963, Lawton Wolf, a principal officer of Kitchens, mixed the chaff from walnuts ("nut dust" he called it) in his chocolate chip cookie batter. This, as the judge found, "produced a distinctive flavor. It was an immediate commercial success." Lawton Wolf, in his testimony, described what nut dust did for his cookies in rhapsodic terms: "Miraculous." Sales, he said, "took off immediately. It did to the cookies what butter does to popcorn or salt to a pretzel. It really made the flavor sing."

The judge found that, from the beginning of its use, Kitchens carefully guarded the cookie recipe. One copy of the recipe was locked in an office safe. A duplicate was secured in the desk of William Wolf, Lawton's son. To satisfied customers who asked for the recipe, Kitchens wrote that the formula was a trade secret. For workday use, Kitchens broke down the formula into baking ingredients, small ingredients (e.g., the nut dust), and bulk ingredients. The three components were kept on separate cards, which contained gross weights. Even though those cards concealed the true proportions of the ingredients, access to the cards was limited to long-time trusted employees. The defendant Terence Hogan, whose responsibilities at Kitchens were plant and equipment maintenance and safety, was not among those entrusted with the ingredients cards. Hogan, the judge found, had gained access to the cards through a pretext, and after Hogan left Kitchens' employ, a master key, which could open the vault and the office in which William Wolf's desk was located, was found in Hogan's desk.

Figure 2–14 Sample State Case.

Hogan and his wife organized a bakery business to sell prepackaged bakery products under the trade name Hogie Bear. Among the first products Hogie Bear made was a chocolate chip cookie. It had the same recipe, including the miraculous nut dust. The judge found that about forty brands of chocolate chip cookies were sold in New England. Except for those made by Kitchens and Hogie Bear, no two are alike. The judge found Hogie Bear's cookie "similar in appearance, color, cell construction, texture, flavor and taste. They are 'formulated' in a similar fashion. They are the same."

. . . [T]he judge described the evidence as too vague and speculative to support a finding. A judgment was entered **enjoining** the defendants from making, baking, and selling chocolate chip cookies, which use the plaintiff's formula. . . . A further judgment adverse to the defendants was entered on their counterclaim, which alleged various unfair practices by the plaintiff Kitchens. We affirm. . . .

1. <u>Was there a trade secret?</u> No doubt, the basic ingredients, flour, sugar, shortening, chocolate chips, eggs, and salt, would be common to any chocolate chip cookie. The combination in which those ingredients are used, the diameter and thickness of the cookie, and the degree to which it is baked would, however, constitute a formula which its proprietor could protect from infringement by an employee who either gains access to the formula in confidence or by improper means. . . . In any event, the insertion of the nut dust into the mix served to add that modicum of originality, which separates a process from the every day and so characterizes a trade secret. . . . Lawton Wolf's testimony that "sales took off immediately" supports a determination that the improved recipe had competitive value so far as Kitchens was concerned.

2. <u>Conduct of the defendants.</u> Once information qualifies as a trade secret, determination of whether the trade secret has been misused steers the inquiry to examining the conduct of the defendant, and the legal character of that conduct, in turn, is much affected by the steps taken by the proprietor of the trade secret to protect it. . . . Here, as we have seen, the holder of the secret took reasonable steps to maintain its mystery and to narrow the circle of those privy to its essentials. We do not think that the absence of admonitions about secrecy or the failure to emphasize secrecy in employment contracts (if there were any in this relatively small business) is fatal to the plaintiff. That Hogan brought no experience in volume baking to his employment with Kitchens and that he employed a ruse to examine the ingredients cards and may have helped himself to a look at the formula tucked away in Kitchens' safe or William Wolf's desk are relevant factors. Listing of nut meal on the plaintiff's label does not constitute publication of the recipe because it discloses nothing about the proportions in which the ingredients are used, nor does it say what kind of nuts or what part of the nuts imparted special zing to Kitchens' cookies.

3. <u>The length and breadth of the injunction.</u> The **injunction** against use of the plaintiff's recipe was permanent and without limit as to area. Injunctions of that length and breadth are unusual, but not without precedent. We do not think the judge was bound to calibrate a more precise area and duration for an injunction as limited as the one imposed. It does not drive Hogan or Hogie Bear Snacks, Inc., out of the cookie business; the injunction forbids only use of Kitchens' precise formula. Other recipes — and the evidence included many — are available to Hogie Bear. There is no limitation on Hogie Bear's packaging or marketing methods.

Judgments affirmed.

Figure 2–14 (continued)

Review Questions

1. Describe the federal government structure and operation.
2. By what process does the legislature enact laws? How do bicameral legislative houses differ?
3. What is a legislative committee? What is its purpose? Name some federal legislative committees.
4. What is a legislative term?
5. What happens if proposed legislation is not passed by the end of a legislative session?
6. What is a bill?
7. What is an act or public law?
8. Why is it important to know legislative bill numbers?
9. What is the federal executive department? List its component parts.
10. How do executive departments operate?
11. What are regulations? What are their purpose? How are regulations enacted?
12. What is an executive order?
13. What is the federal judiciary? List its component parts.
14. How does the federal judiciary operate?
15. Describe the process of litigation and appeal
16. How does the judiciary create law?

Exercise

Find out about the structure, operation, and authority of your state government. Describe its various components, structure, and operation (Hint: Often the statehouse or the Governor's office have brochures or other materials describing state government authority, structure, and operation).

Glossary

Act: Same as **public law**.

Affirm: To agree with or enforce a lower court decision.

Amended: Changed.

Appellant: Party losing in the lower court decision.

Appellate appendix: A copy of necessary parts of the trial court record.

Appellate brief: A written document setting out the case factual and procedural background and making legal arguments for reversing or affirming a lower court decision.

Bicameral: "Of two houses," as compared to unilateral, "of one house."

Bill: Proposed legislation.

Bill of Rights: First ten amendments to the United States Constitution.

Circuit: A geographical region covered by an appellate court.

Codify: Include in topically arranged published laws.

Common law: Court-made law.

Congress: The federal legislature.

Court rule: Rule of procedure governing court actions.

Defendant: The party defending against or opposing a lawsuit.

Deliberative Process: A process by which a body makes decisions.

Educative Process: A process by which one is educated.

Enjoining: Prohibition by a judicial order. See **injunction**.

Executive Agency, Department: An executive department or officer empowered to carry out the purposes of one or more statutes.

Executive orders: Statements of executive policy issued by the executive branch of government.

House of Representatives: One of two houses in the federal legislature. Members of House of Representatives include varying numbers (based on district population) of state-elected representatives serving two-year terms.

Injunction: Court order to do (or stop doing) a certain action.

Judgment: A final decision in a case after trial.

Jurisdiction: The power of a court to act. Jurisdiction includes the power to act in certain geographical regions, subject areas, and over persons and things.

Plaintiff: The complaining party or government (in a criminal case); the party bringing the lawsuit.

Pocket veto: When an executive refuses to act on a bill and the legislature adjourns during the ten days for executive action, the bill is said to be "pocket vetoed."

Promulgating: Enacting agency rules and regulations.

Public Law: A bill passed by both congressional houses. Same as **act**.

Regulations: Rules issued by government agencies setting out agency procedure and interpretation and generally "filling in" the blanks left by the legislature in enacting legislation.

Remand: Return a case for further action.

Reverse: Overturn a lower court decision and either enter a proper decision, or if more evidence is necessary, remand the case for further action by the lower court.

Senate: One of two houses in the federal legislature. Members of Senate include two elected senators from each state serving six-year terms.

Separation of powers: The principle that each branch of government is independent and may not intrude on other branches' duties.

Slip law: The pamphlet form of a law when first enacted.

United States Circuit Courts of Appeal: Intermediate appellate courts for the federal government. Each of the thirteen circuit courts hears appeals from the federal district courts in its region.

United States District Courts: Federal trial courts. Numbering more than ninety, the federal district courts try cases involving federal questions or diversity of citizenship.

United States Statutes at Large: Compilation of slip laws.

United States Supreme Court: Highest federal court. Nine justices hear appeals from the thirteen national circuit courts of appeal in cases involving federal questions.

Verdict: The jury's decision.

Veto: Act of an executive officer declining to enact legislation passed by the legislature.

Writ of certiorari: A request to appeal to the highest court in a jurisdiction, usually the United States Supreme Court.

Notes

[1]Although each state has its own process of legislation, many are like the well-defined federal legislative process.

[2]Automotive Parts & Accessories Assn. v. Boyd, 407 F.2d 330, 338 (D.C. Cir. 1968).

[3]For example, if in a racial discrimination case, 51 nuns testified that they heard the defendant employer use a racial slur when referring to the employee but the employer denied that, a jury could permissibly decide, based on the employer's testimony, that the name-calling did not occur. That determination of witness credibility (i.e., believing the employer rather than the 51 nuns) will not be changed or even reviewed by the appellate court. If, however, the trial judge erroneously told the jury that even if the employer used a racial slur that was not evidence of racial discrimination, the appellate court might remand the case to the trial court for application of the correct statement of the law.

Finding the Law: Books I

Chapter Outline

Learning Objectives

Upon completing this chapter, the student should be able to

* Describe the layout of a typical law library and collection
* Describe the major legal publishers and the importance of distinguishing between them
* Describe various legal research books
* Name, explain, and describe the use of the different types of primary materials
* Describe the American Law Reports and its importance

Introduction

Once you've obtained and organized the preliminary facts, it is time to start gathering the information necessary to advise the client.

Law Libraries and Collections

Although society is in the midst of a technological revolution, with many computer legal research services and products (e.g., Westlaw®, Lexis, the Internet, and CD-ROMs), most legal research is still done using legal research books. The cost of maintaining a law library, while substantial, is often less costly than the cost of **computer-assisted legal research** services. As a result, smaller law firms, legal service providers, and many government law offices continue to rely on legal research books for their research. Fortunately, thanks in no small part to John West (who, in 1872, began to index and cross-reference Illinois legal cases, and whose company, West Group®, has since indexed and cross-referenced most American law), legal research materials are the most up-to-date and comprehensively indexed and cross-referenced materials published.

Legal research materials may be found in law libraries (in law schools, courthouses, or state houses). These libraries may also be **federal depository libraries**, home to large amounts of federal government information. Typically, a comprehensive law library will include both federal and state materials. Law libraries are often organized geographically or by "source type," as shown in Figure 3–1.

Other college libraries (e.g., universities, colleges, and community colleges) and locations (including small courthouses, law firms, etc.) have smaller **legal collections** rather than full scale law libraries. Legal collections typically include state and local materials, a few legal treatises, a legal encyclopedia, and limited federal materials. For example, a typical law collection, such as that required by the American Bar Association for a certified paralegal program, might be arranged as shown in Figure 3–2.

Legal Publishers

Many publishers publish legal books. Indeed, it is useful to notice the publisher of research books you are using because publishers often use consistent indexing, cross-referencing methods, and topics in all of their books. West Group, for instance, publishes the following national legal research materials:

Encyclopedia (Corpus Juris Secundum®)
Case Reporters
Digests
Statute Books
Treatises

West® publications are indexed by **topic and key numbers**, which categorize legal issues addressed in cases, statutes, treatises, and encyclopedias. For instance, the

BASEMENT

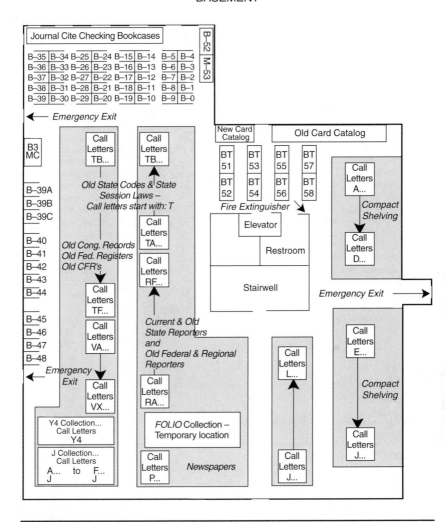

Figure 3–1 Map of Stanford University's Robert Crown Law Library. Courtesy of Stanford University.

West topic *Limitations of Actions*, key number *95(1)* deals with the statute of limitations for professional malpractice in all West books. A case dealing with a malpractice statute of limitations might contain a reference to Lim of Actions ☞ 95(1), as would a digest or encyclopedia entry, or a treatise on medical (or legal) malpractice. Thus, once the researcher locates a relevant West topic and key number, other West published materials on that topic can be readily located. Reed, another major legal

FIRST FLOOR

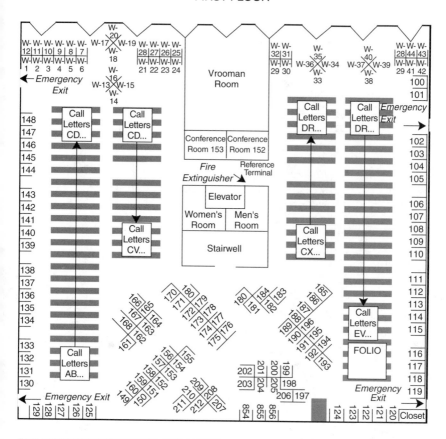

Figure 3–1 (continued)

publisher, indexes and cross-references its materials by topic and section numbers. Other legal publishers may use consistent indexing and cross-referencing systems as well. Other publishers of legal materials include the following:

Commerce Clearing House
John Wiley and Sons
Bureau of National Affairs
Pearson Education

Finally, governments (federal and state) publish primary legal materials (statutes, judicial and agency decisions, regulations) and other official documents. A document published by the government is referred to as its **official publication.** While privately published materials (**unofficial publications**) faithfully reproduce the law, those mate-

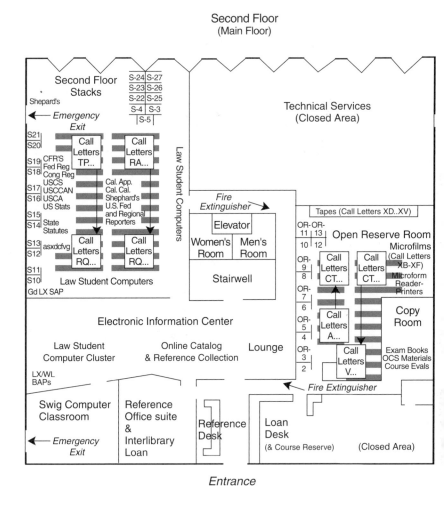

Figure 3–1 (continued)

rials also provide helpful editorial features which assist the legal researcher to find other, related materials. For example, three versions of the Supreme Court case *McBoyle v. United States*, 283 U.S. 25 (1931) demonstrate a few publisher-supplied **editorial features**, as shown in Figure 3–3a on page 51, Figure 3–3b on page 53, and Figure 3–3c on page 54.

Legal Research Books

Legal research sources are of three types: (1) **primary sources**, which contain the law, (2) **secondary sources**, which describe the law, and (3) **finding aids**, which help the

Third Floor

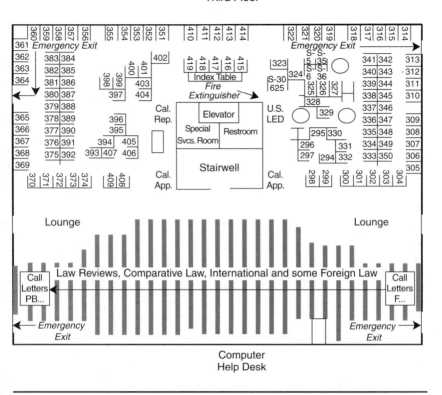

Figure 3–1 (continued)

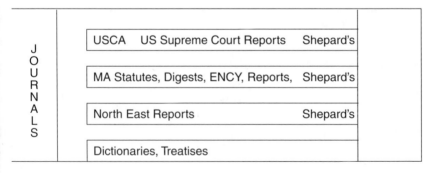

Figure 3–2 Law collection "map."

McBOYLE *v.* UNITED STATES.

15   Opinion of the Court.

U. S. 192; *Jacob Ruppert* v. *Caffey*, 251 U. S. 264; *Lambert* v. *Yellowley*, 272 U. S. 581. *Affirmed.*

McBOYLE *v.* UNITED STATES.

CERTIORARI TO THE CIRCUIT COURT OF APPEALS FOR THE TENTH CIRCUIT.

No. 552.   Argued February 26, 27, 1931.—Decided March 9, 1931.

The National Motor Vehicle Theft Act, U. S. C., Title 18, § 408, which punishes whoever transports, or causes to be transported, in interstate or foreign commerce a motor vehicle knowing it to have been stolen, and which defines "motor vehicle" as including "an automobile, automobile truck, automobile wagon, motor cycle, or any other self-propelled vehicle not designed for running on rails," does not apply to aircraft. P. 26.

43 F. (2d) 273, reversed.

CERTIORI, 282 U. S. 835, to review a judgment affirming a conviction under the Motor Vehicle Theft Act.

Mr. Harry F. Brown for petitioner.

Mr. Claude R. Branch, Special Assistant to the Attorney General, with whom *Solicitor General Thacher, Assistant Attorney General Dodds* and *Messrs. Harry S. Ridgely* and *W. Marvin Smith* were on the brief, for the United States.

MR. JUSTICE HOLMES delivered the opinion of the Court.

The petitioner was convicted of transporting from Ottawa, Illinois, to Guymon, Oklahoma, an airplane that he knew to have been stolen, and was sentenced to serve three years' imprisonment and to pay a fine of $2,000. The judgment was affirmed by the Circuit Court of Appeals for the Tenth Circuit. 43 F. (2d) 273. A writ of certiorari was granted by this Court on the question whether the National Motor Vehicle Theft Act applies to aircraft.

Opinion of the Court.   283 U.S.

Act of October 29, 1919, c. 89, 41 Stat. 324; U. S. Code, Title 18, § 408. That Act provides: "Sec. 2. That when used in this Act: (a) The term 'motor vehicle' shall include an automobile, automobile truck, automobile wagon, motor cycle, or any other self-propelled vehicle not designed for running on rails; . . . Sec. 3. That whoever shall transport or cause to be transported in interstate or foreign commerce a motor vehicle, knowing the same to have been stolen, shall be punished by a fine of not more than $5,000, or by imprisonment of not more than five years, or both."

Section 2 defines the motor vehicles of which the transportation in interstate commerce is punished in § 3. The question is the meaning of the word 'vehicle' in the phrase "any other self-propelled vehicle not designed for running on rails." No doubt etymologically it is possible to use the word to signify a conveyance working on land,

Figure 3–3a McBoyle v. United States (official).

water or air, and sometimes legislation extends the use in that direction, e. g., land and air, water being separately provided for, in the Tariff Act, September 22, 1922, c. 356, § 401 (b), 42 Stat. 858, 948. But in everyday speech 'vehicle' calls up the picture of a thing moving on land. Thus in Rev. Stats. § 4, intended, the Government suggests, rather to enlarge than to restrict the definition, vehicle includes every contrivance capable of being used "as a means of transportation on land." And this is repeated, expressly excluding aircraft, in the Tariff Act, June 17, 1930, c. 997, § 401 (b); 46 Stat. 590, 708. So here, the phrase under discussion calls up the popular picture. For after including automobile truck, automobile wagon and motor cycle, the words "any other self-propelled vehicle not designed for running on rails" still indicate that a vehicle in the pupular sense, that is a vehicle running on land, is the theme. It is a vehicle that runs, not something, not commonly called a vehicle, that flies. Airplanes were well known in 1919, when this statute was passed; but it is admitted that they were not mentioned in the reports or in the debates in Congress.

25   Syllabus.

It is impossible to read words that so carefully enumerate the different forms of motor vehicles and have no reference of any kind to aircraft, as including airplanes under a term that usage more and more precisely confines to a different class. The counsel for the petitioner have shown that the phraseology of the statute as to motor vehicles follows that of earlier statutes of Connecticut, Delaware, Ohio, Michigan and Missouri, not to mention the late Regulations of Traffic for the District of Columbia, Title 6, c. 9, § 242, none of which can be supposed to leave the earth.

   Although it is not likely that a criminal will carefully consider the text of the law before he murders or steals, it is reasonable that a fair warning should be given to the world in language that the common world will understand, of what the law intends to do if a certain line is passed. To make the warning fair, so far as possible the line should be clear. When a rule of conduct is laid down in words that evoke in the common mind only the picture of vehicles moving on land, the statute should not be extended to aircraft, simply because it may seem to us that a similar policy applies, or upon the speculation that, if the legislature had thought of it, very likely broader words would have been used. *United States* v. *Thind*, 261 U. S. 204, 209. *Judgment reversed.*

Figure 3–3a (continued)

researcher find primary materials. Most often a legal researcher seeking answers to legal issues is seeking primary materials; however, secondary and finding materials are an important source of legal background and help to locate primary materials.

Primary Sources

Constitutions.   Both official and unofficial legal publishers publish state and federal constitutions. Typically, official versions of constitutions and other primary materials are published without cross-references to other relevant research materials. Figure 3–4a on page 57, Figure 3–4b on page 58, and Figure 3–4c, beginning on page 59, show pages from the United States Constitution as they appear in the **United States Code** (U.S.C.) Amendment IV, the **United States Code Annotated**® (U.S.C.A. ®; West Group) and the **United States Code Service** (U.S.C.S.; Reed), and may include relevant **annotations** to each version.

(*Text continues on page 57.*)

U. S. 25)
McBOYLE v. UNITED STATES.
No. 552

Argued Feb. 26, 27, 1931.
Decided March 9, 1931.

Automobiles ⇐ **341.**

Airplane *held* not "motor vehicle" within [missing text] relating to transportation in interstate foreign commerce of motor vehicle knowing the same to have been stolen (National Motor Vehicle Theft Act [18 USCA § 408]).

National Motor Vehicle Theft Act, Oct. 29, 1919, c. 89, § 2, 41 Stat. 324 (18 USCA § 408), provides that, when used in the act, the term "motor vehicle" shall include an automobile, automobile truck, automobile wagon, motorcycle, or any other self-propelled vehicle not designed for running on rails.

[Ed. Note.—For other definitions of "Motor Vehicle," see Words and Phrases.]

Automobiles ⇐ **341.**

"Vehicle" as used in law relating to transportation of stolen automobiles in interstate or foreign commerce is limited to vehicles running on land (National Motor Vehicle Theft Act [18 USCA § 408]).

[Ed. Note.—For other definitions of "Vehicle," see Words and Phrases.]

On Writ of Certiorari to the Unites States Circuit Court of Appeals for the Tenth Circuit.

William W. McBoyle was convicted of transporting between states an airplane known to have been stolen, judgment being affirmed by the Circuit Court of Appeals [43 F.(2d) 273], and he brings certiorari.

Reversed.

Mr. Harry F. Brown, of Guthrie, Okl., for petitioner.

The Attorney General and Mr. Claude R. Branch, of Providence, R. I., for the United States.

Mr. Justice HOLMES delivered the opinion of the Court.

[1] The petitioner was convicted of transporting from Ottawa, Illinois, to Guymon, Oklahoma, an airplane that he knew to have been stolen, and was sentenced to serve three years' imprisonment and to pay a fine of $2,000. The judgment was affirmed by the Circuit Court of Appeals for the Tenth Circuit. 43 F.(2d) 273. A writ of certiorari was granted by this Court on the question whether the National Motor Vehicle Theft Act applies to aircraft. *Act of October 29,

*26

1919, c. 89, 41 Stat. 324, U. S. Code, title 18, § 408 (18 USCA § 408). That Act provides: "Sec. 2. That when used in this Act: (a) The term 'motor vehicle' shall include an automobile, automobile truck, automobile wagon, motor cycle, or any other self-propelled vehicle not designed for running on rails. * * * Sec. 3. That whoever shall transport or cause to be transported in interstate or foreign commerce a motor vehicle, knowing the same to have been stolen, shall be punished by a fine of not more than $5,000, or by imprisonment of not more than five years, or both."

[2] Section 2 defines the motor vehicles of which the transportation in interstate commerce is punished in Section 3. The question is the meaning of the word "vehicle" in the phrase "any other self-propelled vehicle not designed for running on rails." No doubt etymologically it is possible to use the word to signify a conveyance working on land, water or air, and sometimes legislation extends the use in that direction, e. g., land and air, water being separately provided for, in the Tariff Act, September 21, 1922, c. 356, § 401 (b), 42 Stat. 858, 948 (19 USCA § 231 (b). But in everyday speech "vehicle" calls up the picture of a thing moving on land. Thus in Rev. St. § 4 (1 USCA § 4) intended, the Government suggests, rather to enlarge than to restrict the definition, vehicle includes every contrivance capable of being used "as a means of transportation on land." And this is repeated, expressly excluding aircraft, in the Tariff Act, June 17, 1930, c. 497, § 401 (b), 46 Stat. 590, 708 (19 USCA § 1401). So here, the phrase under discussion calls up the

⇐ For other cases see same topic and KEY-NUMBER in all Key-Numbered Digests and Indexes

Figure 3–3b McBoyle v. United States. From the *Supreme Court Reporter*; reprinted with the permission of West Group.

popular picture. For after including automobile truck, automobile wagon and motor cycle, the words "any other self-propelled vehicle not designed for running on rails" still indicate that a vehicle in the popular sense, that is a vehicle running on land is the theme. It is a vehicle that runs, not something, not commonly called a vehicle, that flies. Airplanes were well known in 1919 when this statute was passed, but it is admitted that they were not mentioned in the reports or in the debates in

*27

Congress. *It is impossible to read words that so carefully enumerate the different forms of motor vehicles and have no reference of any kind to aircraft, as including airplanes under a term that usage more and more precisely confines to a different class. The counsel for the petitioner have shown that the phraseology of the statute as to motor vehicles follows that of earlier statutes of Connecticut, Delaware, Ohio, Michigan and Missouri, not to mention the late

Regulations of Traffic for the District of Columbia, title 6, c. 9, § 242, none of which can be supposed to leave the earth.

Although it is not likely that a criminal will carefully consider the text of the law before he murders or steals, it is reasonable that a fair warning should be given to the world in language that the common world will understand, of what the law intends to do if a certain line is passed. To make the warning fair, so far as possible the line should be clear. When a rule of conduct is laid down in words that evoke in the common mind only the picture of vehicles moving on land, the statute should not be extended to aircraft simply because it may seem to us that a similar policy applies, or upon the speculation that if the legislature had thought of it, very likely broader words would have been used. United States v. Bhagat Singh Thind, 261 U. S. 204, 209, 43 S. Ct. 338, 67 L. Ed. 616.

Judgment reversed.

Figure 3–3b (continued)

WILLIAM W. McBOYLE, Petitioner,
v.
UNITED STATES
OF AMERICA.

(283 U. S. 25–27.)

Aeroplanes, § 1 — transportation of stolen plane.
The transportation of an airplane, knowing it to have been stolen, is not a violation of the National Motor Vehicle Theft Act of October 29, 1919, 41 Stat. at L. 324, chap. 89, U. S. C. title 18, § 408, imposing a penalty upon anyone who shall transport, or cause to be transported, in interstate or foreign commerce, a motor vehicle knowing it to have been stolen, and providing that "the term 'motor vehicle' shall include an automobile, . . . motorcycle, or any other

self-propelled vehicle not designed for running on rails."

[No. 552.]

Argued February 26 and 27, 1931.
Decided March 9, 1931.

ON WRIT of Certiorari to the United States Circuit Court of Appeals for the Tenth Circuit to review a judgment affirming a judgment of the District Court of the United States for the Western District of Oklahoma upon a conviction of violating the National Motor Vehicle Theft Act by transporting an airplane knowing it to have been stolen. Reversed.

See same case below, 43 F. (2d) 273.

The facts are stated in the opinion.

Figure 3–3c McBoyle v. United States. From Lawyer's Cooperative Publishing; reprinted with the permission of West Group.

Mr. **Harry F. Brown**, of Guthrie, Oklahoma, argued the cause and filed a brief for petitioner:

The term "motor vehicle," as used in the National Motor Vehicle Theft Act, does not include or embrace airplanes, and the indictment does not state a Federal offense, and is therefore void, and the trial court is without jurisdiction.

Being a penal statute, the act must be strictly construed.

25 R. C. L. 1083, 1084; United States v. Wiltberger, 5 Wheat. 76, 5 L. ed. 37; First Nat. Bank v. United States, 46 L.R.A. (N.S.) 1139, 124 C. C. A. 256, 206 Fed. 374.

The language of the act does not clearly indicate the crime charged.

United States v. Noveck, 271 U. S. 201, 70 L. ed. 904, 46 S. Ct. 476; United States v. Lacher, 134 U. S. 624, 628, 33 L. ed. 1080, 1083, 10 S. Ct. 625; Todd v. United States, 158 U. S. 278, 282, 39 L. ed 982, 983, 15 S. Ct. 889; Fasulo v. United States, 272 U. S. 620, 629, 71 L. ed. 443, 445, 47 S. Ct. 200; Donnelley v. United States, 276 U. S. 511, 72 L. ed. 678, 48 S. Ct. 400.

The language of the act, in the light of both legal and general usage, shows conclusively that airplanes were not intended to be embraced therein.

39 Cyc. 1125; Duckwall v. New Albany, 25 Ind. 283; Baltimore & O. R. Co. v. District of Columbia, 10 App. D. C. 111; 19 R. C. L. 677.

Under the doctrine of ejusdem generis the act cannot be construed to embrace airplanes.

36 Cyc. 1119; First Nat. Bank v. United States, 46 L.R.A. (N.S.) 1139, 124 C. C. A. 256, 206 Fed. 374; Parman v. Lemmon, 120 Kan. 370, 44 A.L.R. 1507, 244 Pac. 232; North American Acci. Ins. Co. v. Pitts, 213 Ala. 102, 40 A.L.R. 1171, 104 So. 21.

The debates of Congress at the time of the enactment of the law clearly and conclusively show that airplanes were not intended to be included in the term "motor vehicle," as used therein.

Work v. Braffet, 276 U. S. 560, 566, 72 L. ed. 700–703, 48 S. Ct. 363; Blake v. National City Bank, 23 Wall. 307–321, 23 L. ed. 119-121.

Mr. **Claude R. Branch**, of Washington, D. C., argued the cause, and with Solicitor General Thacher, Assistant Attorney General Nugent Dodds, and Messrs. Harry S. Ridgely and W. Marvin Smith, also of Washington, D. C., filed a brief for respondent:

The term "motor vehicle," as defined in the National Motor Vehicle Theft Act, should be construed to include an airplane. This construction does not extend the words of the statute beyond their letter, or add to them by inference, or attribute to them a purpose which it is clear that Congress did not intend them to have.

Donnelley v. United States, 276 U. S. 505, 512, 72 L. ed. 676, 678, 48 S. Ct. 400; Fasulo v. United States, 272 U. S. 620, 71 L. ed. 443, 47 S. Ct. 200; United States v. Noveck, 271 U. S. 201, 70 L. ed. 904, 46 S. Ct. 476; Mason v. United States, 260 U. S. 545, 554, 67 L. ed. 396, 400, 43 S. Ct. 200; Mid-Northern Oil Co. v. Walker, 268 U. S. 45, 49, 50, 69 L. ed. 841, 843, 45 S. Ct. 119; Caminetti v. United States 242 U. S. 470, 487, 61 L. ed. 442, 453, L.R.A.1917F, 502, 37 S. Ct. 192, Ann. Cas. 1917B, 1168; United States v. Mescall, 215 U. S. 26, 31, 54, L. ed. 77, 79, 30 S. Ct. 19; Cutler v. Kouns, 110 U. S. 720, 728, 28 L. ed. 305, 307, 4 S. Ct. 274; United States v. Briggs, 9 How. 351, 13 L. ed. 170.

Mr. Justice **Holmes** delivered the opinion of the court:

The petitioner was convicted of transporting from Ottawa, Illinois, to Guymon, Oklahoma, an airplane that he knew to have been stolen, and was sentenced to serve three years' imprisonment and to pay a fine of $2,000. The judgment was affirmed by the circuit court of appeals for the tenth circuit. 43 F. (2d) 273. A

Figure 3–3c (continued)

56 ✳ *Chapter 3*

writ of certiorari was granted by this court on the question whether the National Motor Vehicle Theft Act applies to aircraft. **[26]** Act of October 29, 1919, chap. 89, 41 Stat. at L. 324, U. S. C. title 18, § 408. That act provides: "Sec. 2. That when used in this act: (a) The term 'motor vehicle' shall include an automobile, automobile truck, automobile wagon, motorcycle, or any other self-propelled vehicle not designed for running on rails; . . . Sec. 3. That whoever shall transport or cause to be transported in interstate or foreign commerce a motor vehicle, knowing the same to have been stolen, shall be punished by a fine of not more than $5,000, or by imprisonment of not more than five years, or both."

Section 2 defines the motor vehicles for which the transportation in interstate commerce is punished in § 3. The question is the meaning of the word "vehicle" in the phrase, "any other self-propelled vehicle not designed for running on rails." No doubt etymologically it is possible to use the word to signify a conveyance working on land, water or air, and sometimes legislation extends the use in that direction, e. g., land and air, water being separately provided for in the Tariff Act, September 22, 1922, chap. 356, § 401 (b), 42 Stat. at L. 858, 948, U. S. C. title 19, § 231. But in everyday speech "vehicle" calls up the picture of a thing moving on land. Thus, in Rev. Stat. § 4, title 1, §4, intended, the government suggests, rather to enlarge than to restrict the definition, "vehicle" includes every contrivance capable of being used "as a means of transportation on land." And this is repeated, expressly excluding aircraft, in the Tariff Act, June 17, 1930, chap. 497, § 401 (b), 46 Stat. at L590, 708, U. S. C. title 19, § 1401. So, here, the phrase under discussion calls up the popular picture. For, after including automobile truck, automobile wagon and

motorcycle, the words "any other self-propelled vehicle not designed for running on rails" still indicate that a vehicle in the popular sense, that is a vehicle running on land, is the theme. It is a vehicle that runs, not something, not commonly called a vehicle, that flies. Airplanes were well known in 1919 when this statute was passed, but it is admitted that they were not mentioned in the reports or in the debates in Congress. **[27]** It is impossible to read words that so carefully enumerate the different forms of notor vehicles and have no reference of any kind to aircraft, as including airplanes under a term that usage more and more precisely confines to a different class. The counsel for the petitioner have shown that the phraseology of the statute as to motor vehicles follows that of earlier statutes of Connecticut, Delaware, Ohio, Michigan and Missouri, not to mention the late Regulations of Traffic for the District of Columbia, title 6, chap. 9, § 242, none of which can be supposed to leave the earth.

Although it is not likely that a criminal will carefully consider the text of the law before he murders or steals, it is reasonable that a fair warning should be given to the world in language that the common world will understand, of what the law intends to do if a certain line is passed. To make the warning fair, so far as possible the line should be clear. When a rule of conduct is laid down in words that evoke in the common mind only the picture of vehicles moving on land, the statute should not be extended to aircraft simply because it may seem to us that a similar policy applies, or upon the speculation that if the legislature had thought of it, very likely broader words would have been used. United States v. Bhagat Singh Thind, 261 U. S. 204, 209, 67 L. ed. 616, 617, 43 S. Ct. 338.

Judgment reversed.

Figure 3–3c (continued)

RELIGION AND FREE EXPRESSION

FIRST AMENDMENT

Congress shall make no law respecting an establishment of religion, or prohibiting the free exercise thereof; or abridging the freedom of speech, or of the press; or the right of the people peaceably to assemble, and to petition the Government for a redress of grievances.

RELIGION

An Overview
Madison's original proposal for a bill of rights provision concerning religion read: "The civil rights of none shall be abridged on account of religious belief or worship, nor shall any national religion be established, nor shall the full and equal rights of conscience be in any manner, or on any pretence, infringed."[1] The language was altered in the House to read: "Congress shall make no law establishing religion, or to prevent the free exercise thereof, or to infringe the rights of conscience."[2] In the Senate, the section adopted read: "Congress shall make no law establishing articles of faith, or a mode of worship, or prohibiting the free exercise of religion, . . ."[3] It was in the conference committee of the two bodies, chaired by Madison, that the present language was written with its

---

[1] 1 *Annals of Congress* 434 (June 8, 1789).

[2] The committee appointed to consider Madison's proposals, and on which Madison served, with Vining as chairman, had rewritten the religion section to read: "No religion shall be established by law, nor shall the equal rights of conscience be infringed." After some debate during which Madison suggested that the word "national" might be inserted before the word "religion" as "point[ing] the amendment directly to the object it was intended to prevent," the House adopted a substitute reading: "Congress shall make no laws touching religion, or infringing the rights of conscience." 1 *Annals of Congress* 729-731 (August 15, 1789). On August 20, on motion of Fisher Ames, the language of the clause as quoted in the text was adopted. Id., 766. According to Madison's biographer, "[t]here can be little doubt that this was written by Madison." I. Brant, *James Madison — Father of the Constitution 1787-1800* (Indianapolis: 1950), 271.

[3] This text, taken from the Senate *Journal* of September 9, appears in 2 B. Schwartz (ed.), *The Bill of Rights: A Documentary History* (New York: 1971), 1153. It was at this point that the religion clauses were joined with the freedom of expression clauses.

Figure 3–4a Constitution: Amendment I (official).

Legislative Materials

Statutes. The **Government Printing Office** (GPO) officially publishes federal statutes in the U.S.C. West Group and Reed also publish unofficial versions of the United States Code (the U.S.C.A. and the U.S.C.S., respectively) that include annotations to interpretive materials. Figure 3–5a, beginning on page 62, Figure 3–5b, beginning on page 64, and Figure 3–5c, beginning on page 66, show examples of the federal Gun-Free Schools Act as published officially and unofficially.

(Text continues on page 68.)

FREEDOM OF RELIGION Amend. 1

Amendment I. Freedom of Religion
Congress shall make no law respecting an establishment of religion, or prohibiting the free exercise thereof; * * *

LIBRARY REFERENCES
Administrative Law
Aid to sectarian schools, see West's Federal Practice Manual § 13482.
Public office, clerical disqualification, see West's Federal Practice Manual § 13485.
Public schools, use of church facilities, see West's Federal Practice Manual § 13165.
Segregated sectarian schools, see West's Federal Practice Manual § 13351.

Law Reviews
A restatement of the intended meaning of the establishment clause in relation to education and religion. John Remington Graham, 1981 Brigham Young U.L.Rev. 333.
Public aid to parochial schools. Paul A. Freund, 82 Harvard L.Rev. 1680 (1969).
Religion as a concept in constitutional law. Kent Greenawalt, 72 Cal.L.Rev. 753 (1984).
Religion, equality, and the Constitution: An equal protection approach to establishment clause adjudication. Michael A. Paulsen, 61 Notre Dame L.Rev. 311 (1986).
Supreme Court and First Amendment rights of students in the public school classroom. Brian A. Freeman (1984) 12 Hast.Const.L.Q. 1.
Supreme Court, compulsory education, and the first amendment's religion clauses. Philip B. Kurland, 75 W.Va.L.Rev. 213 (1973).

Texts and Treatises
Discovery, scope of and relevancy to subject matter of litigation, see Wright & Miller, Federal Practice and Procedure: Civil § 2009.
Freedom of religion, see Rotunda, Nowak & Young, Treatise on Constitutional Law: Substance and Procedure § 21.1 et seq.
Propriety of summary judgment in constitutional and civil rights litigation, see Wright, Miller & Kane, Federal Practice and Procedure: Civil 2d § 2732.2.
Res judicata, effect upon civil rights actions, see Wright, Miller & Cooper, Federal Practice and Procedure: Jurisdiction § 4471.
Rights of religious autonomy, see Tribe, American Constitutional Law § 14-1 et seq.
Ripeness doctrine, see Wright, Miller & Cooper, Federal Practice and Procedure: Jurisdiction 2d § 3532 et seq.
Substantiality of federal claim, see Wright, Miller & Cooper, Federal Practice and Procedure: Jurisdiction 2d § 3564.

WESTLAW ELECTRONIC RESEARCH
See WESTLAW guide following the Explanation pages of this volume.

NOTES OF DECISIONS
 I. **GENERALLY 1-60**
 II. **DISTRIBUTION OF LITERATURE AND SOLICITATION OF FUNDS 61-120**
 III. **ECCLESIASTICAL DISPUTES 121-160**
 IV. **MILITARY SERVICE 161-200**

Figure 3–4b Constitution: Amendment I. From *United States Code Annotated*; reprinted with the permission of West Group.

AMENDMENTS

**ARTICLES IN ADDITION TO, AND IN AMENDMENT OF, THE CONSTITU-
TION OF THE UNITED STATES**

Proposed by Congress, and Ratified by the Several States, Pursuant to the Fifth
Article of the Original Constitution

HISTORY; ANCILLARY LAWS AND DIRECTIVES

Explanatory notes:
In the original, the amendments are set out as "articles in addition to, and amendatory
of, the Constitution . . . ." Since they are usually referred to simply as "amendments,"
that term is used herein instead of the word "Article," so as to avoid confusion with the
body of the Constitution.

The first ten amendments to the Constitution of the United States were proposed to
the legislatures of the several states by the First Congress, on the 25th of September,
1789. They were ratified by the following states, and the notifications of ratification by
the governors thereof were successively communicated by the President to Congress:
Delaware, January 28, 1790; Maryland, December 19, 1789; New Hampshire, January
25, 1790; New Jersey, November 20, 1789; New York, March 27, 1790; North Carolina,
December 22, 1789; Pennsylvania, March 10, 1790; Rhode Island, June 15, 1790; South
Carolina, January 19, 1790; Vermont, November 3, 1791; and Virginia, December 15,
1791. The following of the thirteen original states did not ratify until the year 1939:
Connecticut, April 19; Georgia, March 18; Massachusetts, March 2.

AMENDMENT 1

Religious and political freedom.
Congress shall make no law respecting an establishment of religion, or prohibiting the
free exercise thereof; or abridging the freedom of speech, or of the press; or the right of
the people peaceably to assemble, and to petition the Government for a redress of
grievances.

CROSS REFERENCES

States as prohibited from depriving persons of due process of law, generally, USCS
Constitution, Amendment 14, § 1.
Expression of views as not constituting unfair labor practice, generally, 29 USCS §
158(c).

RESEARCH GUIDE

Federal Procedure L Ed:
6 Fed Proc L Ed, Civil Rights §§ 11:26, 39, 40, 61, 110, 111, 127, 128, 305, 312,
918.
8 Fed Proc L Ed, Criminal Procedure §§ 22:146, 170, 220, 383, 454, 457.
9 Fed Proc L Ed, Criminal Procedure §§ 22:1312–1318.
10 Fed Proc L Ed, Discovery and Depositions §§ 26:228 et seq.
10A Fed Proc L Ed, Elections and Elective Franchise § 28:66 et seq.
12 Fed Proc L Ed, Evidence § 33:340.
15 Fed Proc L Ed, Government Contracts §§ 38:443, 447.

Figure 3–4c Constitution: Amendment I. From Lawyer's Cooperative
Publishing; reprinted with the permission of West Group.

Mirsky. Civil Religion and the Establishment Clause. 95 Yale L J 1237, May, 1986.
Emerson. Freedom of Association and Freedom of Expression. 74 Yale LJ 1.
Conspiracy and the First Amendment. 79 Yale LJ 872.
Toward a Uniform Valuation of the Religion Guarantees. 80 Yale LJ 77.
Privacy and the First Amendment. 82 Yale LJ 1462.

Auto-Cite®: Cases and annotations referred to herein can be further researched through the Auto-Cite® computer-assisted research service. Use Auto-Cite to check citations for form, parallel references, prior and later history, and annotation references.

INTERPRETIVE NOTES AND DECISIONS

I. IN GENERAL
  A. Amendments to Constitution; Bill of Rights (note 1)
  B. First Amendment, Generally (notes 2-8)
II. ESTABLISHMENT OF RELIGION; FREE EXERCISE OF RELIGION
  A. In General (notes 9-21)
  B. Particular Matters
    1. In General (notes 22-81)
    2. Religion in Public Schools (notes 82-93)
    3. Sectarian or Parochial Schools (notes 94-104)
    4. Taxation (notes 105-116)
    5. Military Service (notes 117-123)
III. FREEDOM OF SPEECH AND PRESS
  A. In General (notes 124-148)
  B. Contents of Utterance
    1. In General (notes 149-176)
    2. Sexually explicit material (notes 177-199)
    3. Defamation (notes 200-219)
  C. Manner and Place of Utterance
    1. In General (notes 220-253)
    2. Advertising (notes 254-271)
    3. Use of Public Property (notes 272-287)
  D. Access to and Coverage of Government Activities
    1. In General (notes 288-295)
    2. Judicial Proceedings (notes 296-307)
  E. Labor and Employment
    1. In General (notes 308-322)
    2. Picketing and Boycotts (notes 323-332)
    3. Public Officers and Employees, Generally (notes 333-374)
    4. Educational employees
      a. Teachers, Professors (notes 375-386)
      b. Others (note 387)
  F. Education, In General (notes 388-400)
  G. Political Activities (notes 401-411)
  H. Licensing (notes 412-421)
  I. Mail Regulation (notes 422-432)
  J. Other Regulation or Infringement (notes 433-467)
IV. FREEDOM OF ASSEMBLY (notes 468-478)
V. FREEDOM TO PETITION FOR REDRESS OF GRIEVANCES (notes 479-494)
VI. FREEDOM OF ASSOCIATION
  A. In General (notes 495-506)
  B. Government Interference (notes 507-511)
  C. Right to Associational ties,

Figure 3–4c (continued)

adoption, and not interfering at all with its spirit, and such exceptions were obviously intended to be respected. Mattox v United States (1895) 156 US 237, 39 L Ed 409, 15 S Ct 337.

If there is any conflict between provisions of Constitution and of Amendments, Amendments must control. Schick v United States (1904) 195 US 65, 49 L Ed 99, 24 S Ct 826.

Conduct controlled by hair-length regulations is not analogous to conduct in privacy of bedroom and is not protected within penumbra of specific guarantees of Bill of Rights. Freeman v Flake (1971, CA10 Utah) 448 F2d 258, cert den (1972) 405 US 1032, 31 L Ed 2d 489, 92 S Ct 1292.

First ten amendments to federal Constitution apply only to procedure and trial of causes in federal courts and do not impose limitations upon such action in state courts, but where violation of rights enumerated in these amendments amounts to denial of due process of law, within meaning of Fourteenth Amendment to Federal Constitution, conduct of that character by state is forbidden and condemned by that amendment. State ex rel. Cosner v See (1947) 129 W Va 722, 42 SE2d 31.

B. First Amendment, Generally
2. Generally

First Amendment gives freedom of mind same security as freedom of conscience. Thomas v Collins (1945) 323 US 516, 89 L Ed 430, 65 S Ct 315, 15 BNA LRRM 777, 9 CCH LC ¶ 51192, reh den (1945) 323 US 819, 89 L Ed 650, 65 S Ct 557.

Prison inmate retains those First Amendment rights that are not inconsistent with his status as prisoner or with legitimate penological objectives of corrections system. Pell v Procunier (1974) 417 US 817, 41 L Ed 2d 495, 94 S Ct 2800, 71 Ohio Ops 2d 195, 1 Media L R 2379 (superseded by statute on other grounds as stated in Hamilton v Schriro (1994, WD Mo) 1994 US Dist LEXIS 14885).

Economically motivated expression or association is not disqualified from protection under First Amendment. International Union, United Auto., etc. International Union, United Auto., etc. v National Right to Work Legal Defense & Education Foundation, Inc. (1978) 192 US App DC 23, 590 F2d 1139, 99 BNA LRRM 3181, 84 CCH LC ¶ 10904, 26 FR Serv 2d 582.

First Amendment is intended to assure privilege that in itself must be so actual

Figure 3–4c (continued)

and certain that fear and doubt are absent from individual's mind, or freedom is but abstraction. NLRB v Montgomery Ward & Co. (1946, CA8) 157 F2d 486, 19 BNA LRRM 2008, 11 CCH LC ¶ 63406.

4. Standing, generally

First Amendment, standing alone, cannot be interpreted to command payment of money damages; it does not provide persons aggrieved by governmental action with action for damages in absence of some other jurisdictional basis. United States v Connolly (1983, CA FC) 716 F2d 882, cert den (1984) 465 US 1065, 79 L Ed 2d 740, 104 S Ct 1414.

While general rule is that person to whom statute may constitutionally be applied cannot challenge that statute on ground that it may conceivably be applied unconstitutionally to others, if statute purports to regulate First Amendment rights one who does not come within constitutional protection may nevertheless attack it. State v Woodworth (1975, ND) 234 NW2d 243.

State statute which prohibits marriage of persons of same sex, does not offend First Amendment to United States Constitution. Baker V Nelson (1971) 291 Minn 310, 191 NW2d 185, app dismd (1972) 409 US 810, 34 L Ed 2d 65, 93 S Ct 37.

Right to marry underlies purposes of Constitution, although not mentioned therein, and is fundamental right afforded protection by First, Fifth, Ninth, and Fourteenth Amendments to United States Constitution; personal rule which establishes system of classification of employees that is based upon and affects exercise of fundamental right can only be sustained if it promotes compelling governmental interest. Voichahoske v Grand Island (1975) 194 Neb 175, 231 Nw2d 124, 10 CCH EPD ¶ 10247.

No citizen has right to challenge constitutionality of law or regulation based upon First Amendment by obstructing police officer charged with enforcing law or regulation; proper place to challenge constitutionality of law or regulation is in

Figure 3–4c (continued)

(Pub. L. 89-10, title XIV, § 14514, as added Pub. L. 103-382, title I, § 101, Oct. 20, 1994, 108 Stat. 3907.)

REFERENCES IN TEXT

The Goals 2000: Educate America Act, referred to in text, is Pub. L. 103-227, Mar. 31, 1994, 108 Stat. 125 (except titles V and IX), as amended, which is classified principally to chapter 68 (§ 5801 et seq.) of this title (except subchapters V (§ 5931 et seq.) and IX (§6001 et seq.)). For complete classification of this Act to the Code, see Short Title not set out under section 5801 of this title and Tables.

Part F—Gun Possession

Part Referred to in Other Sections

This part is referred to in section 8802 of this title.

§ 8921. Gun-free requirements

(a) Short title

This section may be cited as the "Gun-Free Schools Act of 1994".

(b) Requirements

(1) In general

Except as provided in paragraph (3), each state receiving Federal funds under this chapter shall have in effect a State law requiring local educational agencies to expel from school for a period of not less than one year a student who is determined to have brought a weapon to a school under the jurisdiction of local educational agencies in that State, except that such State law shall allow the chief administering officer of such local educational agency to modify such expulsion

Figure 3–5a Gun-Free Schools Act (official).

requirement for a student on a case-by-case basis.

(2) Construction

Nothing in this subchapter shall be construed to prevent a State from allowing a local educational agency that has expelled a student from such a student's regular school setting from providing educational services to such student in an alternative setting.

(3) Special rule

(A) Any State that has a law in effect prior to October 20, 1994, which is in conflict with the not less than one year expulsion requirement described in paragraph (1) shall have the period of time described in subparagraph (B) to comply with such requirement.

(B) The period of time shall be the period beginning on October 20, 1994, and ending one year after such date.

(4) "Weapon" defined

For the purpose of this section, the term "weapon" means a firearm as such term is defined in section 921 of title 18.

(c) Special rule

The provisions of this section shall be construed in a manner consistent with the Individuals with Disabilities Education Act [20 U.S.C. 1400 et seq.].

(d) Report to State

Each local educational agency requesting assistance from the State educational agency that is to be provided from funds made available to the State under this chapter shall provide to the State, in the application requesting such assistance—

(1) an assurance that such local educational agency is in compliance with the State law required by subsection (b) of this section; and

(2) a description of the circumstances surrounding any expulsions imposed under the State law required by subsection (b) of this section, including—

(A) the name of the school concerned;

(B) the number of students expelled from such school; and

(C) the type of weapons concerned.

(e) Reporting

Each State shall report the information described in subsection (c) of this section to the Secretary on an annual basis.

(f) Report to Congress

Two years after October 20, 1994, the Secretary shall report to Congress if any State is not in compliance with the requirements of this subchapter.

(Pub. L. 89-10, title XIV, § 14601, as added Pub. L. 103-382, title I, § 101, Oct. 20, 1994, 108 Stat. 3907.)

REFERENCES IN TEXT

The Individuals with Disabilities Education Act, referred to in subsec. (c), is title VI of Pub. L. 91-230, Apr. 13, 1970, 84 Stat. 175, as amended, which is classified generally to chapter 33 (§ 1400 et seq.) of this title. For complete classification of this Act to the Code, see section 1400 of this title and Tables.

APPLICABILITY OF INDIVIDUALS WITH DISABILITIES EDUCATION ACT

Section 314(b) of Pub. L. 103-382 provided that: "Nothing in the Individuals with Disabilities Education Act [20 U.S.C. 1400 et seq.] shall supersede the provisions of section 14601 of the Elementary and Secondary Education Act [of 1965] [20 U.S.C. 8921] if a child's behavior is unrelated to such child's disability, except that this section [amending section 1415 of this title and enacting provisions set out as a note under section 1415 of this title] shall be interpreted in a manner that is consistent with the Department's final guidance concerning State and local responsibilities under the Gun-Free Schools Act of 1994 [20 U.S.C. 8921]."

§ 8922. Policy regarding criminal justice system referral

(a) In general

No funds shall be made available under this chapter to any local educational agency unless such agency has a policy requiring referral to the criminal justice or juvenile delinquency system of any student who brings a firearm or weapon to a school served by such agency.

(b) Definitions

For the purpose of this section, the terms "firearm" and "school" have the same meaning given to such terms by section 921(a) of title 18.

(Pub. L. 89-10, title XIV, § 14602, as added Pub. L. 103-382, title I, § 101, Oct. 20, 1994, 108 Stat. 3908.)

Figure 3–5a (continued)

§ 8921. Gun-free requirements

(a) Short title

This section may be cited as the "Gun-Free Schools Act of 1994".

(b) Requirements

(1) In general

Except as provided in paragraph (3), each State receiving Federal funds under this chapter shall have in effect a State law requiring local educational agencies to expel from school for a period of not less than one year a student who is determined to have brought a weapon to a school under the jurisdiction of local educational agencies in that State, except that such State law shall allow the chief administering officer of such local educational agency to modify such expulsion requirement for a student on a case-by-case basis.

(2) Construction

Nothing in this subchapter shall be construed to prevent a State from allowing a local educational agency that has expelled a student from such a student's regular school setting from providing educational services to such student in an alternative setting.

(3) Special rule

(A) Any State that has a law in effect prior to October 20, 1994 which is in conflict with the not less than one year expulsion requirement described in paragraph (1) shall have the period of time described in subparagraph (B) to comply with such requirement.

(B) The period of time shall be the period beginning on October 20, 1994 and ending one year after such date.

(4) Definition

For the purpose of this section, the term "weapon" means a firearm as such term is defined in section 921 of Title 18.

(c) Special rule

The provisions of this section shall be construed in a manner consistent with the Individuals with Disabilities Education Act [20 U.S.C.A. § 1400 et seq.].

(d) Report to State

Each local educational agency requesting assistance from the State educational agency that is to be provided from funds made available to the State

Figure 3–5b Gun-Free Schools Act. From *United States Code Annotated*; reprinted with the permission of West Group.

under this chapter shall provide to the State, in the application requesting such assistance—
  (1) an assurance that such local educational agency is in compliance with the State law required by subsection (b) of this section; and
  (2) a description of the circumstances surrounding any expulsions imposed under the State law required by subsection (b) of this section, including—
    (A) the name of the school concerned;
    (B) the number of students expelled from such school; and
    (C) the type of weapons concerned.

(e) Reporting

Each State shall report the information described in subsection (c) of this section to the Secretary on an annual basis.

(f) Report to Congress

Two years after October 20, 1994, the Secretary shall report to Congress if any State is not in compliance with the requirements of this subchapter.

(Pub.L. 89-10, Title XIV, § 14601, as added Pub.L. 103-382, Title I, § 101, Oct. 20, 1994, 108 Stat. 3907.)

HISTORICAL AND STATUTORY NOTES

Revision Notes and Legislative Reports
1994 Acts. House Report No. 103-425 and House Conference Report No. 103-761, see 1994 U.S. Code Cong. and Adm. News, p. 2807.

References in Text
The Individuals with Disabilities Education Act, referred to in subsec. (c), is Pub.L. 91-230, Title VI, Apr. 13, 1970, 84 Stat. 175, as amended, which is classified generally to chapter 33 (section 1400 et seq.) of this title. For complete classification of this Act to the Code, see section 1400 of this title and Tables.

Effective Dates
1994 Acts. Section effective July 1, 1995, except that provisions that apply to programs under subchapter VIII of this chapter, and to programs that are conducted on a competitive basis, effective with respect to appropriations for use under such programs for fiscal year 1995 and for subsequent fiscal years, see section 3(a)(1)(A) of Pub.L. 103-382, set out as a note under section 6301 of this title.

Applicability of Individuals with Disabilities Education Act
Section 314(b) of Pub.L. 103-382 provided that: "Nothing in the Individuals with Disabilities Education Act [Pub.L. 91-230, Title VI, Apr. 13, 1970, 84 Stat. 175, classified to section 1400 et seq. of this title] shall supersede the provisions of section 14601 of the Elementary and Secondary Education Act [this section] if a child's behavior is unrelated to such child's disability, except that this section [section 314 of Pub.L. 103-382, which amended section 1415 of this title and enacted provisions set out as notes under this section and section 1415 of this title] shall be interpreted in a manner that is consistent with the Department's final guidance concerning State and local responsibilities under the Gun-Free Schools Act of 1994 [Pub.L. 103-227, Title X, Part B, Mar. 31, 1994, 108 Stat. 270, classified to section 3381 et seq. of this title]." [Section 314(b) of Pub.L. 103-382 effective July 1, 1995, see section 3(a)(3)(A) of Pub.L. 103-382, set out as a note under section 1411 of this title.]

Figure 3–5b (continued)

LIBRARY REFERENCES

American Digest System
  Schools ⇐ 177.
Encyclopedias
  Schools and School Districts, see C.J.S. § 798 et seq.

WESTLAW ELECTRONIC RESEARCH

Schools cases: 345k⇐.
See WESTLAW guide following the Explanation pages of this volume.

Notes of Decision

1. Construction with other laws

Provision of Gun-Free Schools Act requiring each state receiving federal funds to have in effect state law requiring expulsion from school for not less than one year of student who brings weapon to campus did not permit or require expulsion of handicapped student without adherence to procedural safeguards of Individuals with Disabilities Education Act (IDEA), and did not eliminate district's obligation to provide student with free appropriate public education (FAPE) following his expulsion; final Congressional guidance concerning state and local responsibilities under Gun-Free Schools Act stated that children with disabilities removed from school pursuant to Act must be provided with alternative programming during disciplinary exclusion, and Act specifically stated that its provisions must be construed consistently with IDEA. Magyar By and Through Magyar v. Tucson Unified School Dist., D.Ariz. 1997, 958 F.Sup. 1423.

Figure 3–5b (continued)

GUN POSSESSION

§ 8921. Gun-free requirements

(a) Short title. This section may be cited as the "Gun-Free Schools Act of 1994".

(b) Requirements. (1) In general. Except as provided in paragraph (3), each State receiving Federal funds under this Act [20 USCS §§ 6301 et seq.] shall have in effect a State law requiring local educational agencies to expel from school for a period of not less than one year a student who is determined to have brought a weapon to a school under the jurisdiction of local educational agencies in that State, except that such State law shall allow the chief administering officer of such local educational agency to modify such expulsion requirement for a student on a case-by-case basis.

(2) Construction. Nothing in this title shall be construed to prevent a State from allowing a local educational agency that has expelled a student from such a student's regular school setting from providing educational services to such student in an alternative setting.

(3) Special rule. (A) Any State that has a law in effect prior to the date of enactment of the Improving American's Schools Act of 1994 [enacted Oct. 20, 1994] which is in conflict with the not less than one year expulsion requirement described in paragraph (1) shall have the period of time described in subparagraph (B) to comply with such requirement.

Figure 3–5c Gun-Free Schools Act. From Lawyer's Cooperative Publishing; reprinted with the permission of West Group.

(B) The period of time shall be the period beginning on the date of enactment of the Improving America's Schools Act [enacted Oct. 20, 1994] and ending one year after such date.

(4) **Definition.** For the purpose of this section, the term "weapon" means a firearm as such term is defined in section 921 of title 18, United States Code.

(c) Special rule. The provisions of this section shall be construed in a manner consistent with the Individuals with Disabilities Education Act [20 USCS §§ 1400 et seq.].

(d) Report to State. Each local educational agency requesting assistance from the State educational agency that is to be provided from funds made available to the State under this Act [20 USCS §§ 6301 et seq.] shall provide to the State, in the application requesting such assistance—

(1) an assurance that such local educational agency is in compliance with the State law required by subsection (b); and

(2) a description of the circumstances surrounding any expulsions imposed under the State law required by subsection (b), including—

(A) the name of the school concerned;

(B) the number of students expelled from such school; and

(C) the type of weapons concerned.

(e) Reporting. Each State shall report the information described in subsection (c) to the Secretary on an annual basis.

(f) Report to Congress. Two years after the date of enactment of the Improving America's Schools Act of 1994 [enacted Oct. 20, 1994], the Secretary shall report to Congress if any State is not in compliance with the requirements of this title.

(April 11, 1965, P. L. 89–10, Title XIV, Part F, § 14601, as added Oct. 20, 1994, P. L. 103–382, Title I, § 101, 108 Stat. 3907.)

HISTORY; ANCILLARY LAWS AND DIRECTIVES

References in text:
With respect to the references in subsecs. (b)(2) and (f) to "this title", this section is part of Title XIV of Act April 11, 1965, P. L. 89–10, which appears as 20 USCS §§ 8801 et seq. However, Congress may have intended such references to read "this part" (i.e., Part F of Title XIV of Act April 11, 1965, P. L. 89–10, which appears as 20 USCS §§ 8921 et seq.).

Effective date of section:
Act April 11, 1965, P. L. 89–10 (20 USCS §§ 6301 et seq.), as added by Title I of Act Oct. 20, 1994, P. L. 103–382, takes effect July 1, 1995, except that provisions applicable to programs under Title VIII of the 1965 Act (20 USCS §§ 7701 et seq.), and to programs under such Act that are conducted on a competitive basis, shall be effective with respect to appropriations for use under such programs for fiscal year 1995 and for subsequent fiscal years, as provided by § 3(a)(1)(A) of Act Oct. 20, 1994, P. L. 103–382, which appears as 20 USCS § 6301 note.

Other provisions:
Relationship with Individuals with Disabilities Education Act. Act Oct. 20, 1994, P. L. 103–382, Title III, Part A, § 314(b), 108 Stat. 3937, provides: "(b) Limitation. Nothing in the Individuals with Disabilities Education Act [20 USCS §§ 1400 et seq.] shall supersede the provisions of section 14601 of the Elementary and Secondary Education Act [this section] if a child's behavior is unrelated to such child's disability, except that this section shall be interpreted in a manner that is consistent with the Department's final guidance concerning State and local responsibilities under the Gun-Free Schools Act of 1994 [this section].".

§ 8922. Policy regarding criminal justice system referral

(a) In general. No funds shall be made available under this Act [20 USCS §§6301 et seq.] to any local educational agency unless such agency has a policy requiring refer-

Figure 3–5c (continued)

ral to the criminal justice or juvenile delinquency system of any student who brings a firearm or weapon to a school served by such agency.
(b) Definitions. For the purpose of this section, the terms "firearm" and "school" have the same meaning given to such terms by section 921(a) of title 18, United States Code. (April 11, 1965, P. L. 89–10, Title XIV, Part F, § 14602, as added Oct. 20, 1994, P. L. 103–382, Title I, § 101, 108 Stat. 3908.)

HISTORY; ANCILLARY LAWS AND DIRECTIVES

Effective date of section:
Act April 11, 1965, P. L. 89–10 (20 USCS §§ 6301 et seq.), as added by Title I of Act Oct. 20, 1994, P. L. 103–382, takes effect July 1, 1995, except that provisions applicable to programs under Title VIII of the 1965 Act (20 USCS §§ 7701 et seq.), and to programs under such Act that are conducted on a competitive basis, shall be effective with respect to appropriations for use under such programs for fiscal year 1995 and for subsequent fiscal years, as provided by § 3(a)(1)(A) of Act Oct. 20, 1994, P. L. 103–382, which appears as 20 USCS § 6301 note.

Figure 3–5c (continued)

Federal statutes are topically arranged and numbered (**titled**). Both official and unofficial versions of the United States Code are fully indexed. Those indices include *Popular Names Tables* that cross-reference statutory popular names to their federal titles. Statutes are updated annually by **pocket parts**, paperback supplements stored in the back of each volume. Like their hardbound volumes, statutory pocket parts are arranged by title and section number. *Shepard's* (Reed) Statutory Citations updates statutes by indicating if the statute has been amended or repealed and by collecting citations to other legal materials (cases, law review articles, treatises, and services) interpreting the statutes.

Legislative History. Legislative history (including early bill versions, committee and house debates, and presidential action) are published in the following books:

U.S.C., U.S.C.A., and U.S.C.S. (historical data)
U.S. Code Congressional and Administrative News (includes text of public laws, Congressional committee reports, tables of U.S. Code and Statutes at Large, administrative regulations, executive orders)
Commerce Clearing House Congressional Index
Congressional Information Service Annual
Digest of Public General Bills and Resolutions
House and Senate Journals
Congressional Quarterly
Congressional Monitor
Congressional Record (daily digest of Congressional activities)

In addition, cases interpreting statutes may discuss their legislative history and some agencies maintain legislative histories to their **enabling acts**.

To trace the legislative history of a statute, first identify its **public law** and Congressional bill numbers. Once proposed legislation is introduced, it is assigned a **bill number** (either an "H.R." number for bills introduced in the House of Representatives or an "S." number for Senate bills) that it keeps throughout the legislative session. A federal statute's bill number can be found in annotations to the U.S.C.A. or the U.S.C.S. Those annotations also cite the statute's public law numbers (its congressional session number followed by the act's sequential introduction number). For instance, the Individuals with Disabilities Education Act (I.D.E.A.) was the 603rd act considered by the 92nd Congress; its public law number was therefore 92–603.

Executive Materials

Executive Orders and Proclamations.   From time to time, the chief executive may issue an **executive order** which dictates executive branch practice and procedure. Figure 3–6 is a 1963 Presidential executive order integrating the public schools of Alabama.

Executive Proclamations, on the other hand, although also issued by the president, are statements without binding legal effect. Typically, executive proclamations are issued for public relations or public awareness purposes at an important event or ceremony. Figure 3–7 is former President Bush's 1992 proclamation establishing National D.A.R.E. Day (September 10, 1992).

Federal executive orders and proclamations are published in several research sources, including the following:

U.S. Code Congressional & Administrative News®
Federal Register
Code of Federal Regulations

Weekly compilation of presidential documents, orders, signings, announcements and interviews appear in the following:

U.S. Statutes at Large
Lexis and Westlaw
U.S.C., U.S.C.A., and U.S.C.S., (historical data)
U.S. Code Congressional and Administrative News®
Commerce Clearing House Congressional Index
Congressional Information Service Annual
Digest of Public General Bills and Resolutions
House and Senate Journals
Congressional Quarterly
Congressional Monitor
Congressional Record (a daily digest of congressional activities)

Federal Regulations.   In the early 1930s, the Panama (Oil) Refining Company sued to restrain federal officials from enforcing certain "New Deal" regulations. The

Copr. (C) West® 2000 No Claim to Orig. U.S. Govt. Works Exec. Order
No. 11118
28 FR 9863, 1963 WL 8187 (Pres.)

Executive Order 11118

PROVIDING ASSISTANCE FOR REMOVAL OF UNLAWFUL OBSTRUC-
TIONS OF JUSTICE IN THE STATE OF ALABAMA

September 10, 1963

WHEREAS, on September 10, 1963, I issued a proclamation entitled
'Obstructions of Justice in the State of Alabama' pursuant in part to the provisions of Section 334 of Title 10 of the United States Code; and

WHEREAS the commands contained in that proclamation have not been
obeyed, and the unlawful obstructions of justice, assemblies, combinations,
and conspiracies referred to therein continue:

NOW, THEREFORE, by virtue of the authority vested in me by the
Constitution and laws of the United States, including Chapter 15 of Title 10 of
the United States Code, particularly Sections 332, 333 and 334 thereof, and
Section 301 of Title 3 of the United States Code, it is hereby ordered as follows:

SECTION 1. The Secretary of Defense is authorized and directed to take
all appropriate steps to remove obstructions of justice in the State of
Alabama, to enforce the laws of the United States within that State, including any orders of United States Courts relating to the enrollment and attendance of students in public schools in the State of Alabama, and to suppress
unlawful assemblies, combinations, conspiracies, and domestic violence
which oppose, obstruct, or hinder the execution of the law or impede the
course of justice under the law within that State.

SEC. 2. In furtherance of the authorization and direction contained in
Section 1 hereof, the Secretary of Defense is authorized to use such of the
Armed Forces of the United States as he may deem necessary.

SEC. 3. I hereby authorize and direct the Secretary of Defense to call into
the active military service of the United States, as he may deem appropriate
to carry out the purposes of this order, any or all of the units of the Army
National Guard and of the Air National Guard of the State of Alabama to
serve in the active military service of the United States for an indefinite
period and until relieved by appropriate orders. In carrying out the provisions of Section 1, the Secretary of Defense is authorized to use the units, and
members thereof, of the Army National Guard and of the Air National Guard
of the State of Alabama called into the active military service of the United
States pursuant to this section or otherwise.

SEC. 4. The Secretary of Defense is authorized to delegate to the
Secretary of the Army or the Secretary of the Air Force, or both, any of the
authority conferred upon him by this order.

JOHN F. KENNEDY
THE WHITE HOUSE,
September 10, 1963.

Exec. Order No. 11118, 28 FR 9863, 1963 WL 8187 (Pres.)

Figure 3–6 Executive order. From *Westlaw*; reprinted with the permission of
West Group.

Proclamation 6466

National D.A.R.E. Day, 1992

August 26, 1992

By the President of the United States of America

A Proclamation

Millions of young Americans who have wisely decided to stay off drugs, out of gangs, and in school are living testimony to the effectiveness of Drug Abuse Resistance Education (Project D.A.R.E.). Together with their parents, teachers, and teams of dedicated law enforcement personnel, these children are taking a firm stand against illicit drug use while also demonstrating their determination to make the most of their God-given talent and potential. At the same time, by setting examples of personal responsibility and respect for authority, graduates of Project D.A.R.E. are making an important contribution to the success of our National Drug Control Strategy.

Led by experienced law enforcement officers, Project D.A.R.E. equips students with basic facts about drugs and alcohol and about the devastating effects that these substances can have on the mind and body. In order that children might avoid the dangers of trying drugs and alcohol, D.A.R.E. also equips participants with practical decision-making skills, helping them to recognize that actions have consequences and that personal accountability and self-control are signs of strong moral character and maturity.

By befriending students and by helping them to grow in self-confidence, the law enforcement officers who conduct the D.A.R.E. program build strong bonds of mutual understanding and trust between themselves and young people in their communities. Yet the success of Project D.A.R.E. also depends on the cooperation of parents, who are encouraged to talk with, and to listen to, their children—and to set positive examples for them. This partnership among parents, children, law enforcement officers, and educators continues to change lives for the better in all 50 States and at Department of Defense Dependent Schools around the world.

Through innovative public-private partnerships such as Project D.A.R.E., our Nation has made significant progress in reducing the demand for drugs—a priority of our National Drug Control Strategy. Since we launched this strategy in 1989, overall drug use in the United States has dropped by more than 10 percent. Statistics cited by the Partnership for a Drug-Free America show a decline of 48 to 56 percent in drug use by juveniles between the ages of 13 and 17, and three separate studies indicate that adolescent use of cocaine dropped even more dramatically—by 63 percent—between 1988 and 1991. These trends are encouraging, and they offer reason to believe that our National Drug Control Strategy will continue to bear fruit.

Because Project D.A.R.E. brings drug abuse prevention to the classroom, it not only meets a key objective of our National Drug Control Strategy but also complements America 2000, our national strategy to achieve excellence in our schools. One of the six National Education Goals that form the basis of America 2000 calls for every school in the United States to be free of drugs

Figure 3–7   Presidential Proclamation.

and violence. If we are to achieve that goal, all Americans must work together to create safe, drug-free communities where learning can happen. Reaching an estimated 25 million young Americans every year, Project D.A.R.E. provides an outstanding example of cooperation among parents, educators, law enforcement personnel, business owners, and civic and religious leaders. On this occasion, we celebrate their efforts and congratulate each of the young Americans who have chosen to say "No!" to drugs and "Yes!" to opportunity through education.

The Congress, by Senate Joint Resolution 295, has designated September 10, 1992, as "National D.A.R.E. Day" and has requested the President to issue a proclamation in observance of this day.

NOW, THEREFORE, I, GEORGE BUSH, President of the United States of America, do hereby proclaim September 10, 1992, as National D.A.R.E. Day. I encourage all Americans to observe this day with appropriate programs and activities in celebration of Drug Abuse Resistance Education and in honor of the many dedicated professionals and volunteers who have made it possible. I also invite Americans to observe this occasion by joining in community-based partnerships in support of America 2000 and our National Drug Control Strategy.

IN WITNESS WHEREOF, I have hereunto set my hand this twenty-sixth day of August, in the year of our Lord nineteen hundred and ninety-two, and of the Independence of the United States of America the two hundred and seventeenth.

GEORGE BUSH

Figure 3–7 (continued).

case reached the United States Supreme Court before the United States Attorney realized that the regulations being challenged had been repealed. Soon after *Panama Refining Co. v. Ryan*[1] Congress enacted the **Federal Register** Act requiring that:

> *any document . . . prescribing a penalty or course of conduct, conferring a right, privilege, authority, or immunity, or imposing an obligation, and relevant or applicable to the general public, members of a class, or persons in a locality, as distinguished from individuals or organizations be published in the Federal Register, a daily newspaper of proposed and final regulations, agency announcements and agency policy statements.*

Each daily Federal Register issue has a table of contents listing the agencies and documents in that issue. Following the table of contents, separate sections include presidential documents, regulations, proposed regulations, agency notices, **Sunshine Act** ("open meeting") notices, regulatory agenda (anticipated regulatory action; published in April and October), and reader aids. Information in the Federal Register is cited by annual volume and page number, such as the following: 58 Fed. Reg. 33690 (1993). A cumulative topical index is published monthly.

In 1937, Congress amended the Federal Register Act to require that promulgated regulations be published in the **Code of Federal Regulations** (C.F.R.). Like statutes in the United States Code, federal regulations in the C.F.R. are numerically titled; each federal agency has its own title. Each C.F.R. title is divided into chapters, sub-chapters, parts, and sections. Regulations are cited by C.F.R. title and section number as follows: **34 C.F.R. § 76.100 (2001)** which is an I.D.E.A. Regulation. The C.F.R. is published annually, in quarterly installments (titles 1–6 in January, 17–27 in April, 28–41 in July, and 42–50 in October) and is indexed topically by volumes following the regulations.[2]

The C.F.R. is updated by the Federal Register. Monthly, the GPO publishes a cumulative **List of C.F.R. Sections Affected (L.S.A.)**, which lists, by C.F.R. title and section, Federal Register pages updating the C.F.R. As well, each daily Federal Register includes C.F.R. **Parts Affected Tables** listing C.F.R. titles updated in that issue. Finally, Shepard's C.F.R. Citations lists court cases and other C.F.R. interpretive materials arranged by C.F.R. title and section number.

Agency Decisions. Although the **Federal Administrative Procedure Act** requires agencies to publish their decisions,[3] agencies are inconsistent in publishing those decisions. Some agency decisions and rulings are published officially by the GPO and are available in federal depository libraries, others are published unofficially by commercial publishers like the Bureau of National Affairs (BNA) and appear in bound or loose-leaf "services." These private services are better indexed and digested than most official agency reporters. As well, many include recent event and case summaries, agency statutes and regulations, agency decision **head notes** and summaries, indexes, and Digests. Agency decisions may also be located through U.S.C.S. annotations, through service topical indexes, and through *Shepard's* United States Administrative Citations.[4]

Judicial Materials

Cases. Courts, as well, are important sources of law through publication of their cases. Figure 3–8 shows an example of a federal circuit court case involving the expulsion of a student in Ohio.

Court Rules. Additionally, courts publish rules governing their procedures. The highest court in each jurisdiction may promulgate procedural rules binding all courts and litigation in that jurisdiction. For instance, the United States Supreme Court has issued civil and criminal rules governing federal court procedure. Those rules prescribe preliminary litigation procedures, discovery, jury selection, motions, and entry of judgment in civil and criminal actions, and appeals. Rules may be quite general, like the rule governing summary judgment shown in Figure 3–9 on page 87.

They may also be quite specific, like the rule regarding preparation of appellate briefs shown in Figure 3–10 on page 88.

Court rules may be published in books containing rules applying to all or only individual courts. Court rulebooks are comprehensively indexed and thumb

(Text continues on page 88.)

United States District Court,
S.D. Ohio,
Eastern Division.

Jerrie TURNER, et al., Plaintiffs,

v.

SOUTH-WESTERN CITY SCHOOL DISTRICT, et al., Defendants.

No. C2-99-1229.

82 F.Supp.2d 757 (1999)

High school student, expelled for bringing look-alike gun to school and for disruptive conduct, sued school district seeking preliminary injunction compelling reinstatement, to allow him to graduate on schedule. The District Court, Marbley, J., held that: (1) procedural due process requirements associated with suspension and expulsion of student were complied with; (2) handbook provision barring look-alike weapons was not unconstitutionally overbroad or vague; (3) student failed to show irreparable injury; and (4) student failed to show that public interest would be furthered through reinstatement.

Injunction denied.

West Headnotes

Injunction
☞ **138.1**
212k138.1

In deciding whether to grant preliminary injunction, court is to consider: (1) whether there is strong or substantial likelihood of success on merits; (2) whether movant has established irreparable harm; (3) whether issuance of preliminary injunction would cause substantial harm to others; and (4) whether public interest would be served by issuance of injunction.

Constitutional Law
☞ **278.5(7)**
92k278.5(7)

Procedural due process requirements for suspension of student lasting ten days or less include oral or written notice of charges against him, and if he denies them, explanation of evidence authorities have an opportunity to present his side of story. U.S.C.A. Const.Amend. 14.

Constitutional Law
☞ **278.5(7)**
92k278.5(7)

Schools
☞ **177**
345k177

Constitutional and statutory due process requirements for suspending student were followed in case of student who had toy replica of weapon in car and acted disruptively

Figure 3–8 Federal appellate case (edited). From the *Federal Reporter*; reprinted with the permission of West Group.

when confronted with it; student was presented with charges when first detained and given opportunity to explain, and parent was given notice of intent to suspend, together with counseling regarding procedural steps available to her. U.S.C.A. Const.Amend. 14; Ohio R.C. § 3313.66(A)(1, 2), (D, E).

Constitutional Law
⚷ **278.5(7)**
92k278.5(7)

To satisfy federal due process requirements, student faced with expulsion for disciplinary reasons must be given oral or written notice of charges against him, and if he denies them, explanation of evidence authorities have an opportunity to present his side of story, and also right to pre-expulsion hearing before impartial trier of fact. U.S.C.A. Const.Amend. 14.

Constitutional Law
⚷ **278.5(7)**
92k278.5(7)

Schools
⚷ **177**
345k177

Constitutional and statutory due process requirements for expelling student were observed in case of student who had toy replica of weapon in car and acted disruptively when confronted with it; student was presented with charges when first detained and given opportunity to explain, and parent was given notice of intent to suspend, together with counseling regarding procedural steps available to her, there was pre-expulsion hearing before impartial official and detailed state statutory requirements for expulsion procedural were followed. U.S.C.A. Const.Amend. 14; Ohio R.C. § 3313.66(B).

Constitutional Law
⚷ **42.2(1)**
92k42.2(1)

Overbreadth is an exception to the doctrine of standing for First Amendment claims that allows a plaintiff to facially attack a statute. U.S.C.A. Const.Amend. 1.

Constitutional Law
⚷ **90(3)**
92k90(3)

In analyzing constitutional claim that statute is overbroad, court is first to consider whether substantial amount of constitutionally protected speech is involved, and if not, is then to consider whether statute is substantially overbroad and constitutionally invalid under void for vagueness doctrine. U.S.C.A. Const.Amends. 1, 5, 14.

Constitutional Law
⚷ **82(4)**
92k82(4)

Figure 3–8 (continued)

Statute is unconstitutional on its face on overbreadth grounds if there is realistic danger that statute itself will significantly compromise recognized First Amendment protections of parties not before court. U.S.C.A. Const.Amend. 1.

Constitutional Law
◉⌐ **90.1(1.4)**
92k90.1(1.4)
Publications.

Schools
◉⌐ **172**
345k172

School handbook prohibition on bringing of weapons or objects that could reasonably be considered weapons to school was not overbroad, on grounds that it would chill permissible speech by deterring persons from bringing pictures of guns or props for school dramatic productions. U.S.C.A. Const.Amend. 1.

Constitutional Law
◉⌐ **251.4**
92k251.4

Constitutional Law
◉⌐ **258(2)**
92k258(2)
Ordinance can be void for vagueness, on due process grounds, by denying citizen fair notice of standard of conduct to which he or she is held accountable, or by providing for unrestricted delegation of power to law enforcement officers, in practice leaving to them definition of ordinance's terms and inviting arbitrary, discriminatory and overzealous enforcement. U.S.C.A. Const.Amends. 5, 14.

Municipal Corporations
◉⌐ **594(2)**
268k594(2)

Under requirement that ordinance must give fair notice of applicable standard of conduct, ordinance is void for vagueness if person of ordinary intelligence cannot reasonably interpret what is prohibited. U.S.C.A. Const.Amends. 5, 14.

Municipal Corporations
◉⌐ **594(2)**
268k594(2)

Ordinance will be deemed unconstitutionally vague if it delegates decision making to law enforcement officers by being insufficiently precise to void involvement of so many factors of varying effect that neither person to decide in advance nor jury after fact can safely and certainly judge result. U.S.C.A. Const.Amends. 5, 14.

Schools
◉⌐ **172**
345k172

Figure 3–8 (continued)

Provision of student handbook prohibiting bringing of weapon to school, with term further defined to include "look-alike gun," was not unconstitutionally vague; student of ordinary intelligence would know what was meant, and there was no question of interpretation delegated to enforcement official. U.S.C.A. Const.Amends. 5, 14.

Injunction
©⁓ **138.54**
212k138.54

Expelled student failed to satisfy likelihood of success on merits requirement for issuance of preliminary injunction restoring him to school; student was not likely to prevail on claim that expulsion from bringing look-alike gun to school was unconstitutional, and even if he did obstreperous conduct of student after being confronted with gun would sustain expulsion. U.S.C.A. Const.Amends. 1, 5, 14.

Schools
©⁓ **172**
345k172

There was no constitutional requirement that school handbook prohibition on bringing of weapons to school contain scienter element. U.S.C.A. Const.Amend. 14.

Injunction
©⁓ **138.54**
212k138.54

Expelled high school student seeking preliminary injunction reinstating him failed to satisfy irreparable injury requirement, despite claim that he would not graduate on schedule unless allowed back in school; school offered him alternative schooling and reinstatement that would keep him on schedule, which was declined for insufficiently stated reasons.

Injunction
©⁓ **138.54**
212k138.54

High school student expelled for bringing look-alike gun to school, seeking injunction requiring reinstatement, failed to make necessary showing that injunction would be in public interest; public would be better served if children could attend schools safe from fear of guns.

*759 Jack L. Moser, Adams, Rosenberg & Associates, Columbus, Ohio, Danny W. Bank, Columbus, Ohio, for plaintiffs.

Richard Wayne Ross, Means, Bichimer, Burkholder & Baker, Columbus, Ohio, for defendants.

MARBLEY, District Judge.

I. *INTRODUCTION*

This case was originally brought before the Franklin County Court of Common Pleas by Stephen E. Koser, a high school student, and his mother Jerrie Turner, after Koser

Figure 3–8 (continued)

was expelled from Westland High School for bringing a look-alike gun to school and for disruptive behavior. The case was removed to this Court by the Defendant, South-Western City School District. Koser claims that his constitutional right to procedural due process was denied when he was suspended and expelled, and that the student handbook provision prohibiting look-alike guns is constitutionally vague and over-broad. This matter is presently before the Court on Plaintiffs' Motion for a Preliminary Injunction. For the following reasons, Plaintiffs' Motion is hereby **DENIED**.

II. *FACTS*

The Plaintiff, Stephen E. Koser, is a seventeen-year-old student at Westland High School ("Westland"), in Galloway, Ohio. On September 23, 1999, Deputy Cooper, of the Franklin County Sheriff's Department, was patrolling Westland's student parking lot checking cars for parking permits. Cooper approached Koser's car to issue him a parking violation for not having a parking permit. After placing the citation on Koser's windshield, he saw a partially concealed gun protruding from under the front driver's side seat of Koser's car. The gun looked like a Smith & Wesson 9mm gun; it was silver in color and appeared to have a wood grain grip. The Deputy contacted the Assistant Principal's office to inform him that he had found the gun.

Assistant Principals Grube and McLaughlin, and Deputy Cooper located Koser in the high school library. The three officials escorted Koser to the principal's office, where Deputy Cooper conducted a pat-down of Koser. Deputy Cooper found a box of cigarettes and a pager on Koser's person. Deputy Cooper asked Koser for permission to search his car, which Koser granted. All four individuals, Grube, McLaughlin, Cooper and Koser, went to the high school parking lot where Koser's car was parked. Cooper opened Koser's car and examined the gun. The gun turned out to be a plastic toy gun that had a bright orange tip. The orange tip had been concealed from view.

When Koser was asked to return to the Assistant Principal's office, he became belligerent and hostile, and refused to return to school. Eventually, he was persuaded to return to the building, but on the walk back, he began to use profanity, was disruptive and started to make veiled threats. Upon returning to the principal's office, Koser sat in front of Assistant Principal Grube's desk with clenched fists and pounded on the arms of his chair. Koser also leaned on the desk, toward Grube.

During the time he spent in the office, Koser made threatening statements such as: "this is how I solve my problems," "if I wanted to bring a real gun to school, I would have brought a gun and blown holes in this mother," "you're my problem and I get rid of my problems," and "every dog has his day and you'll get yours." To Deputy Cooper, Koser said, "if you take your gun and badge off, you want to get froggy, leap," which Cooper took as a direct threat and an attempt by Koser to instigate a fight.

At the informal hearing on September 23, 1999, Koser was given the opportunity to explain his side of what happened. Koser said that the car was his mother's and that the toy gun had been left in the back seat of her car by a neighborhood child. Koser said that the first time he saw the toy gun was when he was escorted to the car by Deputy Cooper and the Assistant Principals.

At the same hearing, Koser was given a "Notice of Intent to Suspend," which indicated that he was being suspended for: "look-a-like gun in students car," "student used profanity repeatedly and refused to calm down after repeated requests," "threats directed

Figure 3–8 (continued)

at school officials," and "student also had cigarettes and a pager in his possession." The notice also stated:

> You are hereby suspended 10 school days beginning 9/23/99 for the above-stated violation(s) of the adopted Code of Conduct and School Board Policy. You should return to school on 10/7/99. You have the right to appeal this suspension to the principal, to be granted a hearing on appeal, and to be represented in all appeal proceedings. If you wish to exercise the right of appeal, contact the principal's office immediately. If you fail to file an appeal within ten (10) days, you forfeit your right to appeal.

Koser refused to sign the notice.

Koser was also given a "Notice of Intended Expulsion" at the September 23, 1999, meeting. The reasons checked for Koser's potential expulsion were: "Disruption of Schools," and "Weapons/Dangerous Instruments." The notice also stated:

> You and your parents, guardian, custodian, or representative will have the opportunity to appear in person for a hearing to be held at 2:00 p.m. on 9/29/9 [9] at Westland High School. You are not required to attend this meeting; however, it offers you the opportunity to challenge the reason(s) for the expulsion or explain your actions.

Koser also refused to sign this notice. Assistant Principal Grube contacted Jerrie Turner, Koser's mother, and she came to pick him up from school. Turner was given a copy of both notices at that time.

On September 24, 1999, Turner delivered a notice to school officials indicating that she was going to appeal her son's suspension. The suspension appeal hearing was held on September 29, 1999. Principal Voyles, Deputy Sheriff Cooper, and Assistants Principals McLaughlin and Grube attended the appeal. Turner stated that the car was hers and that the toy gun was left in the car by a child who lived in the neighborhood. Following the hearing, Principal Voyles upheld the suspension.

On September 30, 1999, Turner attended her son's pre-expulsion hearing.[1] Also in attendance were Assistant Principals Grube and McLaughlin, and Shawn Koser, Stephen's older brother. Following the hearing, it was recommended that Koser be expelled. On October 4, 1999, Superintendent Hamilton issued Koser's Expulsion Notice. By letter dated October 5, 1999, and received by the Superintendent's office on October 6, 1999, Turner filed a request to appeal the expulsion.

Dr. Rinehart sent Turner a letter, dated October 12, 1999, scheduling a hearing for October 18, 1999, to appeal Koser's expulsion.[2] The hearing was held by Robert B. St. Clair, an independent hearing office, on October 26, 1999. The hearing included cross-examination and arguments by counsel. By report dated October 29, 1999, St. Clair recommended to the South-Western City School Board that Koser be expelled. On November 8, 1999, the school board met by regular meeting and adopted St. Clair's recommendation to expel Koser.

On October 14, 1999, Defendant's counsel sent a letter to Turner outlining the terms for readmitting Koser to class. Koser would have to attend alternative school until January 18, 1999. Starting on January 18, 1999, Koser would have to attend Westland High School from approximately 9:00 a.m. to 3:00 p.m., then attend alternative high school from 3:00 p.m. until 5:00 p.m. Koser would also have to complete a one-half credit class in anger management. After talking to Koser's psychologist, Turner

---

[1]The hearing was originally scheduled for September 29, 1999, but was rescheduled to accommodate the appeal of Koser's suspension which was instead scheduled for that date.

[2]Dr. Rinehart was the hearing officer assigned to Koser's case. Rinehart's duties would have been to hear the appeal of Koser's expulsion; however, Koser was assigned an independent hearing officer to hear his expulsion appeal.

Figure 3–8 (continued)

rejected the terms. Turner was concerned that Koser would have to attend classes from 9:00 a.m. to 5:15 p.m. starting on January 18, 2000. Turner did not think that Koser could have handled that type of school schedule. Since his expulsion, Koser has been working thirty-five hours per week at Kohl's Department Store.

Koser is prohibited from returning to class and from being on South-Western City School property until January 18, 2000.

III. PRELIMINARY INJUNCTION STANDARD

A preliminary injunction is an extraordinary remedy which should only be granted if the movant carries his or her burden of persuasion. Stenberg v. Cheker Oil Co., 573 F.2d 921, 925 (6th Cir.1978) (citations omitted; Penetone Corp. v. Palchem, Inc., 627 F.Supp. 997, 1004 (N.D.Ohio 1985). To grant an injunction, the Court must consider: (1) whether there is a strong or substantial likelihood of success on the merits; (2) whether the movant has established irreparable harm; (3) whether the issuance of a preliminary injunction would cause substantial harm to others; and (4) whether the public interest is served by the issuance of an injunction. *See, e.g.*, Washington v. Reno, 35 F.3d 1093, 1099 (6th Cir.1994); Keweenaw Bay Indian Community v. Michigan, 11 F.3d 1341, 1348 (6th Cir.1993); Basicomputer Corp. v. Scott, 973 F.2d 507, 511 (6th Cir.1992); Shell v. R.W. Sturge, 850 F.Supp. 620, 632 (S.D.Ohio 1993) (citations omitted). The four elements are "[f]actors to be balanced, not prerequisites that must be met." Shell, 850 F.Supp. at 632 (citing In re DeLorean Motor Co., 755 F.2d 1223, 1229 (6th Cir.1985)). See also Dayton Area Visually Impaired Persons, Inc. v. Fisher, 70 F.3d 1474, 1480 (6th Cir.1995).

In issuing a preliminary injunction, the first factor to consider is whether the Plaintiffs have a substantial likelihood of success on the merits. Here, the Plaintiffs have brought two claims in their Motion for a Preliminary Injunction. First, the Plaintiffs argue that their right to procedural due process under the Fourteenth Amendment to the United States Constitution was abrogated when Koser was suspended and expelled from high school. Secondly, the Plaintiffs argue that school handbook's prohibition on bringing a "look-alike gun" onto school property is constitutionally vague and overbroad. The Plaintiffs' claims will be examined, in turn, to determine the likelihood of success on the merits for each claim.

IV. LIKELIHOOD OF SUCCESS ON THE MERITS
A. Procedural Due Process

The first issue is whether Koser is likely to succeed on his claim that his suspension and expulsion violated his right to procedural due process under the Fourteenth Amendment to the United States Constitution. Koser's suspension will be addressed separately from his expulsion as there are different procedural due process requirements for each action that the high school took.

1. *Ten Day Suspension.*

The Supreme Court has directly addressed the process due a student who is suspended from school for ten days or less. In Goss v. Lopez, 419 U.S. 565, 581, 95 S.Ct. 729, 42 L.Ed.2d 725 (1975), the Court found that "i]n connection with a suspension of 10 days or less, [ ] the student [should] be given oral or written notice of the charges against

Figure 3–8 (continued)

him and, if he denies them, an explanation of the evidence the authorities have and an opportunity to present his side of the story."

In addition, the Ohio legislature has established specific procedures that schools must follow before suspending a student from school. *See* Ohio Rev.Code § 3313.66(A).

> No student shall be suspended unless prior to the suspension such superintendent or principal does both of the following: (1) Give the pupil written notice of the intention to suspend him and the reason for the intended suspension ... and (2) provide the pupil an opportunity to appear at an informal hearing before the principal, assistant principal, superintendent, or superintendent's designee and challenge the reason for the intended suspension or otherwise to explain his actions.

Ohio Rev.Code § 3313.66(A)(1)-(2).

> Furthermore:
> (D) The superintendent ... *within one school day* after the time of a pupil's expulsion or suspension, shall notify in writing the parent ... and the treasurer of the board of education of the expulsion or suspension. The notice shall include the reasons for the expulsion or suspension, notification of the right of the pupil or his parent, guardian, or custodian to appeal the expulsion or suspension to the board of education....
> (E) A pupil or his parent ... may appeal the expulsion or suspension by the superintendent ... to the board of education or to its designee.

Ohio Rev.Code § 3313.66(D)-(E) (emphasis added).

Here, Koser's suspension meets the procedural due process required for a suspension established by Goss and section 3313.66(A) of the Ohio Revised Code, which mirrors Goss. Koser was given written notice of the school's intent to suspend him for ten days. The notice documented the reasons for Koser's suspension, including, "look-a-like gun in students car," "student used profanity repeatedly and refused to calm down after repeated requests," "threats directed at school officials," and "student also had cigarettes and a pager in his possession." Koser refused to sign the notice. Following the September 23, 1999, search of Koser's car, Koser was taken to the Assistant Principal's office where he was given an opportunity to explain his side of the story. Koser told Grube that the car belonged to Koser's mother. Koser also explained that a child from the neighborhood was playing in the back seat of his mother's car and had left the toy gun there. Koser said that he did not know the toy gun was in the car until it was searched by Officer Cooper.

The officials of Westland High School also met the requirements established by section 3313.66(D)-(E) the Ohio Revised Code when they suspended Koser. Turner was called from the Assistant Principal's office after Koser was suspended. When Turner arrived at the school to pick up her son, she was given a copy of the Notice of Intent to Suspend, which included the reasons for Koser's suspension. The notice also informed Koser and Turner that they had a "[r]ight to appeal this suspension to the principal, to be granted a hearing on appeal, and to be represented in all appeal proceedings. If you wish to exercise the right of appeal, contact the principal's office immediately." Turner obviously understood her right to appeal Koser's suspension, as the next day, on September 24, 1999, she sent a letter to Principal Voyles appealing the suspension of Koser. On September 29, 1999, Principal Voyles conducted a suspension appeal hearing. See Ohio Rev.Code § 3313.66(D). Koser's constitutional procedural due process rights were preserved and the Ohio Revised Code requirements were met when school officials suspended Koser for ten days.

2. Expulsion.

Goss did not directly address what process is due for suspension of more than ten days. The Court, however, did recognize that suspensions longer than ten days require "more formal procedures," Goss, 419 U.S. at 584, 95 S.Ct. 729. In Newsome v. Batavia Local Sch. Dist., 842 F.2d 920, 921 (6th Cir.1988), where the Plaintiff was expelled from school for the remainder of the fall semester for allegedly possessing and attempting

Figure 3–8 (continued)

to sell marijuana, the Court noted in dicta that "[a] student faced with expulsion has the right to a pre-expulsion hearing before an impartial trier-of-fact—he does not have the right to a full-blown administrative appellate process." Id. at 927 (citing Brewer v. Austin Indep. Sch. Dist., 779 F.2d 260 (5th Cir.1985)); *see also* Hall v. Medical College of Ohio at Toledo, 742 F.2d 299, 309 (6th Cir.1984) (citing with favor Dixon v. Alabama State Bd. of Educ., 294 F.2d 150, 158-59 (5th Cir.1961), which held that a hearing which gives school authorities an opportunity to hear both sides is required in expulsion cases, but that a full-dress judicial hearing is not required).

Following Goss and Newsome, the Sixth Circuit held in Ashiegbu v. Williams, No. 97-3173, 1997 WL 720477 at *1 (6th Cir. Nov. 12, 1997), that a student faced with expulsion for disciplinary reasons must be given the pocedural requirements established by Goss, and in addition, "[t]he right to a pre-expulsion hearing before an impartial trier of fact." Id. at *3 (citing Newsome, 842 F.2d at 927).

Section 3313.66(B) of the Ohio Revised Code establishes the procedures to be used in student expulsions, which are:

(4) No pupil shall be expelled under division (B)(1), (2), or (3) of this section unless, prior to his expulsion, the superintendent does both of the following:
(a) Gives the pupil and his parent, guardian, or custodian written notice of the intention to expel the pupil;
(b) Provides the pupil and his parent ... an opportunity to appear in person before the superintendent or his designee ... to challenge the reason for the intended expulsion or otherwise to explain the pupil's actions.
The notice required in this division shall include the reasons for the expulsion, notification of the opportunity of the pupil and his parent ... to appear before the superintendent or his designee to challenge the reasons for the intended expulsion or otherwise to explain the pupil's actions, and notification of the time and place to appear. The time to appear shall not be earlier than three nor later than five school days after the notice is given, unless the superintendent grants an extension of time at the request of pupil or parent....

Ohio Rev.Code § 3313.66(B)(4)(a)-(b) (emphasis added).[3]

In this case, Westland High School officials gave Koser the process that was due prior to expelling him. First, as established, the requirements of Goss were met when Koser was suspended from school, and therefore, since the expulsion was based on the same conduct, those requirements were also met when Koser was expelled. Koser was given an opportunity to be heard and to explain his version of the events. Koser was also given written "Notice of Intended Expulsion." That notice indicated that Koser would have the opportunity for a hearing on September 29, 1999, at Westland High School. The notice gave the reasons for Koser's possible expulsion which included: "Disruption of Schools," and "Weapons/Dangerous Instruments."

The next issue is whether Koser's expulsion satisfied the additional due process requirements as established by Newsome and Ashiegbu which include a pre-expulsion hearing before an independent trier of fact. Koser's expulsion hearing was held on September 30, 1999, at Westland High School. Present at the hearing were Assistant Principals Grube and McLaughlin, Shawn Koser, Stephen's older brother, and Koser's mother. Assistant Principal McLaughlin presided over the pre-expulsion hearing.[4] Koser's pre-expulsion

---

[3]In addition, Ohio Revised Code § 3313.66(D)-(E) apply to expulsions.
[4]In Newsome, the court noted that if the student had shown that the school officials had pre-existing animosity toward him that they would not have been permitted to preside over the pre-expulsion hearing. 842 F.2dat 926-27. Koser and Turner did not make such an assertion against Westland School officials. Assistant Principal McLaughlin was present during the September 23, 1999, search of Koser's car, and was present as a witness during Koser's suspension hearing. However, McLaughlin maintained his impartiality as he did not make the decision to suspend Koser, nor did he make the decision to issue the pre-expulsion notice.

Figure 3–8 (continued)

hearing satisfied Newsome 's requirement, that there should be a hearing and that it should be held in front of an independent trier of fact. Under the circumstances of this case, the Court finds that Koer was accorded his due process rights pursuant to the United States Constitution prior to his expulsion from Westland High School. Koser's expulsion also met the more stringent requirements of the Ohio Revised Code.

First, Koser was given written notice of the school's intent to expel him. *See* Ohio Rev.Code § 3313.66(B)(4)(a). Second, Koser and his mother had an opportunity to appear before Assistant Principal McLaughlin to challenge the reasons for his expulsion. *See* Ohio Rev.Code § 3313.66(B)(4)(b). Koser was given notice of the reasons for his potential expulsion, and the notice indicated that Turner and/or Koser could appear before the superintendent's designee to challenge the reasons for Koser's expulsion. *See* Ohio Rev.Code § 3313.66(B)(4)(b). The time set for the hearing also met the requirements established by the Code. The pre-expulsion hearing "shall not be earlier than three nor later than five school days after the notice is given...." Ohio Rev.Code § 3313.66(B)(4)(b). Here, Koser was given notice on September 23, 1999. The hearing was originally set for September 29, 1999, but was rescheduled for September 30, 1999, to accommodate the Plaintiff's appeal of his suspension. Three school days after Thursday, September 23, 1999, would have been September 28, 1999; five days after notice was given would have been September 30, 1999.[5] Koser's pre-expulsion hearing, which was held on September 30, 1999, fell within the time requirement established by section 3313.66(B)(4)(b) of the Ohio Revised Code.

Westland High School officials also met the requirements of section 3313.66(D) of the Ohio Revised Code. Following the pre-expulsion hearing, on Thursday, September 30, 1999, it was recommended that Koser be expelled.[6] Ohio statutes require parental notice within one school day after the pupil's pre-expulsion hearing. *See* Ohio Rev.Code § 3313.66(D). On Monday October 4, 1999, Superintendent Hamilton issued an expulsion notice and mailed it to Turner. Although the notice may have been one day late, this fact, in itself, is not a violation of the statute. *See* Stuble v. Board of Educ. of the Cuyahoga Valley Joint Vocational Sch. Dist., No. 44412, 1982 WL 5953 at *5 (Ohio Ct.App. Oct. 7, 1982) (finding that "[w]here delay by a public official with respect to the precise time in which a statutory act is performed does not affect the rights of the parties involved, that technical defect does not invalidate the officials subsequent action.") (citations omitted); The State v. Board of Educ. of Hamilton City Sch. Dist., 20 Ohio App.2d 154, 252 N.E.2d 318 (1969). In addition, as required by the Code, the notice gave the reasons for the expulsion: "[d]isruption and being in possession of a weapon/look-alike." See Ohio Rev.Code § 3313.66(D). The notice also stated, "I wish to advise you that according to the law the parent has the right to appeal this action within ten (10) days from the date of this letter. If you wish to do this, contact Dr. Rinehart in this office." *See* Ohio Rev.Code § 3313.66(D).

By letter dated October 5, 1999, Turner and her attorney informed Dr. Rinehart that she wished to appeal Koser's suspension. By letter dated October 12, 1999, Dr. Rinehart set an expulsion appeal hearing for October 18, 1999. *See* Ohio Rev.Code § 3313.66(E). The hearing was held by the board's designee, Robert B. St. Clair, an independent hearing officer, on October 26, 1999. The hearing included cross-examination and arguments by counsel. By report dated October 29, 1999, St. Clair recommended

---

[5]Ohio statutes also provide that the superintendent may grant an "extension of time at the request of the pupil or his parent ..." Ohio Rev.Code § 3313.66(4)(b). Such an extension was given in this case to accommodate Koser's appeal of his suspension.
[6]According to Turner's letter to Dr. Rinehart, the expulsion hearing took place on Friday October 1, 1999.

Figure 3–8 (continued)

to the South-Western City School Board that Koser be expelled. On November 8, 1999, the School Board met by regular meeting and adopted St. Clair's recommendation. *See* Ohio Rev.Code § 3313.66(E).

The Court finds that Westland High School officials met the detailed requirements of the Ohio Revised Code when they expelled Koser from school until January 18, 2000. Based on the Court's finding that Koser was given the process due in both his suspension and expulsion and that the applicable Ohio Revised Code provisions were met, the Court finds that there is little likelihood of success on the merits on the Plaintiffs' claim that his right to procedural due process under the Fourteenth Amendment of the United States Constitution was violated when he was suspended and expelled from school.

B. Overbreath Doctrine

The Plaintiff argues that the "Weapons and Dangerous Instruments," provision of student handbook is overbroad. That provision provides: "[a] student shall not possess, handle, or transmit any object that can reasonably be considered a weapon. Weapons include any type of ... look-alike gun ... This guideline applies: 1. On the school grounds during and before and after school hours...." Specifically, the Plaintiff takes issue with the language "look-alike gun," and with the fact that the handbook does not have a scienter requirement for possession of a weapon.

There are two steps in analyzing a constitutional claim of overbreath.[7] "The first step is to 'determine whether the regulation reaches a substantial amount of constitutionally protected speech.' " Dambrot v. Central Michigan Univ., 55 F.3d 1177, 1182 (6th Cir.1995); Triplett Grille, Inc. v. City of Akron, 40 F.3d 129, 135 (6th Cir.1994).[8] Under this step, "[a] statute is unconstitutional on its face on overbreath grounds if there is 'a realistic danger that the statute itself will significantly compromise recognized First Amendment protections of parties not bfore the court....' " Dambrot, 55 F.3d at 1182 (quoting Members of City Council v. Taxpayers for Vincent, 466 U.S. 789, 801, 104 S.Ct. 2118, 80 L.Ed.2d 772 (1984)). The second step is to determine whether the statute is " 'substantially overbroad and constitutionally invalid under the void for vagueness doctrine.' " Dambrot, 55 F.3d at 1183 (quoting Leonardson v. City of East Lansing, 896 F.2d 190, 195-96 (6th Cir.1990)).

The Plaintiffs argue that the prohibition against bringing a look-alike gun onto school premises implicates First Amendment rights, as the provision could possibly prohibit bringing pictures of weapons in magazines ad books to school, and also prohibit props in student dramas. The Plaintiffs' argument lacks merit. Here, it is unclear how a prohibition against transporting a "look-alike gun" onto school premises implicates any free speech concerns—as it is neither speech nor expression that is regulated, but conduct. Furthermore, the handbook language prohibits the "possess[ion], hand[ling] or transmit[ting] any object that can reasonably be considered to be a weapon." A pic-

---

[7]In count four of his Complaint, the Plaintiff appears to combine several concepts—the overbreath doctrine, void for vagueness, due process requirements under the Fifth and Fourteenth Amendments, the Equal Protecton clause of the Fourteenth Amendment, and substantive due process. From oral argument, it appears that the Plaintiff is simply arguing that the language violates the overbreath doctrine which includes both protection of speech and also includes notice and due process requirements based on the Fifth and Fourteenth Amendments of the United States Constitution.

[8]Typically, overbreath is an exception to the doctrine of standing for First Amendment claims that allows a plaintiff to facially attack a statute. *See* Triplett Grille, Inc. v. City of Akron, 40 F.3d 129, 135 (6t Cir.1994).

Figure 3–8 (continued)

ture in a magazine or book is not an "object" and hardly could be considered a weapon. The student handbook which prohibits specific conduct implicates no First Amendment rights.

The thrust of Plaintiffs' argument lies in the second step. The void for vagueness doctrine has its foundation in the due process clause of the Fifth Amendment to the Constitution. Columbia Natural Resources, In. v. Tatum, 58 F.3d 1101, 1104 (6th Cir.1995). As the Court noted in Leonardson :

> Vagueness may take two forms, both of which result in a denial of due process. A vague ordinance denies fair notice of the standard of conduct to which a citizen is held accountable. At the same time an ordinance is void for vagueness if it is an unrestricted delegation of power, which in practice leaves the definition of its terms to law enforcement officers, and thereby invites arbitrary, discriminatory and overzealous enforcement.

896 F.2d at 196 (citation omitted). Essentially, there must be fair notice and there must not be an unrestricted delegation of power. Dambrot, 55 F.3d at 1184.

Under the fair notice requirement, "[a]n ordinance is void for vagueness if a person or ordinary intelligence cannot reasonably interpret what is prohibited." Deja Vu v. Metro Gov't (In re State of Tennessee Pub. ndecency Statute), No. 96-6512, 1999 WL 55276 at *4 (6th Cir. Jan. 13, 1999) (citing Grayned v. City of Rockford, 408 U.S. 104, 108, 92 S.Ct. 2294, 33 L.Ed.2d 222 (1972)). *See also* Connally v. General Const. Co., 269 U.S. 385, 391, 46 S.Ct. 126, 70 L.Ed. 322 (1926) (finding that for a statute to be vague, it must use "terms so vague that men of common intelligence must necessarily guess at its common meaning."). "[T]he statute need not define with mathematical precision the conduct forbidden." Deja Vu, 1999 WL 55276 at *4 (citing Columbia Natural Resources, 58 F.3d at 1108.)

The second half of the test encompasses a notice requirement to those who may enforce the law, including judges, police officers, and juries. Columbia Natural Resources, 58 F.3d at 1105. Here, the law must be "prcise enough to void 'involving so many factors of varying effect that neither the person to decide in advance nor the jury after the fact can safely and certainly judge the result.' " Id. at 1105 (citing Cline v. Frink Dairy Co., 274 U.S. 445, 465, 47 S.Ct. 681, 71 L.Ed. 1146 (1927)).

Plaintiffs argue that "look-alike" is undefinable, ambiguous and vague. The Plaintiffs' argument fails. Students at Westland High School are on notice of what conduct is prohibited. In unambiguous terms, the handbook prohibits the possession, transmission or handling of any object that looks like a gun, or could "reasonably be considered to be a weapon." An individual of common intelligence can glean from reading the handbook what conduct is prohibited. Based on this, the Court concludes that the relevant portion of the student handbook is not vague.[9]

Additionally, the handbook does not provide for an unrestricted delegation of power to school officials, since under the look-alike provision of the school handbook, school officials can only discipline students for doing precisely what the handbook prohibits. Because of the specificity of the language as to what is prohibited, there is no danger that school officials will interpret the provision arbitrarily. Sanctions will only be imposed upon those students possessing, *inter alia*, objects which look like guns. Since guns are clearly definable, objects which look like guns are as easily definable.

---

[9]Koser acknowledged receiving a copy of the handbook.

Figure 3–8 (continued)

Typically, overbreath refers to state and federal criminal laws. And, although there are many comparisons between a criminal code and a school handbook, the Supreme Court has held that "[g]iven the school's need to be able to impose disciplinary sanctions for a wide range of unanticipated conduct disruptive of the educational process, the school disciplinary rules need not be as detailed as a criminal code which imposes criminal sanctions." Bethel Sch. Dist. v. Fraser, 478 U.S. 675, 686, 106 S.Ct. 3159, 92 L.Ed.2d 549 (1986). Following the guidelines established by the Supreme Court in Fraser, the handbook need not be as detailed as a criminal code.

Even if the Court were to find that this portion of the student handbook violates the Plaintiffs' First Amendment rights, Koser's suspension and expulsion stand independently of his bringing a toy gun to school. At the preliminary injunction hearing, Assistant Principal Grube testified that Koser probably would not have been expelled for simply bringing the toy gun to school, but that Koser's disruptive and threatening behavior caused the ten day suspension to rise to an expellable offense. Certainly, Koser was on notice that profanity and abusive language directed at teachers and school employees and disruption of class were expellable offenses. Based on this, the Court finds that the Plaintiffs have no likelihood of success on the merits of their claim that the student handbook is either vague or overbroad or both.

As for the Plaintiffs' argument that the handbook lacks a scienter requirement, given strict liability crimes, there is no constitutional requirement that school handbooks, or criminal statutes for that matter, have as one of their elements actual knowledge. And even if the Court finds that knowledge must be an element of student possession of a gun, the Court finds it incredulous that Koser did not "know" that there was a toy gun lying partially exposed under the front driver's seat of the car that he drove to school that morning.

V. *IRREPARABLE INJURY*

The second element the Court needs to address is whether the Plaintiffs have demonstrated irreparable injury. In their Complaint, the Plaintiffs allege that Koser's irreparable injuries are that he cannot graduate in the spring, that he cannot further his academic career, and that he cannot attend a secondary institution next year. However, the Court find that Koser's injuries were not irreparable.

At the time of his suspension, Koser was given an opportunity to further his academic career, graduate in the spring and possibly attend a secondary institution next year. The plan provided by the school would have had Koser attending an alternative school for two hours a day until January 18, 2000. On January 18, 2000, Koser would have attended Westland High School from approximately 9:00 a.m. to 3:00 p.m. and then would have attended an alternative high school from 3:00 p.m. until 5:00 p.m. Koser would have also had to have completed a one-half credit class in anger management. This plan would have allowed Koser to graduate on time.

Turner rejected these terms after talking to Koser's psychologist; however, Koser's psychologist did not testify in this case. The Court must rely on Turner's assertion that Koser could not have handled attending classes from 9:00 a.m. to 5:15 p.m. The Court views this assertion inconsistent with the fact that Koser has been working thirty-five hours a week for Kohl's Department Store since he was expelled. Given that Koser had an alternative to not graduating in the spring, the Court finds that he did not suffer irreparable injury.

Figure 3–8 (continued)

VI. *SUBSTANTIAL HARM TO OTHERS AND PUBLIC INTEREST*

The third and fourth factors the Court must consider involve balancing the harm to others against the public interest in issuing an injunction. The Plaintiffs argue that the issuance of a preliminary injunction would not cause substantial harm to others in that it would allow the school to abide by compulsory attendance laws, provide education to children in the South-Western City School district, and allow the rules and regulations of Ohio schools to be followed. The Plaintiffs also argue that the public interest will be served in that the issuance of a preliminary injunction will avoid willful, unreasonable, and malicious expulsions within the school systems of Ohio, and will prevent the bad faith expulsions of students.

The Plaintiffs' arguments are not well taken. The Court finds the contrary to be the case. The public interest will be served if our children are allowed to attend safe schools—free from guns, disruption and profanity. The public interest will be served if school officials are permitted to regulate conduct which relates to school safety and discipline; to ensure the safety of the student body. It is in the interest of all students that weapons not be allowed to be brought into school. School officials should not be required to perform a detailed analysis to determine if a student's gun is real or fake. Furthermore, school officials should be allowed to complete their duties free from abusive behavior and from threats of violence from students.

The Court concludes that the public interest will not be served in issuing an injunction. The public interest is served by maintaining safe schools, by ensuring discipline and by the abeyance of abusive student behavior.

VII. *CONCLUSION*

The Court finds that there is no basis for the issuance of a preliminary injunction. The Plaintiffs' Motion for a Preliminary Injunction is **DENIED**.

IT IS SO ORDERED.

Figure 3–8 (continued)

Rule 56. Summary Judgment

A party seeking to recover upon a claim, counterclaim, or cross-claim or to obtain a declaratory judgment may, at any time after the expiration of 20 days from the commencement of the action or after service of a motion for summary judgment by the adverse party, move with or without supporting affidavits for a summary judgment in the party's favor upon all or any part thereof.... The judgment sought shall be rendered forthwith if the pleadings, depositions, answers to interrogatories, and admissions on file, together with the affidavits, if any, show that there is no genuine issue as to any material fact and that the moving party is entitled to a judgment as a matter of law.

Figure 3–9 Federal Rule of Civil Procedure 56. From *Federal Civil Judicial Procedure and Rules*; reprinted with the permission of West Group.

Rule 32. Form of Briefs, the Appendix and Other Papers

(a) Form of Briefs and the Appendix. Briefs and appendices may be produced by standard typographic printing or by any duplicating or copying process which produces a clear black image on white paper. Carbon copies of briefs and appendices may not be submitted without permission of the court, except in behalf of parties allowed to proceed in forma pauperis. All printed matter must appear in at least 11 point type on opaque, unglazed paper. Briefs and appendices produced by the standard typographic process shall be bound in volumes having pages 6 1/8 by 9 1/4 inches and type matter 4 1/6 by 7 1/6 inches. Those produced by any other process shall be bound in volumes having pages not exceeding 8 1/2 by 11 inches and type matter not exceeding 6 1/2 by 9 1/2 inches, with double spacing between each line of text. In patent cases the pages of briefs and appendices may be of such size as is necessary to utilize copies of patent documents. Copies of the reporter's transcript and other papers reproduced in a manner authorized by this rule may be inserted in the appendix; such pages may be informally renumbered if necessary.

If briefs are produced by commercial printing or duplicating firms, or, if produced otherwise and the covers to be described are available, the cover of the brief of the appellant should be blue; that of the appellee, red; that of an intervenor or amicus curiae, green; that of any reply brief, gray. The cover of the appendix, if separately printed, should be white. The front covers of the briefs and of appendices, if separately printed, shall contain: (1) the name of the court and the number of the case; (2) the title of the case (see Rule 12(a)); (3) the nature of the proceeding in the court (e.g., Appeal; Petition for Review) and the name of the court, agency, or board below; (4) the title of the document (e.g., Brief for Appellant, Appendix); and (5) the names and addresses of counsel representing the party on whose behalf the document is filed.

(b) Form of Other Papers. Petitions for rehearing shall be produced in a manner prescribed by subdivision (a). Motions and other papers may be produced in like manner, or they may be typewritten upon opaque, unglazed paper 8 1/2 by 11 inches in size. Lines of typewritten text shall be double spaced. Consecutive sheets shall be attached at the left margin. Carbon copies may be used for filing and service if they are legible.

A motion or other paper addressed to the court shall contain a caption setting forth the name of the court, the title of the case, the file number, and a brief descriptive title indicating the purpose of the paper.

Figure 3–10 Federal Rule of Appellate Procedure 32. From *Federal Civil Judicial Procedure and Rules*; reprinted with the permission of West Group.

tabbed to ease access to a particular rule. Rulebooks may be hardbound and updated annually by supplement or pocket part, or published annually softbound, fully updated.

American Law Reports (A.L.R.s)

The American Law Reports (A.L.R.), published by West Group, is a bridge between primary and secondary legal research materials. The A.L.R. selects a timely legal issue, reports a leading case on the subject, and follows that case with an article, much like an encyclopedia topic or law review article, fully annotating the case with information from around the United States. For topics covered by the A.L.R., the A.L.R. offers comprehensive coverage. Thus, as a starting place for legal research, the A.L.R. is an invaluable research tool.[5]

Figure 3–11 shows an excerpt from an A.L.R. article regarding school discipline.

---

79 A.L.R.5th 1

IMPOSITION OF STATE OR LOCAL PENALTIES FOR THREATENING TO USE EXPLOSIVE DEVICES AT SCHOOLS OR OTHER BUILDINGS   Erin Masson Wirth, J.D.

SUMMARY

The Columbine school tragedy has focused attention on the fact that schools and other public buildings are uniquely vulnerable to bomb threats, stemming from the threat alone, because of the panic and disruption that can result from such bomb scares. A variety of state and local measures have been employed to penalize such threats, but the statutes in question are often strictly construed to protect the rights of those accused of such misdeeds. The court in State ex rel. R.T., 748 So. 2d 1256, 79 A.L.R.5th 711 (La. Ct. App. 2d Cir. 1999), held that the evidence was not sufficient to support the delinquency adjudication of the juvenile defendant for the communication of a bomb threat towards the school he attended, as neither of the two students to whom the alleged threat was communicated were shown by the state to have reacted in any manner to demonstrate that they were actually threatened, and the only direct participant in the conversation with the defendant denied ever being threatened by the defendant's statement. Other cases have reached contrary results depending on the particular circumstances presented and the varying rules applied by the courts. This annotation collects and analyzes cases in which the courts have dealt with the imposition of state and local penalties for threats to use explosive devices at schools or other buildings.

TABLE OF CONTENTS

Article Outline

Research References

- Total Client-Service Library References

- Research Sources

Index

Jurisdictional Table of Cited Statutes and Cases

Article

ARTICLE OUTLINE

I. PRELIMINARY MATTERS

s 1. Introduction

[a] Scope

Figure 3–11 Excerpts from an A.L.R. article on school discipline. From *American Law Reports 5th*; reprinted with the permission of West Group.

[b] Related annotations

s 2. Summary and comment

II. SCHOOL SUSPENSIONS, EXPULSIONS, OR TEACHER DISCHARGE

s 3. Evidence insufficient to expel student

s 4. Suspension or expulsion

[a] Upheld

[b] Overturned

. . . .

JURISDICTIONS

JURISDICTIONAL TABLE OF CITED STATUTES AND CASES

UNITED STATES

Edwards For and in Behalf of Edwards v. Rees, 883 F.2d 882, 55 Ed. Law Rep. 856—s 2

New Jersey v. T.L.O., 469 U.S. 325, 105 S. Ct. 733, 83 L. Ed. 2d 720, 21 Ed. Law Rep. 1122—s 2

Tinker v. Des Moines Independent Community School Dist., 393 U.S. 503, 89 S. Ct. 733, 21 L. Ed. 2d 731—s 2

ALABAMA

Robinson v. State, 484 So. 2d 1197—s 9

. . . .

OHIO

Foster, In re, 128 Ohio App. 3d 566, 716 N.E.2d 223—s 14[a]

. . . .

ARTICLE

I. PRELIMINARY MATTERS

SUMMARY s 1

s 1. Introduction

SUMMARY s 1(a)

[a] Scope

This annotation[1] collects and analyzes those cases in which the courts have imposed state or local penalties for threatening to use explosive devices at schools or other buildings. The annotation does not discuss cases in which individuals, airlines, or other vehicles have been threatened, nor does it discuss the application of federal remedies. The annotation also does not include cases regarding threats to use firearms or weapons, threats to burn buildings, or penalties for the possession or use of explosive devices.

Figure 3–11 (continued)

II. SCHOOL SUSPENSIONS, EXPULSIONS, OR TEACHER DISCHARGE

TEXT s 3

s 3. Evidence insufficient to expel student

It has been held that there was insufficient evidence to expel a student for making a false bomb threat to a school.

The court in Goldwire v. Clark, 234 Ga. App. 579, 507 S.E.2d 209, 130 Ed. Law Rep. 1352 (1998), reconsideration denied, (Sept. 30, 1998), held that there was no evidentiary support to find that the plaintiff student, challenging his expulsion, took an active role in persuading another student to make a false telephone call to 911 stating that there was a bomb in school, and the student therefore could not be suspended and placed on permanent probation for violating the Code of Student Discipline and Conduct. The evidence showed that on a Monday, a group of four students, including the plaintiff, discussed calling in a bomb threat so they would get out of school for a little while. The plaintiff testified that he thought they were joking. On the following Wednesday, the plaintiff told a substitute teacher that there was going to be a bomb threat that day; however, the teacher decided to just shrug it off. The group of students discussed calling in the bomb threat again later on Wednesday and the plaintiff observed the other students go over to a telephone booth. The plaintiff testified that he assumed that they were calling in the bomb threat and was later told that they had made the call to 911. The student who made the call testified that he remembered the plaintiff being present and encouraging him to make the call, but he could not recall anything specific that the plaintiff said. The court held that this was insufficient to convict the plaintiff, even under the "any evidence" standard of review, because knowledge and presence alone are insufficient to support a finding of guilt.

TEXT s 4

s 4. Suspension or expulsion

TEXT s 4(a)

[a] Upheld

Expulsion has been upheld as a punishment for making a false bomb threat to a school.

The court in Keith D. v. Ball, 177 W. Va. 93, 350 S.E.2d 720, 36 Ed. Law Rep. 231 (1986), denied a writ in mandamus by four students who were expelled from school for one year for making false bomb threats, because the students had temporarily forfeited their right to an education by their actions. Although students have a fundamental constitutional right to an education, when conduct materially disrupts classwork and impedes other students' rights to receive their education, the court held that a school board may constitutionally suspend the students from school. The court noted that the school setting requires an easing of some constitutional restrictions to maintain discipline.

Figure 3–11 (continued)

Review Questions

1. Which agency publishes official federal statutes and agency decisions?
2. Into how many "titles" are federal statutes divided? Name some of those titles.
3. Name some of the publishers of unofficial federal statutes and agency decisions.
4. What are the differences between official and unofficial publications of federal materials?
5. Name three publications of federal statutes.
6. Where is the legislative history of federal statutes published?
7. What is the Federal Register?
8. Name the sections of the Federal Register.
9. The Federal Register was not published until the late 1930s. What prompted its publication?
10. Which publications publish federal regulations?
11. Which publications update the C.F.R.?
12. What is the List of C.F.R. Sections Affected (L.S.A.)? Which publication(s) include an L.S.A.?

Exercises

Research the following issues:

1. Is a child expelled from school for behavioral problems entitled to alternative education:? What types of alternative education are available in your state?
2. May a non-lawyer advocate to recover fees for representing a child under the Individuals with Disabilities Education Act?
3. Must a child be identified as a special needs student before being expelled from school to receive alternative education under the Individuals with Disabilities Education Act?

Glossary

American Law Reports (A.L.R.): Reports of selected cases with accompanying annotations analyzing the law of the case nationally.

Bill number: A number issued proposed legislation.

Code of Federal Regulations (C.F.R.): Official publication of federal agency regulations.

Editorial features: Publisher-created aids to legal research.

Executive Order: Statement of executive policy issued by the chief executive.

Executive Proclamations: Chief executive's statements commemorating a public event.

Federal Administrative Procedure Act: Statute governing procedure before federal agencies.

Federal depository library: Library storing federal government documents.

Federal Register: A daily publication of agency activities, including proposed rules, final rules, notices, regulatory agenda, Presidential documents.

Funding aids: A remark, note, case summary, or commentary on some passage of a book, statute, or case intended to illustrate or explain its meaning.

Government Printing Office (GPO): Official publisher of federal government legal materials.

Head notes: Publisher's summary of a single point of law addressed in a case.

List of C.F.R. Sections Affected (L.S.A.): Publication of Federal Register documents affecting the Code of Federal Regulations.

Official publication: Legal materials published by the government.in permanent, hardbound volumes.

Parts Affected Tables: A section of the Federal Register which daily lists updates to federal regulations.

Pocket parts: Paperback supplements stored in the back of legal research books.

Primary sources: Research materials containing the law.

Public Law: First published form of enacted legislation.

Secondary materials : Research materials about the law.

Sunshine Act: Open Meeting Law; requires that government meetings be open to the public.

Titled: Labeled according to the numbering system for federal statutes.

Topic and key number: West's system of indexing and cross-referencing legal materials.

United States Code Annotated® (U.S.C.A.): West publication of federal statutes.

United States Code Service (U.S.C.S.): Reed publication of federal statutes.

United States Code (U.S.C.): Official publication of federal statutes.

Unofficial publications: Legal materials published by a private publisher.

Notes

[1]293 U.S. 388 (1935).

[2]Capital Services, Inc. monthly indexes the Federal Register and the Congressional Record monthly.

[3]5 U.S.C. § 552 (a) (2) (A).

[4]Shepard's also publishes citations volumes for the following, specialized administrative decisions: Federal Labor Law Citations, Environmental Law Citations, Federal Energy Law Citations, Federal Tax Law Citations, Immigration and Naturalization Citations, OSHA Citations, and United States Patents and Trademarks Citations.

[5]The A.L.R. is published in six volumes, the A.L.R., the A.L.R. 2d, A.L.R. 3d, A.L.R. 4th and A.L.R. 5th, which are consecutive, and the A.L.R. Fed, which covers leading federal issues and cases. The A.L.R. is topically indexed by individual indexes for each set of volumes and a combined index for the A.L.R. 3d, A.L.R. 4th, and A.L.R. 5th. The A.L.R. is updated by annual pocket parts and occasional hardbound supplements.

CHAPTER 4

Legal Research Books II

Chapter Outline

Secondary sources
    Dictionaries
    Encyclopedias
    Treatises
    Law Journals and Reviews
    Legal Newspapers
    Law Finders

Learning Objectives

Upon completing this chapter, the student should be able to

* Explain secondary sources of legal materials
* Name, explain, and describe the different types of secondary materials
* Name, explain, and describe the use of law finders

Secondary Sources

As already mentioned, secondary legal authority contains information about the law rather than the law itself. Nevertheless, secondary materials are invaluable aids to finding primary materials because of the footnotes and citation they provide. Among secondary materials are: dictionaries, encyclopedias, treatises, law journals and reviews, legal newspapers, and digests.

Dictionaries

One source of general information about a legal topic is a dictionary, either general or legal. A legal dictionary is an alphabetically arranged collection of definitions. Just as any researcher might look up the definition of "agoraphobia" in a standard dictionary such as *Merriam-Webster's Collegiate Dictionary*, the legal researcher might look up terms like "disability" or phrases like "nunc pro tunc" in a legal dictionary. The legal dictionary long the standard in the legal profession is *Black's Law Dictionary®*. Another well-known legal dictionary is *Ballentine's Law Dictionary*. Both dictionaries, in addition to providing word spelling, pronunciation, and definitions, identify cases defining or using the words or phrases. Dictionaries may be hardbound or softbound, abridged, unabridged, or "simplified" for non-lawyers.

Encyclopedias

Legal encyclopedias are also very useful. West Group's **Corpus Juris Secundum®** **(CJS)** and Lawyer's Cooperative Publishing **American Jurisprudence 2d (Am.Jur.2d)** are national legal encyclopedias containing articles (organized and indexed by topic) about various legal subjects. States, as well, may have legal encyclopedias. Articles in a legal encyclopedia are liberally footnoted with references to cases and other supporting legal materials. Figure 4–1 shows an example of part of an article appearing in C.J.S.® A similar article in Am.Jur. 2d is shown in Figure 4–2 on page 103.

Treatises

Finally, many, many books (**treatises**) have been written on various legal topics. Treatises, including textbooks, **hornbooks,** and **loose-leaf services,** are usually individually indexed and provide much background subject matter. Examples of legal treatises include *Prosser and Keeton on Torts,* and *Tribe on Constitutional Law.* Treatises include narrative explanations of particular legal areas and footnote relevant primary and secondary materials. Commonly, treatises include tables of contents and cases. Treatises may be updated by annual **pocket parts,** supplements, regular revisions, or, if the treatise is published in loose-leaf volumes, by replacement pages. Figure 4–3 on page 107 shows an example of a page from Edmund Reutler, Jr.'s treatise on the *Law of Public Education* (4ᵗʰ ed., 1994).

Sometimes private publishers, like West Group and Matthew Bender publish single or multi-volume treatises in loose-leaf binders. Like other treatises, loose-leaf

(Text continues on page 108.)

Factors considered.

Factors to be considered in determining whether corporal punishment is reasonable are the age and physical condition of the student,[57] the seriousness of the misconduct soliciting the punishment,[58] the nature and severity of the punishment,[59] the attitude and past behavior of the student,[60] and the availability of a less severe but equally effective means of discipline.[61]

2. Expulsion and Suspension
§ 798. In General

A student may be constitutionally suspended or expelled for misconduct whenever the conduct is of a type the school may legitimately prohibit.

Library References

Schools ☞ 177.

School boards and officials have inherent authority to suspend or expel a student when necessary to maintain order and discipline,[62] as long as the authority is exercised in a manner that will satisfy the statutory and constitutional standards for disciplinary proceedings.[63] As a general rule, a student may be constitutionally suspended or expelled for misconduct whenever the conduct is of a type the school may legitimately prohibit.[64]

A student may be suspended or expelled without regard to whether delinquency or criminal proceedings are pending as a result of the same conduct.[65] The grant of authority to suspend or expel is not expressly limited to suspensions from the regular classroom, but contemplates suspension from the entire system.[66]

In order to constitute a lawful expulsion of a student, there must be a deprivation of school privileges on proper grounds by the person or persons authorized under the law to expel.[67] A refusal to promote to a school or grade for which the student has not attained the required standard of scholarship is not an expulsion where the school or grade for which the student is fitted is open to him.[68] Suspension through the time of graduation ceremonies is not equivalent to an expulsion, although there is no return to school, where the student is in fact graduated.[69]

In the absence of a statute so providing,[70] the school authorities have no affirmative duty to provide an alternative educational program for suspended students.[71]

La.—LeBlanc v. Tyler, App., 381 So.2d 908.

Use of paddle
Teachers did not violate nine-year-old student's substantive due process rights by spanking her with paddle a total of seven times on three separate occasions in 30-minute period, notwithstanding that doctor and policewoman stated that bruises received by student were excessive; although student was severely bruised, she was not physically injured to the point that would "shock the conscience" of court.
U.S.—Brown by Brown v. Johnson, E.D.Ky., 710 F.Supp. 183.
57. La.—LeBoyd v. Jenkins, App., 381 So.2d 1290, writ denied 386 So.2d 341.
58. La.—LeBoyd v. Jenkins, App., 381 So.2d 1290, writ denied 386 So.2d 341.
59. La.—LeBoyd v. Jenkins, App., 381 So.2d 1290, writ denied 386 So.2d 341.
60. La.—LeBoyd v. Jenkins, App., 381 So.2d 1290, writ denied 386 So.2d 341.

61. La.—LeBoyd v. Jenkins, App., 381 So.2d 1290, writ denied 386 So.2d 341.
62. Ala.—Scoggins v. Henry County Bd. of Educ., Civ.App., 549 So.2d 99.
N.C.—Matter of Jackson, 352 S.E.2d 449, 84 N.C.App. 167.
W.Va.—Keith D. v. Ball, 350 S.E.2d 720, 177 W.Va. 93.

Rules and regulations
Ky.—Clark County Bd. of Ed. v. Jones, App., 625 S.W.2d 586.
Miss.—Clinton Mun. Separate School Dist. v. Byrd, 477 So.2d 237.
Vt.—Rutz v. Essex Junction Prudential Committee, 457 A.2d 1368, 142 Vt. 400.
63. Cal.—Abella v. Riverside Unified School Dist., 135 Cal.Rptr. 177, 65 C.A.3d 153.
64. Del.—Rucker v. Colonial School Dist., Super., 517 A.2d 703.
N.C.—Matter of Jackson, 352 S.E.2d 449, 84 N.C.App. 167.

Figure 4–1 C.J.S. article on school discipline. From *Corpus Juris Secundum*; reprinted with the permission of West Group.

Who may exercise power.

As a general rule the power of expelling or suspending a student is in the school board[72] or school committee[73] having the power of controlling and governing the school, and such power may be exercised by a school superintendent when conferred by statute.[74]

Liability.

As a general rule, a school official, in suspending or expelling a student, is liable in damages only if he acts with such an impermissible motivation or with such disregard of the student's constitutional rights that the action cannot be reasonably characterized as being in good faith.[75] A teacher and the members of a school board in exercising the power of expelling or suspending a pupil must exercise judgment and discretion, and are not liable in damages for errors of judgment in that respect if they act without malice, wantonness, or intention to wrong the pupil.[76] They are not liable even though they act with malice if the expul-

sion is based on lawful grounds and made in a lawful manner.[77]

§ 799. Grounds

A refusal to comply with a reasonable rule or regulation may constitute ground for expulsion or suspension.

Library References

Schools ☞ 177.

A student may properly be expelled or suspended for an infraction of, or for a refusal to comply with, a reasonable rule or regulation of the school authorities,[78] or he may be expelled or suspended for misconduct for which no formal rule is prescribed, but which has an injurious effect on the discipline and government of the school,[79] and it is within the power of the board to determine what constitutes disobedience or misconduct justifying expulsion or suspension.[80] A student may be suspended or expelled for insulting language and behavior toward the teacher in the presence of

---

65. Ohio—Schank v. Hegele, 521 N.E.2d 9, 36 Ohio Misc.2d 4.
66. N.C.—Matter of Jackson, 352 S.E.2d 449, 84 N.C.App. 167.
67. Wis.—State ex rel. Smith v. Board of Education of City of Eau Claire, 71 N.W. 123, 96 Wis. 95.
68. Mass.—Barnard v. Inhabitants of Shelburne, 102 N.E. 1095, 216 Mass. 19.
69. Pa.—Mifflin County School Dist. v. Stewart by Stewart, 503 A.2d 1012, 94 Pa.Cmwlth. 313.
70. U.S.—Mrs. A. J. v. Special School Dist. No. 1, D.C.Minn., 478 F.Supp. 418.
71. Fla.—Walter v. School Bd. of Indian River County, App., 518 So.2d 1331.
N.C.—Matter of Jackson, 352 S.E.2d 449, 84 N.C.App. 167.
72. Ga.—Cartersville Board of Education v. Purse, 28 S.E. 896, 101 Ga. 422.
73. Mass.—Antell v. Stokes, 191 N.E. 407, 287 Mass. 103.
74. Ky.—Byrd v. Begley, 90 S.W.2d 370, 262 Ky. 422.
75. Neb.—French v. Cornwell, 276 N.W.2d 216, 202 Neb. 569.
76. Ill.—McCormick v. Burt, 95 Ill. 263.
Neb.—French v. Cornwell, 276 N.W.2d 216, 202 Neb. 569.
77. N.H.—Sweeney v. Young, 131 A. 155, 82 N.H. 159.
78. U.S.—Dillon v. Pulaski County Special School Dist., D.C.Ark., 468 F.Supp. 54, affirmed 594 F.2d 699.
Cal.—Abella v. Riverside Unified School Dist., 135 Cal.Rptr. 177, 65 C.A.3d 153.
Ga.—Leoles v. Landers, 192 S.E. 218, 184 Ga. 580, appeal dismissed 58 S.Ct. 364, 302 U.S. 656, 82 L.Ed. 507.

Ky.—Byrd v. Begley, 90 S.W.2d 370, 262 Ky. 422.
Mass.—Antell v. Stokes, 191 N.E. 407, 287 Mass. 103.
N.D.—Stromberg v. French, 236 N.W. 477, 60 N.D. 750.
79. Mass.—Antell v. Stokes, 191 N.E. 407, 287 Mass. 103.
80. Minn.—State ex rel. Stone v. Probst, 206 N.W. 642, 165 Minn. 361.
81. Ga.—Board of Education v. Purse, 28 S.E. 896, 101 Ga. 422.
82. Wyo.—Clements v. Board of Trustees of Sheridan County School Dist. No. 2, In Sheridan County, 585 P.2d 197.
83. N.J.—State v. Conk, 434 A.2d 602, 180 N.J.Super. 140.
84. N.J.—State v. Conk, 434 A.2d 602, 180 N.J.Super. 140.
85. La.—Labrosse v. St. Bernard Parish School Bd., App. 4 Cir., 483 So.2d 1253.
86. U.S.—Pollnow v. Glennon, D.C.N.Y., 594 F.Supp. 220, affirmed 757 F.2d 496.
87. N.Y.—Sabin v. State University of New York Maritime College at Fort Schuyler, 460 N.Y.S.2d 332, 92 A.D.2d 831.
88. Cal.—Slayton v. Pomona Unified School Dist., 2 Dist., 207 Cal. Rptr. 705, 161 C.A.3d 538.
Ill.—Robinson v. Oak Park and River Forest High School, 1 Dist., 571 N.E.2d 931, 156 Ill.Dec. 951, 213 Ill.App.3d 77.
Ky.—Clark County Bd. of Ed. v. Jones, App., 625 S.W.2d 586
N.Y.—Board of Educ. of Millbrook Central School Dist., Dutchess County v. Ambach, 3 Dept., 465 N.Y.S.2d 77, 96 A.D.2d 637, appeal denied 460 N.E.2d 1360, 61 N.Y.2d 603, 472 N.Y.S.2d 1026.

Figure 4–1 (continued).

the other students,[81] and under some statutory provisions, for behavior which in the judgment of the school authorities is detrimental to education, welfare, safety, and morals of other students.[82] Also, a student may be suspended or expelled for a continued and willful disobedience,[83] or open defiance of authority.[84]

Except where punishment is limited by statute to offenses occurring on school grounds or property,[85] off-campus, non-school-related conduct may be a sufficient basis for suspension.[86] Suspension or expulsion on grounds unrelated to academic achievement requires conformity by the school with its own rules.[87]

A student cannot be arbitrarily expelled or suspended,[88] or suspended or expelled for a refusal to comply with a rule or regulation that is not needful for the government, good order, or efficiency of the school.[89] Also, a student cannot be suspended or expelled for the exercise of First Amendment rights,[90] or because of a parent's failure to pay textbook fees,[91] or for a careless act, no matter how negligent, which is not willful or malicious.[92]

Flag salute.

Since students cannot be compelled to participate in a flag-salute ceremony contrary to their religious belief, as discussed supra § 781, their expulsion based on their refusal so to participate is invalid.[93] A statute which merely requires the state superintendent of public instruction to prepare a program for a flag-salute ceremony does not authorize expulsion of a pupil for refusing to participate in such ceremony because of sincere religious beliefs.[94]

§ 800. —— Particular Grounds

Various particular matters have been held to constitute or not to constitute grounds for suspension or expulsion of a student.

Library References

Schools ☞ 177.

In accordance with the principles discussed supra § 799, various particular matters have been held to constitute grounds for suspension or expulsion of a

---

89. Wis.—State ex rel. Bowe v. Board of Education of City of Fond Du Lac, 23 N.W. 102, 63 Wis. 234.

90. U.S.—Dodd v. Rambis, D.C.Ind., 535 F.Supp. 23.

Vulgar gesture outside school
Student's making of vulgar gesture toward teacher which occurred off school premises and after school hours was too attenuated to support discipline of student for violating rule which provided suspension for vulgar or extremely inappropriate language or conduct directed to staff member.
U.S.—Klein v. Smith, D.Me., 635 F.Supp. 1440.

91. U.S.—Carder v. Michigan City School Corp., D.C.Ind., 552 F.Supp. 869.

92. Mich.—Holman v. School Trustees of Avon, 43 N.W. 996, 77 Mich. 605.

93. U.S.—West Virginia State Board of Education v. Barnette, W.Va., 63 S.Ct. 1178, 319 U.S. 624, 87 L.Ed. 1628.
Kan.—State v. Smith, 127 P.2d 518, 155 Kan. 588.
Pa.—Commonwealth v. Crowley, 35 A.2d 744, 154 Pa.Super. 116.
S.D.—State v. Davis, 10 N.W.2d 288, 69 S.D. 328.

94. Kan.—State v. Smith, 127 P.2d 518, 155 Kan. 588.

95. U.S.—Bahr v. Jenkins, D.C.Ky., 539 F.Supp. 483.
Ala.—Scoggins v. Henry County Bd. of Educ., Civ.App., 549 So.2d 99.
Ark.—Springdale Bd. of Educ. v. Bowman by Luker, 740 S.W.2d 909, 294 Ark. 66.
Fla.—Jones v. Brevard County School Bd., App. 5 Dist., 470 So.2d 760.

Ill.—Donaldson v. Board of Ed. for Danville School Dist. No. 118, 424 N.E.2d 737, 53 Ill.Dec. 946, 98 Ill.App.3d 438.
Mo.—Consolidated School Dist. No. 2 v. King By Dresselhaus, App., 786 S.W.2d 217.
N.Y.—Hogan v. Board of Ed. of North Colonie Central School Dist., 442 N.Y.S.2d 623, 83 A.D.2d 729.

Refusal to remove sunglasses
U.S.—Cole By and Through Cole v. Newton Special Mun. Separate School Dist., S.D.Miss., 676 F.Supp. 749, affirmed 853 F.2d 924.

Bringing alcohol to school
Ala.—Adams v. City of Dothan Bd. of Educ., Civ.App., 485 So.2d 757.

Bringing knife to school
Mo.—Consolidated School Dist. No. 2 v. King by Dresselhaus, App., 786 S.W.2d 217.

Distribution of unofficial newspaper
Suspension of students from school for three days for distribution on high school premises of unofficial newspaper did not violate the First Amendment where disruption of classes resulted, not in original distribution but as result of other student's circulating, reading, and reacting to the publication during classes, where publication contained sexually explicit, indecent and lewd language, and where publication advocated violence against teachers, though not in such fashion as was likely to incite or produce imminent lawless action.

Figure 4–1 (continued).

student[95] such as insubordination,[96] assault[97] or battery[98] on another student, conspiring to and threatening to assault a teacher,[99] false reports concerning bombs or other explosive devices[1], and carrying a weapon and ammunition to school.[2] Additional grounds for suspension or expulsion include the sale of drugs at school,[3] use or possession of drugs,[4] possession of drug paraphernalia,[5] and use or possession of alcoholic beverages on school property or at school functions.[6] Other particular matters which have been held to constitute grounds for suspension or expulsion include continued absences without satisfactory excuses[7] and refusal to obey proper orders or regulations.[8]

On the other hand, various particular matters have been held not to constitute grounds for suspension or expulsion of a student.[9]

§ 801. Proceedings for Expulsion; Interference by Court

Proceedings for expulsion must be in accordance with law.

Library References

Schools ☞ 177.

Where express provision is made by statute therefor, the expulsion or suspension of a student must be made in the manner prescribed.[10] Ordinarily a school board may adopt any mode of procedure in obtaining information or evidence of the conduct of a student which it deems best.[11] As a general rule the student is entitled to notice of the charges against him and must be granted a hearing on the charges before he can be suspended or expelled.[12]

The notice must be timely,[13] and must be sufficiently specific to apprise the student of the charges against him.[14] However, a failure to observe the technical requirements of a statute which does not rise to the level of a constitutional violation is not fatal.[15]

A hearing must be held even absent a demand for it,[16] and cannot be excused by later proof that the student is guilty of the offense charged.[17]

U.S.—Bystrom By and Through Bystrom v. Fridley High School, D.Minn., 686 F.Supp. 1387, affirmed 855 F.2d 855.

96. Use of profanity
Student's admission at hearing that she used obscenity aimed at school officials was sufficient to support decision superintendent of school district for suspending student for insubordination and affirmance of such determination by district's board of education.

N.Y.—Underwood v. Board of Educ. of City School Dist. of City of Kingston, 3 Dept., 498 N.Y.S.2d 907, 117 A.D.2d 897.

97. Mo.—Reasoner by Reasoner v. Meyer, App., 766 S.W.2d 161.
N.J.—State v. Conk, 434 A.2d 602, 180 N.J.Super. 140.
Pa.—Porter v. Board of School Directors for Clairton School Dist., 445 A.2d 1386, 67 Pa.Cmwlth. 147.
98. U.S.—Gonzales v. McEuen, D.C.Cal., 435 F.Supp. 460.
99. La.—Williams v. Turner, App., 382 So.2d 1040.
1. W.Va.—Keith D. v. Ball, 350 S.E.2d 720, 177 W.Va. 93.
2. Ill.—Lusk By and Through Lusk v. Triad Community Unit No. 2, 5 Dist., 551 N.E.2d 660, 141 Ill.Dec. 473, 194 Ill.App.3d 426.
3. U.S.—Salazar v. Luty, S.D.Tex., 761 F.Supp. 45.

Vt.—Rutz v. Essex Junction Prudential Committee, 457 A.2d 1368, 142 Vt. 400.

Marijuana cigarette

Mich.—Birdsey v. Grand Blanc Community Schools, 344 N.W.2d 342, 130 Mich.App. 718.
4. U.S.—Palmer v. Merluzzi, D.N.J., 689 F.Supp. 400, affirmed 868 F.2d 90.
Ill.—Wilson on Behalf of Wilson v. Collinsville Community Unit School Dist. No. 10, 5 Dist., 451 N.E.2d 939, 71 Ill.Dec. 785, 116 Ill.App.3d 537.
Miss.—Jones v. Board of Trustees of Pascagoula Mun. Separate School Dist., 524 So.2d 968.
Pa.—Abremski v. Southeastern School Dist. Bd. of Directors, 421 A.2d 485, 54 Pa.Cmwlth. 292.
5. U.S.—Brewer by Dreyfus v. Austin Independent School Dist., C.A.5(Tex), 779 F.2d 260.
Ohio—Cross v. Princeton City School Dist. Bd. of Educ., 550 N.E.2d 219, 49 Ohio Misc.2d 1.
6. U.S.—Board of Educ. of Rogers, Arkansas v. McCluskey, Ark., 102 S.Ct. 3469, 458 U.S. 966, 73 L.Ed.2d 1273, rehearing denied 103 S.Ct.16, 458 U.S. 1132, 73 L.Ed.2d 1402, on remand 688 F.2d 596—Wood v. Strickland, Ark., 95 S.Ct. 992, 420 U.S. 308, 43 L.Ed.2d 214, rehearing denied 95 S.Ct. 1589, 421 U.S. 921, 43 L.Ed.2d 790, on remand Strickland v. Inlow, 519 F.2d 744.
Anable v. Ford, W.D.Ark., 653 F.Supp. 22, modified on

Figure 4–1 (continued).

When so required by statute, a hearing must be conducted within the time prescribed by statute,[18] but the full formality of traditional legal proceedings,[19] or the technicalities of a criminal prosecution,[20] need not be followed.

Interference by court.

The decision of school authorities in expelling or suspending a student is not subject to judicial interference[21] except where lack of power is shown,[22] or the school authorities act arbitrarily or maliciously.[23] Hence, if there is evidence to support the decision of the school board, it is improvident for the court to render a contrary judgment.[24] However, a school board could be enjoined from expelling a child in need of services where the child would suffer irreparable injury if not permitted to return to school.[25]

---

other grounds 663 F.Supp. 149.
Pa.—Appeal of McClellan, 475 A.2d 867, 82 Pa.Cmwlth. 75.
7. Ark.—Williams v. Board of Ed. for Marianna School Dist., 626 S.W.2d 361, 274 Ark. 530.
Mass.—Wulff v. Inhabitants of Wakefield, 109 N.E. 358, 221 Mass. 427.
8. Ky.—Byrd v. Begley, 90 S.W.2d 370, 262 Ky. 422.
Mass.—Antell v. Stokes, 191 N.E. 407, 287 Mass. 103.
9. N.Y.—Matter of Blackman, 419 N.Y.S.2d 796, 100 Misc.2d 566.
Wash.—Quinlan v. University Place School Dist. 83, 660 P.2d 329, 34 Wash.App. 260.

Knife as Christmas Gift
Under school regulation providing for mandatory expulsion for possession of knife used to intimidate, student could not be expelled for bringing boxed commemorative knife to school to give to her boyfriend from her father as Christmas gift.
Fla.—C.J. v. School Bd. of Broward County, App. 4 Dist., 438 So.2d 87.
10. U.S.—Mrs. A.J. v. Special School Dist. No. 1, D.C.Minn., 478 F.Supp. 418.
Fla.—W.A.N. v. School Bd. of Polk County, App. 2 Dist., 504 So.2d 529.
11. Neb.—Vermillion v. State ex rel. Englehardt, 110 N.W. 736, 78 Neb. 107.
12. U.S.—Goss v. Lopez, Ohio, 95 S.Ct. 729, 419 U.S. 565, 42 L.Ed.2d 725.
Cal.—Abella v. Riverside Unified School Dist., 135 Cal.Rptr. 177, 65 C.A.3d 153.
Mass.—Morrison v. City of Lawrence, 72 N.E. 91, 186 Mass. 456.
Ohio—Rossman v. Conran, 572 N.E.2d 728, 61 Ohio App.3d 246.

Formal hearing not required
(1) A formal hearing in true adversary context is not required prior to suspension of child from public school for entire school year for disciplinary reasons.
U.S.—Whiteside v. Kay, D.C.La., 446 F.Supp. 716.

(2) High school student is entitled to hearing, informal in nature, before he can be suspended from school.
Ohio—Menke v. Ohio High School Athletic Ass'n, 441 N.E.2d 620, 2 Ohio App.3d 244, 2 O.B.R. 266.

Informal discussion as sufficient
In connection with suspension of student for drinking from cup containing whiskey mixed with a soft drink, school officials complied with requirement that student be given oral or written notice of charges against him and opportunity to present his side of story, where student and principal informally discussed incident shortly after it occurred, principal asked student to admit he had been drinking, and student admitted cup contained alcohol.
U.S.—Lamb v. Panhandle Community Unit Dist. No. 2, C.A.7(Ill.), 826 F.2d 526.

Delivery of notice by hand
Notice of expulsion procedure by "registered or certified mail" as provided by statute was not jurisdictional prerequisite, and, thus, notice delivered to parent by hand was sufficient to vest school board with jurisdiction to act in expulsion proceedings.
Ill.—Stratton v. Wenona Community Unit Dist. No. 1, 551 N.E.2d 640, 141 Ill.Dec. 453, 133 Ill.2d 413.

Evidence not presented at open hearing
School administrator's disclosure to board, during its closed deliberations, of evidence not previously presented at open hearing on student's expulsion violated student's due process rights by depriving him of opportunity to rebut evidence.
U.S.—Newsome v. Batavia Local School Dist., C.A.6(Ohio), 842 F.2d 920.

Hearsay testimony
Admission of hearsay testimony from school employees at expulsion hearing did not deprive student of due process.
Miss.—Jones v. Board of Trustees of Pascagoula Mun. Separate School Dist., 524 So.2d 968.
13. Ill.—Stratton v. Wenona Community Unit Dist. No. 1, 551 N.E.2d 640, 141 Ill.Dec. 453, 133 Ill.2d 413.
14. Ill.—Stratton v. Wenona Community Unit Dist. No. 1, 551 N.E.2d 640, 141 Ill.Dec. 453, 133 Ill.2d 413.

15. Failure to serve notice on pupils
To extent that school officials failed to observe technical requirements of statute in that written notice was not served on pupils at or before time suspension was to take effect, but was mailed to students' parents on the afternoon of their suspensions, this did not rise to level of constitutional violation and was de minimus, and thus did not violate statute.
U.S.— Bystrom By and Through Bystrom v. Fridley High School, D.Minn., 686 F.Supp. 1387, affirmed 855 F.2d 855.

Figure 4–1 (continued).

§ 802. Students with Disabilities

The **Individuals with Disabilities Education Act** prohibits the expulsion of a handicapped student for misbehavior that results from or is a manifestation of the handicap.

Library References

Schools ☜ 177.

By enacting the Individuals with Disabilities Education Act, and prior versions thereof,[26] one of the evils Congress sought to remedy was the unilateral exclusion of disabled children by schools.[27] The expulsion of a handicapped student must be accompanied by a determination as to whether his misconduct bears a relationship to his handicap,[28] as the Act prohibits the expulsion of a handicapped student for misbehavior that results from[29] or is a manifestation of[30] the handicap. This proscription, although nowhere directly stated in the Act, may be inferred from the Act's history, purpose, terms, and accompanying regulations.[31]

However, if the child's misbehavior is properly determined not to be a manifestation of his handicap, the handicapped child can be expelled;[32] and

---

16. N.Y.—Johnson v. Board of Ed., Union Free School Dist. No. 6, Manhasset, 393 N.Y.S.2d 510, 90 Misc.2d 40.
17. U.S.—Doe v. Rockingham County School Bd., W.D.Va., 658 F.Supp. 403.
18. Cal.—Garcia v. Los Angeles County Bd. of Ed., 177 Cal.Rptr. 29, 123 C.A.3d 807.
19. N.Y.—Spencer v. New York City Bd. of Higher Educ., 502 N.Y.S.2d 358, 131 Misc.2d 847.
20. U.S.— Whiteside v. Kay, D.C.La., 446 F.Supp. 716.

Investigator as hearing officer
High school administrator involved in initiation and investigation of charges against student was not thereby disqualified from conducting hearing on charges.
U.S.—Brewer by Dreyfus v. Austin Independent School Dist., C.A.5(Tex.), 779 F.2d 260.
21. Ky.—Byrd v. Begley, 90 S.W.2d 370, 262 Ky. 422.
22. Mo.—Wright v. Board of Education of St. Louis, 246 S.W. 43, 295 Mo. 466.
23. Ill.—Donaldson v. Board of Ed. for Danville School Dist. No. 118, 424 N.E.2d 737, 53 Ill.Dec. 946, 98 Ill.App.3d 438.
Ky.—Cross v. Board of Trustees of Walton Graded Common School, 110 S.W. 346, 129 Ky. 35, 33 Ky.L.472.
N.Y.—Board of Educ. of Millbrook Central School Dist., Dutchess County v. Ambach, 3 Dept., 465 N.Y.S.2d 77, 96 A.D.2d 637, appeal denied 460 N.E.2d 1360, 61 N.Y.2d 603, 472 N.Y.S.2d 1026.
24. U.S.—Smith v. Little Rock School Dist., D.C.Ark., 582 F.Supp. 159.
25. Ind.—Matter of P.J., App. 3 Dist., 575 N.E.2d 22.
26. 20 U.S.C.A. § 1400 et seq.
27. U.S.—Honig v. Doe, Cal., 108 S.Ct. 592, 484 U.S. 305, 98 L.Ed.2d 686.

28. U.S.—S-1 v. Turlington, C.A.Fla., 635 F.2d 342, certiorari denied 102 S.Ct. 566, 454 U.S. 1030, 70 L.Ed.2d 473 and Edwards v. S-1, 102 S.Ct. 566, 454 U.S. 1030, 70 L.Ed.2d 473.
Miss.—Board of Trustees of Pascagoula Mun. Separate School Dist. v. Doe, 508 So.2d 1081.
29. U.S.— S-1 v. Turlington, C.A.Fla., 635 F.2d 342, certiorari denied 102 S.Ct. 566, 454 U.S.1030, 70 L.Ed.2d 473 and Edwards v. S-1, 102 S.Ct. 566, 454 U.S. 1030, 70 L.Ed.2d 473.

Inappropriately placed handicapped student
Expulsion of an inappropriately placed handicapped student for disruptive behavior caused by the handicap is improper, particularly if procedures outlined in the Act for changing educational placement are not followed beforehand.
Cal.—In re John K., 1 Dist., 216 Cal.Rptr. 557, 170 C.A.3d 783, review denied.
30. U.S.—Doe by Gonzales v. Maher, C.A.9(Cal.), 793 F.2d 1470, certiorari granted in part Honig v. Doe, 107 S.Ct. 1284, 479 U.S. 1084, 94 L.Ed.2d 142, affirmed as modified on other grounds 108 S.Ct. 592, 484 U.S. 305, 98 L.Ed.2d 686.
31. U.S.— Doe by Gonzales v. Maher, C.A.9(Cal.), 793 F.2d 1470, certiorari granted in part Honig v. Doe, 107 S.Ct. 1284, 479 U.S. 1084, 94 L.Ed.2d 142, affirmed as modified 108 S.Ct. 592, 484 U.S. 305, 98 L.Ed.2d 686.
32. U.S.—Doe by Gonzales v. Maher, C.A.9(Cal.), 793 F.2d 1470, certiorari granted in part Honig v. Doe, 107 S.Ct. 1284, 479 U.S. 1084, 94 L.Ed.2d 142, affirmed as modified on other grounds 108 S.Ct. 592, 484 U.S. 305, 98 L.Ed.2d 686.

Figure 4–1 (continued).

directed against him, he used excessive force in violation of the students' due process rights and was not entitled to qualified immunity since the students' liberty interest in freedom from arbitrary corporal punishment was clearly established and the principal could not have reasonably believed that his actions were lawful.[97]

§ 296. As violation of Eighth Amendment

The paddling of students in public schools as a means of maintaining school discipline does not constitute cruel and unusual punishment in violation of the Eighth Amendment, because the Eighth Amendment is directed toward the punishment of criminal offenders.[98]

§ 297. Procedural requirements

A school regulation that does not provide for notice and hearing before corporal punishment is administered is not violative of the constitutional right of procedural due process of law guaranteed by the Fourteenth Amendment of the Constitution.[99] However, school authorities, before administering manual corporal punishment, must give the student an opportunity to explain his or her version of the disruptive event, as such an explanation may convince a fair-minded person that corporal punishment is not warranted. Furthermore, in the absence of some extraordinary factor, the administration of corporal punishment must be done in the presence of another adult.[1]

3. SUSPENSION AND EXPULSION [§§ 298-310]

a. IN GENERAL [§§ 298-301]

§ 298. Generally

A student's right to attend the public schools is necessarily conditioned on his or her compliance with the reasonable rules, regulations, and requirements of the school authorities,[2] breaches of which may be punished by sus-

---

97 P.B. v. Koch, 96 F.3d 1298, 112 Ed. Law Rep. 687 (9th Cir. 1996).

98 Ingraham v. Wright, 430 U.S. 651, 97 S.Ct. 1401, 51 L. Ed. 2d 711 (1977) (distinguished on other grounds by, Frost v. City and County of Honolulu, 584 F. Supp. 356 (D. Haw. 1984)) and (distinguished on other grounds by, Gelber By and Through Gelber v. Rozas, 584 F. Supp. 902 (S.D. Fla. 1984)) and (distinguished on other grounds by, Jefferson v. Ysleta Independent School Dist., 817 F.2d 303, 39 Ed. Law Rep. 17 (5th Cir. 1987)) and (declined to extend on other grounds by, Sweaney v. Ada County, Idaho, 119 F.3d 1385, 120 Ed. Law Rep. 149, 38 Fed. R. Serv. 3d (LCP) 1129 (9th Cir. 1997)) and (distinguished on other grounds by, Township of West Orange v. Whitman, 8 F. Supp. 2d 408 (D.N.J. 1998)).

Practice References: Constitutional challenges to corporal punishment. 20 Am Jur POF2d 511, Teacher's Use of Excessive Corporal Punishment § 14.

99 Ingraham v. Wright, 430 U.S. 651, 97 S.Ct. 1401, 51 L. Ed. 2d 711 (1977) (distinguished on other grounds by, Frost v. City and County of Honolulu, 584 F. Supp. 356 (D. Haw. 1984)) and (distinguished on other grounds by, Gelber By and Through Gelber v. Rozas, 584 F. Supp. 902 (S.D. Fla. 1984)) and (distinguished on other grounds by, Jefferson v. Ysleta Independent School Dist., 817 F.2d 303, 39 Ed. Law Rep. 17 (5th Cir. 1987)) and (declined to extend on other grounds by, Sweaney v. Ada County, Idaho, 119 F.3d 1385, 120 Ed. Law Rep. 149, 38 Fed. R. Serv. 3d (LCP) 1129 (9th Cir. 1997)) and (distinguished on other grounds by, Township of West Orange v. Whitman, 8 F. Supp. 2d 408 (D.N.J. 1998)).

1 Smith v. West Virginia State Bd. of Educ., 170 W. Va. 593, 295 S.E.2d 680, 6 Ed. Law Rep. 1138 (1982).

2 Tanton v. McKenney, 226 Mich. 245, 197 N.W. 510, 33 A.L.R. 1175 (1924); Texarkana

---

Figure 4–2 Am.Jur.2d article on school discipline. From *American Jurisprudence 2d;* reprinted with the permission of West Group.

§ 301 SCHOOLS 68 Am Jur 2d

pension or privileges of the school is generally subject to review by the trustees, board of education, or other governing body of the school district.[24]

b. Grounds [§§ 302-307]

§ 302. Generally; Insubordination or disobedience

Subject only to the limitation that their actions must be reasonable and undertaken in the enforcement of the reasonable rules and regulations of the school,[25] school authorities may suspend or expel pupils for any insubordination or misconduct that is subversive of the discipline of the school.[26]

♦ *Observation:* In measuring the reasonableness of student suspensions, the courts must give credence to the role and purpose of the schools, and to the means available to school administrators to deal with their problems.[27]

§ 303. Sale or use of controlled substance or alcohol at school

A school board may, by regulation, provide for the suspension of a student who, while at school, has used, sold, been under the influence of, or been in possession of controlled substances defined as such by state law.[28]

♦ *Illustration:* A school district has the authority to suspend a student for the students were not fairly apprised that they could be expelled for the possession of marijuana off the school campus.[36]

---

22 Vermillion v. State, 78 Neb. 107, 110 N.W. 736 (1907); State v. District Board of School Dist. No. 1, 135 Wis. 619, 116 N.W. 232 (1908).

Under South Carolina law, a principal or superintendent has the inherent power, when the interest of school requires it, to suspend a student in a proper case, unless he or she has been deprived of that power by an affirmative action of the board of Trustees. Phillips v. Anderson County School Dist. Five, 987 F. Supp. 488, 124 Ed. Law Rep. 85 (D.S.C. 1997).

23 State v. District Board of School Dist. No. 1, 135 Wis. 619, 116 N.W. 232 (1908).

24 Richie v. Board of Educ. of Lead Hill School Dist., 326 Ark. 587, 933 S.W.2d 375, 114 Ed. Law Rep. 688 (1996).

25 Board of Education of City of Covington v. Booth, 110 Ky. 807, 23 Ky. L. Rptr. 288, 62 S.W. 872 (1901).

It is within the discretion of a school board to expel a student who is guilty of gross disobedience or misconduct, but such discretion does have limits. Washington v. Smith, 248 Ill. App. 3d 534, 187 Ill. Dec. 970, 618 N.E.2d 561, 84 Ed. Law Rep. 1113 (1st Dist. 1993).

26 Douglas v. Campbell, 89 Ark. 254, 116 S.W. 211 (1909); State v. Conk, 180 N.J. Super. 140, 434 A.2d 602 (App. Div. 1981); Underwood v. Board of Educ. of City School Dist. of City of Kingston, 117 A.D.2d 897, 498 N.Y.S.2d 907, 30 Ed. Law Rep. 832 (3d Dep't 1986).

The three-day suspension of a high school student for insubordination involving the student's unauthorized

performance at a homecoming event did not violate the student's right to equal protection, as a public education is not a fundamental right, and the suspension was supported by a rational basis. Smith on Behalf of Smith v. Severn, 129 F.3d 419, 122 Ed. Law Rep. 106, 39 Fed. R. Serv. 3d (LCP) 1026 (7th Cir. 1997).

A student's gross disrespect and contempt for the officials of an educational institution may be justification not only for suspension, but also for expulsion. Schwartz v. Schuker, 298 F. Supp. 238 (E.D.N.Y. 1969).

As to the enforcement of rules by administrative agencies, generally, see 2 Am Jur 2d, Administrative Law §§ 312-314.

27 Baker v. Downey City Bd. of Educ., 307 F. Supp. 517 (C.D. Cal. 1969).

28 Birdsey v. Grand Blanc Community Schools, 130 Mich. App. 718, 344 N.W.2d 342, 16 Ed. Law Rep. 297 (1983); Adams v. School Bd. of Brevard County, 470 So. 2d 760, 25 Ed. Law Rep. 975 (Fla. Dist. Ct. App. 5th Dist. 1985).

As to disciplinary action taken with respect to use of such substances off campus, see § 305. **Forms:** Complaint, petition, or declaration—

36 Galveston Independent School Dist. v. Boothe, 590 S.W.2d 553 (Tex. Civ. App. Houston 1st Dist. 1979).

37 Donovan v. Ritchie, 68 F.3d 14, 104 Ed. Law Rep. 80 (1st Cir. 1995).

38 Donovan v. Ritchie, 68 F.3d 14, 104 Ed. Law Rep. 80 (1st Cir. 1995).

Figure 4–2 (continued).

Legal Research Books II ✳ **105**

In some jurisdictions, a statute prohibits the suspension of a student for conduct unrelated to school-sponsored activities.[37] Such a statute deals with matters other than actions taken with and aimed toward other students,[38] and does not bar the suspension of a student for his role in distributing an abusive or obscene document about his or her classmates, when the student's admitted off-premises conduct led to the distribution of the document on school premises.[39]

◆ *Observation:* High school athletic events that are held at other schools are "school-sponsored activities" for the purposes of a statute establishing the grounds for the suspension or expulsion of students.[40]

§ 306. Violent behavior or possession of weapons

A student may properly be suspended or expelled for fighting[41] or for possessing a dangerous weapon at school or at a school-sponsored event,[42] so long as the student's constitutional and statutory rights are not abridged.[43] Thus, students have been found properly expelled or suspended for —

—using a stun gun during an altercation with another student during school hours, even though the altercation took place on a campus other than that which the expelled student attended.[44]

—knowingly possessing a knife on school property.[45]

—carrying a pocket knife on a school field trip.[46]

A statute that provides for the expulsion from school for up to 12 months of students who bring weapons to school is facially constitutional under a state constitutional guarantee of a "thorough and efficient school system," since the state has a compelling interest in providing a safe and secure environment to school children under that constitutional guarantee, and such an expulsion is a reasonably necessary and narrowly tailored method to further that interest.[47]

39 Donovan v. Ritchie, 68 F.3d 14, 104 Ed. Law Rep. 80 (1st Cir. 1995).

40 Pirschel v. Sorrell, 2 F. Supp. 2d 930, 127 Ed. Law Rep. 124 (E.D. Ky. 1998).

41 Donaldson v. Board of Ed. for Danville School Dist. No. 118, 98 Ill. App. 3d 438, 53 Ill. Dec. 946, 424 N.E.2d 737 (4th Dist. 1981).

42 Wood By and Through Wood v. Henry County Public Schools, 255 Va. 85, 495 S.E.2d 255, 123 Ed. Law Rep. 373 (1998).

43 Wood By and Through Wood v. Henry County Public Schools, 255 Va. 85, 495 S.E.2d 255, 123 Ed. Law Rep. 373 (1998).
As to what process is required for a suspension, see §§ 302 et seq.

Law Reviews: "Expelled. No excuses. No exceptions."—Michigan's zero-tolerance policy in response to school violence: MCLA Section 380.1311, 74 U Det Mercy LR 2:357 (1997).

44 Fremont Union High Sch. Dist. v. Santa Clara County Bd. of Education, 235 Cal. App. 3d 1182, 286 Cal. Rptr. 915, 70 Ed. Law Rep. 570 (6th Dist. 1991).

45 Kolesnick By and Through Shaw v. Omaha Public School Dist., 251 Neb. 575, 558 N.W.2d 807, 115 Ed. Law Rep. 1054 (1997).

46 Wood By and Through Wood v. Henry County Public Schools, 255 Va. 85, 495 S.E.2d 255, 123 Ed. Law Rep. 373 (1998).

47 Cathe A. v. Doddridge County Bd. of Educ., 200 W. Va. 521, 490 S.E.2d 340, 120 Ed. Law Rep. 1212 (1997).

Figure 4–2 (continued).

68 Am Jur 2d   SCHOOLS   § 308

Similarly, the expulsion of a student from a public school for the knowing possession of a knife on school property is rationally related to the school board's interest in protecting the other students and the staff from violence, and therefore does not violate the student's state or federal constitutional rights.[48]

§ 307. Other grounds

A student may properly be suspended for—
—violating the school's racial harassment and intimidation policy.[49]
—wearing a jacket with the Confederate battle flag on it, when racial incidents have recently occurred in the school and the jacket could cause a disruption.[50]
—wearing sagging pants in violation of school dress code.[51]
Students may not be suspended solely because they silently refuse to rise and stand for the playing or singing of the national anthem, when the conduct of the students is not disorderly and does not materially disrupt the conduct and discipline of the school, and when there is no evidence that it would do so in the future.[52]

C. PROCEDURAL RIGHTS OF STUDENTS FACING SUSPENSION OR EXPULSION [§§ 308–310]

§ 308. Generally

A student does not have fundamental right to a public education so as to trigger a strict scrutiny or analysis whenever school officials determine, in the interest of safety, that his or her misconduct warrants expulsion.[53]

♦ *Caution:* Although student disciplinary hearings are serious and adversarial in nature, students are not entitled to the procedural protections of a criminal trial.[54] The burden of proof and evidentiary rules imposed in a school disciplinary proceeding are not as stringent as in a formal trial, the evidence may consist of hearsay,[55] and any reasonable inferences drawn by the hearing officer will be sustained by a reviewing court if they are supported by the record.[56]

A student is denied due process of the law when the regulation under which the child is excluded from school is so vague and standardless that it leaves the

---

48 Kolesnick By and Through Shaw v. Omaha Public School Dist., 251 Neb. 575, 558 N.W.2d 807, 115 Ed. Law Rep. 1054 (1997).

49 West v. Derby Unified School Dist. No. 260, 23 F. Supp. 2d 1223, 130 Ed. Law Rep. 1186 (D. Kan. 1998).

50 Phillips v. Anderson County School Dist. Five, 987 F. Supp. 488, 124 Ed. Law Rep. 85 (D.S.C. 1997).

51 Bivens By and Through Green v. Albuquerque Public Schools, 899 F. Supp. 556, 104 Ed. Law Rep. 195 (D.N.M. 1995).
As to school dress codes, generally, see §§ 287 et seq.

52 Sheldon v. Fannin, 221 F. Supp. 766 (D. Ariz. 1963).

As to the First Amendment rights of students, generally, see §§ 284 et seq.

53 Doe v. Superintendent of Schools of Worcester, 421 Mass. 117, 653 N.E.2d 1088, 102 Ed. Law Rep. 781 (1995).
As to the strict scrutiny test, generally, see 16A Am Jur 2d, Constitutional Law § 387.

54 Board of Educ. of Monticello Cent. School Dist. v. Commissioner of Educ., 91 N.Y.2d 133, 667 N.Y.S.2d 671, 690 N.E.2d 480, 123 Ed. Law Rep. 876 (1997).

55 § 310.

56 Board of Educ. of Monticello Cent. School Dist. v. Commissioner of Educ., 91 N.Y.2d 133, 667 N.Y.S.2d 671, 690 N.E.2d 480, 123 Ed. Law Rep. 876 (1997).

Figure 4–2 (continued).

Ch. 12   STUDENT PERSONNEL   761

Regulations preventing use of drugs and alcohol on or off campus by student athletes can be enforced on the basis of health and safety concerns.[122] The penalty of suspension or dismissal from the team is the usual penalty. That parents may approve the acts of the students is not releveant here. Of course, the rules cannot be too broad, such as one forbidding an athlete from being in a car where beer is being transported.[123] But presence at an event where alcohol is being consumed by others can be made the basis for an athlete's disqualification.[124]

Activities of students off campus that would clearly threaten the health or safety of students on campus can be the basis for punishment, including long-term exclusions. Thus, drug sales[125] or aggravated assaults[126] off premises have been upheld as reasons for expulsion. The Fourth Circuit Court of Appeals has upheld the validity of a rule providing for disciplinary action against public college students for unlawful use or possession of drugs on or off campus.[127]

Perhaps the oldest appellate case involving discipline for off premises acts was decided in 1859. A high school student, in the presence of other students but after he had returned home following school, called his teacher "old Jack Seaver." The Supreme Court of Vermont upheld punishment for this offense, which had "a direct and immediate tendency to injure the school and bring the master's authority into contempt."[128] The court added that "misbehavior generally, * * * even towards the master in matters in no ways connected with or affecting the school," would not be punishable. In 1976 a United States District Court sustained the disciplining of a high school student for loudly making a vulgar remark in the presence of others about a teacher (who was there to hear it) in a shopping center.[129] In 1986 a United States District Court enjoined punishment of a student who off campus had made a vulgar gesture to a teacher as he passed by the teacher's parked car.[130]

Searches

The Fourth Amendment to the Constitution provides: "The right of the people to be secure in their persons, houses, papers, and effects, against unreasonable searches and seizures, shall not be violated. * * *" This clause and the one following it, which pertains to issuance

---

[122] Braesch v. DePasquale, 200 Neb. 726, 265 N.W.2d 842 (1978), cert. den. 439 U.S. 1068, 99 S.Ct. 836, 59 L.Ed.2d 34 (1979). [Case No. 122]

[123] Bunger v. Iowa High School Athletic Ass'n, 197 N.W.2d 555 (Iowa 1972).

[124] Clements v. Board of Educ. of Decatur Public School Dist. No. 61, 133 Ill.App.3d 531, 88 Ill.Dec. 601, 478 N.E.2d 1209 (1985); Bush v. Dassel–Cokato Bd. of Educ., 745 F.Supp. 562 (D.Minn.1990).

[125] Howard v. Colonial School Dist., 621 A.2d 362 Reutter, Law of Pub. Educ. 4th–18 (Del.Super.1992).

[126] Pollnow v. Glennon, 594 F.Supp. 220 (S.D.N.Y.1984), aff. 757 F.2d 496 (2 Cir.1985).

[127] Krasnow v. Virginia Polytechnic Institute and State Univ., 551 F.2d 591 (4 Cir.1977).

[128] Lander v. Seaver, 32 Vt. 114 (1859).

[129] Fenton v. Stear, 423 F.Supp. 767 (W.D.Pa.1976).

[130] Klein v. Smith, 635 F.Supp. 1440 (D.Me.1986).

Figure 4–3 Page from Edmund Reutler, Jr.'s *Law of Public Education* (4th ed., 1994). Reprinted with the permission of West Group.

services include annotated explanations of the law. Unlike usual hardbound treatises, however, loose-leaf services may include the law itself (relevant statutes, regulations, cases, executive orders, rules, policies, and rulings) or other useful information and tables. As well, loose-leaf services include the following research aids:

Index
Table of Contents
Table of Cases

Loose-leaf services are updated by replacement pages, or in periods when much new material is published (e.g., when large numbers of new cases are decided), by supplements or additional, chronological volumes.

Law Journals and Reviews

Law schools periodically publish "magazines" of scholarly legal articles called law reviews or journals. **Law reviews and journals** are unique in the literature in that they are compiled, edited, published, and partially written by students. *The Western New England College Law Review* is typical. Students join the law review staff following their freshman year of law school; half of those invited to join may be chosen on the basis of their first year grades (i.e., the top ten ranked sophomores); others may "write on," that is prepare a brief, scholarly paper judged by the review's senior editors. First-year staffers complete a student article (usually a case note describing or analyzing a recent important court decision) and perform many editorial tasks, including proofreading, citation checking, spell checking, and index preparation. Second-year editors (the editor in chief, assistant editor, lead article editors) are usually chosen at year-end by the staff.

Law reviews, though initially published in paperback, are periodically hardbound, indexed, and included in the **Index to Legal Periodicals**, a publication similar to the familiar *Cumulative Index to Periodicals*. Figure 4–4 shows excerpts for the title page and an article from the *Akron Law Review*.

As well, legal specialty, support, and bar organizations like the National Academy of Trial Lawyers, the National Association of Legal Assistants, the Criminal Justice Institute, and the California Bar Association publish journals reporting and analyzing recent events of interest to their subscribers.

Legal Newspapers

Finally, a number of publishers produce weekly newspapers of legal events, legislation, and court decisions. Some legal newspapers are national in scope, like the *National Law Reporter*. Others specialize in particular courts, like *The United States*

Akron Law Review

Member, National Conference of Law Reviews

Volume 33 **1999** **Number 1**

Figure 4–4 Title page and article from *Akron Law Review.* Laura Beresh-Taylor, *Preventing Violence in Ohio's Schools*, 33 Akron L. Rev. 311 (1999). Reprinted with the permission of the Akron Law Review.

PREVENTING VIOLENCE IN OHIO'S SCHOOLS*

I. INTRODUCTION

Springfield, Oregon, May 21, 1998: A fifteen-year-old student pulls a semiautomatic rifle from his trench coat and begins mercilessly firing into the crowd gathered in the school cafeteria.[1] Two students are dead and twenty-four others are injured.[2]

Jonesboro, Arkansas, March 24, 1998: Two students in combat gear, ages eleven and thirteen, initiate a massacre as their classmates vacate the building during a false fire alarm.[3] Four students and one teacher are dead, and ten others

---

* This article was written prior to the events at Columbine High School.

[1] John Ritter & Marty Kasindorf, *Nobody Took Him Seriously: Oregon Student "Joked" He Would "Get People,"* USA TODAY, May 22, 1998, at 3A. According to witnesses, at one point, Kip Kinkel approached a classmate cowering underneath a table, put a foot on the boy's body, and shot him in the chest. *Id.* As Kinkel stopped to reload his gun after "mowing down students as they dove under tables for cover," he was tackled by a seriously wounded classmate. *Id.* An investigation of Kinkel's house uncovered the bodies of his parents, several hundred rounds of ammunition on the living room floor, homemade explosives, fireworks, and bomb-making books. Maxine Bernstein, *Police Papers Detail Kinkel Findings,* PORTLAND OREGONIAN, Oct. 2, 1998, at A1. Kinkel was indicted on fifty-eight charges, including four counts of aggravated murder and twenty-five counts of attempted aggravated murder. *Id. See* discussion *infra* note 72. A trial date is scheduled for April 6, 1999, and Kinkel will be tried as an adult in regards to the murder charges. *Id.* Although Kinkel had frequently mentioned that it would be fun to kill, Kinkel's friends proclaimed that he was no different than most of his classmates. Ritter & Kasindorf, *supra.* On the day prior to his rampage, Kinkel was arrested and suspended for bringing a stolen firearm to school. *Id.*

[2] *Suspect in School Shooting Formally Charged,* CHICAGO TRIBUNE, June 17, 1998, at 16.

[3] Peter Katal, *Arkansas Boys Stole Family Guns,* USA TODAY, Mar. 26, 1998, at 1A. Mitchell Johnson held out chairs for girls, regularly attended church, and sang with a choir at a nursing home. Steve Mills, et al., *Jonesboro Boys Called Angels—And Bullies: Adults Knew Pair as Good Kids; Children Saw a Darker Side,* CHICAGO TRIBUNE, Mar. 29, 1998, at 1. However, Johnson also bullied children to tears, bragged about being a member of a Los Angeles gang, and warned his schoolmates tht they would discover who would live and who would die. *Id.* Andrew Golden collected model airplanes and trading cards and was known for his friendliness. *Id.* However, Golden was a bully and often threatened his neighbors while riding his bike. *Id.* On March 25, the boys played hooky from school, loaded Johnson's parents' van with nine handguns and rifles, a crossbow, nine knives, camping gear, and food. *Id.* Johnson and Golden then hid in a grove of trees and waited for their targets. *Id.* The juveniles are serving their sentences at a juvenile detention camp. Carol Morello, *Arkansas Vows to Toughen Laws on Penalizing Young Felons,* USA TODAY,

Figure 4–4 (continued).

Law Week, a legal newspaper of the federal courts, or jurisdictions (like the *Massachusetts Lawyer's Weekly,* a compilation of Massachusetts' legal news events and cases). Legal newspapers periodically publish cumulative topical indexes. Figure 4–5 shows an example of United States Supreme Court entries from a recent *United States Law Week.*

Law Finders

A **digest,** an index to cases, is a topically and alphabetically organized collection of case **headnotes.** As court decisions are released for publication, editors summarize their legal

(Text continues on page 115.)

VOL. 69, NO. 3   *PROCEEDINGS OF THE U.S. SUPREME COURT*   JULY 18, 2000

Term in Review

Individual Rights
Supreme Court Tackles Tough Issues About Families, Abortion, Religion, Gays

For a reputedly conservative body, the U.S. Supreme Court avidly took on contentious individual rights issues during its 1999-2000 term. In two high profile cases it vindicated substantive due process rights, striking down state statutes that impaired parental control over third parties' visitation of their children and barred access to certain kinds of abortions.

Six of these individual rights cases involved the First Amendment. The court upheld a statute restricting protests outside abortion clinics. It rejected a facial challenge to a state statute regulating public access to information about arrestees. And in one of the three cases with a school setting, it rebuffed an attack on a state university's program of distributing mandatory student activities fees to political and ideological groups on a viewpoint-neutral basis.

Schools also figured in two First Amendment establishment clause cases. In one, the court ruled that student-initiated, student-led prayers at public high school football games violate the establishment clause. In the other, it upheld a federal statute authorizing loans to sectarian schools of educational materials and equipment purchased with federal funds.

Another First Amendment decision upheld the Boy Scouts of America's right to exclude gays as an aspect of the private group's freedom of association.

Adding to its equal protection clause jurisprudence, the court made it easier to sue governmental entities for discrimination when it ruled that an individual constituting a "class of one" may state a claim under the 14th Amendment's equal protection clause by alleging that she was intentionally and irrationally treated differently from others similarly situated.

Although it is difficult to categorize each of these nine decisions as either "liberal" or "conservative" or to assess which wing of the court came out on top overall, at least one common thread is discernible: Justice Sandra Day O'Connor was on the prevailing side in every one of them (including once as author of the plurality opinion, and once concurring in the judgment). That was true of no other justice.

Child Visitation Rights. Making a relatively rare venture into family law, the court splintered in ruling that states' authority to grant child visitation rights to grandparents or other nonparental parties over the objection of a custodial parent is limited by the 14th Amendment's due process clause (*Troxel v. Granville,* 68 U.S.L.W. 4458 (U.S.2000)).

Writing for four members of the court, O'Connor said that a Washington State trial court violated a mother's fundamental right to "make decisions concerning the care, custody and control" of her children when it

Figure 4–5 *United States Law Week* entry. Reprinted with the permission of the United States Law Week.

applied a Washington visitation rights statute to award grandparents longer visitation time than the mother had agreed to. O'Connor termed the statute "breath-takingly broad" and said the trial court failed to give proper weight to the mother's status as fit custodian of her children and to her agreement to allow some visitation.

Concurring in the judgment, Justice David H. Souter would have avoided consideration of the specific application of the Washington statute in this case and affirmed the state supreme court's ruling that the statute is unconstitutional on its face.

The statute authorizes "[a]ny person" to petition "at any time" for visitation rights, which may be granted whenever visitation "may serve the best interest of the child." In this case, paternal grandparents went to court to obtain visitation of their deceased son's two young daughters, who were in the custody of their mother. The mother, who had never married the children's father and whose husband had adopted the children, sought to limit the grandparents' visitation to one day per month, plus participation in holiday celebrations.

The trial court granted the grandparents one weekend of visitation per month, one week in the summer, and time on the grandparents' birthdays. The Washington Supreme Court declared the statute unconstitutional on grounds that it allows interference with parental rights without a showing of harm and that it sweeps too broadly by allowing the state to "make significant decisions concerning the custody of children merely because it could make a 'better' decision."

In similar fashion, O'Connor scored the statute's "sweeping breadth," which "effectively permits any third party seeking visitation to subject any decision by a parent concerning visitation of the parent's children to a state-court review."

A parent's interest in the "care, custody, and control" of her children is "perhaps the oldest of the fundamental liberty interests recognized by this Court," O'Connor said, citing *Meyer v. Nebraska,* 262 U.S. 390 (1923). As applied by the trial court, the statute infringed the mother's substantive due process rights by inverting the traditional presumption "that fit parents act in the best interests of their children," O'Connor said. The trial court's determination was not founded on any special factors that might justify the state's interference with the mother's fundamental right to make decisions concerning the rearing of her two children, she said. Instead, the trial court appeared to require the mother to disprove that visitation by the grandparents would be in her daughters' best interest. The trial court also erred, she

Schools
99-1801 Michael C. v. Radnor Township, Pa., School District
IDEA—Pendency rights
Ruling below (3d Cir., 202 F.3d 642, 68 U.S.L.W. 1445):

Department of Education's position—that Individuals with Disabilities Education Act provision requiring child, when relocating, to remain in "then-current educational placement" during pendency of proceedings to find appropriate individual educational plan in new location does not apply to interstate relocations—is entitled to deference; Pennsylvania's regulatory pendency requirement does not require different result, because, although state

Figure 4–5 (continued).

statute expressly requires implementation of existing IEP pending re-evaluation of exceptional student who moves intrastate, it makes no parallel provision for students who move from another state to school district in Pennsylvania, thereby suggesting that Pennsylvania does impose "stay-put" requirement with respect to interstate relocations.

Questions presented: (1) Did Third Circuit err in finding that actions of defendants in unilaterally changing disabled child's educational program and placement did not violate pendency requirement of IDEA and in denying tuition reimbursement to plaintiffs who independently obtained appropriate education program? (2) Did Third Circuit err in finding that denial of pendency rights under IDEA to disabled students who transfer into school district from out-of-state, rather than from within state, is not violative of constitutional protections regarding right to travel? (3) Did Third Circuit err in accepting policy statement of Department of Education that recognizes no pendency rights under IDEA to disabled children who transfer into public school district from another state despite lack of any congrssional authority in IDEA for distinction between in-state and out-of-state transfers? (4) Did Third Circuit err in refusing to find that Pennsylvania's special education standards, as incorporated into federal entitlement under IDEA, provide greater protections concerning pendency than under federal law?

Petition for certiorari filed 5/11/00, by Dennis C. McAndrews, of Wayne, Pa.

99-1862 Kipps v. Caillier
Retaliatory discharge of state university coach—Qualified immunity.

Ruling below (5th Cir., 197 F.3d 765):

University of Southwestern Louisiana officials' firing of assistant football coach because his son decided to play football for Louisiana State University rather than USL, based as it was on desire to mitigate damage that student's attendance at LSU would have on alumni relations and recruiting efforts, was objectively reasonable, and, accordingly, even though officials violated coach's clearly established constitutional liberty interest in familial association, they are qualifiedly immune from coach's suit against them under 42 U.S.C.§ 1983.

Question presented: Did court of appeals misapply doctrine of qualified immunity in contravention of law as announced by this court and as applied by other circuits?

Petition for certiorari filed 5/22/00, by J. Minos Simon, of Lafayette, La.

99-1870 Adler v. Duval County, Fla., School Board
High school graduation ceremonies— Student referendum on unrestricted student messages—Establishment clause.

Ruling below (11th Cir., 206 F.3d 1070, 68 U.S.L.W. 1571):

Public school district's policy of allowing high school students to vote on whether their graduation ceremonies will include unrestricted student messages, which may include prayer, does not violate First amendment's establishment clause.

Question presented: Does respondents' public school district policy permitting student-led prayer at high school graduation exercises, pursuant to results of student referenda, violate religion clauses of First Amendment?

Petition for certiorari filed 5/22/00, by Wm. J. Sheppard, D. Gray Thomas, and Sheppard, White and Thomas PA, all of Jacksonville, Fla.

Figure 4–5 (continued).

99-1877 Linda W. v. Indiana Dep't of Education
IDEA—Reimbursement of parents for unilateral placement—Attorneys' fees.
Ruling below (7th Cir., 200 F.3d 504):

Parents who enrolled their child in private school during pendency of administrative appeals from initial hearing officer's decision concerning their child's individual educational program under Individuals with Disabilities Education Act are not entitled to recover costs of private school, such reimbursement being entirely within district court's discretion, despite their contention that hearing officers determined that IEP in use at time of their child's transfer was flawed; parents who recovered about $1,000 as compensation for private tutoring for their child, which was "paltry" amount compared to what they sought in reimbursement for private school tuition and otherwise, and who lost on all other issues were not prevailing parties and thus are not entitled to attorneys' fees.

Questions presented: (1) When school district could have, but failed to, provide free appropriate public education in least restrictive environment to student eligible for special education services under IDEA, are parents eligible for reimbursement of their expenses in securing more restrictive but otherwise appropriate unilateral placement during pendency of due process proceedings, until such time as school district in fact provides FAPE? (2) Once school district fails to provide FAPE, are parents eligible for reimbursement of unilateral placement if they show that placement was reasonably calculated to confer educational benefit, without showing that student would suffer irreparable

harm unless placed unilaterally, and without showing that unilateral placement is only placement for their child? (3) Under IDEA, when parents are successful in obtaining substantially more than zero relief in due process proceedings, even though they ultimately do not obtain all of relief they seek, are they prevailing parties entitled to award of attorneys' fees?

Petition for certiorari filed 5/22/00, by Margie Best, of Chicago, Ill.

Securities
99-1883 R&W Technical Services Ltd. v. Commodity Futures Trading Commission
Commodity trading recommendations—Commodity Exchange Act.
Ruling below (5th Cir., 205 F.3d 165):

Expensive computer software that made buy and sell recommendations for commodity futures contracts based on real-time financial data provided by users had no purpose except as device for choosing which trades to make, and thus fraudulent advertising claims about its reliability made by software's sellers satisfied requirement of Section 4b(a) of Commodity Exchange Act that any sanctionable fraud be "in connection with" commodities futures contract trading, even though sellers executed no trades for their customers and did not otherwise have direct stake in customers' trading; such sellers are within plain meaning of act's definition of "commodity trading advisors" and are thus subject to act's antifraud provisions.

Questions presented: (1) Under Section 1a(5) of CEA, are publishers of software that provides impersonal commodity trading recommendations "commodity trading advisors"? (2) Are misrepresentations in publishers' advertisements to sell their

Figure 4–5 (continued).

software "in connection with" any order to make or making of any commodity futures contract for or on behalf of any other persons under Section 4b(a) of CEA?

Petition for certiorari filed 5/24/00, by Michael E. Schoeman, and Schoeman, Updike & Kaufman LLP, both of New York, N.Y.

Taxation
99-1675 United States v. Farley

Discharge of indebtedness by insolvent Subchapter S corporations.

Ruling below (3d Cir., 202 F.3d 198, 68 U.S.L.W. 1460):

Cancellation-of-debt income excluded from gross income of Subchapter S corporation under Section 108 of Internal Revenue Code passes through to S corporation shareholders and increases basis of their S corporation stock, enabling tax deductions for suspended losses.

Question presented: Is amount expressly excluded from "income" under 26 U.S.C. § 108(a)(1)(B) nonetheless to be treated as if it were item of "income" that, under 26 U.S.C. § 1366(a)(1)(A), flows through to respondents as shareholders of Subchapter S corporations, thereby increasing their basis in stock of corporations under 26 U.S.C. § 1367(a)(1)(A), and thereby allowing them to deduct losses they previously were unable to deduct because they had exhausted their basis by prior deductions?

Petition for certiorari filed 4/17/00, by Seth P. Waxman, Sol. Gen, Paula M. Junghans, acting Asst. Atty. Gen., Lawrence G. Wallace, Dpty. Sol. Gen., Kent L. Jones, Asst. to Sol. Gen., and Teresa E. McLaughlin and Edward T. Perelmuter, DOJ attys.

99-1693 Witzel v. Commissioner of Internal Revenue

Subchapter S corporations— Cancellation of debt.

Ruling below (7th Cir., 200 F.3d 496, 68 U.S.L.W. 1446):

Section 108(d)(7)(A) of Internal Revenue Code, which provides, in case of subchapter S corporations, that net operating losses are to be reduced by amount of excludable cancellation-of-debt income "at the corporate level," prohibits S corporation shareholder from offsetting corporation's existing suspended losses against his current taxable income.

Questions presented: (1) When subchapter S corporation realizes cancellation of debt income pursuant to reorganization under Chapter 11 of Bankruptcy Code and excludes it from gross income pursuant to 26 U.S.C. § 108(a), is COD income that is excluded at corporate level item of "income" under 26 U.S.C. § 1366 (permitting pass

Figure 4–5 (continued).

holdings in headnotes at the beginning of the decisions. The editors then classify those headnotes by legal topics like negligence, Social Security, and arbitration, and numbered subtopics (**key numbers** or sections.) Figure 4–6 shows an example of a school expulsion headnote (topic: Schools, key: 177).

Digest topics begin with an analysis or outline of key numbers or sections like that shown in Figure 4–7.

Schools 177

Constitutional and statutory due process requirements for suspending student were followed in case of student who had toy replica of weapon in car and acted disruptively when confronted with it; student was presented with charges when first detained and given opportunity to explain, and parent was given notice of intent to suspend, together with counseling regarding procedural steps available to her. U.S.C.A. Const.Amend. 14; Ohio R.C. § 3313.66(A)(1, 2), (D, E).

Figure 4–6 Case headnote. From *West Digests*; reprinted with the permission of West Group.

Digest volumes are updated annually by pocket parts and semiannually by softbound supplements. **Regional reporters** and **advance sheets** (softbound case reporters issued before permanent hardbound volumes are published) include mini-digests, digesting the cases appearing in that volume. These mini-digests update digest pocket parts and supplements.

Digests are indexed by multi-volume **Descriptive Word Indices**, and include a Table of Cases (listing case citations alphabetically by plaintiff's name), and a **Defendant-Plaintiff Table of Cases** (listing case citations alphabetically by defendant's name) following the digest volumes. West Group and Lawyer's Cooperative Publishing publish many and varied legal digests.

Some helpful hints for book research are shown in Figure 4–8 on page 122.

49 10th D Pt 2—1036

SCHOOLS

SUBJECTS INCLUDED

Institutions for instruction below the grade of colleges or universities, whether maintained by private means for individual benefit, or by government as common or public schools

Bodies formed for maintenance of such institutions, whether unincorporated or incorporated by special charters or under general laws, or formed by territorial subdivision of counties, towns, or cities, etc.

Constitutional and statutory provisions relating thereto

Public supervision and regulation of such schools in general

Incorporation and organization of private schools, academies, etc., and public aid and regulation thereof

Creation, organization, boundaries, alteration and dissolution of school districts

School meetings and government and officers of school districts

School lands, funds, buildings, furniture, textbooks, and other property and supplies, and contracts relating thereto

Indebtedness, bonds, warrants, and other securities of school districts

Taxation by school districts

Qualifications, employment and discharge, and compensation of teachers and other specialized officers and employees

Admission and attendance of pupils

Curriculum, rules, discipline and government of schools

SUBJECTS EXCLUDED AND COVERED BY OTHER TOPICS

Public lands reserved as school lands, but not allotted to school districts, see PUBLIC LANDS

Taxation for school purposes, see TAXATION

For detailed references to other topics, see Descriptive-Word Index

---

Analysis

I. Private schools and academies, ☞ 1–8.

II. PUBLIC SCHOOLS, ☞ **9–179.**

    (A) ESTABLISHMENT, SCHOOL LANDS AND FUNDS, AND REGULATION IN GENERAL, ☞ 9–20.

    (B) CREATION, ALTERATION, EXISTENCE, AND DISSOLUTION OF DISTRICTS, ☞ 21–44.

    (C) GOVERNMENT, OFFICERS, AND DISTRICT MEETINGS, ☞ 45–63.

    (D) DISTRICT PROPERTY, ☞ 64–76.

    (E) DISTRICT CONTRACTS, ☞ 77–86.

Figure 4–7 *Schools Digest* analysis. From the *West Digest*; reprinted with the permission of West Group.

Figure 4–7 (continued)

Figure 4–7 (continued)

Figure 4–7 (continued)

(L) PUPILS.

⌾⟿ 148. Nature of right to instruction in general.
 (1). In general.
 (2). Handicapped children and special services therefor.
 (2.1). —— In general.
 (3). —— Mental or emotional handicap; learning disabilities.
 (4). —— Medical services.
148.5. Aid to indigent children.
149. Eligibility.
150. —— In general.
151. —— Race or color.
152. —— Age.
⌾⟿ 153. —— Residence.
154. —— Assignment or admission to particular schools.
 (1). In general.
 (2). Handicapped children.
 (2.1). —— In general.
 (3). —— Home care and residential placement.
 (4). —— Private school and out-of-state placement.
155. Proceedings to compel admission
155.5. Handicapped children, proceedings to enforce rights.
 (1). In general
 (2). Judicial review or intervention.
 (2.1). —— In general.
 (3). —— Exhaustion of remedies.
 (4). Evidence.
 (5). Judgment and relief; damages, injunction, and costs.
156. Health regulations.
157. —— In general.
158. —— Vaccination.
 (1). In general.
 (2). Existence of epidemic.

159. Payment for tuition.
159.5. Transportation of pupils to and from schools or provisions in lieu thereof.
 (1). In general.
 (2). Transportation to private schools or beyond district.
 (3). Transportation for racial integration; busing.
 (4). Handicapped children.
 (5). Contracts.
 (6). Drivers
160. Compulsory attendance.
161. Truants and truant officers and schools.
162. chool terms, vacations, and holidays.
162.1. —— In general.
162.5. —— Summer programs and extended programs for the handicapped.
163. Grades or classes and departments.
164. Curriculum and courses of study.
165. Religious instruction and reading of Scriptures.
166. Text-books.
166.1. —— In general.
167. —— Selection or adoption and change.
168. —— Duty to furnish.
169. Control of pupils and discipline in general.
169.5. Searches and seizures.
170. Rules and regulations.
170.1. —— In general.
171. —— Authority to make.
172. —— Reasonableness and validity.
172.5. —— Construction and operation.
173. Violation of rules and offenses.
174. Punishment.
175. —— In general.
176. —— Corporal punishment.
177. —— Expulsion or suspension.
178. Graduation, and diploma or certificate.

III. INTERSCHOLASTIC ASSOCIATIONS.

⌾⟿ 180. In general.
181. Rules and regulations.
181.1. —— In general.

182. —— Construction, enforcement, and sanctions.
183. Judicial intervention.

For detailed references to other topics, see Descriptive-Word Index

Figure 4–7 (continued)

1. Find a good place to do your research.

In order of preference:
   a. A quiet place, away from the main library traffic.
   b. A place near the books you need.
   c. A place not too far from the copying machine, so you don't have to carry the books too far to copy what you need.
   d. A comfortable place. Remember that you may be there a while, so look for a place that is:
      • warm and big (so you can spread out);
      • near a water fountain:
      • near a bathroom: and
      • near a window with a nice view if possible.

2. Four things you need when you go to the library:
   a. Lots of time. You may find that legal research eats up a lot of time very quickly. There are many reasons this is true, not the least of which is that you may find yourself interested in what you're doing. Enjoy your investigation.
   b. Lots of paper.
   c. Lots of sharp pencils (it's amazing how hard it is to find a pencil sharpener in a library) with erasers; and
   d. Lots of change for the copying machine.

3. Things to remember while doing research:
   a. Research materials are so thoroughly indexed and cross-referenced, there is almost never only one way to find what you are looking for. Don't give up because a book or material you are looking for isn't where it should be, is out of the library, or is otherwise unavailable.
   b. Beware of the quick, simple answer. While many answers are easy, be sure you've gotten to the bottom of your research. Until you are experienced in the law, don't rely on your own notions of the meaning of words or phrases. See what the courts and legal scholars have had to say. Double check things two or three different ways.
   c. Important rights may ride on your research. Beware of short-cuts.
   d. Librarians are bright, friendly, helpful people. Although you should try to find your own way, don't hesitate to ask where things are or for general help.

Figure 4–8 Helpful hints to book research in a law library or legal collection.

Review Questions

1. What are digests?
2. Describe a digest entry.
3. How are digests created?
4. What is a digest topic? What is a digest key number?
5. Who assigns digest topic and key numbers to case headnotes?
6. What is a digest topic analysis?
7. What is a treatise? What sorts of information are in treatises? How is that information presented? Name some treatises.
8. What are loose-leaf services? Why are they called "loose-leaf" services? How are loose-leaf services updated?
9. What are law reviews and journals? How might law reviews and journals be useful to a legal researcher?
10. What are legal newspapers? How might those be useful in legal research?

Exercises

Research the following issues:
1. May school officials search a student's locker without a warrant?
2. What does it mean for a statute of limitations to "accrue?"
3. When did Kitty Barbour's action against Tessa Benson accrue?

Glossary

Advance sheets: Softbound case reporters issued before publication of hardbound reporters.

American Jurisprudence 2d (Am.Jur. 2d): Lawyer's Cooperative Publishing's national legal encyclopedia.

Corpus Juris Secundum (CJS): West Group's national legal encyclopedia.

Defendant-Plaintiff Table of Cases: An alphabetic listing of case citations by defendant's name.

Descriptive Word Indices: Topical indices of legal materials.

Digest: An alphabetically and topically organized collection of case headnotes.

Headnotes: Publisher's summary of a single point of law addressed in a case.

Hornbooks: Text or elementary books on a single legal subject.

Index to Legal Periodicals: Index of legal journals and law reviews.

Key numbers: Numbered digest subtopics.

Law reviews and journals: Student written, edited, and produced journals of articles on current legal topics.

Loose-leaf services: Easily updated three-ring binders of materials.

Pocket parts: Paperback supplements stored in the backs of legal research books.

Regional reporters: West published appellate court opinions grouped geographically.

Treatises: Scholarly books on a single legal subject.

CHAPTER 5

Finding the Law: Computer Assisted Legal Research (CALR)

Chapter Outline

Learning Objectives

Upon completion of this chapter, the student should be able to

* Explain and describe various CALRs available
* Describe the features, advantages and disadvantages of various CALRs
* Explain the CALR "ground rules"
* Describe how to use CALRs to answer particular legal issues
* Explain the following concepts: signing on, searching, browsing, non-legal research, printing and saving information, and signing off as they pertain to each CALR type

Introduction

Book research is the traditional and still most widely used method of legal research. However, much has happened since John West initiated his topic and key number index to legal materials. Since the 1970s, the advent, popularity, and decreasing cost, of computers for business and personal use has brought much legal information to the researcher's personal computer. No longer must researchers conduct their investigations in law libraries or collections with limited resources. Now, legal research can expand to nationwide materials and can be completed much more quickly than "book" research. The name of this technological "investigator": **Computer Assisted Legal Research (CALR).**

What is Computer Assisted Legal Research?

As its name implies, CALR is legal research done with the aid of a computer. CALRs are currently of three varieties: *Computer services*, like **LEXIS**® and **Westlaw**®, compact disk read-only **(CD-Rom)** systems, and the **Internet.** On-line computer services usually involve a large, centrally located computer storing large amounts of data that users access through a telephone line, a **modem**, and a **personal computer.** Both The West Group® (Westlaw) and Reed (LEXIS) offer on-line computer access to federal and state court opinions, statutes, regulations, the Federal Register, agency decisions, and many other materials. Both systems offer on-line access to *Shepard's* or other research verification services. Both offer direct access by citation and descriptive word searching. Westlaw, because it is based on West Group's legal research books, also offers searching by digest topic and key number. Although expensive ($2–3 per minute), because of the breadth and accuracy of their coverage, CALR services provide quick, easy, and timely access to legal research materials. In addition, law schools, paralegal studies programs, and legal studies programs may offer students free or low-cost access to CALR services. Most law libraries and many large law firms have access to Westlaw and LEXIS.

CD-ROM CALRs are entirely local to the researcher. Research information is stored on a compact disk and read by a CD-ROM drive attached to the researcher's personal computer.

The Internet, or **World Wide Web**, is the most recent entrant to the CALR field. Unlike CALR services and CD-ROMs, which consist of a centralized **database** of legal research material and a search mechanism, the Internet is an international "network of networks." Very much like the telephone system, which consists of various **nodes** connected by "paths" (so that if any telephone call attempts to connect by a "path" that is "busy," the call is immediately re-routed along another, "open" path) the Internet consists of individual workstations (i.e., the end-user at his/her personal computer and modem), which are connected into **local area networks** (i.e., LANs), which in turn are joined through regional networks, and finally the World Wide Web network.

The Internet, although it has become widely popular in the last decade, was actually a federal government invention of the Cold War. During that period, the United States Department of Defense (DoD) entered into contracts with various United States colleges and universities to conduct defense research. To secure the information that was transmitted between and among the DoD and the university contractors against loss or theft by foreign governments or foreign nationals, the federal government connected the DoD with the university contractors by "dedicated" connections accessible solely by the DoD and the universities **(ARPANET)**. The ports (i.e., the DoD and the university contractors) exchanged information through an electronic protocol called **TCP/IP** which encoded data sent from the sending node and decoded that data at the receiving node. As colleges and universities were among the first users of the Internet, through their DoD contracts, it is not surprising that colleges and universities were among the first users as the Internet expanded beyond the original ARPANET to connections between the colleges and universities themselves. These Internet connections continued to be used by the colleges and universities to share research and information. With the entry of modem technology, the Internet ceased to be "bound" by dedicated lines and the potential growth of the Internet became suddenly boundless, stretching beyond local and regional networks to the world at large. At the same time, information other than research materials began to be broadly disseminated. Enter business, manufacturing, and service providers to the Web, along with sales, marketers, and advertisers. Today it is possible to contact individuals and businesses throughout the world. Buy cameras from Tokyo, the latest Paris fashions from the hottest designers, in-print and out-of-print books, art, and so on, all with the click of a mouse (and a credit card).

The Web, however, has not lost its basic research emphasis. Web hosts or **Internet Service Providers (ISPs)** accumulate data of various types and offer user access to that information through **Web pages** that may include words, sound, animation, and other communication forms.

The methods of accessing information through the Internet are several.

1. WWW **browsers** are set up to lead the researcher to the information she or he seeks. By accessing a Web browser, a researcher can find information by clicking on various highlighted words (**hypertext**) which transfer the information the researcher seeks. Through hypertext clicking, the researcher moves eventually to the information she or he seeks.

   America Online, Internet Explorer, and Netscape Navigator are examples of Web browsers. Browsing is the slowest way to locate research materials.

2. A second way of accessing data on the Web is by using a **Boolean searching search engine**. There are several search engines available to aid the researcher in his or her research.

Because each search engine uses different search algorithms, information, and locations to search, it is often true that information unavailable through one search engine can be retrieved through another. Recently, in order to address the gaps in searching, **meta-engines** (like DogPile, Ask Jeeves, Google, etc.) have appeared on the Internet. These meta-engines simultaneously run a single query through several search engines at once, so that the researcher gains the advantage of multiple searches by conducting a single search.

3. Look by subject for database guides concerning your topic. For instance, the Cornell University Law School maintains a legal database and search engine which can be searched or browsed using hyperlinks. Other useful legal research sites include the following:

www.findlaw.com

www.lawcrawler.com

www.lectlaw.com/

LEXIS and Westlaw are accessible through the Internet at www.lexis.com and www.westlaw.com.

4. Whether the researcher is searching through a browser or a search engine, the result of the search will be a document or documents on the Web. The researcher must choose the article(s) most relevant to the inquiry.

5. Internet Web page **Uniform Resource Locators (URLs)**, unique "addresses" or "identifiers" of Web pages of information. A URL looks like the following:

(a)   (b)   (c)   (d)

http://library.Berkley.edu/Teaching lib/ Workshops.html

   a. http: HyperText Transfer Protocol — the "language" of data transfer

   b. Web site

   c. subdirectory on the Web site

   d. Documents in html: HyperText Markup Language — the "language" used to create the website

6. The most effective method of finding legal research on the Web is to combine methods. This method, however, is usually reserved to fairly sophisticated researchers who are already familiar with the Internet and with locations on the Internet likely to include the information she or he seeks.

The differences among CALRs are largely as follows:

✳ *Size.* CALR services make vast amounts of information available to the researcher. Because services store data on large, ever-expanding computers, the information available through services is broader than that available on a CD-ROM (each CD-ROM holds approximately five hundred million characters of data). So, while a CD-ROM might allow a researcher to access cases from a particular state, computer services offer access to cases from all jurisdictions, all *Shepard's Citations*, most law reviews, newspapers, statutes, and more.

✳ *Speed.* CALR services and the Internet are much faster than CD-ROMs. For example, although retrieving First Circuit cases determining whether a child can be expelled from public school for possessing weapons might take a minute or two on a CD-ROM, a similar search of all federal circuits would take only seconds on a CALR service.

✳ *Ease of use.* CALR services may be considerably easier to use (more user friendly) than CD-ROMs and the Internet. For instance, CALR services provide menu-driven research and English-language research while the Internet and CD-ROMs may require the researcher to do research by using a more stilted, technical Boolean, language to perform **terms-and-connectors searching**. For instance, the following is an example of a Westlaw **natural language** search or a LEXIS **freestyle search**:

May a School Expel a Student for Possesion of Weapons?

On a CD-ROM or the Internet a search for similar materials would be written as follows:

School Near Student Near Possession Near Weapon

✳ *Cost.* CALR services are considerably more expensive than CD-ROMs. To access a CALR service, the researcher needs a **password** or account number for the service. Each time the researcher accesses the service, his account is billed for his use. Research may be billed by the type of research performed (i.e., $25–50 per search, $2–3 per citation Shepardized) or by time used ($2–3 per minute), and the researcher may be billed for "connect-time" and printing ($.02 per line). CD-ROM researchers, on the other hand, subscribe to their CD-ROMs for an all-inclusive (monthly, quarterly, or annual) subscription fee, and pay the same fee if they never use the CD-ROM or if they use the CD-ROM continuously. Internet access is free or very low cost. Anyone with a personal computer and a modem can have access to information on the Web for a $18–25 monthly access fee to a Web server or free to college or university users.

Figure 5–1 summarizes the differences, advantages, and disadvantages of various CALR types. Figure 5–2 summarizes the ground rules of using CALR.

CALR	DATA		COST	SPEED	EASE OF USE	BEST FEATURE	WORST FEATURE
	COVERAGE	VERIFICATION					
WESTLAW	COMPLETE	EXCELLENT	HIGH	HIGH	EXCELLENT	DATA	COST
LEXIS	COMPLETE	EXCELLENT	HIGH	HIGH	EXCELLENT	DATA	COST
LOIS LAW	LIMITED	EXCELLENT	MODERATE	GOOD	EXCELLENT	DATA VERIFICATION COST	DATA COVERAGE
INTERNET	RECENT MATERIALS	GOOD/POOR	FREE	MODERATE	GOOD	COST	DATA COVERAGE

Figure 5-1 CALR summary chart.

1. *Don't Panic.* Unless you are doing your research with a pickax, screwdriver, hammer, or other heavy, blunt, or pointed object, you need not fear that your work will ruin or break the computer. Computer hardware and software are designed to protect themselves from inadvertent (even some deliberate) ordinary use and misuse. It is, of course, fairly easy to run up a hefty CALR service bill by casual, unplanned use. Therefore, when using services, always

   a. Learn, practice, and experiment with CALR services while in school (at low or no cost).

   b. Always plan your research before signing on. Runaway searches and extensive connect charges are most often caused by no or poor planning. Thus, before you sign onto a CALR service:

      (1) Plan your entire session in detail, including all search queries.

      (2) Do preliminary research in a law library and identify appropriate key and alternative words for your research.

2. *Learn.* Take the time to read CALR manuals, attend training seminars, and use system tutorials before using the CALR. The time you spend learning the system will save time and money later.

3. *Help.* Both CALR services and CD-ROMs offer both off-line (book) and online help. Although help functions, whether on- or off-line, are general rather than specific to your task, they often provide just the "memory-jog" needed for the next step.

As well, CALR manufacturers and support services provide help through manuals and over the telephone. When in doubt, get help.

Figure 5–2 CALR ground rules.

Understanding CALR

It may be useful to think of a CALR as a law library and a runner (I like to think of the legal research runner as a furry little creature — I call him Ralph — whose only desire is to run and find legal research materials relevant to my issue. Once he returns with the requested materials, I imagine him panting at my feet wanting to find more). Just as legal collections and law office libraries are smaller and more limited than courthouse or law school libraries, CD-ROMs are more limited in their materials than CALR services. However, unlike law libraries, where the researcher must locate appropriate research materials, the CALR provides a "runner" to look for and **retrieve** requested legal materials. Just as with book research, when the researcher must know generally where she is looking — that is, the kinds of materials (statutes, cases, jurisdiction, etc.) — and what she is looking for — that is, relevant legal topics (negligence, divorce, contract law, etc.) — the CALR researcher needs to tell the runner where to look and what to look for. It is thus important to understand how information is organized and stored on CALRs. CALR consists of one or more databases (collections of related materials). For instance, a CD-ROM might include all federal First Circuit decisions or a service might include databases for federal District Court, First Circuit, and Supreme Court decisions. Databases contain **documents** like First Circuit decisions or law review articles. Documents may be divided into **fields** such as the **title field**, the **citation field**, the **headnote field**, the **synopsis field**, the **judge or author field**, and the **opinion field**. Fields, in turn, are divided into words, sentences, and paragraphs to increase precision.

Using CALRs

To use a CALR, a reasearcher follows a discrete series of steps which may differ slightly depending on the particular CALR used. These steps include: signing on to the CALR, searching for relevant materials, browsing the results retrieved, printing and saving information, and signing off from the CALR.

Signing on to a CALR

Just as a law library researcher must preliminarily locate and enter a law library to do research, the CALR researcher must enter or "sign on to" the CALR. Usually, this means turning on the computer, monitor, printer, and CD-ROM or modem. Once the computer completes its start-up, the researcher must start the CALR software and follow its instructions. If using a CALR service, the service will ask for a password and billing reference (i.e., a client identifier or case file number; this permits a researcher signing onto a service to do research for clients Brown, Smith, and Jones to keep track of charges for the Brown research under the name "Brown," the Smith research under "Smith," the Jones research under "Jones.")

Searching

CALRs offer various types of searching. For instance, if you provide the runner a citation for a particular legal document, he will retrieve that particular document. Or, if you know the title of a document (*e.g.*, *Turner v. South Western School Dist.*, 82 F.Supp.2d 757 (S.D. Ohio 1999)) CALRs can find the document by title.

By far the most powerful type of CALR searching, however, is **full-text searching**. In full-text searching, the CALR runner "reads" documents looking for "key words" identified by the researcher. The researcher doing full-text searching must tell the runner what key words to look for in a language that the runner understands.[1] Although both Westlaw and LEXIS offer English-language searching, where the researcher need only enter a relevant legal research question, all CALRs provide full text Boolean or terms-and-connectors searching. In Boolean searching, the researcher identifies key words (and alternatives) to build a search query using CALR query **connectors** such as

AND	(words connected by AND must all appear in document)
OR	(one word OR the other appears in the document)
BUT NOT	(one word BUT NOT the second appears in the document)
NEAR/WITHIN x	(one word appears within *x* words of second word).

The researcher can indicate to the runner how close together words must appear in a document before he retrieves it. For instance, suppose the researcher wished to know whether it was lawful for a landlord to refuse to rent to families with children. The Boolean query

Landlord AND Refuse AND Rent

might retrieve useful documents; however, it would also return documents involving the landlord of a commercial rental space in which the judge refused a requested injunction. To narrow that search, the researcher should tell the runner to retrieve cases only if *landlord, refuse,* and *rent* appear in the same paragraph (or within 50 words of each other).

Landlord WITHIN 50 Refuse WITHIN 50 Rent

CALRs may also offer one or more universal characters (usually "!" or "*" or "?") which ask the runner to retrieve documents containing a specified root word followed by any number of characters or a word containing one or more unidentified letters in it (e.g., searching for "wom*n" retrieves documents containing "woman" or "women"; (also "womin," "womon," etc.). CALRs often offer certain automatic options, like automatically searching for plurals and possessives if the singular form of a word is given or searching for Roman numerals or other number forms (e.g. "3" will search for "three" and "third" as well as the numeral "3") if the Arabic number is given.

It may be useful in forming your Boolean search to fill out a query planner like the one shown in Figure 5–3.

Begin with a statement of the issue you wish to research. In Vincent's case, such a statement of the issue might be as follows:

May a School Expel a Student for Possession of Weapons?

Next insert synonyms and other alternatives for key terms on the query planner under their related key terms. For instance, "scholar" and "child" might be alternatives for "student"; "suspended," "excluded," and "dismissed" might be alternatives for "expelled"; "buy" and "sell" for "possessing"; "pipe bomb," "gun," "knife," and "baseball bat" for "weapon." To make use of CALR automatic substitutes use the singular forms of "student," "scholar," and "child."

Where to search
Choose Databases to Search:

What to search for
1. Begin with a concise statement of the issue.

2. Underline issue key terms; insert in query planner.
3. Choose alternative, related terms; insert in query planner.
4. Choose and insert universal characters and root expanders.
5. Choose and insert connectors.

	con-nector	keyword	con-nector	keyword	con-nector	keyword		keyword
related term		related term		related term		related term		related term

6. Complete final query, moving vertically through the query planner chart, connecting alternative terms with "OR."

Figure 5–3 Query planning.

Next, consider whether it is important to use different forms of search terms. For instance, in Vincent's query, the researcher might substitute "suspen?" for suspended or "purch?" for purchasing. Finally, connect the words with query connectors indicating how closely words must appear in a document before the runner should retrieve it. There are no right or wrong choices for connectors, only more or less effective connectors. Choosing broad connectors (like OR or AND) may retrieve too many documents; choosing narrow connectors (like "NEAR WITHIN 2 or 3") will retrieve fewer cases. Figure 5–4 is the completed query planner for Vincent's McCall's research.

To enter the planned query, simply enter search terms, column by column, separating these terms by "OR." Insert connectors as they appear. Thus, a Boolean search for Vincent's problem appear as follows:

```
EXPEL! OR SUSPEND! OR DISMISS! /S STUDENT OR SCHOLAR OR
CHILD! /P POSSES! OR BUY! OR SELL! OR PURCH! /S WEAPON OR
PIPE-BOMB OR GUN OR KNIFE OR "BASEBALL BAT"
```

Figure 5–5 lists some helpful hints for full text searching.

Browsing

Once the runner has completed his search, he will return retrieved documents in reverse chronological order or in descending order by frequency of search terms. In addition, because a CALR presumes the researcher's first post-search task will be to peruse retrieved documents for their usefulness, the CALR will return the documents in a format designed for quick review of document areas where search terms appear. Of course, CALRs permit normal, sequential paging (often by using page-down and page-up keys). CALRs may also allow the researcher to browse documents for terms or phrases other than original search terms. Finally, CALRs keep track of search results so that the researcher can return to documents retrieved in earlier searches.

Figure 5–6 is a screen of information retrieved by Westlaw.

Notice the screen areas and their contents, which although formatted and named differently in different CALRs, are usually provided by all CALRs.

CALR fields are important both in limiting CALR searches to certain fields (e.g., searching only for documents written after a certain date, or cases authored by a certain judge) and for limiting browsing of retrieved documents to certain document areas (e.g., the case summary).

Other Searches

In addition to citation, title, and full-text searching, CALRs offer other, specialized searches including headnote, topic and key number searches, and so on.

Beyond Legal Research

Legal materials are not the only materials available through computers. Materials available on CALRs are extensive, varied, and ever-growing. Dictionaries and encyclopedias are available on CD-ROMs and the Inernet, as are novels, nonfiction,

Where to search
Choose Databases to Search:

OH-CS

What to search for
1. Begin with a concise statement of the issue.

MAY A SCHOOL EXPEL A STUDENT FOR POSSESSION OF WEAPONS?

2. Underline issue key terms; insert in query planner.
3. Choose alternative, related terms; insert in query planner.
4. Choose and insert universal characters and root expanders.
5. Choose and insert connectors.

EXPEL!	/S	STUDENT	/P	POSSES!	/S	WEAPON	con-nector	keyword
SUSPEND!		SCHOLAR!		BUY!		PIPE-BOMB		related term
DISMISS!		CHILD!		SELL!		GUN		
				PURCH!		KNIFE		
						"BASEBALL BAT"		

6. Complete final query, moving vertically through the query planner chart, connecting alternative terms with "OR."

EXPEL! OR SUSPEND! OR DISMISS! /S STUDENT OR SCHOLAR OR
CHILD! /P POSSES! OR BUY! OR SELL! OR PURCH! /S
WEAPON OR PIPE-BOMB OR GUN OR KNIFE OR "BASEBALL BAT"

Figure 5–4 Vincent McCall's query planner.

General suggestions when Boolean searching

When searching for words in a title or for an author's name, remember the following suggestions to make your searching more effective:

- Limit the number of words in a search phrase to one or two unusual words. Multiple word searches require an exact match; therefore, it is better to enter a single word unless you are certain of exact words. Example: To search for *State v. Uqunruh,* use the term "Uqunruh."

- Remove plural possessive words and punctuation from the search phrase.

   Example: To search for Black's Law Dictionary, use the term "black."

- Use part of a word instead of the whole word to retrieve all forms of that word.

   Example: *litigat* will retrieve litigate, litigates, litigated, litigating or litigation.

- Using a single common term may result in long search times. If a common term is necessary, try to combine that common term with other search options.

- Do not use connectors such as OR or AND within text boxes. If you wish to use connectors, choose the desired connector from drop-down list in the More Options Search Form.

Figure 5–5   Tips for full-text searching.

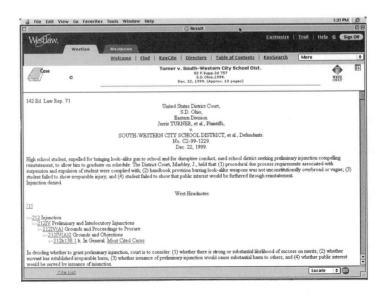

Figure 5–6   Westlaw screen. From Westlaw; reprinted with the permission of West Group.

A. number of documents retrieved
B. number of CALR screens in each document
C. database searched
D. browsing **mode:** T = pressing enter returns to the next page containing search terms, P = displays next sequential page
E. document fields
   1. document title
   2. document citation
   3. date document was authored
   4. document summary
   5. court deciding the case
   6. document headnote
   7. digest topic
   8. document digest entry
   9. names of attorneys involved in the case
  10. name of judge writing the majority opinion in a case
  11. written opinion in a case

Figure 5–6 (continued)

newspapers, and magazines. Even national and local telephone books are available on computers, as are catalogs and regional and local maps.

Additionally, Westlaw and LEXIS offer on-line access to many non-legal materials including newspapers and journals, as part of the subscriber's contract. Other databases, particularly financial, medical, and technological information, are accessible for a separate, additional fee. The following are examples of non-legal databases available through CALR services:

✳ Trademark filings and documents
✳ Patent filings and documents
✳ Dunn & Bradstreet Market Reports
✳ Journal of the American Medical Association
✳ Tax information and filings

Additional information about available non-legal databases is available on-line, through CALR manuals, and by telephone help services.

Printing and Saving Information

All CALRs permit the researcher to **download** (i.e., save) retrieved material to computer disks (either floppy or hard) or print them on a local printer. The CALR's user manuals should explain these functions. Although printing and saving data are free on the Internet and included in the subscription fee for a CD-ROM, printing and downloading data from CALR services can be quite expensive. Both Westlaw and LEXIS charge the researcher $.02 per line of data (over $1.25 per page) saved or printed. Fortunately, CALR services offer a lower cost, though labor intensive, alternative. Both Westlaw and LEXIS allow researchers to print individual screens of data ("Print Screen" option) and "save" screens of data to disk at no per line charge. To save screens to disk, the researcher need only turn on a "logging" function and page through the document she wishes to save. As each screen appears on the computer monitor, the CALR stores it to the researcher's disk. The labor intensive parts of the process are two: (1) the time and effort involved in paging through each document saved, and (2) screens logged to disk are stored in screen format, including copyright information and embedded carriage returns necessary to fit the text on the computer screens; therefore, using information stored to disk is like using the information as it appears on the screen — a tedious and often not terribly useful format.

Signing off from a CALR

Signing off from a CALR is usually just a matter of following the CALR's exit sequence. To sign off from one of the CALR services, the researcher enters a sign-off command ("OFF" or ".SO"). Before the service signs off, it may ask the researcher if she wants to save her research until the end of the day. Once the researcher responds, the CALR will provide certain accounting information and will then download or print saved data. Once downloading and printing are complete, the researcher may need to exit the CALR program and turn off the modem (or CD-ROM), printer, monitor, and computer.

Review Questions

1. What is CALR?
2. List some types of CALR.
3. How do those types differ?
4. What two pieces of information does the researcher need to do a CALR search?
5. What is a CALR database? Give some examples.
6. What is a CALR document?
7. What are some common fields in a CALR document?
8. Describe the process of signing on to a CALR.
9. Name some types of CALR searches. How do they differ?
10. What CALR search is the most powerful? Why?
11. List common search connectors. What do they mean? How are they used?
12. How are CALR universal characters used?
13. Explain different methods of browsing CALR results.
14. Explain some fields on a CALR retrieval screen.
15. Name some ways to update your CALR research.

16. List some non-legal information that may be available on CALRs.
17. Explain how to print and store CALR information.
18. Explain how to sign off from a CALR.
19. List some useful helpful hints in CALR research.

Exercises

1. Using a CALR, find the citation for the federal Pregnancy Discrimination Act. When was the act most recently amended?
2. Find the statute of limitations governing legal malpractice cases in your jurisdiction.
3. Find some recent cases in your jurisdiction discussing limitations of legal malpractice cases.
4. When does a legal malpractice cause of action accrue in your jurisdiction?
5. Can Kitty file her legal malpractice claim against Attorney Braithwaite before the statute of limitations in your jurisdiction runs out? Why or why not?

Glossary

ARPANET: The original "Internet" created by the U.S. Department of Defense to protect research contracts and projects with various universities around the country.

Boolean searching: CALR searching for documents based on key words.

Browsers: Internet programs that help locate information.

Browsing: Looking through retrieved documents.

CD-ROM: Compact disk, read-only memory; a storage device for legal research information.

Citation field: Where a CALR document is located.

Computer Assisted Legal Research (CALR): Legal research accomplished through the use of a computer.

Connectors: AND, OR, NEAR, WITHIN, BUT NOT; words that set the proximity of words in full-text searching.

Database: Collection of related CALR information.

Documents: CALR research materials.

Download: Print or save CALR research off-line.

Fields: Discrete sections of CALR-retrieved documents.

Freestyle search: English-language searching capability offered on LEXIS.

Full-text Searching: Word-for-word searching of documents to determine their relevance to the issue researched.

Hard-wired: Computers wired directly to each other.

Headnote field: Summary of a legal point decided in a case.

HTTP: HyperText Transfer Protocol—the language of the Internet.

Hypertext: Words that link Web pages together.

Internet: A worldwide network of computers sharing information.

Internet service providers (ISPs): Organizations providing access to the Internet or a CALR on-line service.

Judge or author field: The author of a computer document.

LEXIS: CALR service based on official publications.

Local area networks: Networks of computers within offices, businesses, or homes.

Meta-engines: Search engines that use other engines to do multiple searches of a single query.

Mode: Browsing method.

Modem: Device for transmitting data over a telephone line.

Natural language search: English-language searching capability offered on Westlaw.

Nodes: Computers on the Internet.

Opinion field: The court's words in a CALR document.

Page: A computer screen of data.

Password: Code necessary to access and pay for use of CALR service.

Personal computer: A small compact computer for personal use.

Rank: Number of documents retrieved.

Retrieve: Find and return information.

Search engine: Software that searches Web pages for relevant query language.

TCP/IP: Internet communication language or "protocol."

Terms-and-connectors searching: CALR searching for documents based on key words.

Title field: Document name.

Uniform Resource Locators (URLs): Electronic "addresses" for information on the internet.

Web pages: Information documents on the Internet.

Westlaw: CALR service based on the West Group publications.

World Wide Web: The Internet. Also, the Web or "www."

Notes

[1] Full-text searching, if not carefully done, can result in retrieval of many more documents than necessary or in no or too few results to be useful.

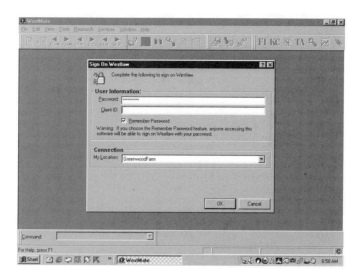

Sign-on screen

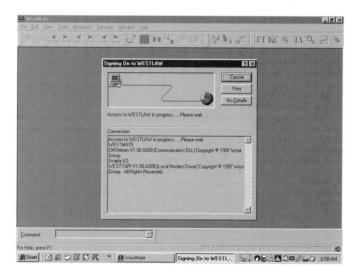

Connection screen

Figure 5–7 Westlaw commands and examples. From Westlaw; reprinted with the permission of West Group.

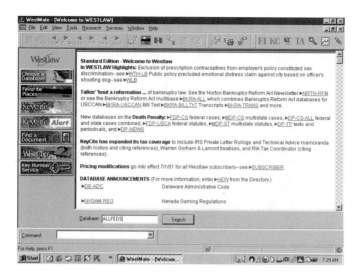

Welcome page

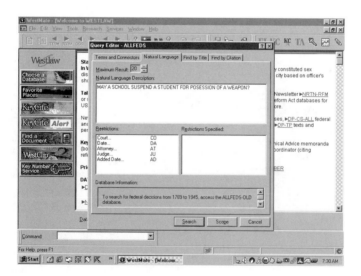

Natural language search screen

Figure 5–7 (continued)

First page of first document retrieved

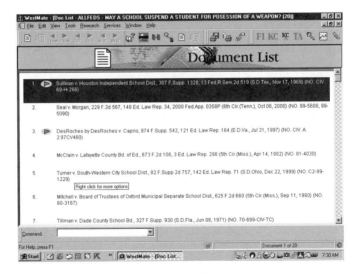

Document list

___

Figure 5–7 (continued)

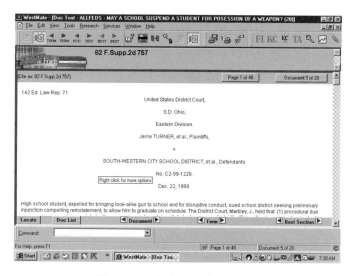

First page of relevant document

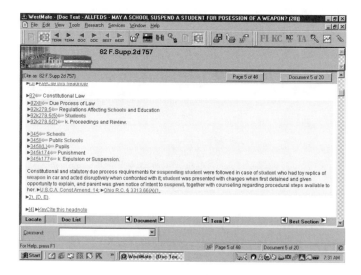

First occurence of search terms

Figure 5–7 (continued)

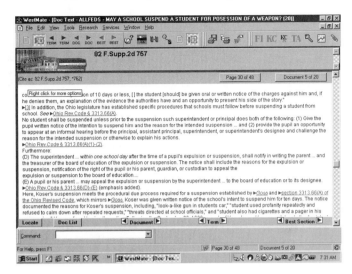

More search terms

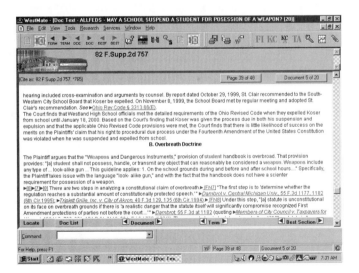

More search terms

Figure 5–7 (continued)

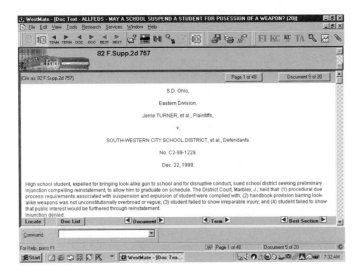

First page

Second page

Figure 5–7 (continued)

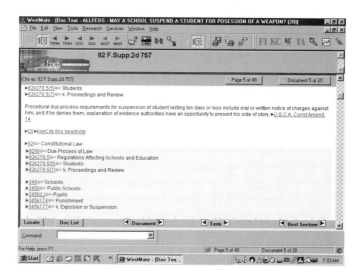

Location of greatest number of search terms (Best)

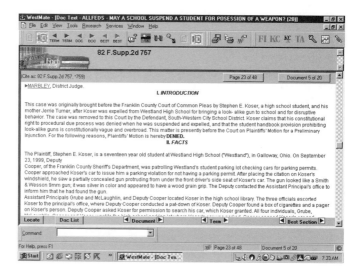

First page of opinion

Figure 5–7 (continued)

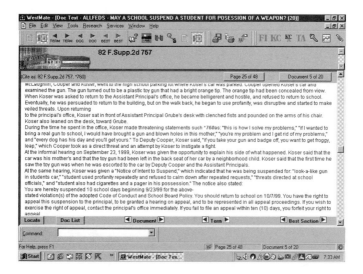

Opinion page

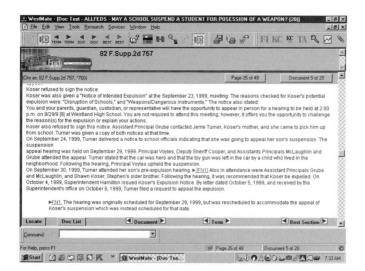

Opinion page

Figure 5–7 (continued)

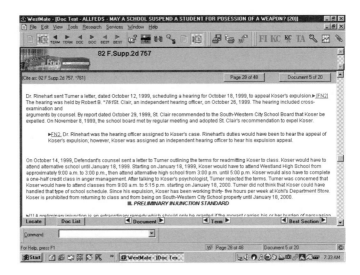

Opinion page

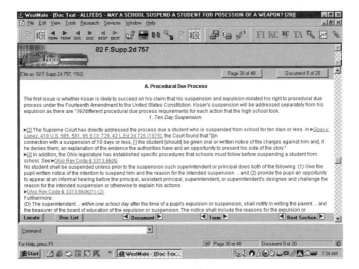

Opinion page

Figure 5–7 (continued)

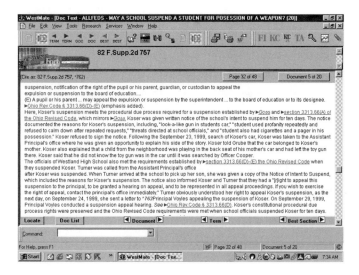

Opinion page

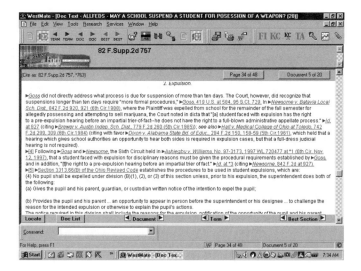

Opinion page

Figure 5–7 (continued)

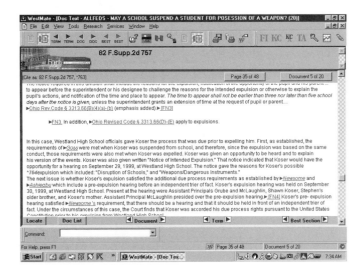

Opinion page

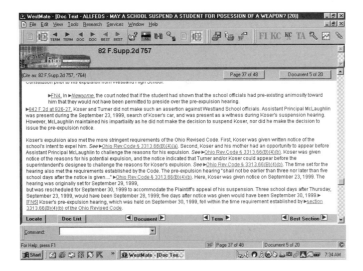

Opinion page

Figure 5–7 (continued)

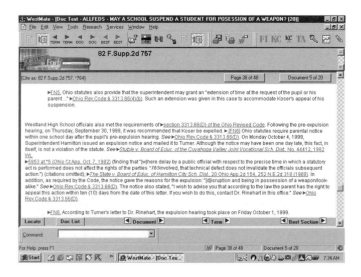

Opinion page

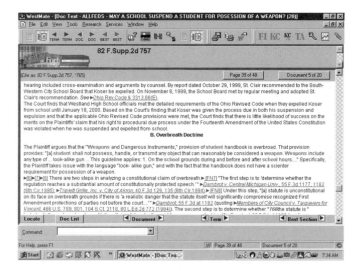

Opinion page

Figure 5–7 (continued)

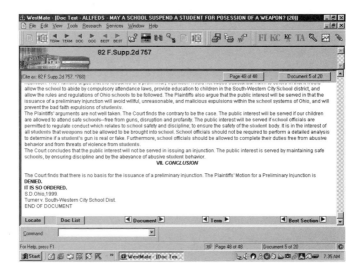

Opinion page

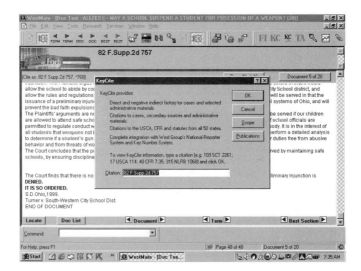

Result verification: KeyCite

Figure 5–7 (continued)

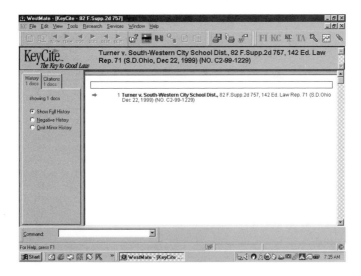

Result verification

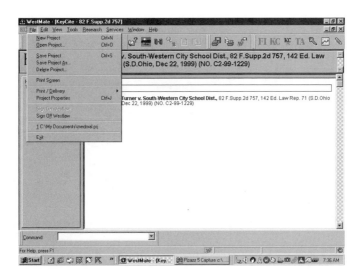

Sign-off

Figure 5–7 (continued)

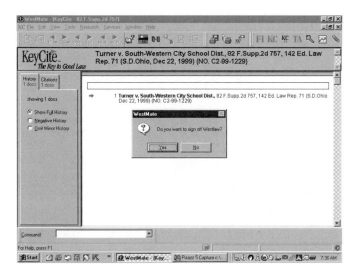

Sign-off

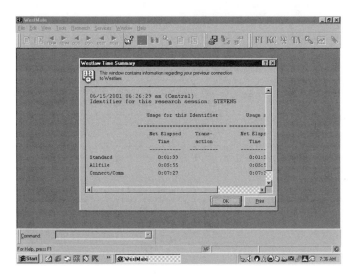

Accounting page

Figure 5–7 (continued)

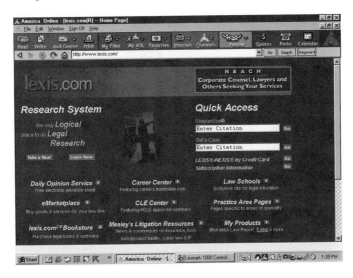

Lexis.com welcome screen

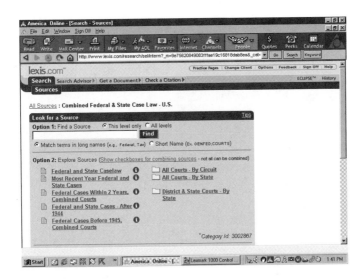

Database selection

Figure 5–8 LEXIS commands and examples. Reprinted with the permission of LEXIS-NEXIS, a division of Reed Inc. LEXIS-NEXIS, *lexis.com* and *Shepard's* are registered trademarks of Reed, used with the permission of LEXIS-NEXIS. AOL screenshots © 2001 America Online, Inc.

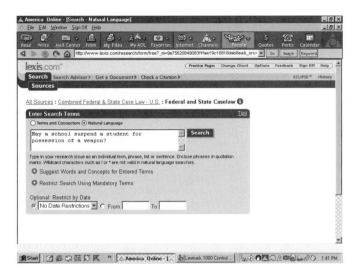

Freesstyle search

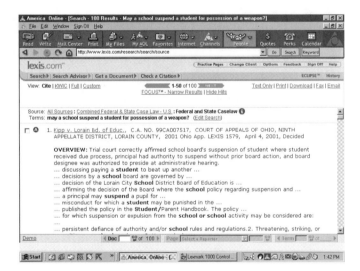

Quik result list

Figure 5–8 (continued)

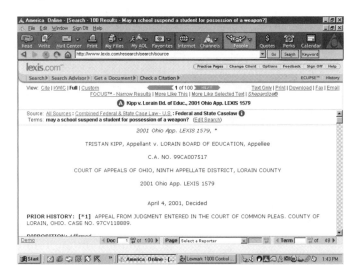

First page of relevant opinion

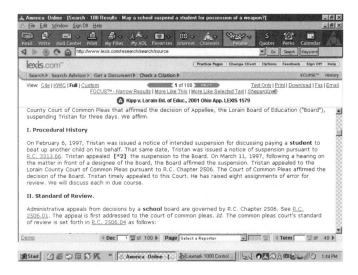

Opinion page

Figure 5–8 (continued)

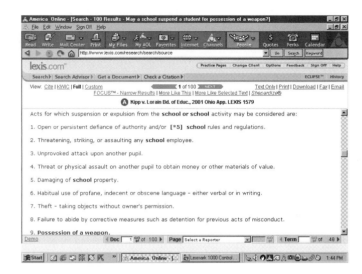

Citation list

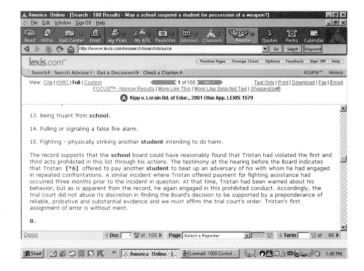

Citation list continued

Figure 5–8 (continued)

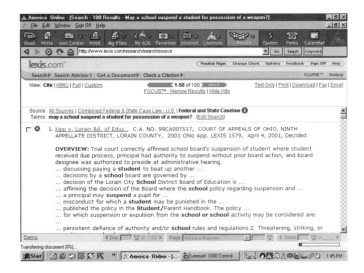

Quik screen

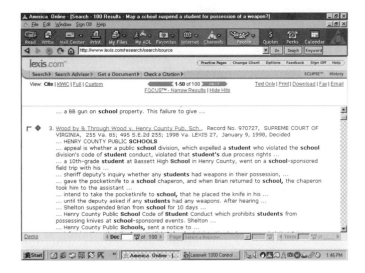

Quik screen

Figure 5–8 (continued)

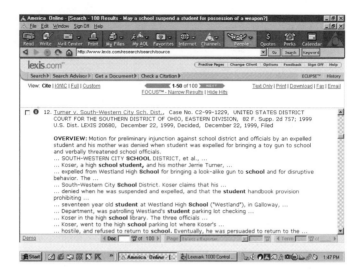

Quik screen

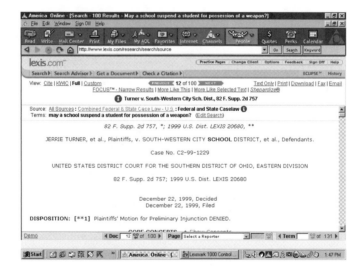

First page of relevant opinion

Figure 5–8 (continued)

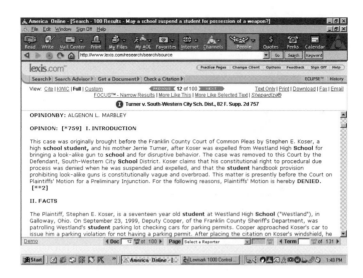

First page of opinion

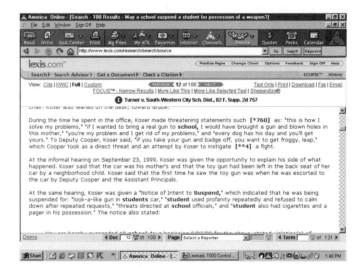

Opinion page

Figure 5–8 (continued)

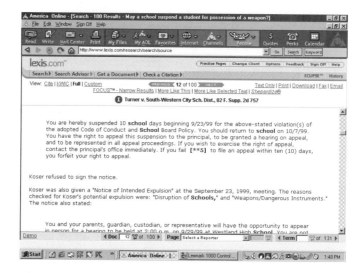

Opinion page

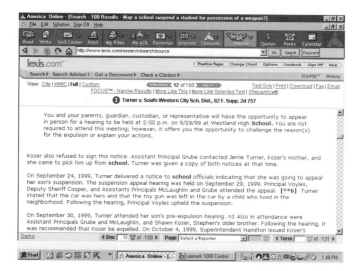

Opinion page

Figure 5–8 (continued)

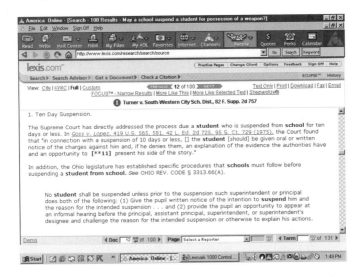

Opinion page — jump to statute

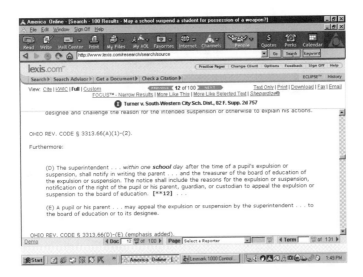

Statute page

Figure 5–8 (continued)

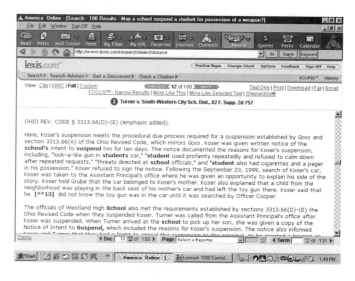

Statute page

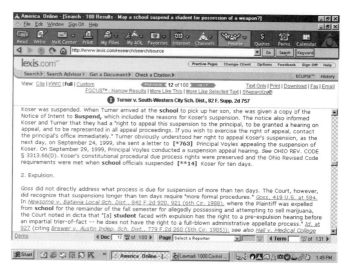

Statutory annotations

Figure 5–8 (continued)

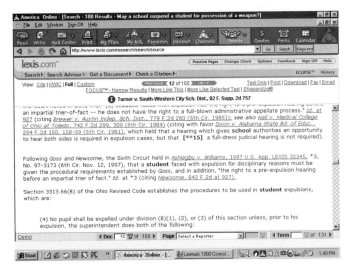

Return to citing case

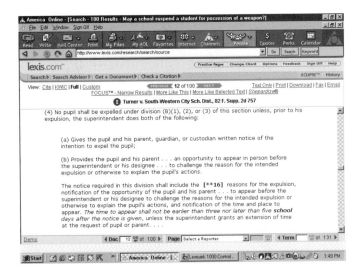

Opinion page

Figure 5–8 (continued)

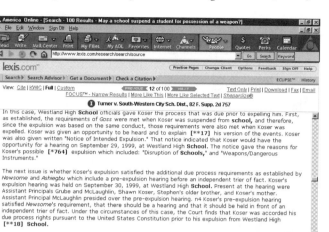

Opinion page

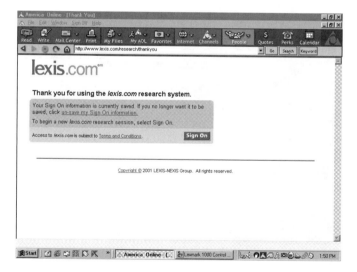

Sign-off

Figure 5–8 (continued)

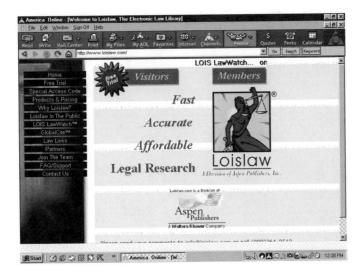

Loislaw welcome screen

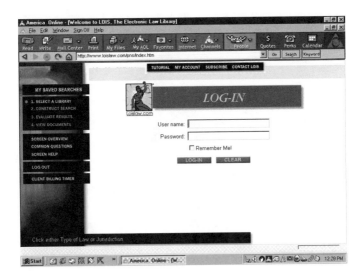

Log-in screen

Figure 5–9 Loislaw commands and examples. Courtesy of Loislaw.com, Inc. AOL screenshots © 2001 America Online, Inc. Used with permission.

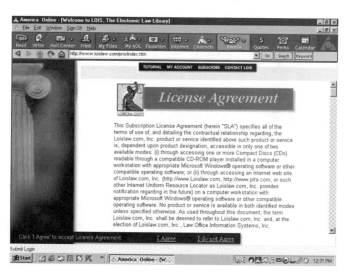

License agreement

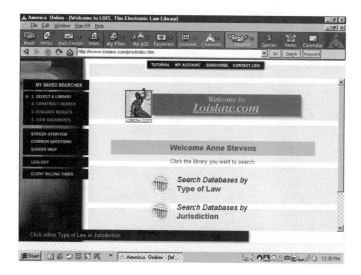

Database selection

Figure 5–9 (continued)

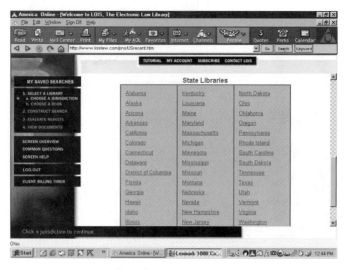

State database selection

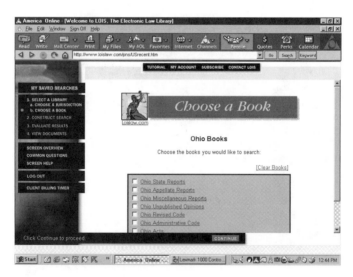

Specific materials selection

Figure 5–9 (continued)

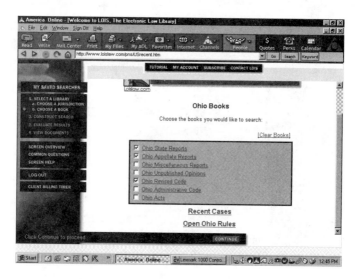

Specific materials selection

Search screen

Figure 5–9 (continued)

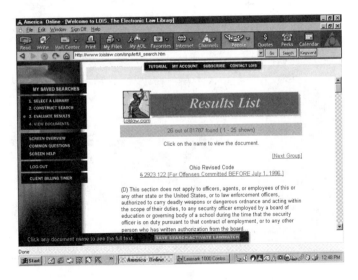

Results list

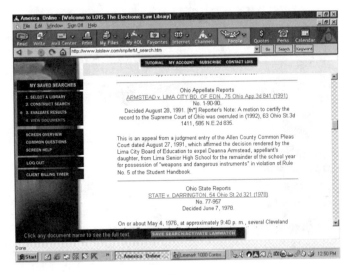

Result page

Figure 5–9 (continued)

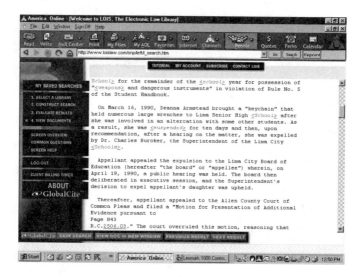

Result page

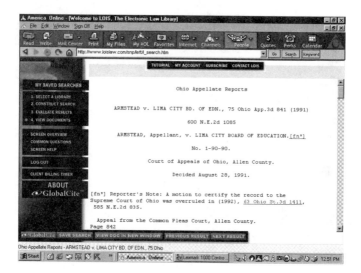

First page of relevant case

Figure 5–9 (continued)

Opinion page

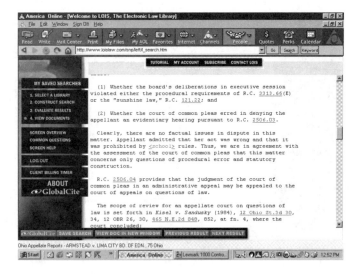

Opinion page

Figure 5–9 (continued)

Opinion page

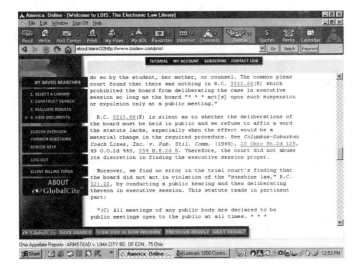

Opinion page

Figure 5–9 (continued)

Opinion page

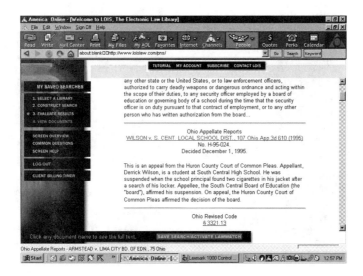

Result list

Figure 5–9 (continued)

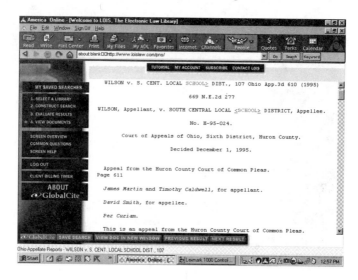

First page of relevanr decisions

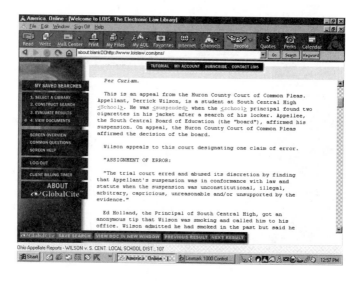

Opinion page

Figure 5–9 (continued)

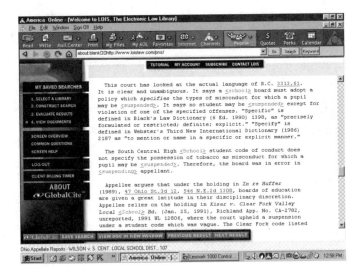

Opinion page

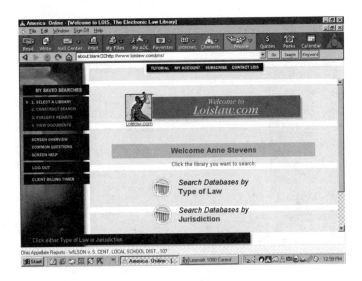

Outcome screen

Figure 5–9 (continued)

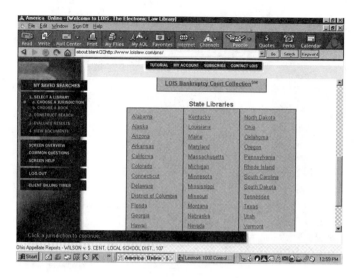

Database selection

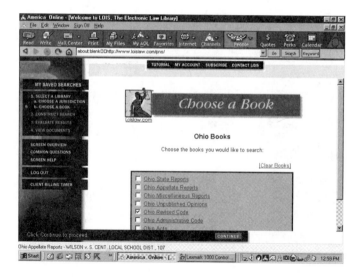

Specific database selection

Figure 5–9 (continued)

Search page

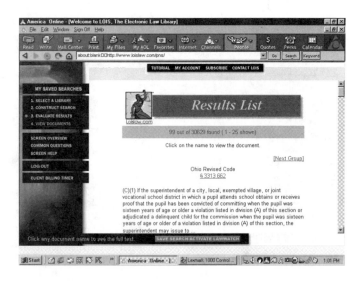

Results list

Figure 5–9 (continued)

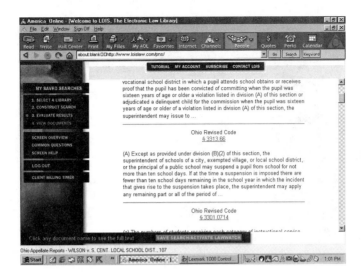

Results list

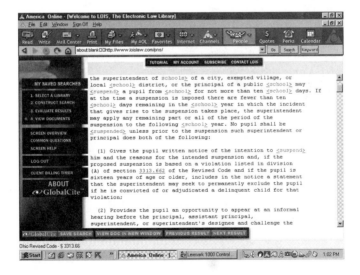

Opinion page

Figure 5–9 (continued)

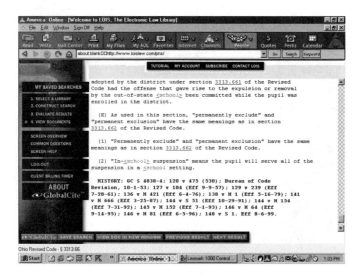

Opinion page

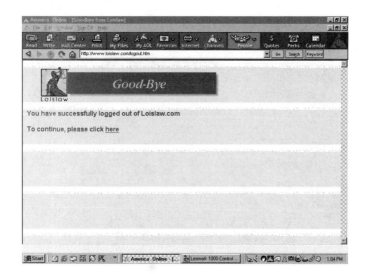

Sign-off

Figure 5–9 (continued)

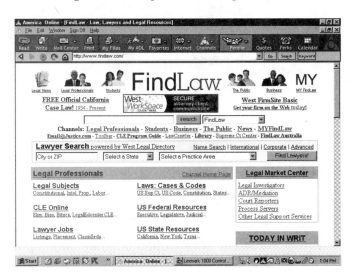

Internet/FindLaw welcome screen

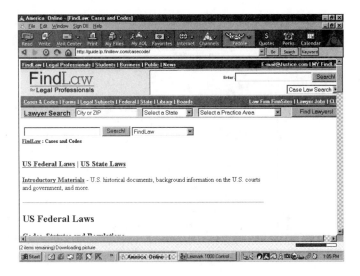

Database selection

Figure 5–10 FindLaw commands and examples. Reprinted by permission of FindLaw. AOL screenshots © 2001 America Online, Inc. Used with permission.

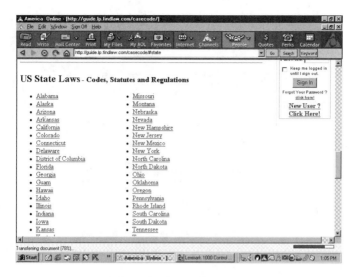

State database selection

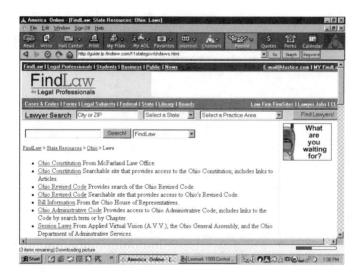

Specific database selection

Figure 5–10 (continued)

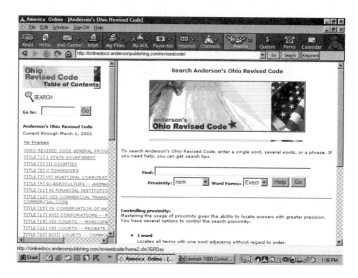

Statute table of contents

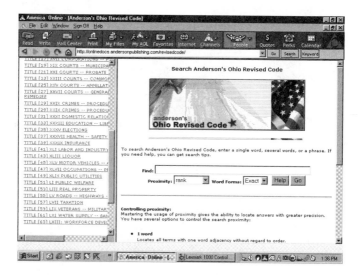

Statute table of contents

Figure 5–10 (continued)

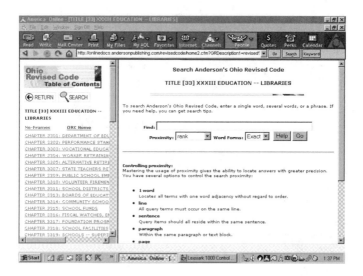

Statute table of contents

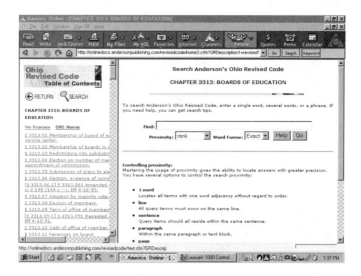

Statute table of contents

Figure 5–10 (continued)

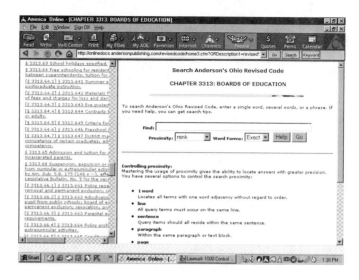

Statute table of contents

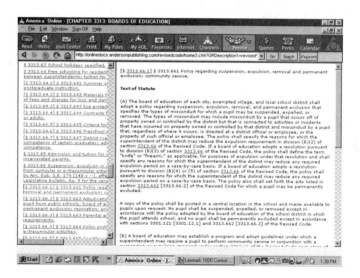

Statute

Figure 5–10 (continued)

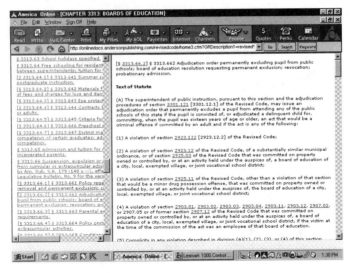

Statute

Figure 5–10 (continued)

An Approach to Legal Research and an Example

Chapter Outline

Learning Objectives:

Upon completing this chapter, the student should be able to

* List the steps in researching a legal issue
* List background resources if the issue is novel
* Explain why statutes are a good place to begin research
* Explain why digests are helpful in legal research
* List other sources of research materials
* Describe the proper way to integrate book and CALR research
* Know when to stop researching

An Approach to Legal Research and an Example

Legal reference books (except case reporters) are indexed topically. Therefore, to research a legal issue it is useful to think of possible index topics. A method of legal research based on index topics follows.

Begin with a Concise Statement of the Issue

Try to state the legal issue you wish to research in one or two concise sentences. For instance, the legal issue in Vincent's case might be phrased as follows:

> *May a Public School Expel a Student for Possessing Weapons?*

Choose Key Terms

Choose three to five key terms from the issue statement. For instance, in Vincent's case, the following key terms may be useful:

> public school
> student
> expel
> possessing
> weapon

Choose Alternative Terms

Next, think of synonyms and terms related to those key terms that might appear in materials addressing your issue. For instance, in Vincent's case, consider the related terms shown in Figure 6–1.

These key and related terms are possible index topics.

Begin with Legal Encyclopedias, Dictionaries, and/or Treatises

If you have no idea what it means to **expel** a student, a good start is reading its dictionary definition. Merriam-Webster's Collegiate® Dictionary (Tenth Edition) defines *expel* as a transitive verb meaning "to force to leave (as a place or organization) by official action: take away rights or privileges of membership <expelled from college>." Legal dictionaries also define ordinary words and may provide citations to relevant legal sources.

If you want general background information on school discipline, you might thus turn to the index of a legal encyclopedia and look up key words and alternates, like *school, expel, discipline, suspend,* and *suspension,* depending on the topic you need more general information about.

Education treatises like Edmund Reutler, Jr.'s *Law of Public Education* (4ᵗʰ ed., 1994) also treat school discipline. For instance, Reutler's treatise at 764 notes that:

Key Term	Related Terms
Public School	school
	academy
Student	scholar
	pupil
Expel	suspend
	throw out
	dismiss
Possessing	purchasing
	bartering
	borrowing
	trading
	receiving
	taking
Weapons	pipe bombs
	guns
	knives
	bats
	explosives
	bombs
	brass knuckles

Figure 6–1 Sample alternative related terms

The most serious penalty is exclusion from school. Although usage is not consistent, "suspension generally connotes a temporary exclusion for a specific period or until something is done by student or parent, and "expulsion" connotes permanent separation . . . . Most states have statutes related to expulsion, covering causes and sometimes procedures. This penalty may be imposed only by the school board on evidence it has itself considered."[148]

n. 148: *Lee v. Macon County Bd. Of Educ.*, 490 F.2d 458 (5 Cir. 1974)

Additionally, West publishes a multi-volume *Education Law Digest*, which indexes, cross-references, and digests education law decisions. Under "Schools — Expulsion or suspension," the reporter lists the following cases dealing with suspension and expulsion:

Donovan v. Ritchie, 68 F.3d 14 (1st Cir. 1995).

Newson v. Batavia Local Sch. Dist., 842 F.2d 920 (6th Cir. 1988).

Draper v. Columbus Pub. Schools, 760 F. Supp. 131 (S.D. Ohio 1991).

Finally, loose-leaf services may be useful. For instance, Matthew Bender publishes a seven-volume treatise on *Education Law*, that reports, indexes, and digests education cases. That loose-leaf service includes the following features:

✴ Topical Index
✴ Table of Contents
✴ Laws

"Control of student conduct" in the treatise table of contents suggests that, for purposes of discipline, bringing weapons to school should be defined broadly and notes the following decision:

M.K. v. School Bd. Of Brevard County, 708 So. 2d 340 (Fla. App. 1998).

Move to the Statutes

If a statute is involved in the issue, the statute itself may shed light on research issues, and statutory annotations provide a quick, direct route to cases interpreting the statute. In Vincent's case, those statutes include the federal Individuals with Disabilities Education Act (IDEA), the Gun Free School Act of 1994, and the Ohio Education Statute. If you do not know the code title for the Gun Free School Act, look up "Gun Free School Act" in a **Popular Names Table** of the United States Code (U.S.C.), the United States Code Annotated (U.S.C.A.), or the United States Code Service (U.S.C.S.). The Popular Names Table identifies the "Gun Free School Act" as title 20 § 8921 of the U.S. Code. That act mandates a one-year minimum expulsion of students caught with weapons at school, as follows:

> Except as provided in paragraph (3), each State receiving Federal funds under this chapter shall have in effect a State law requiring local educational agencies to expel from school for a period of not less than one year a student who is determined to have brought a weapon to a school under the jurisdiction of local educational agencies in that State, except that such State law shall allow the chief administering officer of such local educational agency to modify such expulsion requirement for a student on a case-by-case basis.

It also defines a weapon as "a firearm as such term is defined in section 921 of Title 18." Beginning research with an unofficial statutory compilation — the U.S.C.A. or U.S.C.S. — is useful because those compilations include notes to interpretive cases and materials. Notes following § 8921 (including appropriate pocket parts) list the following weapon-related case:

> Provision of Gun-Free Schools Act requiring each state receiving federal funds to have in effect state law requiring expulsion from school for not less than one year of student who brings weapon to campus did not permit or require expulsion of handicapped student without adherence to procedural safeguards of Individuals with Disabilities Education Act (IDEA), and did not eliminate district's obligation to provide student with free appropriate public education (FAPE) following his expulsion; final Congressional guidance concerning state and local responsibilities under Gun-Free Schools Act stated that children with disabilities removed from school pursuant to Act must be provided with

alternative programming during disciplinary exclusion, and Act specifically stated that its provisions must be construed consistently with IDEA. *Magyar By and Through Magyar v. Tucson Unified School Dist.*, 958 F.Supp. 1423 (D.Ariz.1997).

Look in Digests

Alternatively, digests reference education law cases. Because digests are organized by topic and key number or section, research in the digests is simplified if you have a relevant topic and key number or section. There are several ways to do this.

Use the Descriptive Word Index.   Use key and related terms to access digest topics and key numbers and sections through **the descriptive word index**. Begin with the key terms. If one key term is not helpful, move to related or other key terms. For instance, a search for "Schools" in West's *Tenth Decennial Federal Digest®* index suggests the topic "Schools," key number 177, might be useful.

> Schools
>   Public Schools
>   Pupils
>   Punishment
>   Expulsion or suspension 177

Use the Topic Analysis.   Begin with a pertinent West topic (i.e., Schools). Locate the digest volume containing that topic and turn to the topic analysis, as shown in Figure 6–2. The topic analysis suggests that key number 177 (Expulsion or suspension) may be useful. Digest topic "Schools" suggests that thirteen cases involve suspension or expulsion of students. Of those cases, the following cases are particularly relevant because they involve students suspended or expelled for having weapons in school:

Seal v. Morgan, 229 F.3d 567 (6th Cir. 2000).

McClain v. Lafayette County Bd. of Educ., 687 F.2d 121 (5th Cir. 1982).

Turner v. South-Western City School Dist., 82 F. Supp. 2d 757 (S.D. Ohio 1999).

Colvin ex rel Colvin v. Lowndes County, Mississippi School Dist., 114 F. Supp. 2d 504 (N.D. Miss. E. Div.1999).

Peterson v. Independent School Dist. No. 811, 999 F. Supp. 665 (D. Minn. 1998).

James By and Through James v. Unified School Dist. No. 512, Johnson County, Kan., 899 F. Supp. 530 (D. Kan. 1995).

Carey ex rel. Carey v. Maine School Administrative Dist. No. 17, 754 F. Supp. 906 (D. Me. 1990).

SCHOOLS

SUBJECTS INCLUDED

Institutions for instruction below the grade of colleges or universities, whether maintained by private means for individual benefit, or by government as common or public schools

Bodies formed for maintenance of such institutions, whether unincorporated or incorporated by special charters or under general laws, or formed by territorial subdivision of counties, towns, or cities, etc.

Constitutional and statutory provisions relating thereto

Public supervision and regulation of such schools in general

Incorporation and organization of private schools, academies, etc., and public aid and regulation thereof

Creation, organization, boundaries, alteration and dissolution of school districts

School meetings and government and officers of school districts

School lands, funds, buildings, furniture, textbooks, and other property and supplies, and contracts relating thereto

Indebtedness, bonds, warrants, and other securities of school districts

Taxation by school districts

Qualifications, employment and discharge, and compensation of teachers and other specialized officers and employees

Admission and attendance of pupils

Curriculum, rules, discipline and government of schools

SUBJECTS EXCLUDED AND COVERED BY OTHER TOPICS

Public lands reserved as school lands, but not allotted to school districts, see PUBLIC LANDS
Taxation for school purposes, see TAXATION

For detailed references to other topics, see Descriptive-Word Index

---

Analysis

I. Private schools and academies, ☞ 1–8.

II. PUBLIC SCHOOLS, ☞ 9–179.
    (A) ESTABLISHMENT, SCHOOL LANDS AND FUNDS, AND REGULATION IN GENERAL, ☞ 9–20.
    (B) CREATION, ALTERATION, EXISTENCE, AND DISSOLUTION OF DISTRICTS, ☞ 21–44.
    (C) GOVERNMENT, OFFICERS, AND DISTRICT MEETINGS, ☞ 45–63.
    (D) DISTRICT PROPERTY, ☞ 64–76.
    (E) DISTRICT CONTRACTS, ☞ 77–86.

Figure 6–2 West topic analysis. From *West Digests*; reprinted with the permission of West Group.

(F) DISTRICT LIABILITIES, ☞ 87–89.19.
(G) FISCAL MATTERS, ☞ 90–110.
(H) TAXPAYERS' SUITS AND OTHER REMEDIES, ☞ 111.
(I) CLAIMS AGAINST DISTRICT, ☞ 112.
(J) ACTIONS, ☞ 113–126.
(K) TEACHERS, ☞ 127–147.54.
    1. IN GENERAL, ☞ 127–147.
    2. ADVERSE PERSONNEL ACTIONS, ☞ 147.2–147.54.
(L) PUPILS, ☞ 148–179.

III. INTERSCHOLASTIC ASSOCIATIONS, ☞ 180–183.

I. PRIVATE SCHOOLS AND ACADEMIES.

1. Establishment and status in general.
2. Incorporation and organization.
3. Public aid.
4. Regulation and supervision.
5. Property, funds, and liabilities in general.
6. Governing boards and officers.
7. Teachers and other instructors.
8. Pupils, tuition, and discipline.

II. PUBLIC SCHOOLS.

(A) ESTABLISHMENT, SCHOOL LANDS AND FUNDS, AND REGULATION IN GENERAL.
9. Power to establish and maintain in general.
10. Constitutional and statutory provisions.
11. School system, and establishment or discontinuance of schools and local educational institutions in general.
12. Application of school system to cities and incorporated towns and villages.
13. Separate schools for racial groups.
    (1). In general.
    (2). Existence and propriety of segregated system.
    (3). Equality within segregated system.
    (4). Desegregation and integration and duty to desegregate in general.
    (5). De facto or de jure segregation.
    (6). Desegregation plans in general.
    (7). Role of courts.
    (8). Role of federal or statewide agencies and local committees.
    (9). Time for desegregation.

(10). Justification for delay or failure.
(11). Step-by-step desegregation; transitional period.
(12). School location; districts and attendance zones.
(13). School pairing or clustering.
(14). Freedom of choice; transfer.
(15). Disregard of district boundaries.
(16). Private schools; state involvement and abandonment or nonsupport of public system.
(17). Particular schools; related facilities and activities.
(18). Actions.
(18.1). —— In general.
(19). —— Evidence.
(20). —— Judgment and relief; retained jurisdiction.
(21). —— Review.
14. State and county educational institutions.
15. Application to school purposes of school lands and proceeds thereof.
16. School funds.
16.1. —— In general.
17. —— Creation and sources.
18. —— Investment and administration.

Figure 6–2 (continued)

III. INTERSCHOLASTIC ASSOCIATIONS.

For detailed references to other topics, see Descriptive-Word Index

Figure 6–2 (continued)

Use A Relevant Case. A case involving students suspended or expelled from school will include an appropriate headnote topic and key number. For instance, the case of *Turner v. South Western School District*, 82 F. Supp. 2d 757 (S.D. Ohio 1999) includes the following relevant headnote:

Schools ☞ 177

Constitutional and statutory due process requirements for expelling student were observed in case of student who had toy replica of weapon in car and acted disruptively when confronted with it; student was presented with charges when first detained and given opportunity to explain, and parent was given notice of intent to suspend, together with counseling regarding procedural steps available to her, there was pre-expulsion hearing before impartial official and detailed state statutory requirements for expulsion procedural were followed. U.S.C.A. Const.Amend. 14; Ohio R.C. § 3313.66(B).

Use the relevant topic and key or section number to locate additional relevant primary materials in the digests.

Agency Regulations and Decisions

If statutes and digests do not clearly resolve the right of a school district to expel a student for possession of a pipe bomb, **regulations** and decisions may be helpful. While school regulations and decisions involving suspension or expulsion of students are not generally available, a useful resource in public school discipline cases is the school student handbook. Schools cannot expel or suspend students for disciplinary reasons unless a rule in the student handbook is violated. The *Cuyahoga Public School Student Handbook* (obtainable from the school administrative offices), includes statements about suspension and expulsion of students shown in Figure 6–3.

CALR Research

Finally, Westlaw, LEXIS, Internet, and Loislaw federal and state databases may include cases involving suspension and expulsion of public school students for disciplinary reasons. A natural language search for

May a Public School Expel a Student for Possessing Weapons?

retrieves many cases (some duplicated). Browsing those cases suggests the following are most useful because they involve expulsion of students for possession of weapons:

Doe v. Superintendent of Schools of Worcester, 421 Mass. 117, 653 N.E.2d 1088 (1995).

Wood By and Through Wood v. Henry County Public Schools, 255 Va. 85, 495 S.E.2d 255 (1998).

WHAT WE EXPECT OF YOU

．
．
．

Weapons

All weapons including but not limited to knives or any kind of guns are banned from school . . .

Disciplinary Terms Used At The Middle School . . .

Expulsion from school

State law provides the principal with the authority to recommend the expulsion of any student from shool under the conditions stated below.

• Any student who is found on school premises or at school-sponsored or school-related events, including athletic games, in possession of a dangerous weapon, including, but not limited to, a gun or a knife; or a controlled substance as defined in Chapter 94C, including but not limited to, marijuana, cocaine, and heroin, may be subject to expulsion from the school or school district by the principal.

• Any student who assaults a principal, assistant principal, teacher, teacher's aide or other educational staff on school premises or at school sponsored or school-related events, including athletic games, may be subject to expulsion from the school or school district by the principal.

• Any student who is charged with a violation of either paragraph (1) or (2) shall be notified in writing of an opportunity for a hearing; provided, however, that the student may have representation, along with the opportunity to present evidence and witnesses at said hearing before the principal.

• After said hearing, a principal may, in his/her discretion, decide to suspend rather than expel a student who has been determined by the principal to have violated either paragraph (1) or (2); provided, however, that any principal who decides that said student should be suspended shall state in writing to the school committee his reasons for choosing the suspension instead of the expulsion as the most appropriate remedy. In this statement, the principal shall represent that, in her opinion, the continued presence of this student in the school will not pose a threat to the safety, security and welfare of the other students and staff in the school.

• Any student who has been expelled from a school district pursuant to these provisions shall have the right to appeal to the superintendent. The expelled student shall have ten days from the date of the expulsion in which to notify the superintendent of his appeal. The student has the right to counsel at a hearing before the superintendent. The subject matter of the appeal shall not be limited solely to a factual determination of whether the student has violated any provisions of this section.

• When a student is expelled under the provisions of this section and applies for admission to another school for acceptance, the superintendent of the sending school shall notify the superintendent of the receiving school of the reasons for the pupil's expulsion.

Behaviors that may result in suspension and/or recommendation for expulsion . . .

• Possession of a weapon

Figure 6–3 Excerpts from the *Cuyahoga Public School Student Handbook.*

Kolesnick By and Through Shaw v. Omaha Public School Dist., 251 Neb. 575, 558 N.W.2d 807 (1997).

Davis v. Hillsdale Community School Dist., 226 Mich. App. 375, 573 N.W.2d 77 (1997).

In re F.B., 555 Pa. 661, 726 A.2d 361 (1999).

Spencer By and Through Spencer v. Omaha Public School Dist., 252 Neb. 750, 566 N.W.2d 757 (1997).

Board of School Trustees of Muncie Community Schools v. Barnell by Duncan, 678 N.E.2d 799 Ind. (1997).

D.B. v. Clarke County Bd. of Educ., 220 Ga. App. 330, 469 S.E.2d 438 (1996).

Phillip Leon M. v. Greenbrier County Bd. of Educ., 199 W.Va. 400, 484 S.E.2d 909 (1996).

Cathe A. v. Doddridge County Bd. of Educ., 200 W.Va. 521, 490 S.E.2d 340 (1997).

J.M. v. Webster County Bd. of Educ., 534 S.E.2d 50 (W. Va. 2000).

Lyons v. Penn Hills School Dist., 723 A.2d 1073 (Pa. 1999).

Washington v. Smith, 248 Ill. App. 3d 534, 618 N.E.2d 561 (1993).

Board of Educ. v. School Committee of Quincy, 415 Mass. 240, 612 N.E.2d 666 (1993).

Note Taking and Following up on Likely Resources

Once you have noted likely research materials, review those materials in order of relevance and reverse-chronologically: often more recent materials summarize and cite earlier resources, so that more recent materials may save reading earlier materials.

As you review your research materials, take notes on what you've found. Start a new page of notes (and identify the source) for each source (e.g., encyclopedia, treatise, case, etc.). Keeping notes on separate pages allows easy weeding of irrelevant information and organizing relevant information into a convenient written framework. Read and note additional resources. Highlight particularly relevant sources. For instance, initial research into Vincent's case might result in the following notes:

> *Matthew Bender, Education Law — "Control of Student Conduct" § 9.01*
>   *9.01 Control of Student Conduct*
>   *Authority*
>   *Constitutional Perspective*
>   *Extent of control*
>   *On-Campus or School Related Activities*
>   *Off-Campus or Non-School Related Activities*

Establishing Rules of Student Conduct and Discipline
In general
Specificity
Development and Dissent
Implementation

Weapons are broadly defined in suspension or school discipline cases

 M.K. v .School Bd. Of Brevard County, 708 So. 2d 340 (Fla. App. 1998).
 Washington v. Smith, 248 Ill. App. 3d 539, 618 N.E.2d 561 (1993).

School districts can forbid presence of weapons in schools

 Doe v. Superintendent of Schools of Worcester, 421 Mass. 117, 653 N.E.2d
 1088 (1995).

-- --------

West Education Law Reporter® Digest

 Schools
  Verona Sch. Dist. 47J v. Acton, 515 U.S. 646 (1995) (search and seizure).
  Tarter v. Raybuck, 742 F.2d 977 (1984) (school discipline constrained by
  constitution).
  Ray v. Wilmington College, 106 Ohio App. 3d 707, 667 N.E.2d 39
  (1995) (punishment of off campus activities).
  In re. Adam, 120 Ohio App. 3d 364, 697 N.E.2d 1100 (1997).
  In re suspension of Hupfer from Circlassville H.S., 47 Ohio St. 3d 12, 546
  N.E.2d 1308 (1989).

 169.5 Search and seizure
  Morgan v. Girard City Sch. Dist. Bd. Of Educ., 90 Ohio App. 3d 627,
  630 N.E.2d 71 (1993) (relative blameworthiness of joint enterprisers).

 177 Expulsion or Suspension
  Donovan v. Ritchie, 8 F.3d 14 (D. Mass. 1995).
  Newson v. Batavia Local Sch. Dist., 842 F.2d 920 (6th Cir. 1988).
  Draper v. Columbus Pub. Schools, 760 F. Supp. 131 (S.D. Ohio 1991).

CFR/OAC/School Handbook info here

 Once you've completed your initial research notes, look up additional possible
sources. Consider how those resources impact your research. Incorporate relevant
additional research into your legal analysis.

Integrating Book and CALR Service (Westlaw, LEXIS) Research

Because of the expense of CALR service research, it is very important to carefully
plan CALR research before signing on to a service.

Begin your research in the library. Use books to determine likely legal topics and jurisdictions for your research issue. Develop a CALR "game plan" detailing the databases and searches you wish to perform on-line. Sign on to the CALR service and follow your plan, browsing through retrieved documents to determine whether your search was helpful. If it was not, revise and rerun your search until the CALR retrieves useful results. Note documents available in printed form in the library and log other key documents to disk. Sign off from the CALR service.

Complete your research in the library. Shepardize important documents for which you have printed *Shepard's Citations.* Plan additional necessary on-line research. Sign on to the CALR and complete your research. Shepardize materials not available in print. Finally, before relying on your research, update and verify that research through available books or on-line.

Knowing When to Stop

It doesn't take many hours of legal research before the researcher realizes the end-lessness of the task: sources lead to sources, which lead to other sources. Knowing when to safely stop researching an issue is as much an art as a science. If you specialize in a legal area, eventually you will become sufficiently familiar with the law in that area to know when enough research is enough. Until you reach that desired familiarity (or develop other successful methods), one of the following methods may help you determine when to stop researching.

Time's Up

Time may limit research. For instance, suppose Vincent and his family handled the early stages of his expulsion (e.g., meetings with school officials, responding to let-ters, etc.) but the weekend before his administrative hearing developed a case of nerves and sought legal help. With the hearing imminent (postponement is not possible), the time for legal research is limited to the research that will "get to the bottom line" as quickly as possible. In this case, the researcher may have to be sat-isfied with some cases on public school expulsion, relevant statutes, and relevant regulations until time permits further research.

You're Out of Money

Often, a practical concern — money — may limit research. For a client like Vincent who may recover only a few hundred dollars in benefits, the amount at stake may not warrant extensive witness interviews, research, discovery, document preparation, and appeals.

Tripping Over Yourself

Eventually, the legal researcher not limited by time or money will begin encoun-tering the same materials over and over. When this happens, the researcher can be confident that she has found all (or most) available relevant materials. Indeed, this happened in researching Vincent's issue, as all resources eventually pointed to the following cases:

Doe v. Superintendent of Schools of Worcester, 421 Mass. 117, 653 N.E.2d 1088 (1995).

Wood By and Through Wood v. Henry County Public Schools, 255 Va. 85, 495 S.E.2d 255 (1998).

Davis v. Hillsdale Community School Dist., 226 Mich. App. 375, 573 N.W.2d 77 (1997).

Board of School Trustees of Muncie Community Schools v. Barnell by Duncan, 678 N.E.2d 799 (Ind. 1997).

Washington v. Smith, 248 Ill. App. 3d 534, 618 N.E.2d 561 (1993).

Board of Educ. v. School Committee of Quincy, 415 Mass. 240, 612 N.E.2d 666 (1993).

Seal v. Morgan, 229 F.3d 567 (6th Cir. 2000).

McClain v. Lafayette County Bd. of Educ., 687 F.2d 121 (5th Cir. 1982).

Turner v. South-Western City School Dist., 82 F.Supp.2d 757 (S.D. Ohio. 1999).

James By and Through James v. Unified School Dist. No. 512, Johnson County, Kan., 899 F.Supp. 530 (D. Kan., 1995).

Carey on Behalf of Carey v. Maine School Administrative Dist. No. 17, 754 F.Supp. 906 (D. Me. 1990).

Review Questions

1. List the steps in researching a legal issue. If the issue is new to you, list some resources that might give you background information on the issue.

2. Why are statutes a good place to begin research?

3. Why are digests helpful in legal research?

4. If an agency is involved in a research issue, list some other sources of research materials.

5. Describe the proper way to integrate book and CALR research.

6. If your initial research leads to other resources, what should you do?

7. How do you know when to stop researching?

Exercises

Complete the following exercises using your state's research sources:

1. Draft a concise statement of a legal issue in Kitty Barbour's case.

2. List key terms in that issue.

3. Choose alternate terms.

4. Define any unfamiliar terms.

5. Look up background information in legal encyclopedias.

6. Does a statute govern Kitty's problem? Find that statute. Are annotations to the statute helpful in resolving Kitty's problem? What other information might be useful?

7. Find an appropriate digest topic to Kitty's issue. Do the digest cases resolve Kitty's problem? Why or why not?

8. Research Kitty's issue on a CALR. What new resources did you locate on the CALR that you did not find in books? What book resources were not retrieved in the CALR?

Glossary

Descriptive word index: Digest topical index.

Expel: To force to leave (as a place or organization) by official action: take away rights or privileges of membership <expelled from college>.

Popular Names Table: A table cross-referencing statutes' common names to their official citation.

Regulations: Rules promulgated by a government agency regulating rights and procedures before the agency.

Topic Analysis: Outline of key numbers or sections in a digest topic.

CHAPTER 7

Finding the Current Law: Updating and Verifying Legal Research and Examples

Chapter Outline

Learning Objectives

Upon completing this chapter, the student should be able to

* Describe how to update and verify legal research using the digests and the mini-digests in the case reports and advance sheets
* Explain *Shepard's Citations* — how they came about, their coverage, and their use
* Describe how to update to verify legal research using *Shepard's Citations*
* Describe how to update and verify legal research using CALR
* Explain the integration of digest, Shepard's, and CALR citators to update and verify legal research

Introduction

Just as the thorough detective checks and rechecks his evidence, looking for discrepancies and the truth, the legal researcher must **update** and verify the research materials she relies on. **Research verification** usually involves the following two tasks:

1. determining whether relevant research materials are accurately cited; and
2. determining that materials relied on in legal analysis are current and have not been modified, overruled, or otherwise disfavored

Fortunately[1], by using already familiar digests, CALR systems, and books such as **Shepard's Citations,** this most essential part of legal research — updating and verification — can be done simply, accurately, and quickly.

Legal research verification is an ongoing process. Most often, the researcher uses legal research verification tools early in research to identify sources of research materials. Later, after research is completed and the researcher has settled on the materials she intends to use in her analysis, the researcher returns to those verification tools to recheck the validity of her research.

Updating Legal Research through Digests and Mini-Digests

By identifying a digest **topic** and **key number** relevant to your research, it is possible to find recent relevant research materials by looking up that topic and key number in digests, their pocket parts, and semi-annual supplements. At any given time, however, digests may be as much as six months old. Fortunately, West Group® publishes **mini-digests** in case reporter volumes, which digest cases appearing in that volume. Mini-digests appear in the back of hardbound reporter volumes, and in the front of reporter **advance sheet** pamphlets. It is thus possible to determine the case reporter volumes included in the digests, its pocket parts, and its supplements, and beginning with the reporter volume following those digested volumes, to search the mini-digests of more recent reporters (and advance sheets) for more recent cases digested.

For instance, to find cases post-dating the *Tenth Federal Decennial Digest,* its pocket parts, and supplements, begin with the most recent digest supplement. The second page of that supplement is a **Closing Table** which indicates the most recent reporter volumes digested in that supplement. For instance, in Figure 7–1, the *Tenth Federal Decennial Digest* supplement closing table suggests that updating research beyond materials digested in that supplement should begin with 936 *Federal Reporter*® *Second,* (F.2d) and 765 *Federal Supplement*® (F. Supp.).

Figure 7–2 shows the steps in updating research material using digests.

REPORTERS AND REPORTS

COVERED BY

TENTH DECENNIAL DIGEST

PART 1

REPORTER OR REPORT	From	To
Atlantic	.511 A.2d 310	592 A.2d 148
Bankruptcy Reporter	.61 B.R. 631	128 B.R. 319
California Reporter	.228 Cal. Rptr. 159	283 Cal. Rptr. 380
Claims Court Reporter	.10 Cl.Ct. 191	23 Cl.Ct. 233
Federal	.794 F.2d 688	935 F.2d 1297
Federal Rules Decisions	.110 F.R.D.213	136 F.R.D. 497
Federal Supplement	.636 F.Supp. 484	764 F. Supp. 1567
Illinois Decisions	.99 Ill.Dec. 1	158 Ill.Dec. 488
Military Justice	.22 M.J. 271; 840	32 M.J. 458; 1061
New York Supplement	.504 N.Y.S.2d 72	571 N.Y.S.2d 417
North Eastern	.495 N.E.2d 66	574 N.E.2d 601
North Western	.389 N.W.2d 643	471 N.W.2d 320
Pacific	.721 P.2d 40	812 P.2d 597
South Eastern	.345 S.E.2d 575	405 S.E.2d 647
Southern	.490 So.2d 1228	581 So.2d 413
South Western	.712 S.W.2d 275	810 S.W.2d 326
Supreme Court	.107 S.Ct. 1	111 S.Ct. 2923

Figure 7–1 *Decennial Digest* closing page. From *West Digests*; reprinted with the permission of West Group.

1. Check each relevant digest volume, pocket part, and supplement for cases digested under the relevant topic and key number.
2. From the most recent digest supplement, identify the supplement's closing reporter volume from that supplement's closing table.
3. Beginning with the reporter volume following that closing volume, check each following volume and mini-digest for cases digested under the relevant topic and key number. Note each relevant case.
4. Look up noted cases and determine whether and how they affect the research and their usefulness in analyzing the research issue.

Figure 7–2 Steps in updating research material through digests.

Updating and Verifying Legal Research Using *Shepard's Citations*

In 1873, Frank Shepard, an Illinois newspaper publisher, began keeping track of Illinois appellate court decisions on stickers. For instance, when the *Nudd v. Matsoukas*, 7 Ill. 2d 608, 131 N.E.2d 525 (1956) decision was released, Shepard would have created a sticker containing the case name and citation[2]

> *Nudd v. Matsouskas*, 7 Ill. 2d 608, 131 N.E.2d 525 (1956).

As later decisions were released, Shepard did two things: (1) Start a sticker for the case, and (2) search through those decisions for references to earlier case citations. For instance, when a later case, *Graham v. General U. S. Grant Post*, 43 Ill, 2d 1, 248 N.E.2d 657 (1969) was released, Shepard would have created a sticker for *Graham*:

> *Graham v. General U. S. Grant Post*, 43 Ill, 2d 1, 248 N.E.2d 657 (1969).

Shepard would then have looked through the *Graham* decision for references to other cases. On page 6 of the official report of the *Graham* decision, Shepard would have found a citation to *Nudd v. Matsoukas*. He would have pulled out the *Nudd* sticker and added to that sticker the citation for the *Graham* page where *Nudd* was cited.[3]

> 43 Il 2d[3]6

In this fashion, it became very easy to find more recent cases citing to *Nudd*. Figure 7–3 shows current Shepard's citations for *Nudd v. Matsoukas*.

Shepard would not, however, have been through with his citations. It had occurred to him that if he were going to the trouble of reading **citing material,** it might help the researcher to know how a later citing case affected the cited material and for which specific issue in the cited case. Therefore, Shepard developed a series of one-letter codes indicating the cited case's later **history** (what happened on appeal) and **treatment** (by a later decision). Important **Shepard's history codes** and **Shepard's treatment codes** can be found in Figure 7-4.

As well, Shepard indicated the relevant **headnote number** of the cited case by a raised headnote number (a superscript) in the treating case citation. For instance, the citing case, *Graham*, discusses *Nudd* headnote 3 — indicated in the following Shepard's citation:

> 43 Il2d[3]6

Over the years, *Shepard's Citations* moved from stickers to computers, and expanded from Illinois appellate decisions to the appellate decisions of the federal and state courts (both official and unofficial versions), and to various special and topical reporters. Today, there are *Shepard's Citations* for the following:

all official publications of state appellate decisions
all unofficial publications of state appellate decisions

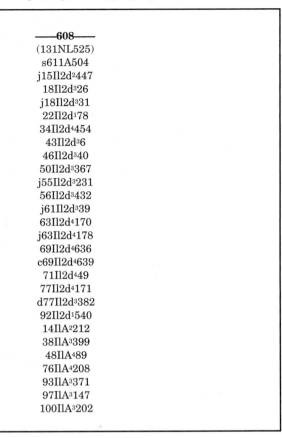

Figure 7–3 *Shepard's* citations for *Nudd.* Reprinted with the permission of McGraw-Hill.

federal court decisions
federal rules decisions
special topical decisions, including (though not limited to)
    West's® Military Law Reporter
    West's Education Law Reporter

In addition, there are Shepard's volumes for statutes, federal regulations, and law review and journal articles. Finally, McGraw-Hill now publishes volumes called **Case Name Citators,** which list cases citations alphabetically by plaintiff and defendant names, so the legal researcher wishing to locate a case (when she knows only one party name) can quickly and easily locate the case.

Shepard's History Codes	
a	Case affirmed on appeal
cc	Connected case, different cases raising same issue
m	Case modified on appeal
r	Case reversed on appeal
s	Same case earlier decided
v	Case vacated on appeal
cert. den.	Petition for certiorari denied
cert. dis.	Petition for certiorari dismissed
reh. den.	Rehearing denied
reh. dis.	Rehearing dismissed
app. pendg.	Appeal pending
Shepard's Treatment Codes	
c	Later case criticized cited case
f	Later case followed cited case
d	Later case distinguished cited case
h	Later case harmonized cited case
j	Case cited in dissenting opinion
L	Later case limited cited case
o	Later case overruled cited case
q	Later case questioned cited case

Figure 7–4 Important *Shepard's* history and treatment codes.

Shepard's Citations are often multiple volumes. For instance, *Shepard's Federal Citations* is a set of books containing citations for federal circuit court cases. The *Shepard's* volumes are sequential, each covering a range of federal case reporters, the reporter volumes included in each *Shepard's* volume are listed on the volume spine. The twenty-*one Shepard's Federal Citations* volumes are divided as shown in Figure 7–5.

Citations in *Shepard's* are arranged numerically by the volume and page numbers of the **cited material**. Thus the researcher wishing to verify and update an identified case will look up that case citation in *Shepard's*. Below the citation for the case, the researcher will find the name and date of the case and a list of materials, citing the case. *Shepard's Citations* are updated monthly by red, softbound supplements.

Using *Shepard's Citations* to Update Legal Research: An Example

Assume a researcher wishes to use *Shepard's Citations* to update and check the validity[4] of *Turner v. South-Western City Sch. Dist.*, 82 F. Supp. 2d 757 (S.D. Ohio 1999), one of the cases she located in Victor's case. She would begin by locating the relevant *Shepard's* volumes. These are listed on the most recent supplement cover. For *Turner*,

Shepard's Volume	Federal Reporter Volumes Covered
1	1-97 F.
2	98-237 F.
3	238-300 F.; 1-40 F.2d
4	41-116 F.2d
5	117-193 F.2d
6	192-283 F.2d
7	284-372 F.2d
8	373-441 F.2d
9	442-506 F.2d
10	507-575 F.2d
11	576-654 F.2d
12	655-736 F.2d
13	737-813 F.2d
14	814-902 F.2d
15	903-999 F.2d; 1-49 F.3d
16	1-152 F.Supp.
17	153-313 F.Supp
18	314-446 F.Supp
19	447-609 F.Supp
20	610-809 F.Supp
21	810-877 F.Supp 1-159 Federal Rules Decisions; 1-231 Federal Claims Rptr; 1-26 Claims Court Rptr; 27-32 Court of Claims Rptr

Figure 7–5 *Shepard's Federal Citations* volumes.

she determines she needs to look at the hardbound volumes of the *Federal Citations*, the red hardbound supplement that updates *Shepard's Federal Citations* to 1996, and the most recent red, softbound supplement that updates *Shepard's Federal Citations* from 1996 to the present. At the top of a page in every *Shepard's* volume, the researcher will see the name of the reporter and the case volume being Shepardized. Using this, the researcher locates the volume (82) and reporter (F. Supp. 2d) for her citation in each volume of *Shepard's*.

Under the volume and reporter name on each page are six columns of citations divided by bold numbers, as shown in Figure 7–6. These numbers represent the starting pages for decisions in that volume. In *Turner*, that is page 757. Under the starting page number is the case name. Under the case name are the citations to any cases that have cited the case being Shepardized. From the pages of *Shepard's Federal Citations*, the researcher learns that only one other case has cited *Turner*, a case from the 11th circuit that appears at 93 F. Supp. 2d 1234.[5]

FEDERAL SUPPLEMENT, 2d SERIES   Vol. 82

—612—	2000USDist.	[LX12758	98FS2d1029	2000	2000USDist
Christmon v	[LX9355	Cir. 2	c) 98FS2d1030	m)	[LX10509
Allstate Ins.	—723—	212F3d996	—997—	2000USDist	105FS2d1336
Co.	Ruffin-	—879—	3M v Beautone	[LX10129	—1354—
2000	Steinback v De	United States	Specialties, Co.	m) 103FS2d	Gill v Kostroff
57FS2d380	Passe	ex rel. Hindi v	2000	[1233	2000
Cir. 5	2000	Warden of	(53PQ2d1878)	—1190—	Cir. 11
97FS2d773	(53PQ2d1823)	McHenry	—1012—	Beerheide v	2000BankrLX
—616—	s) 2000USDist	County Jail	K&K Jump	Suthers	[1022
Jim Sowell	[LX10468	2000	Start/	2000	—1366—
Constr. Co. v	cc) 17FS2d699	cc) 291IlA1051	Chargers, Inc.	s) 997FS1405	Wolf v Coca-
City of Coppell	—757—	cc) 684NL1089	v Schumacher	—1220—	Cola Co.
1998	Turner v	—892—	Elec. Corp.	Aetna Health	1998
i) 2000USDist	South-Western	Perry v	2000	Mgmt. v Mid-	a) 200F3d1337
[LX9869	City Sch. Dist.	Community	s) 98FS2d1108	America	—1379—
g) 2000USDist	1999	Action Servs.	—1024—	Health	Agricredit
[LX9869	Cir. 11	2000	United States	Network	Acceptance,
s) 61FS2d542	93FS2d1234	Cir. 7	v Guarino	2000	LLC v Hendrix
Cir. 5	—788—	2000USDist	1999	s) 975FS1382	2000
f) 27FS2d942	United States	[LX7747	N J	—1279—	s) 32FS2d1361
—626—	Fire Ins. Co. v	—901—	332NJS468	Wright v	
Cricchio v	Vanderbilt	Payton v Rush-	f) 332NJS470	Circuit City	**Vol. 83**
Dyckman	Univ.	Presbyterian	753A2d1188	Stores, Inc.	
2000	2000	St. Luke's	f) 753A2d1189	2000	—1—
Cir. 5	cc) 18FS2d786	Med. Ctr.	—1098—	Cir. 5	Davis v
2000USDist	cc) 174FRD396	2000	In re	2000USDist	Latschar
[LX7769	—801—	s) 184F3d623	Indefinite	[LX12174	1998
—631—	McDonald's	Cir. 7	Detention	Cir. 8	a) 202F3d359
Herman v	Corp. v Shop	96FS2d812	Cases	2000USDist	Cir. DC
Tyson Foods,	At Home, Inc.	—911—	2000	[LX12125	42FS2d15
Inc.	2000	Love v Cook	Cir. 9	—1288—	—15—
2000	(53PQ2d1959)	County	208F3d1121	Barron v	Butera v
Cir. 4	—817—	2000	—1105—	Trans Union	District of
87FS2d¹460	Chang v TVA	Cir. 7	Speaker v	Corp.	Columbia
162ALRF581n	1999	2000USDist	County of San	2000	1999
—667—	Cir. 8	[LX11444	Bernardino	Cir. 5	s) 83FS2d25
Rock Bit Int'l,	2000USDist	—936—	2000	d) 194FRD252	Cir. 8
Inc. v Smith	[LX13615	United States	Cir. 2	—1326—	2000USApp
Int'l, Inc.	—823—	v Baker	2000USDist	Johnson v	[LX17760
1999	Christman v	1999	[LX9390	GMC	—25—
s) 82FS2d677	Brauvin	a) 2000USApp	194FRD445	1997	Butera v
—677—	Realty	[LX23568	—1121—	Cir. 11	District of
Rock Bit Int'l,	Advisors	—945—	Young Hak	96FS2d1356	Columbia
Inc. v Smith	1998	United States	Song v INS	—1331—	1999
Int'l, Inc.	s) 134F3d374	v McNeal	2000	Federal Ins.	s) 83FS2d15
1999	s) 185FRD251	2000	Cir. 9	Co. v Bill	Cir. 7
s) 82FS2d667	—844—	Cir. 7	2000USApp	Harbert	2000USDist
—689—	Kendall-	2000USDist	[LX22626	Constr. Co.	[LX9523
Lowery v	Jackson	[LX7750	—1151—	1999	Cir. DC
University of	Winery, Ltd. v	—966—	Kapiolani	Cir. 2	2000USDist
Houston	Branson	Bailey v	Med. Ctr. for	f) 2000USDist	[LX13429
2000	2000	Canan	Women &	[LX10065	—42—
s) 50FS2d648	Cir. 2	2000	Children v	f) 106FS2d513	Proriver, Inc. v
Cir. 5	f) 2000USDist	Cir. 7	Hawaii	Cir. 11	Red River

Figure 7–6 *Shepard's* citations for *Turner v. South-Western Sch. Dist.* Reprinted with the permission of Reed.

Verifying and Updating Research Using CALRs

Among the services CALRs provide are the simple, thorough, and current verification of research results. One method common to all CALRs, whether on-line services or CD-ROMs, is **using the CALR as a citator**, to update legal materials. For instance, suppose you wish to determine whether *Turner v. South-Western City Sch. Dist.* has been altered or overruled by later cases. One way to determine that information is to search for later cases mentioning *Turner*. A sample Westlaw terms and connectors CALR search for cases citing *Turner* might appear as follows:

Turner /s (South /5 School)

Lexis and Westlaw have automated the process of drafting an appropriate search query based on the document name and citation (i.e., **QuickCite®** on Westlaw, **Lexcite®** on LEXIS), when the researcher requests that service.

McGraw-Hill makes *Shepard's Citations* available on CD-ROM for automated citation checking. LEXIS offers on-line Shepardizing that consolidates all *Shepard's* volumes and supplements and decodes Shepard's history and treatment codes. Also, CALR services offer additional citator services that trace the previous and subsequent history of documents (**AutoCite®**) and update *Shepard's*. Finally, the on-line services offer automatic citation checking programs, which search for citations in legal memos and documents and automatically check those citations through one or more CALR citators (e.g., **WestCheck®**, **CheckCite™**).

In addition, Westlaw has introduced a new citation service (**KeyCite**) based on its databases and its topic and key numbering research technique. KeyCite provides the history of a case and retrieves all current and comprehensive citing references. It is an easy-to-use service that goes beyond current citation services to provide the researcher with information needed to determine the validity of research and find additional useful authority. It provides the full text of headnotes from a case so that the researcher can research relevant issues directly from KeyCite. KeyCite alerts the researcher to the reliability of research results by providing status flags (red status flag = material has been reversed, overruled, repealed, or reversed; yellow status flag = caution, material may have been called into question or pending legislation may affect validity). Useful information about the depth of discussion is also available through the use of stars (more stars = deeper discussion: 4 stars = examined, 3 stars = discussed; 2 stars = cited; 1 star = mentioned).

KeyCite sorts citations by topic and key number so that the researcher can quickly find cases that support his or her position by jumping to the full text of a relevant headnote or from a headnote to the full case text on Westlaw. And, because key numbers group similar cases, the researcher can be confident that s/he has not missed important cases.

Finally, a Table of Authorities service operates as a mirror image of KeyCite. It displays a list of all cited cases and includes status flags for cases having negative authority. Thus, the Table of Authorities service can help the researcher uncover hidden weaknesses in the opponent's cited cases even when there is no negative history in KeyCite.

CALR updating techniques duplicate digest and *Shepard's* verification techniques. However, although updating research through a CD-ROM is included in the CD-ROM subscription price, because the CD-ROMs are never completely up-to-date, it is impossible for the researcher to be certain her research is current using only CD-ROM updating and verification techniques. On the other hand, on-line services updating is the most up-to-date method of verifying research, because it includes cases and materials added within days or hours of release. However, CALR service updating techniques are expensive. For instance, a complete updating and verification process on **Westlaw** involves KeyCite and searching for more recent relevant cases. Most CALR services charge a flat rate (commonly $2–3) for each citator. Thus, updating and verifying a single citation on LEXIS will cost $4.00 (for AutoCite, *Shepard's* and LexCite) plus search costs (for LexCite). Unless you are verifying only a few citations, on-line updating and verification is an expensive (though very convenient) process.

Integrating Digest, Shepard's, and CALR Citators

Students often ask, if CALRs are not available, whether to use *Shepard's* or the digest methods to update their research. Both *Shepard's* and digest updating techniques are incomplete. *Shepard's* relies on judges to cite earlier relevant cases in later opinions; a judge overruling or modifying an earlier line of cases may cite only one or a few of those earlier cases and may miss citing the very case the researcher wishes to check. Likewise, digesting depends on a publishing editor identifying and properly categorizing a legal issue; a slight variation in assigning a topic and key number may well result in a missed critical case. To compensate for each technique's weakness, I recommend that students use both methods of updating their research, though at different times during their research.

During initial legal research, researchers often use the digest method to identify recent, relevant cases. Once the researcher identifies relevant materials, she then Shepardizes those materials to ensure that they have not been called into question or overruled. Then, when all research is complete and the researcher knows the materials she intends to use in her analysis, she should once again Shepardize those materials thoroughly and carefully. See Figure 7–7 for the steps in Shepardizing research material.

1. Note the full citation for the material relied on. Note headnote numbers of headnotes relevant to the research issue.
2. Choose the Shepard's volumes, including hard and softbound volumes listed on the most recent supplement cover.
3. Look up the citation in all relevant Shepard's volumes, oldest to newest.
4. Note the following relevant citations:
   a. Citations containing a relevant headnote number
   b. Citations indicating that they reverse (Shepard's code "r"), vacate ("v"), overrule ("o"), criticize ("c"), distinguish ("d"), or modify ("m") the cited case and cases indicating that further appellate review has been granted.
   c. Citations with no headnote, history, or treatment code.
5. Analyze those noted cases to determine how they affect the research and their usefulness in the legal analysis.

Figure 7–7 Steps in Shepardizing Found Research Material

Review Questions

1. Name three methods of updating research. When should each method be used?
2. Why is it important to update legal research?
3. What are *Shepard's Citations*?
4. Name some kinds of citations updated by Shepard's.
5. List the volumes of *Shepard's Federal Citations*.
6. List the steps in Shepardizing a case.
7. List some features of *Shepard's Citations*.
8. When should you Shepardize research material?
9. How current is *Shepard's Citations* in print? On-line?
10. What are legal digests?
11. How can digests be used to update research?
12. What is a digest "closing table?"
13. What is a "mini-digest?"
14. List the steps in updating research using digests to update research.
15. When should you use digests and mini-digests to update research?
16. Is it necessary to both Shepardize and update through digests? Why?
17. How can CALR be used to update legal research?
18. How does CALR updating differ from "book" updating?
19. How is CALR updating similar to "book" updating?
20. Should CALR updating be used instead of or in addition to "book" updating?

Exercise

1. Use *Shepard's* and any necessary case reporters to answer the following question: Shepardize a state statute that interests you. Has that statute been amended or repealed? What gave you that answer?

2. Use the digests and any necessary case reporters to answer the following questions.

   a. Your client is the leader of a gang that recently murdered a member of a rival gang. You would like to know if the gang leader can be charged as a joint venturer in the murder even if he did not participate in the crime. Using the topic Homicide, ☞ 234 (4), give the correct citation for the recent court opinions bearing on that issue.

   b. Your clients are gay men living together in a long-term committed relationship. They wish to adopt a child and want to know if a homosexual couple can petition for adoption of a child. Using the topic Adoption, ☞ 4, give the correct citation for recent court opinions bearing on that issue.

3. Update the issues in excises 1 and 2 using CALR services and products. Were your results any different? How were they different? Why were they different?

Glossary

Advance sheets: A paperback pamphlet containing very recent decisions not yet officially (or unofficially) bound.

AutoCite: Reed's automated service for retrieving and validating cited material.

Case Name Citator: Volumes listing cases alphabetically by plaintiff and defendant name.

Cited material: Material whose validity and currentness the researcher wishes to check.

Citing material: More recent material citing and cited material.

Closing Table: Chart in digest supplements indicating the most current reporter volume available when supplement was published.

Headnote number: One of a series of numbers identifying headnotes to a case.

History: Treatment of the case on appeal and/or remand.

LexCite: Reed's CALR tool for gathering the previous and subsequent history of cited material.

Mini-digests: Short digests in case reporters digesting only decisions appearing in that volume.

QuickCite: West's automated system for using Westlaw as a citator.

Research Verification: Checking the validity of documents relevant to an issue.

Shepardizing®: Checking the validity of research materials through *Shepard's Citations.*

Shepard's supplements: Red softbound volumes updating bound *Shepard's Citations.*

Shepard's Citations: Listings of the citations of materials citing earlier legal materials.

Shepard's history codes: Code letters describing a cited document's history before and after its existence.

Shepard's treatment codes: Code letters describing a document's treatment by other, more recent materials.

Topic and Key Number: Topic and subtopic indicator assigned to decided legal issues.

Treatment: The way later research materials use earlier materials.

Update: Find the most recent references for a legal issue.

Using the CALR as a citator: Using a CALR to search for subsequent references to a cited document.

WestCheck: West Group's automated service for retrieving and validating cited material.

Notes

[1]Due in no small part to the vision of John West and Frank Shepard, late nineteenth-century legal research pioneers.

[2]The *Nudd* example is found in *How to Shepardize: Your Guide to Complete Legal Research through Shepard's Citations* (McGraw-Hill, 1993).

[3]Shepard's citations are abbreviated to save space, so that citations in *Shepard's* appear slightly different than *Bluebook* citations.

[4]This process is also known as **"Shepardizing"** the case.

[5]Note that if later federal cases do not cite *Turner* no entry will appear for volume 82, page 757 in the *Shepard's* supplements.

CHAPTER 8

Understanding the Results of Legal Research: Reading the Law

Chapter Outline

Learning Objectives

Upon completing this chapter, the student should be able to

* Name two types of written law
* Explain the goal in interpreting a statute
* Describe the structure of a typical statute and the uses of each part in interpreting the statute
* List some things to consider in interpreting a statute
* List and explain some rules of statutory construction
* Explain what a case brief is
* Explain why is it important to brief appellate court decisions
* Explain what it means to say that a "published appellate decision signals some change in the law"
* List and explain the parts of a good case brief
* List some helpful hints in reading the law

Introduction

Just as research was a matter of learning the purpose and contents of various legal materials and then finding particular materials in a logical series of steps, understanding the results of the research, reading and understanding the law, is also logical. This chapter explains the method of law and describes a beginning method of reading and understanding the law. Just like legal research, however, legal interpretation is most difficult initially; with practice and experience, it becomes much easier.

Written law is of two types: (1) legislation (statutes, executive regulations, orders, and the like), written to direct future conduct, and (2) adjudication (both agency and court decisions), which applies existing legal principles to past conduct.

Reading the Law: Statutes

The goal in reading a statute is to determine the legislature's intent in drafting the statute and predict the outcome of a case not expressly addressed by the statute.

Structure of Statutes

Law, whether legislation or adjudication, has structure and form. Understanding that structure and form aids in its interpretation. Consider the excerpt from the Ohio Education Act shown in Figure 8–1.

In reading and interpreting a statute, look at its various parts.

1. The *Title of the Statute.* Often the **statutory title** (in this case, "Permanent exclusion of pupils; revocation; probationary admission" and "Suspension, expulsion, and removal from premises") provides important information about the legislature's intent in enacting the law.
2. *The Statute's Preamble.* The preamble to legislation is another important indication of the legislature's intent in passing the law. As well, the **statutory preamble** often explains its audience and the conduct it requires, permits, or prohibits. For instance, the Ohio Constitution, in Art. I, § 7, states that the Ohio Education Act was enacted to "encourage schools and the means of instruction."
3. *The Language of the Statute.* The language of the statute is its primary source of interpretation. It is, after all, the legislature's statement of what the law is.
4. *Other Statutory Stuff.* Additionally, various publishers provide statutory annotations, which direct the reader to other resources helpful to interpreting the statute. Some of these annotations include cross-references to other relevant statutes, to relevant encyclopedia and law review/journal references, and to cases interpreting the statute.

Interpretation of Statutes

Statutory interpretation is a primary function of courts. The following excerpt from *McBoyle v. United States*, 283 U.S. 25, (1931) is an example of the United States

(A) The superintendent of public instruction, pursuant to this section and the adjudication procedures of section 3301.121 of the Revised Code, may issue an adjudication order that permanently excludes a pupil from attending any of the public schools of this state if the pupil is convicted of, or adjudicated a delinquent child for, committing, <u>when the pupil was sixteen years of age or older</u>, an act that would be a criminal offense if committed by an adult and if the act is any of the following:

(1) A violation of section 2923.122 of the Revised Code;

(2) A violation of section 2923.12 of the Revised Code, of a substantially similar municipal ordinance, or of section 2925.03 of the Revised Code that was committed on property owned or controlled by, or at an activity held under the auspices of, a board of education of a city, local, exempted village, or joint vocational school district;

(3) A violation of section 2925.11 of the Revised Code, other than a violation of that section that would be a minor drug possession offense, that was committed on property owned or controlled by, or at an activity held under the auspices of, the board of education of a city, local, exempted village, or joint vocational school district;

(4) A violation of section 2903.01, 2903.02, 2903.03, 2903.04, 2903.11, 2903.12, 2907.02, or 2907.05 or of former section 2907.12 of the Revised Code that was committed on property owned or controlled by, or at an activity held under the auspices of, a board of education of a city, local, exempted village, or joint vocational school district, if the victim at the time of the commission of the act was an employee of that board of education;

(5) Complicity in any violation described in division (A)(1), (2), (3), or (4) of this section that was alleged to have been committed in the manner described in division (A)(1), (2), (3), or (4) of this section, regardless of whether the act of complicity was committed on property owned or controlled by, or at an activity held under the auspices of, a board of education of a city, local, exempted village, or joint vocational school district.

Figure 8–1 Ohio Revised Code § 3313.662 Permanent exclusion of pupils; revocation; probationary admission.

Supreme Court's interpretation of the National Motor Vehicle Theft Act (NMVTA), which prohibited interstate transportation of known stolen motor vehicles. McBoyle was convicted of violating the NMVTA when he transported a known stolen airplane from Illinois to Oklahoma. In determining whether the statute applied to interstate transportation of stolen airplanes, the Court made the decision excerpted in Figure 8–2.

Notice how, in interpreting the statute, the court looked at (1) the plain language of the statute, (2) the definition of "motor vehicle," (3) what the statute did not say, (4) the use of "motor vehicle" in other statutes, and (5) a rule or **canon of statutory construction** that criminal statutes be strictly interpreted, that is, not

... [The NMVTA] provides: 'Sec. 2. That when used in this Act: (a) The term 'motor vehicle' shall include an automobile, automobile truck, automobile wagon, motor cycle, or any other self-propelled vehicle not designed for running on rails. * * * Sec. 3. That whoever shall transport or cause to be transported in interstate or foreign commerce a motor vehicle, knowing the same to have been stolen, shall be punished by a fine of not more than $5,000, or by imprisonment of not more than five years, or both.'

Section 2 defines the motor vehicles of which the transportation in interstate commerce is punished in § 3. The question is the meaning of the word 'vehicle' in the phrase 'any other self-propelled vehicle not designed for running on rails.' No doubt etymologically it is possible to use the word to signify a conveyance working on land, water or air, and sometimes legislation extends the use in that direction, e. g., land and air, water being separately provided for, in the Tariff Act ... 19 USCA § 231(b). But in everyday speech 'vehicle' calls up the picture of a thing moving on land. Thus ... the NMVTA intended, the Government suggests, rather to enlarge than to restrict the definition, vehicle includes every contrivance capable of being used 'as a means of transportation on land.' So here, the phrase under discussion calls up the popular picture. For after including automobile truck, automobile wagon and motor cycle, the words 'any other self-propelled vehicle not designed for running on rails' still indicate that a vehicle in the popular sense, that is a vehicle running on land is the theme. It is a vehicle that runs, not something, not commonly called a vehicle that flies. Airplanes were well known in 1919 when this statute was passed, but it is admitted that they were not mentioned in the reports or in the debates in Congress. It is impossible to read words that so carefully enumerate the different forms of motor vehicles and have no reference of any kind to aircraft, as including airplanes under a term that usage more and more precisely confines to a different class. The counsel for the petitioner have shown that the phraseology of the statute as to motor vehicles follows that of earlier statutes of Connecticut, Delaware, Ohio, Michigan and Missouri, not to mention the late Regulations of Traffic for the District of Columbia, none of which can be supposed to leave the earth.

Although it is not likely that a criminal will carefully consider the text of the law before he murders or steals, it is reasonable that a fair warning should be given to the world in language that the common world will understand, of what the law intends to do if a certain line is passed. To make the warning fair, so far as possible the line should be clear. When a rule of conduct is laid down in words that evoke in the common mind only the picture of vehicles moving on land, the statute should not be extended to aircraft simply because it may seem to us that a similar policy applies, or upon the speculation that if the legislature had thought of it, very likely the picture of vehicles moving on land.

Figure 8–2 Excerpt from McBoyle v. United States.

expanded beyond their express language. All of these are common aids to determining the meaning of legislation.

Aids to Statutory Interpretation

Just as the court did in analyzing the Federal Motor Vehicle Theft Act in the *McBoyle* case, Figure 8–3 lists a number of useful rules to consider and apply whenever interpreting a statute.

1. plain language of the statute
2. definitions — dictionary and statutory
3. what the statute doesn't say
4. how the language is used elsewhere in the statute or in other statutes
5. regulations — the agency rules interpreting the statute
6. legislative history and intent
7. canons of statutory construction

Figure 8–3 Aids to statutory interpretation.

Another Example of Statutory Construction

Applying *McBoyle* principles (and other relevant aids to statutory construction), let's determine whether Vincent can be permanently expelled from school.

Legislative History and Intent. From the title and preamble to the Ohio Education Act, the statute was enacted to "encourage schools and the means of education," and if need be, to expel students to accomplish that goal.

The Plain Language of the Statute. In Vincent's case, the relevant statutory language, Ohio Rev. Cod Ann. § 3313.662 (West Group®, 1999) says that a student can be expelled from school under the circumstances given in Figure 8–1.

As Vincent is not yet 16, he does not meet one of the **preconditions** for being permanently excluded from school; therefore, the school district's attempt to permanently expel him will fail. In this case, however, it is important to determine whether Vincent, as a 14-year-old, might be otherwise suspended or expelled from school. Another section of the Ohio Education Act, shown in Figure 8–4, may be helpful.

As is common with statutes, Ohio Rev. Code Ann. § 3313.66 (West® 1996) sets out preconditions or **elements** that must be satisfied before Vincent can be expelled. To expel Vincent, the school district must show three things:

1. Vincent brought a firearm to school,
    and
2. the superintendent gave Vincent and his parents
   three days' written notice of the intention to expel Vincent
   and
3. an opportunity to appear in person to challenge the reasons for the
   intended expulsion
   or
   otherwise explain Vincent's behavior

Some elements must be met in all situations (usually separated by an express or implied *and*), other elements may be met in different ways (separated by *or*). To

(B)(1) Except as provided under division (B)(2), (3), or (4) of this section, the superintendent of schools of a city, exempted village, or local school district may expel a pupil from school for a period not to exceed the greater of eighty school days or the number of school days remaining in the semester or term in which the incident that gives rise to the expulsion takes place, unless the expulsion is extended pursuant to division (F) of this section. If at the time an expulsion is imposed there are fewer than eighty school days remaining in the school year in which the incident that gives rise to the expulsion takes place, the superintendent may apply any remaining part or all of the period of the expulsion to the following school year.

(2)(a) Unless a pupil is permanently excluded pursuant to section 3313.662 of the Revised Code, the superintendent of schools of a city, exempted village, or local school district shall expel a pupil from school for a period of one year for bringing a firearm to a school operated by the board of education of the district or onto any other property owned or controlled by the board, except that the superintendent may reduce this requirement on a case-by-case basis in accordance with the policy adopted by the board under section 3313.661 of the Revised Code.

(b) The superintendent of schools of a city, exempted village, or local school district may expel a pupil from school for a period of one year for bringing a firearm to an interscholastic competition, an extracurricular event, or any other school program or activity that is not located in a school or on property that is owned or controlled by the district. The superintendent may reduce this disciplinary action on a case-by-case basis in accordance with the policy adopted by the board under section 3313.661 of the Revised Code.

(c) Any expulsion pursuant to division (B)(2) of this section shall extend, as necessary, into the school year following the school year in which the incident that gives rise to the expulsion takes place. As used in this division, "firearm" has the same meaning as provided pursuant to the "Gun-Free Schools Act of 1994," 108 Stat. 270, 20 U.S.C. 8001(a)(2).

(3) The board of education of a city, exempted village, or local school district may adopt a resolution authorizing the superintendent of schools to expel a pupil from school for a period not to exceed one year for bringing a knife to a school operated by the board, onto any other property owned or controlled by the board, or to an interscholastic competition, an extracurricular event, or any other program or activity sponsored by the school district or in which the district is a participant, or for possessing a firearm or knife at a school, on any other property owned or controlled by the board, or at an interscholastic competition, an extracurricular event, or any other school program or activity, which firearm or knife was initially brought onto school board property by another person. The resolution may authorize the superintendent to extend such an expulsion, as necessary, into the school year following the school year in which the incident that gives rise to the expulsion takes place.

(4) The board of education of a city, exempted village, or local school district may adopt a resolution establishing a policy under section 3313.661 of

Figure 8–4 Ohio Revised Code § 3313.66 Suspension, expulsion, and removal from premises. From *Baldwin's Ohio Revised Code Annotated*®; reprinted with the permission of West Group.

the Revised Code that authorizes the superintendent of schools to expel a pupil from school for a period not to exceed one year for committing an act that is a criminal offense when committed by an adult and that results in serious physical harm to persons as defined in division (A)(5) of section 2901.01 of the Revised Code or serious physical harm to property as defined in division (A)(6) of section 2901.01 of the Revised Code while the pupil is at school, on any other property owned or controlled by the board, or at an interscholastic competition, an extracurricular event, or any other school program or activity. Any expulsion under this division shall extend, as necessary, into the school year following the school year in which the incident that gives rise to the expulsion takes place.

(5) No pupil shall be expelled under division (B)(1), (2), (3), or (4) of this section unless, prior to the pupil's expulsion, the superintendent does both of the following:

(a) Gives the pupil and the pupil's parent, guardian, or custodian written notice of the intention to expel the pupil;

(b) Provides the pupil and the pupil's parent, guardian, custodian, or representative an opportunity to appear in person before the superintendent or the superintendent's designee to challenge the reasons for the intended expulsion or otherwise to explain the pupil's actions. The notice required in this division shall include the reasons for the intended expulsion, notification of the opportunity of the pupil and the pupil's parent, guardian, custodian, or representative to appear before the superintendent or the superintendent's designee to challenge the reasons for the intended expulsion or otherwise to explain the pupil's action, and notification of the time and place to appear. The time to appear shall not be earlier than three nor later than five school days after the notice is given, unless the superintendent grants an extension of time at the request of the pupil or the pupil's parent, guardian, custodian, or representative. If an extension is granted after giving the original notice, the superintendent shall notify the pupil and the pupil's parent, guardian, custodian, or representative of the new time and place to appear. If the proposed expulsion is based on a violation listed in division (A) of section 3313.662 of the Revised Code and if the pupil is sixteen years of age or older, the notice shall include a statement that the superintendent may seek to permanently exclude the pupil if the pupil is convicted of or adjudicated a delinquent child for that violation.

(6) A superintendent of schools of a city, exempted village, or local school district shall initiate expulsion proceedings pursuant to this section with respect to any pupil who has committed an act warranting expulsion under the district's policy regarding expulsion even if the pupil has withdrawn from school for any reason after the incident that gives rise to the hearing but prior to the hearing or decision to impose the expulsion. If, following the hearing, the pupil would have been expelled for a period of time had the pupil still been enrolled in the school, the expulsion shall be imposed for the same length of time as on a pupil who has not withdrawn from the school.

Figure 8–4 (continued)

meet the statutory requirements, the school district must therefore show that it met all required elements and necessary alternative elements; that is, that Vincent possessed a firearm in school and that it (1) gave Vincent and his parents three days' written notice of a hearing to determine whether to expel Vincent and (2) provided Vincent and his parents the opportunity to appear in person before the superintendent "to challenge the reasons for the intended expulsion [or] otherwise to explain [Vincent's] actions."

It is clear that the superintendent did not properly expel Vincent, as apparently the attempted "expulsion" occurred the same day as the pipe-bomb incident, so Vincent and his parents did not have the required three days' notice before appearing for a hearing. Nevertheless, most courts would consider the "three-day notice" requirement as giving Vincent and his parents an opportunity to prepare for the hearing, rather than as being a protected substantive right. That procedural infirmity would thus be remediable by allowing Vincent and his parents three days' notice before they need appear and respond to the charges. In the meantime, Vincent could be suspended from school (which does not require notice and a hearing, § 3313.66(A)(1)) for a long enough period to give Vincent and his parents an opportunity to prepare for their formal hearing. At issue, nevertheless, is whether Vincent did the following:

    a. *possessed*
    b. a *firearm* at school

As § 3313.66 does not specifically address those issues, other available materials may help.

Possess. Merriam-Webster's Collegiate Dictionary defines "possess" as holding, carrying, or being in control of. Thus, the definition suggests that to bring something, you must carry it or at least transport it in some fashion. Vincent had no part in bringing the pipe bombs to school. Indeed, had the legislature wished to punish Vincent's behavior, it would have been a small matter to have inserted "buy" or "receive" or "possess" in the statute.

Firearm. Section 3313.66 (B)(2) says "'firearm' has the same meaning as provided in the 'Gun-Free Schools Act of 1994,' . . . 20 U.S.C. [8921]."

Other statutory sections. The Gun-Free Schools Act defines a "firearm" as such term is defined in section 921 of Title 18, as shown in Figure 8–5.

What the statute doesn't say. Significantly, neither the Ohio Education Act nor the Federal Gun-Free Schools Act mentions "pipe bombs." Moreover, cases interpreting those statutes do not include pipe bombs as firearms.

Regulations. Often in passing legislation, the legislature may delegate authority to apply and enforce the legislation to a new or existing executive agency. The agency may enact rules or regulations to fill the gaps left by the legislature. While

---

The term "firearm" means (A) any weapon (including a starter gun) which will or is designed to or may readily be converted to expel a projectile by the action of an explosive; (B) the frame or receiver of any such weapon; (C) any firearm muffler or firearm silencer; or (D) any destructive device. Such term does not include an antique firearm.
. . . .

(4) The term "destructive device" means—

  (A) any explosive, incendiary, or poison gas—

    (i) bomb,

    (ii) grenade,

    (iii) rocket having a propellant charge of more than four ounces,

    (iv) missile having an explosive or incendiary charge of more than one- quarter ounce,

    (v) mine, or

    (vi) device similar to any of the devices described in the preceding clauses;

  (B) any type of weapon (other than a shotgun or a shotgun shell which the Secretary finds is generally recognized as particularly suitable for sporting purposes) by whatever name known which will, or which may be readily converted to, expel a projectile by the action of an explosive or other propellant, and which has any barrel with a bore of more than one-half inch in diameter; and

  (C) any combination of parts either designed or intended for use in converting any device into any destructive device described in subparagraph (A) or (B) and from which a destructive device may be readily assembled.

The term "destructive device" shall not include any device which is neither designed nor redesigned for use as a weapon; any device, although originally designed for use as a weapon, which is redesigned for use as a signaling, pyrotechnic, line throwing, safety, or similar device; surplus ordnance sold, loaned, or given by the Secretary of the Army pursuant to the provisions of section 4684(2), 4685, or 4686 of title 10; or any other device which the Secretary of the Treasury finds is not likely to be used as a weapon, is an antique, or is a rifle which the owner intends to use solely for sporting, recreational or cultural purposes.

Figure 8–5 Definition of "firearm" from 20 U.S.C. 921.

those agency rules or regulations are themselves a form of legislation subject to "statutory" construction, they may provide important clues to the statutes they implement. For instance, 27 CFR, § 178.11 (April 9, 1999) defines a "firearm" as "[A]ny weapon, including a starter gun, which will or is designed to or may readily be converted to expel a projectile by the action of an explosive; the frame or receiver of any such weapon; any firearm muffler or firearm silencer; or any destructive device" and § 47.11 of the same chapter defines "[F]irearms, a weapon, and all components and parts therefor, not over .50 caliber which will or is designed to or may be readily converted to expel a projectile by the action of an explosive." Thus, the regulations seemingly define firearm as a device designed to expel a projectile. It may thus be necessary for the school to demonstrate that a pipe bomb was designed to expel a projectile to expel Vincent under its "weapons" rule.

Canons of Statutory Construction. To those regulations, it may be helpful to apply certain judicially created rules of statutory construction. In *McBoyle v. United States*, 283 U.S. 25 (1931), the Court focused on the construction rule that certain statutes (including criminal, licensing, and statutes **in derogation of** the common law) must not be construed beyond their plain language[1]; this rule may be useful in Vincent's case, for although expulsion from school is not a criminal matter, § 3313.66 relies on a federal criminal statute in defining "firearm;" hence, similar concerns to those of interpreting a criminal law may apply in this non-criminal context. As well, other rules of construction may be useful in interpreting the Act. For instance, the rule of construction **expressio unis est exclusio alternus**, the expression of one context requires denial of other contexts, suggests that Congress' failure to include pipe bombs with other named firearms suggests an intent to exclude a pipe bomb from that definition.

Other, though less relevant to Vincent's situation, rules of construction also include the following:[2]

1. statutes **in pari materia** (related to the same subject) should be read consistently; and
2. **ejusdem generis**, meaning that if a statute specifically enumerates items followed by a catchall phrase (e.g., apples, pears, and other products), the catchall phrase applies only to items in the same class. Thus, the example would be construed to refer only to fruit.

The facts of Vincent's situation suggest that to be expelled, Vincent must have "possessed" at school a "firearm." It appears, from the facts given, that Vincent did not possess a "firearm" at school on the day of the incident.

Reading the Law: Briefing Cases

Like statutes, court decisions have structure and form that aid in their reading and interpretation. Consider again the *McBoyle* case shown in Figure 8–6.

Components of a Court Decision

The *McBoyle* case includes the sections shown in Figure 8–7.

Briefing a Case

A **case brief**, or structured summary, of a court decision summarizes the decision in a particular style so that the researcher can recall and apply the case without

McBOYLE

v.

UNITED STATES.

283 U.S. 25, 51 S.Ct. 340, 71 L.Ed. 816 (1931)

On Writ of Certiorari to the United States Circuit Court of Appeals for the Tenth Circuit.

William W. McBoyle was convicted of transporting between states an airplane known to have been stolen, judgment being affirmed by the Circuit Court of Appeals (43 F.(2d) 273), and he brings certiorari.

Reversed.

[1] AUTOMOBILES key 341

Airplane held not "motor vehicle" within law relating to transportation in interstate or foreign commerce of motor vehicle knowing the same to have been stolen. National Motor Vehicle Theft Act, 18 U.S.C.A. § 408.

[2] AVIATION key 16

Airplane held not "motor vehicle" within law relating to transportation in interstate or foreign commerce of motor vehicle knowing the same to have been stolen. National Motor Vehicle Theft Act, 18 U.S.C.A. § 408.

[3] AUTOMOBILES key 341

"Vehicle" as used in law relating to transportation of stolen automobiles in interstate or foreign commerce is limited to vehicles running on land. National Motor Vehicle Theft Act, 18 U.S.C.A. §§ 10, 2311-2313.

Mr. Harry F. Brown, of Guthrie, Oki., for petitioner.

The Attorney General and Mr. Claude R. Branch, of Providence, R. I., for the United States.

Mr. Justice HOLMES delivered the opinion of the Court.

The petitioner was convicted of transporting from Ottawa, Illinois, to Guymon, Oklahoma, an airplane that he knew to have been stolen, and was sentenced to serve three years' imprisonment and to pay a fine of $2,000. The judgment was affirmed by the Circuit Court of Appeals for the Tenth Circuit. 43 F.(2d) 273. A writ of certiorari was granted by this Court on the question whether the National Motor Vehicle Theft Act applies to aircraft. . . .That Act provides: 'Sec. 2. That when used in this Act: (a) The term 'motor vehicle' shall include an automobile, automobile truck, automobile wagon, motor cycle, or any other self-propelled vehicle not designed for running on rails. * * * Sec. 3. That whoever shall transport or cause to be transported in interstate or foreign commerce a motor vehicle, knowing the same to have been stolen, shall be punished by a fine of not more than $5,000, or by imprisonment of not more than five years, or both.'

Section 2 defines the motor vehicles of which the transportation in interstate commerce is punished in § 3. The question is the meaning of the word 'vehicle' in the

Figure 8–6 McBoyle v. United States, 283 U.S. 25 (1931).

phrase 'any other self-propelled vehicle not designed for running on rails.' No doubt etymologically it is possible to use the word to signify a conveyance working on land, water or air, and sometimes legislation extends the use in that direction, e. g., land and air, water being separately provided for, in the Tariff Act . . . 19 USCA § 231(b). But in everyday speech 'vehicle' calls up the picture of a thing moving on land. Thus . . . 1 USCA § 4 intended, the Government suggests, rather to enlarge than to restrict the definition, vehicle includes every contrivance capable of being used 'as a means of transportation on land.' And this is repeated, expressly excluding aircraft, in the Tariff Act, . . . 19 USCA § 1401. So here, the phrase under discussion calls up the popular picture. For after including automobile truck, automobile wagon and motor cycle, the words 'any other self-propelled vehicle not designed for running on rails' still indicate that a vehicle in the popular sense, that is a vehicle running on land is the theme. It is a vehicle that runs, not something, not commonly called a vehicle that flies. Airplanes were well known in 1919 when this statute was passed, but it is admitted that they were not mentioned in the reports or in the debates in Congress. It is impossible to read words that so carefully enumerate the different forms of motor vehicles and have no reference of any kind to aircraft, as including airplanes under a term that usage more and more precisely confines to a different class. The counsel for the petitioner have shown that the phraseology of the statute as to motor vehicles follows that of earlier statutes of Connecticut, Delaware, Ohio, Michigan and Missouri, not to mention the late Regulations of Traffic for the District of Columbia, . . . none of which can be supposed to leave the earth.

Although it is not likely that a criminal will carefully consider the text of the law before he murders or steals, it is reasonable that a fair warning should be given to the world in language that the common world will understand, of what the law intends to do if a certain line is passed. To make the warning fair, so far as possible the line should be clear. When a rule of conduct is laid down in words that evoke in the common mind only the picture of vehicles moving on land, the statute should not be extended to aircraft simply because it may seem to us that a similar policy applies, or upon the speculation that if the legislature had thought of it, very likely the picture of vehicles moving on land. United States v. Bhagat Singh Thind, 261 U. S. 204, 209, 43 S. Ct. 338, 67 L. Ed. 616.

Judgment reversed.

Figure 8–6 (continued)

rereading it. A case brief summarizes the elements of a court decision in a sensible and simple manner that ensures full understanding of the court's reasoning and decision-making. It is not uncommon for researchers to brief all cases relevant to their research issue. A good case brief includes the case's factual background, the court's decision and its reasoning.

There are many methods of case briefing, none right or wrong. The key to understanding court decisions is first to understand what court decisions do and do not do. All appellate courts have methods of summarily disposing of cases raising no novel issue of law or a clear error of law. There is, after all, no point in publishing multiple decisions saying the same thing. Therefore, a published appellate decision signals a change in the law, either (1) some new common law, (2) a new

Case Name: *McBoyle v. United States*

Citation: The case citation tells you where to find the case. Some publishers list all places the case can be found (most usually, a publisher will list where, in its own reference materials the case can be found first). Case citations, whether, singular or plurals (so-called parallel citations) follow the same general format:

**Volume # Reporter Name Beginning Page Number
(Court and Decision Date)**

McBoyle's citation, 283 U.S. 25, 51 S.Ct. 340, 71 L.Ed. 816 (1931), tells the researcher that it was decided by the U.S. Supreme Court and can be located in three different Supreme Court reporters: the U.S. (official) reports, the Supreme Court (west) reports, and the Lawyers Edition (Law, Co-op) Supreme Court reports.

Case Synopsis: Often, publishers of cases include a synopsis paragraph, that summarizes the case background, what a lower court decided, who that judge was, and what was decided on appeal. The following is *McBoyle's* case synopsis:

On Writ of Certiorari to the United States Circuit Court of Appeals for the Tenth Circuit.

William W. McBoyle was convicted of transporting between states an airplane known to have been stolen, judgment being affirmed by the Circuit Court of Appeals (43 F.2d 273), and he brings certiorari.

Reversed.

Headnotes: Summaries of individual legal principles stated in the decision. In *McBoyle*, there are three headnotes:

[1] AUTOMOBILES key 341

Airplane held not "motor vehicle" within law relating to transportation in interstate or foreign commerce of motor vehicle knowing the same to have been stolen. National Motor Vehicle Theft Act, 18 U.S.C.A. § 408.

[2] AVIATION key 16

Airplane held not "motor vehicle" within law relating to transportation in interstate or foreign commerce of motor vehicle knowing the same to have been stolen. National Motor Vehicle Theft Act, 18 U.S.C.A. § 408.

[3] AUTOMOBILES key 341

"Vehicle" as used in law relating to transportation of stolen automobiles in interstate or foreign commerce is limited to vehicles running on land. National Motor Vehicle Theft Act, 18 U.S.C.A. §§ 10, 2311-2313.

Attorneys: This is a list of attorneys representing various parties before this court. Occasionally, if different counsels are representing parties on appeal than below, trial attorneys will be mentioned here, as well. In *McBoyle*, the attorneys were:

Figure 8–7 Parts of an appellate case.

Mr. Harry F. Brown, of Guthrie, Oki., for petitioner.

The Attorney General and Mr. Claude R. Branch, of Providence, R. I., for the United States.

Opinion: The opinion section of a reported case begins with the name of the judge writing the decision (in *McBoyle*, Mr. Justice Holmes), and ends with the case order ("Judgment reversed"). This is the actual text of the decision.

Court Order: The court order is the judicial "bottom line." It resolves the case and informs the parties what will next happen. In *McBoyle*, the order "Judgment reversed" tells the parties (and the world) that the court has overturned McBoyle's conviction for violating the NMVTA, and, that the government must set McBoyle free and clear his criminal record of this conviction.

Figure 8–7 (continued)

interpretation of law, (3) a new application of the law, or (4) a reiteration of long past law. The following briefing method focuses on that legal "change."

A good case brief has at least six parts: the case citation, its factual and procedural background, the old rule, the issue being decided, the court's holding, and its reasoning.

Citation: The name of the case, where it is located, and the decision date so that a researcher can quickly find the decision. Include all available parallel citations.

Facts: A summary of case facts — the who did what to whom, when, and where of the case; not the reasons for the events, only the events themselves—and the case procedural history — what the trial court decided, what appellate courts (including this court) decided.

Old Rule: A concise statement of the applicable legal rule before this decision was made. After reading the case at least once, ask whether the court is (1) explaining the law, (2) changing the law, or (3) applying the law. Once you have determined what the court is doing to the law, the old rule is simply the law.

Issue: The issue has three parts: the word "Whether," the facts of the case, and its old rule. Do not adopt the court's statement of issue; prepare the issue from the identified facts and old rule.

Holding: The court's answer to the issue: Yes or No and the facts of the case. Again, do not be misled by the court's statement of its holding; write the holding based on the court's decision.

Reasoning: Once you have identified the facts, rule, issue, and holding in a case, the court's reasoning is all that remains in the decision. The court's reasoning is its explanation for its decision. That reasoning is the best hint to the court's rulings in future similar cases. (Hint: If you are having trouble summarizing the court's reasoning, try summarizing each paragraph of reasoning in a sentence.)

Finally, think critically about the case. Do you agree with the decision? Did the court give the only or the best reasons for its decision? It may be helpful to imagine what the loser might say about the decision or what the court might decide if the next litigant had a similar problem with slightly different facts.

The example shown in Figure 8–8 may help to illustrate a case brief.

See Figure 8–9 for general advice in reading the law.

The following is a brief of the U.S. Supreme Court Case, *McBoyle* v. *United States*:

CITATION: *McBoyle* v. *United States*, 283 U.S. 25, 51 S.Ct. 340, 71 L.Ed. 816 (1931).

Note: Although Bluebook form requires only the official citation of United States Supreme Court decisions (i.e., 283 U.S. 25), when briefing cases, include all parallel citations so you can locate the case in *any* law library.

FACTS: McBoyle transported a known stolen airplane from Illinois to Oklahoma. The trial court convicted McBoyle of violating the NMVTA. Reversed.

Note: Include both substantive facts (first sentence) and procedural facts (last two "sentences"). After briefing a case, return to the statement of facts and add necessary or eliminate unnecessary facts.

OLD RULE: The NMVTA prohibits interstate transportation of stolen motor vehicles, including: automobiles, trucks, wagons motor cycles or other self-propelled vehicles not designed for running on rails.

Note: The case rule is the law before this decision. Write the rule in your own words, unless particular words (particularly statutory words) are important.

ISSUE: *Whether* McBoyle is guilty of violating the *NMVTA which prohibits interstate transportation of stolen motor vehicles, including automobiles, trucks, wagons motor cycles or other self-propelled vehicles not designed for running on rails* when *he transported a known stolen airplane from Illinois to Oklahoma?*

Note: The statement of the issue includes: "Whether," the case rule (the NMVTA), and its facts. This method of issue writing clearly (though not necessarily succinctly) sets out what the court is deciding.

Figure 8–8 A sample case brief.

HOLDING: No. McBoyle did not violate the NMVTA when he transported a known stolen airplane from Illinois to Oklahoma.

Note: The holding, which includes: Yes/No and a restatement of the case facts, answers the question asked in the issue.

REASONING: The NMVTA defines the motor vehicles as "a self-propelled vehicle not designed for running on rails." While it is possible to use the word to mean a land, water or air vehicle, see, e.g., the Tariff Act, 19 USCA § 231(b), in everyday speech 'vehicle' suggests a thing moving on land. While the NMVTA includes every contrivance capable of being used "as a means of transportation on land," in the context of this statute, which first describes a motor vehicle as automobiles, trucks, wagons, motor cycles or other self-propelled vehicles not designed for running on rails suggests land-running vehicles. Airplanes were well known in 1919 when this statute was passed, but were not mentioned in congressional reports or debates. Statutes of Connecticut, Delaware, Ohio, Michigan and Missouri and the District of Columbia traffic regulations use the term motor vehicles to indicate land-running vehicles.

Finally, criminal statutes must give fair warning of their prohibitions. When a statute's words evoke land-running vehicles, it should not be extended to aircraft just because a similar policy applies.

Note: All that remains of the case is the court's reasoning for its holding. Summarize that reasoning in your own words.

Finally, think critically about the case. What holes are there in the court's decision? What might the loser say about the court's decision? The next client? For instance, this decision would seem to imply that transporting a stolen boat (or a helicopter, or a hovercraft) interstate would not violate the NMVTA. Is this a reasonable result? Has the government no further argument to make?

Figure 8–8 (continued)

1. In part because of the length and process of lawmaking, law is often very difficult to read and understand. Lengthy and involved sentences (containing many connectors and negatives) and use of vague words and references are primary culprits. It is therefore always useful to obtain hard copy (from a computer or by photocopying) of the law and underline or highlight relevant phrases.

2. Read the law several times. If you need to interpret a part of the law, read that part first. Look up unfamiliar words and phrases. Once you've done your initial analysis, reread the law to ensure that your thinking "squares" with the written law.

3. Abbreviate common terms ("P" for plaintiff, "D" for defendant, "J" for judgment) Cross reference areas of the law to pages or paragraphs of the law.

Figure 8–9 Helpful hints in reading the law.

Review Questions

1. Name two types of written law.
2. What is the goal in interpreting a statute?
3. Describe the structure of a typical statute.
4. How might the title of a statute be useful in its interpretation?
5. How might the statutory preamble be useful to interpret a statute?
6. List some things to consider in interpreting a statute.
7. Explain the following common statutory connectors: *and, or*
8. List and explain some rules of statutory construction.
9. What is a case brief?
10. Why is it important to brief appellate court decisions?
11. What does it mean to say that a "published appellate decision signals some change in the law?"
12. List and explain the parts of a good case brief.
13. What is the old rule? Why is it important?
14. What are case substantive facts? Procedural facts?
15. What are the components of the case issue? Case holding?
16. What is the case reasoning?
17. List some helpful hints in reading the law.

Exercises

1. How many crimes are defined in the following statute? List the elements of those crimes. Under what circumstances could one person (Justin) be found guilty of killing another (McKenzie)?

   A person who kills another without justification commits murder if, in acting:

   (1) He either intends to kill or do great bodily harm to the other or knows that such acts will cause death to the other; or

   (2) He knows that such acts create a strong probability of death or great bodily harm to the other; or

   (3) He is attempting or committing a forcible felony other than voluntary manslaughter.

   A person who kills an individual without justification commits voluntary manslaughter if at the time of the killing he is acting under a sudden and intense passion resulting from serious provocation by:

(1) The individual killed, or

(2) Another whom the offender endeavors to kill, but he negligently or accidentally causes the death of the individual killed.

A person who kills another without justification commits involuntary manslaughter if his acts are such as are likely to cause death or great bodily harm to some individual, and he performs them recklessly. If the acts, which cause the death, consist of the driving of a motor vehicle, the person may be prosecuted for reckless homicide or if he is prosecuted for involuntary manslaughter, he may be found guilty of the included offense of reckless homicide.

2. Brief the following case:

Carlton *BARNES, Appellant,*

v.

CLAYTON HOUSE MOTEL, *Appellee*

435 S.W.2d 616(1968)

Summary judgment for defendant was rendered in plaintiff's libel action. Defendant's sole contention concerns the question of whether there was a publication of the asserted libelous letter

The undisputed facts are as follows: Defendant operates a motel. An unknown person registered under the name of Burne, giving a fictitious address and falsely stating his automobile license number to be that of a vehicle registered in plaintiff's name. This guest left the motel without paying his bill. Motel property was missing from his room.

Defendant's manager traced the automobile registration and wrote a letter on the bottom of an itemized statement addressed to plaintiff at his residence. It stated in effect that plaintiff had registered under the name of Burne, had left without making payment, and had "accidentally packed" listed items of motel property with his own belongings. The letter requested restitution, or suggested the plaintiff contact a lawyer.

The letter was sent as certified mail with return receipt requested. The maid at plaintiff's residence, who signed the receipt but did not open the letter, received it. The maid delivered the letter to plaintiff's wife, who opened and read it. The wife showed it to the maid and called her husband, who read it. No other person saw the letter.

Defendant's manager did not know plaintiff, and did not know he was married. Plaintiff and his wife had been married more than 20 years. She frequently opened mail addressed to him. The manager testified:

Q. Did you not know that someone other than Mr. Barnes might receive it?

A. Yes, but it was certified to him personally.

Q. Why did you not send it to the addressee only?

A. No particular reason.

Q. Did you not in fact intend for Mr. Barnes' wife to see the letter?

A. It was addressed to him personally.

Q. You recognized that she might have seen it, did you not?

A. Yes.

Q. What was the purpose for this? Does this sometimes produce collections that otherwise would not be forthcoming?

A. Yes. But if it is addressed certified to a party, my chances for collection are better.

And again,

Q. When you mailed the letter who did you intend to receive it?

A. Mr. Barnes.

Q. Did you intend for anyone else to receive it?

A. No.

Q. Did you intend, expect or suspect that anyone else would read it?

A. No.

The applicable principle of the law of libel, uniformly recognized, is relatively simple of statement: If one sends a libelous statement through the mails, addressed to the person defamed, with the expectation or intention that it will be read by another person as a matter of course, and such other person so reads it, there is a publication; but where the sender is "not reasonably chargeable with knowledge that a third person might 'intercept' and read the libelous matter before it reached the person allegedly defamed," there is no publication. . . .

The evidence shows that the sender considered it possible that some third person might intercept and read the letter; that some person other than the addressee 'might receive' it. This falls far short of a showing he was reasonably chargeable with appreciation or knowledge of likelihood that it would be opened and read by another. It is not sufficient, to constitute publication, that there is a mere conceivable possibility or chance of such eventuality. That chance may nearly always exist when a letter is transmitted through the mails. Here the sender did not know plaintiff. The sender did not know he was married. There is simply no evidence to show reasonable grounds to anticipate the reading by a third person so as to constitute a publication. Cases relied on by plaintiff rest on special circumstances, as where it is known the letter must be translated, or where the addressee is blind, or where the sender knows of the habit or custom of a third person to open and read the mail. These cases must be distinguished on the facts.

The judgment is affirmed.

3. Based on the decision in *McBoyle v. United States*, could McBoyle have been convicted under the NMVTA had he taken a stolen yacht on Lake Eerie from Cleveland, OH to Detroit, MI? Why or why not?

Glossary

Case brief: A structured summary of an appellate court decision.

Elements: Stated preconditions to operation of the statute.

Ejusdem generis: Where a statute specifically enumerates items followed by a catchall phrase, the catchall phrase applies only to items in the same class.

Expressio unis est exclusio alternus: The expression of one context requires denial in other contexts;

In derogation of the common law: Statutes changing the common law.

In pari materia: Statutes related to the same subject should be read consistently.

Preconditions: Necessary conditions that must be met before statute will operate.

Statutory title: Title of legislation.

Statutory preamble: Legislature's statement of purpose in enacting a statute.

Canon of statutory construction: Rule developed over the years to aid in statutory interpretation.

Notes

[1]That rule, as applied to criminal statutes, is based on the notion that, particularly as to statutes prohibiting criminal conduct, courts should not read the statute beyond its plain language because criminal statutes should clearly inform the public of prohibited conduct so the public can properly conform to the dictates of law. Notice also in *McBoyle* the Court "winks" at, but nevertheless adheres to, this principle of statutory construction: "Although it is not likely that a criminal will carefully consider the text of the law before he murders or steals, it is reasonable that a fair warning should be given to the world in language that the common world will understand, of what the law intends to do if a certain line is passed. To make the warning fair, so far as possible the line should be clear. When a rule of conduct is laid down in words that evoke in the common mind only the picture of vehicles moving on land, the statute should not be extended

to aircraft simply because it may seem to us that a similar policy applies, or upon the speculation that if the legislature had thought of it, very likely the picture of vehicles moving on land.

[2]As Mr. Justice K.B. Smith noted in a recent Massachusetts Appeals Court case, "Canons of statutory construction are like greeting cards — there seems to be one for every occasion." A.C. Cruise Line, Inc. v. Alcoholic Beverages Control Comm. 29 Mass. App. Ct. 319, 560 N.E.2d 145 (1990). Indeed, canons of statutory constructions may even conflict with each other. Consider the following:

"Statutes in derogation of the common law will not be extended by construction"

and:

"Such acts will be liberally construed if their nature is remedial."

K. Llewellyn, *The Common Law Tradition: Deciding Appeals*, App. C 323-335 (1960).

Using the Law: Legal Analysis

Chapter Outline

Learning Objectives

Upon completing this chapter, the student should be able to

* Explain legal analysis
* Explain analytical thinking
* List the steps in analytical headwork
* List the steps in written analysis
* Explain legal synthesis
* Explain how legal synthesis differs from legal analysis
* List and describe the four types of legal synthesis

Introduction

Now that the research is complete, it's time to piece the law and the facts of the research problem together to determine the client's legal rights. This piecing-together process is called **legal analysis** and involves applying research results (the law) to the facts of the client's situation. Legal analysis involves two processes: **Thinking**[1] and **written legal analysis**. By far the most difficult part of legal analysis is its thinking, which applies the law to the client's situation and answers the questions being asked. Once thinking is complete, writing the analysis is a simple matter of gathering up the puzzle pieces (already assembled during thinking) and moving them to paper.

Ninety Percent of Legal Analysis Happens in the Head

There are many approaches to legal analysis. As you become adept at manipulating the tools of legal analysis, you will no doubt develop your own methods of legal analysis. This book offers one approach — a direct, "cookbook" approach — to legal analysis that works in most situations and ensures that important facts and issues are not missed.

Legal analysis begins with the question being asked. That question should be a general one, often phrased from the client's point of view, such as:

"Can Vincent be expelled for possessing a pipe bomb in school?"

The question is very important because it defines the contours and bounds of the legal analysis. Write it at the top of a piece of paper and refer to it often.

Next, because legal analysis involves applying the law to the *facts* of a client's situation, jot down these facts. Bare bones phrases are sufficient, as long as the facts include all those relevant to the question being asked. A statement of facts in Vincent's case might be as follows:

Vincent's difficulties began when he was a 14- year-old student at the Cuyahoga Public Middle School. One day, a friend called Vincent over to his locker and showed him a number of metal "tubes" that the friend explained were some really fine fireworks. The friend asked if Vincent was interested in buying a couple. Vincent asked their price and agreed to buy three later that afternoon. In the meantime, the boys selling these "super fireworks" sawed the lock off a nearby locker and stowed their "fireworks" in the other locker – locked, of course with the boys' lock. When the owner of the storage locker came by to get the books he needed for class, he couldn't open his locker. He went to the school office to ask for help. Help came in the form of a janitor who "snipped" the lock off with wire-cutters. When the janitor saw what looked like (and indeed, were) pipe bombs in the locker, he called the local bomb squad, who quietly removed the devices for testing and re-locked the locker with yet a third lock. The police then simply staked out the locker corridor until a number of youngsters (including Vincent) gathered around the locker. When they were unable to unlock the lock, the police moved in and took the boys, including Vincent, into custody. They were later released to their parents' custody pending the initiation of criminal charges. The school was evacuated for the remainder of the day so that the bomb specialists could ensure that there were no other bombs or incendiary devices on the premises (there were not). An emergency school committee meeting was held that night; the school committee summarily expelled the boys indefinitely.

Now, it is time to determine which law to apply. If the law to be applied is a statute, identify its elements; if it is one or more cases, reduce the facts and holding of each case to a one or two sentence "bullet." Vincent's question involves analysis of Ohio Rev. Code Ann. §§ 3313.66 and 3313.662 (West 1996).

Next, identify the issues involved in the client's situation. An issue occurs when application of the law to the facts of the client's situation yields no clear answer. For instance, in Vincent's case, his age is not an issue: Vincent is not 16 or older. Therefore, the school cannot permanently expel him under § 3313.662.

Nevertheless, some issues remain, as follows:

Did Vincent possess a firearm at school?

Were Vincent and his parents given three days' written notice of the intent to expel Vincent?

Were Vincent and his parents given an opportunity to appear in person and contest the charges against Vincent or otherwise explain his behavior?

Let's look at one of the remaining issues:

Did Vincent possess a pipe bomb at school?

Because the school bears the burden of proving that Vincent possessed a firearm at school, think first of the school's likely argument. This step may be difficult because the legal professional usually recognizes quite easily the client's available arguments. Seeing things from the opponent's side is difficult. But this step is crucial — the opponent will most likely make the best argument imagined and the legal professional must be prepared to respond to that argument. In Vincent's case, for instance, the school might argue as follows.

The boys who brought the bombs to school would not have done so had there been no "market" for the bombs. As Vincent was part of that "market" he possessed the bombs at school.

Next, based on the law as researched, for that issue, think of Vincent's best argument supporting his position.[2] For example, we might argue as follows:

The definition of possess implies a holding or controlling of something. It is clear that the boys who transported the bombs to the school "brought" the bombs to school. Vincent never touched, picked-up, moved the bombs, nor had control of the bombs.

Next, consider how a court might decide the issue. Why do you think that outcome is most likely? What relevant law gave you that answer? In reaching a conclusion, draw from the purpose of the law, the legislature's or court's reasons for the law, and relevant public policy. For instance, in Vincent's case, we might conclude as follows:

> *Vincent did not "possess" the bombs at school.*

Because the criteria for expulsion are based on the criminal definition of firearm, a judge would likely apply the rule that criminal statutes be narrowly read, and conclude that Vincent did not possess firearms at school.

Finally, based on the likely outcome of all relevant issues, what is the answer to the original question? Can Vincent be expelled from school for possessing a pipe bomb?

> *In Vincent's case, a court would most likely find that because Vincent did not possess the pipe bombs at school, he cannot be expelled for possessing a firearm at school under Ohio Rev. Code Ann. § 3313.66 (West 1996).*

In summary, the steps in the thinking part of legal analysis include those shown in Figure 9–1.

The Remaining Ten Percent: Written Legal Analysis

Once the more difficult "thinking" of legal analysis is complete, it is relatively simple to reduce that thinking to written form for the benefit of others. As was true for analytical thinking, there are many, many different forms for writing legal analysis. The following approach is a common one that works in most situations and ensures complete analysis: It consists of stating the **issue, rule, application, and conclusion (IRAC).**

---

1. Begin with the question.
2. Summarize the facts of the client's situation.
3. Quote or paraphrase the relevant law.
4. Identify the issues.
5. For each issue:
   - Identify the client's best argument[1] based on the law.
   - Identify the adversary's best argument based on the law.
     Based on those arguments, what might a court decide, and why might it decide that way?
6. Based on the outcome for all issues, answer the original question.

[1] In advanced legal analysis, the legal professional will identify all relevant arguments on both sides. As a start, try to identify one good argument on each side.

Figure 9–1 Legal analysis: thinking.

Begin with an introductory paragraph that sets out the facts and client's question. Set up the issues involved in answering that question. In Vincent's case, such an introductory paragraph might be as follows:

> *Vincent's difficulties began when he was a 14- year-old student at the Cuyahoga Public Middle School. One day, a friend called Vince over to his locker and showed him a number of metal "tubes" that the friend explained were some really fine fireworks. The friend asked if Vincent was interested in buying a couple. Vincent asked their price and agreed to buy three later that afternoon. In the meantime, the boys selling these "super fireworks" sawed the lock off a nearby locker and stowed their "fireworks" in the other locker – locked, of course with the boys' lock. When the owner of the storage locker came by to get the books he needed for class, he couldn't open the lock anymore. He went to the school administrative office to ask for help. Help came in the form of a janitor who "snipped" the lock off with wire-cutters. When the janitor saw what looked like (and indeed, were) pipe bombs, he called the local bomb squad, who quietly removed the devices for testing and re-locked the locker with yet a third lock. The police then simply staked out the locker corridor until a number of youngsters (including Vincent) gathered around the locker. When they were unable to unlock the lock, the police moved in and took the boys, including our client Vincent, into custody. They were later released to their parents' custody pending the initiation of criminal charges. The school was evacuated for the remainder of the day so that the bomb specialists could ensure that there were no other bombs or incendiary devices on the premises (there were not). An emergency school committee meeting held that night; the school committee summarily expelled the boys indefinitely. Determining whether Vincent can be expelled for possessing a pipe bomb at school involves answering the following question:*

> *Did Vincent possess a pipe bomb at school?*

Next, for each issue involved, write an IRAC paragraph, as described in Figure 9–2. Begin with a statement of the *issue*. Set out the *rule* bearing on that issue — that is, summarize the applicable law. Follow the rule with the *application* of that rule to the client's facts — most often, this will be a summary of the party arguments. Finally, how would the court likely *conclude*? Why would the court conclude that way? If there is more than one issue, include a transitioning sentence to other issues. An IRAC paragraph in Vincent's case might be as follows:

> *Whether Vincent possessed the pipe bombs at school is straightforward. The Merriam-Webster Collegiate Dictionary (Tenth Edition) defines "possess" as: holding, carrying, or being in control of. The school may argue that the boys who brought the bombs to school would not have done so had there been no "market" for the bombs; because Vincent was part of that market, he possessed the bombs at school. Vincent can point out that the definition of possess involves holding or having control of, yet he neither touched, picked up, nor moved the bombs.*

Write an introductory paragraph that sets out the facts of the client's situation and the legal issues being analyzed

1. For each issue, write an IRAC paragraph:
   a. Begin with a statement of the *issue.*
   b. State the *rule* applicable to that issue.
   c. *Apply* the law to the facts of the client's situation. Often, the application part of the IRAC analysis is a full statement (including necessary explanation) of each party's arguments.
   d. What would a court likely *conclude* on the issue?
2. Transition to the next paragraph.
3. Based on your resolution of all issues, state the likely overall result in the client's situation in a concluding paragraph.

Figure 9–2 Legal analysis: writing (IRAC).

Because the criteria for expulsion are based on the criminal definition of firearm, a judge would likely apply the rule that criminal statutes be narrowly read, and conclude that Vincent did not "bring" the pipe bombs to school.

Finally, based on the likely outcome of all relevant issues, what is the answer to the original question? Can Vincent be expelled from school for possessing a pipe bomb?

As Vincent will likely be able to demonstrate that he did not possess a pipe bomb at school, he will not be expelled under Ohio Rev. Code Ann. § 3313.66.

Examples

The following are examples (in order of complexity) of several different types of legal analysis.

Simple Legal Analysis: Single Law Source

The decision in *McBoyle v. United States* is a good example of a simple legal analysis of a statute. Let's assume Mr. McBoyle has come to our office seeking legal advice. He tells the following story:

On May 7, 1930, I was arrested and charged with transporting an airplane which I knew was stolen, from Ottawa, Illinois, to Guymon, Oklahoma, in violation of the National Motor Vehicle Theft Act ("NMVTA"). I wish to know if I could be convicted of violating the NMVTA.

A thinking analysis outline for McBoyle's situation might appear as in Figure 9–3.

See Figure 9–4 for the *McBoyle* court's written analysis of McBoyle's situation and determine whether the court agrees with our analysis (components of legal analysis are bracketed).

Question Asked	Can McBoyle be convicted under the National Motor Vehicle Theft Act?
Facts	On May 7, 1930, McBoyle was arrested and charged with transporting from Ottawa, Illinois, to Guymon, Oklahoma, an airplane that he knew was stolen, in violation of the National Motor Vehicle Theft Act.
Applicable Rules	That whoever shall transport or cause to be transported in interstate or foreign commerce a motor vehicle, knowing the same to have been stolen, shall be punished by a fine of not more than $5,000, or by imprisonment of not more than five years, or both. The term 'motor vehicle' shall include an automobile, automobile truck, automobile wagon, motor cycle, or any other self-propelled vehicle not designed for running on rails.
Legal Elements	Transports In interstate commerce Known stolen Motor vehicle
Issue	Whether an airplane is a motor vehicle under the NMVTA.
Other useful interpretive rules	Canons of statutory construction: Plain meaning; use of term motor vehicle in other statutes; strict interpretation of criminal statutes.
McBoyle's best argument that he should not be convicted under the NMVTA	The statute was intended to punish people transporting land-running stolen motor vehicles across state lines. Since an airplane is not a land-running motor vehicle, McBoyle is not guilty.
U.S. government's best argument that McBoyle is guilty	The statute is non-specific. Thus, it covers all "self propelled vehicles not designed for running on the rails." Since an airplane is such a "self propelled vehicle not designed for running on rails," McBoyle is guilty.
Likely conclusion and why	An airplane is a motor vehicle under the NMVTA.
Overall conclusion	As McBoyle admits to all statutory elements of the crime save the "motor vehicle" element, and the government will likely prevail on its argument that an airplane is a motor vehicle, McBoyle will likely be convicted under the NMVTA.

Figure 9–3 McBoyle analysis.

MCBOYLE

v.

UNITED STATES

283 U.S. 25, 15 S. Ct. 340, 71 L.Ed. 816 (1931)

On Writ of Certiorari to the United States Circuit Court of Appeals for the Tenth Circuit.

Mr. Harry F. Brown, of Guthrie, Okl., for petitioner.

The Attorney General and Mr. Claude R. Branch, of Providence, R. I., for the United States.

Mr. Justice HOLMES delivered the opinion of the Court.

Introductory Paragraph

The petitioner was convicted of transporting from Ottawa, Illinois, to Guymon, Oklahoma, an airplane that he knew to have been stolen, and was sentenced to serve three years' imprisonment and to pay a fine of $2,000. The judgment was affirmed by the Circuit Court of Appeals for the Tenth Circuit. 43 F.(2d) 273. A writ of certiorari was granted by this Court on the question [whether the National Motor Vehicle Theft Act applies to aircraft]. . .[That Act provides: 'Sec. 2. . . :

Issue:

(a) The term 'motor vehicle' shall include an automobile, automobile truck, automobile wagon, motor cycle, or any other self-propelled vehicle not designed for running on rails. Sec 3. That whoever shall transport or cause to be transported in interstate or foreign commerce a motor vehicle, knowing the same to have been stolen, shall be punished by a fine of not more than $5,000, or by imprisonment of not more than five years, or both.']

Rule:

Analysis:

[Section 2 defines the motor vehicles of which the transportation in interstate commerce is punished in § 3. The question is the meaning of the word 'vehicle' in the phrase 'any other self-propelled vehicle not designed for running on rails.' No doubt etymologically it is possible to use the word to signify a conveyance working on land, water or air, and sometimes legislation extends the use in that direction, e.g., land and air, water being separately provided for, in the Tariff Act . . . But in everyday speech 'vehicle' calls up the picture of a thing moving on land. Thus . . . [the NMVTA] intended, the

Figure 9–4 McBoyle analysis, part 2.

	Government suggests, rather to enlarge than to restrict the definition, vehicle includes every contrivance capable of being used 'as a maeans of transportation on land.' And this is repeated, expressly excluding aircraft, in the Tariff Act, . . . So here, the phrase under discussion calls up the popular picture. For after including automobile truck, automobile wagon and motor cycle, the words 'any other self-propelled vehicle not designed for running on rails' still indicate that a vehicle in the popular sense, that is a vehicle running on land is the theme. It is a vehicle that runs, not something, not commonly called a vehicle, that flies. Airplanes were well known in 1919 when this statute was passed, but it is admitted that they were not mentioned in the reports or in the debates in Congress. It is impossible to read words that so carefully enumerate the different forms of motor vehicles and have no reference of any kind to aircraft, as including airplanes under a term that usage more and more precisely confines to a different class. The counsel for the petitioner has shown that the phraseology of the statute as to motor vehicles follows that of earlier statutes of Connecticut, Delaware, Ohio, Michigan and Missouri, not to mention the late Regulations of Traffic for the District of Columbia, . . . none of which can be supposed to leave the earth.
Conclusion:	Although it is not likely that a criminal will carefully consider the text of the law before he murders or steals, it is reasonable that a fair warning should be given to the world in language that the common world will understand, of what the law intends to do if a certain line is passed. To make the warning fair, so far as possible the line should be clear.] [When a rule of conduct is laid down in words that evoke in the common mind only the picture of vehicles moving on land, the statute should not be extended to aircraft simply because it may seem to us that a similar policy applies, or upon the speculation that if the legislature had thought of it, very likely the picture of vehicles moving on land.]

Figure 9–4 (continued)

Complex Legal Analysis: Many Law Sources, Legal Synthesis

Legal Synthesis Examples — Parental Immunity. John Doncaster seeks legal advice in the problem described in Figure 9–5.

When dealing with multiple legal sources, statutes, cases, regulation, rules, and so on, bearing on a legal problem, it is not enough to apply each law source to the client's situation. Rather, the legal professional must try to read the sources

While his four-year-old daughter, Hester, was visiting her mother Cathy (John and Cathy separated acrimoniously about six months ago; John and Cathy nevertheless share joint custody of Hester with equal rights of visitation), Cathy invited her family to the house for a several day visit. Since the house was overflowing with people, Cathy set up a futon for Hester in her room. Cathy and Hester slept together without mishap for two nights. On the third night, Cathy woke at about 2 A.M. to the sound of Hester falling down the metal spiral staircase that connects Cathy's second floor room to the first floor. Hester had hit her head on the way down. Fortunately, after paramedics, emergency room doctors, and a plastic surgeon finished, Hester recovered from the incident. However, she was left with a four-inch scar on her forehead.

John has sued Cathy on Hester's behalf for medical and psychological damages based on the incident, as well as for the lasting damages of Hester's scar. Cathy has moved to dismiss John's complaint based on the doctrine of parental immunity, which says that children cannot sue their parents for torts. The cases listed in Figure 9–6 may bear on John's problems.

Figure 9–5 Legal synthesis problem.

A v. A — 12-year-old child injured in car accident may sue parent causing the accident.

B v B — 23-year-old child injured in car accident may sue parent causing accident.

C v C — 3-year-old child injured when she stuck a fork in electrical outlet may not sue parent who was in kitchen cooking dinner.

D v D — 28-year-old child injured in fist fight with father over politics may sue parent.

E v. E — 12-year-old child raped by father may sue father for physical and psychological damages.

F v. F — 19-year-old child scalded when parent accidentally dropped a pot of boiling water may sue parent.

Figure 9–6 Cases bearing on legal synthesis problem.

together and resolve the sources to each other, as well as apply them in the client's situation. This process of **harmonizing** multiple legal sources to each other and to the client's situation is **legal synthesis**. Legal synthesis comes in four varieties (in increasing order of value and strength of synthesis).

1. no synthesis.
2. arguing conflicting sources.
3. harmonizing multiple (seemingly conflicting) sources.
4. arguing for a change in the law based on legal trends.

In the following examples, the professional's synthesis comes out primarily in her written analysis. Therefore, thinking for all four types of legal synthesis would be similar.

No Synthesis. The no-synthesis method of synthesizing legal sources is a method of analysis often used by legal novices and lazy professionals. In this method, the researcher simply sets out the issues, states available authorities and leaves the legal synthesis to the reader. Figure 9–7 shows an example of no-synthesis legal synthesis.

Introductory Paragraph	While his four-year-old daughter, Hester, was visiting her mother Cathy (John and Cathy separated acrimoniously about six months ago; John and Cathy nevertheless share joint custody of Hester with equal rights of visitation), Cathy invited her family to the house for a several day visit. Since the house was overflowing with people, Cathy set up a futon for Hester in her room. Cathy and Hester slept together without mishap for two nights. On the third night, Cathy woke at about 2 A.M. to the sound of Hester falling down the metal spiral staircase that connects Cathy's second floor room to the first floor. Hester had cracked her head on the way down. Fortunately, after paramedics, emergency room doctors, and a plastic surgeon finished, Hester recovered from the incident. However, she was left with a four inch scar on her forehead. John has sued Cathy on Hester's behalf for medical and psychological damages based on the incident, as well as for the lasting damages resulting from the scar on Hester's forehead. Cathy has moved to dismiss John's complaint based on the doctrine of parental immunity, that is, that children cannot sue their parents for torts.
IRAC Paragraph **Issue**	John would like to know if indeed, Cathy is immune from suit.
Rule **Application**	Sometimes a child may sue her parent for torts. For instance, in *A v. A*, a 12-year-old child injured in a car accident was allowed to sue her parent who caused the accident. In *B v. B*, a 23-year-old child injured in a car accident was permitted to sue his parent who caused the accident. In *C v. C*, a 3-year-old child injured when she stuck a fork in an electrical outlet was denied the right to sue her parent who was in the kitchen cooking dinner. In *D v. D*, a 28-year-old injured in a fist fight with his father over politics was allowed to sue his father. In *E v. E*, a 12-year-old child raped by her father was allowed to sue him for physical and psychological damages. Finally, in *F v. F*, a 19-year-old child scalded when his parent accidentally dropped a pot of boiling water was allowed to sue his parent.
Conclusion	Thus, it seems that sometimes, though not always, a child may sue her parent for torts.
Concluding Paragraph	John may be successful in defending against Cathy's motion to dismiss.

Figure 9–7 No synthesis.

Notice that all the writer does in her synthesis is set out the issue, the facts, and the holding of the relevant legal sources, and leaves to her reader the harmonization and application of those sources to the facts and arrival at the writer's conclusion.

Arguing Seemingly Conflicting Law Sources. A second, often used, though poor method of synthesizing law sources is to argue both sides of an issue, using law sources favorable to each side and then, in some fashion, concluding which is likely to prevail in the client's situation, as shown in Figure 9–8.

Harmonizing Seemingly Conflicting Law Sources. Inherent in the "arguing conflicting cases" method of legal synthesis is a request that a judge adopt one legal source over other, seemingly conflicting sources. Most judges (particularly trial and intermediate appellate judges) are reluctant to do that; the cases are, after all, the pronouncement of the highest court in the jurisdiction. Judges do not take lightly (nor should any legal professional analyzing a situation based on decisions by a single court) the suggestion that the high court has somehow whimsically or capriciously rendered conflicting decisions on the same legal issue. If, however, the legal professional can extract from the cases a rule that incorporates the holdings in all of the cases, so that the judge is not forced to choose one set of cases over another, the judge will likely adopt that explanation. This extracting of a rule harmonizing seemingly conflicting law sources is the essence of fine legal synthesis. How is that extracting accomplished? Sometimes it is easy: a court may identify the harmonizing rule in its decisions. Other times, when the court does not identify that rule in its decision (as in our parental immunity cases), it is up to the legal professional to extract the rule. It may be useful, in harmonizing cases with no clear harmonizing rule, to chart factual similarities and differences in the cases. For instance, the parental immunity cases seemingly turn on two factors: the age of the child and the nature of the tort. A chart listing those facts might appear as shown in Figure 9–9.

IRAC Paragraph Issue	John would like to know if indeed, Cathy is immune from suit.
Rule Application	Children are sometimes permitted to sue their parents. For example, in the following cases, children were permitted to sue their parents for torts: *A v. A, B v. B, D v. D, E v. E* and *F v. F*. However, in *C v. C*, a 3-year-old child injured when she stuck a fork in electrical outlet was not permitted to sue the parent who was in the kitchen cooking dinner.
Conclusion Concluding Paragraph	Hester will likely be permitted to sue Cathy. In conclusion, because Hester can sue her mother for her injuries, John can successfully defend against Cathy's motion to dismiss.

Figure 9–8 Arguing conflicting legal materials.

CASE	AGE OF CHILD	NATURE OF TORT	OUTCOME
A v. A	12	Negligence (car accident)	Not immune
B v. B	23	Negligence (car accident)	Not immune
C v. C	3	Negligence	Immune
D v. D	28	Intentional	Not immune
E v. E	12	Intentional	Not immune
F v. F	19	Negligence	Not immune

Figure 9–9 Chart of synthesis cases: factual differences.

From the chart in Figure 9–9, two rules emerge: There is no parental immunity for intentional torts or automobile accidents, and parents are immune only for non-automobile negligence to their minor children. Applying those rules to John's situation, the answer is straightforward, as shown in Figure 9–10.

Arguing for a Change in the Law Based on Legal Trends. Does all of this analysis and synthesis leave John (and Hester) without remedy? A fourth method of synthesizing legal sources is to argue that the present law should be changed because

IRAC Paragraph	
Issue	John would like to know if indeed, Cathy is immune from suit.
Rule **Application**	Parents are immune from suit by their minor children only for negligence not involving a car accident. Appellate decisions on parental immunity deny immunity to parents intentionally injuring their child, regardless of the child's age. *D v. D*; *E v. E*. As well, appellate decisions deny immunity to parents injuring their children, regardless of the child's age, in car accidents. *A v. A*, *B v. B*. Moreover, those decisions allow adult children to sue their parents for any sort of negligence. *F v. F*.
Conclusion	Thus, in this state, parents are immune from suit for negligence (other than car accidents) only by their minor children.
Concluding Paragraph	As Hester was only four when she fell down the spiral staircase as a result of her mother's negligent failure to properly supervise and protect her, Cathy will likely prevail on her motion to dismiss John's complaint.

Figure 9–10 Harmonizing seemingly conflicting sources.

of a *trend in the law.* Suppose, for instance, that the law on parental immunity is as stated in the cases. Suppose as well that the state has a common-law rule prohibiting spouses from suing each other, that is, spousal immunity. However, two recent spousal immunity decisions from the state's highest court have begun to erode the doctrine of spousal immunity. In the *G v. G* case, decided seven years ago, Mrs. G sued her husband for injuries she sustained in an automobile accident he caused. In that case, the court modified its spousal immunity rule and allowed Mrs. G to sue her husband, making it very clear that its ruling applied only to automobile accidents. In a case decided only last year, *H v. H*, however, Mrs. H was allowed to sue her husband when she slipped on an icy patch in their driveway, an area Mr. H was responsible for clearing. Saying that it saw no significant difference between car accidents and slip-and-fall accidents, the state's highest court allowed Mrs. H to sue her husband. Based on all eight cases, the argument might proceed as shown in Figure 9–11.

IRAC Paragraph	John would like to know if indeed, Cathy is immune from suit.
Issue	
Rule	Under present legal principles, Cathy would be immune from suit by Hester. However, a developing legal trend in this state would permit Hester's (and John's) suit.
Application	Appellate decisions on parental immunity deny immunity to parents intentionally injuring their child, regardless of the child's age. *D. v. D.; E. v. E.* As well, appellate decisions deny immunity to parents injuring their children, regardless of the child's age, in car accidents. *A. v. A., B. v. B.* The decisions do allow adult children to sue their parents for any sort of negligence. *F. v. F.* Thus, in this state, parents are immune from suit for negligence only by their minor children. A developing trend in spousal immunity cases, however, would suggest that in cases like these, negligence suits by a minor child against her parent, the child ought to be permitted to sue.
	More than seven years ago, spouses were not permitted to sue each other for torts committed during their marriage for largely the same reasons that the present rule of parental immunity prevails (i.e., preservation of peace and harmony in the family, prevention of collusive suits between family members). However, in the *G. v. G.* case, decided seven years ago, Mrs. G. tried to sue her husband for injuries she sustained in an accident caused by her husband. In that case, the court modified its spousal immunity rule and allowed Mrs. G. to sue her husband, while making it very clear that its ruling applied only to suits arising out of automobile accidents. In a case decided only last year, *H. v. H.*, however, Mrs. H was allowed to sue her husband when she slipped on an icy patch in their driveway, an area Mr. H. was responsible for clearing of ice and snow. Saying that it saw no significant difference between car accidents

Figure 9–11 Arguing for a change in the law.

	and slip-and-fall accidents, the state's highest court allowed Mrs. H to sue her husband. We see a similar trend developing in this state in parental immunity cases. Until recently, minor children were not allowed to sue their parents for negligence. Then, three years ago, in *A. v. A.*, this state's highest court for the first time permitted children to sue their parents when the negligence involved a car accident. For the same reasons the courts of this state abrogated spousal immunity in negligence cases (i.e., there is no meaningful difference between car accidents and other forms of negligence), this court should abrogate parental immunity in this case.
Conclusion	Based on a developing trend in the common law doctrines of spousal and parental immunity, the court will allow Hester (and John) to sue Cathy.
Concluding Paragraph	Based on the similar principles underlying spousal and parental immunity, and recent cases abrogating spousal immunity in negligence cases, John will likely succeed in defending against Cathy's motion to dismiss based on parental immunity.

Figure 9–11 (continued)

Review Questions

1. What is legal analysis?
2. What is the hardest part of legal analysis?
3. What is analytical thinking?
4. List the steps in analytical headwork.
5. What's left after analytical headwork in legal analysis?
6. List the steps in written analysis.
7. What is legal synthesis?
8. How does legal synthesis differ from legal analysis?
9. List four types of legal synthesis. Explain their differences.

Exercises

1. Using the methods of this chapter and your research results, prepare the thinking portion of the Kitty Barbour analysis.
2. Using the methods of this chapter, prepare a written analysis of Kitty's case.
3. Consult a local lawyer from one of the key appellate cases you've identified in your research. Talk to him/her about the case — the difficulties he/she encountered and how those difficulties were resolved. Lawyers often enjoy talking about their cases and there is much to be learned from their "war stories."

Glossary

Harmonizing: Resolving seemingly conflicting legal resources into a rule applicable to a broader class of cases.

Issue, rule, application, and conclusion (IRAC): A method of written analysis that consists of stating the *issue* involved, the applicable *rule*, *applying* that rule to the client's factual situation, and *concluding* the likely result in the client's situation.

Legal Analysis: The process of applying legal research (the law) to the facts of a client's situation.

Legal synthesis: Deriving (from a variety of legal sources) and applying a legal rule to a client's situation.

Thinking: That preliminary part of legal analysis that occurs in the legal professional's head before she puts pen to paper.

Written legal analysis: Rendering legal analysis to paper for the benefit of others.

Notes

[1]Although I speak of this part of legal analysis as "thinking," it is useful to take and keep notes during that process.

[2]In advanced legal analysis, the legal professional will identify all relevant arguments on both sides. As a start, try to identify one good argument on each side.

CHAPTER 10

Putting Pen to Paper: Legal Writing

Chapter Outline

Learning Objectives

Upon completing this chapter, the student should be able to

* Describe the four elements of legal citations for cases, statutes, books, and scholarly articles
* Explain what the Bluebook is and how it is organized
* Explain the difference between citation sentences and clauses
* Describe some introductory signals for legal citations
* Describe short citing and when it is used
* Explain the goal of good legal writing; list and describe the characteristics of good legal writing
* List some components of accurate legal writing
* List some quick ways to professionalize legal writing
* Describe the legal research, writing, and revising processes

Legal Writing

Contrary to what you may have believed (or experienced in reading cases, encyclopedias, texts, and other legal documents and materials), legal writing should be good, simple writing. In times past, lawyers, judges, and teachers clung to Latin words and phrases, to old, confusing writing patterns and terms which have no place in modern legal writing. The law makes sense, and must be understood by common people, or a primary purpose of law — preventing illegal acts — is lost. Nearly all legal concepts can be clearly and concisely explained and written. The legal writer's goal is to produce a **concise**, thorough document that the reader can read and understand without pause or further research. Consider the following:

> As Humpty Dumpty (hereinafter "the party of the first part"), a person of somewhat flattened ovular dimension, sat in a semi-reclined position on a protuberance of stone, the children, minors, or infants of the proximately situated Neighbor Brown (hereinafter "the party of the second part") hit, beat, pushed, shoved, jostled, or otherwise displaced said party of the first part. The party of the first part thereafter loosened, jostled, fell, became displaced from his seat, resting spot, perch, protuberance and hit, smashed, crashed, splayed to the terra firma below, beneath, down there. The resulting crash, explosion, implosion, or bang rendered, tore, wrought the party of the first part into myriad particles, pieces, segments, portions. Medical, structural, or other assistance proved fruitless to the party of the first part's struggle to regain his balance, poise, form, and spirit. Indeed, no wise man, architect, doctor, engineer, builder, flora or fauna in the entire realm, world, county, kingdom, fiefdom, and/or universe could restore, reinstate, recreate the party of the first part's balance, poise, form, or spirit. As a result, consequence, remedy, the party of the first part hereby, hereinafter, heretofore brings suit, litigates, and sues the party of the second part for improper, inadequate, negligent, or deliberate failure to supervise, watch, control, discipline, or be responsible for his children, minors, or infants, causing the party of the first part great, grievous, and awful, harm, damage, injury, pain, suffering, mental anguish, lost consortium, loss of income, profits, and interest as well as great, vast, awful loss of wages, inconvenience and other expensive and despicable things.

All that to describe the clean-up of a broken egg?

Fortunately, the legal writer has a friend in her search for clear, simple legal writing. Her name is Celeste and she is a COBRA. Although Celeste can become irate and will "bite" the legal writer who does not heed her five simple rules, as long as the writer follows each of her rules (Citation, Organization, Brevity, Readability, Accuracy), s/he will always achieve her or his goal. But first, a few ground rules, as shown in Figure 10–1.

1. *The writer bears full responsibility for his reader's understanding.* Unlike other exchanges, such as conversations and teaching, where both parties to the exchange bear a responsibility in understanding the message, in writing, the writer bears full responsibility for the message. If the reader does not understand the message, the writer has failed in his duty to explain his message clearly and understandably.

2. *The reader's time and attention are valuable.* It is therefore the writer's responsibility to explain his message simply, straightforwardly, and concisely. The reader need not (indeed, should not) follow the writer's every footstep toward her conclusion. The goal of writing is to guide the reader to the conclusion, not retrace the writer's steps. Writing must be simple so the reader need not interrupt her reading to ponder a sentence, a paragraph, or a word. A good writer lets the reader know early what she has concluded and her path to that conclusion. As well, a good writer posts "signs" (section headings or other indicators) to keep the reader "on track" toward the conclusion.

3. *Never plan to complete a writing in one sitting.* Expect to edit, rewrite, and revise writing several times. Although some writers may be able, in one sitting and without error or misstep, to pen a final writing, those writers are very, very few. Most writers are not such very good writers, as good rewriters and revisers. If you do not know word processing, learn it. That time will be saved many times over in revision time.

4. *Invest in a dictionary and thesaurus.* Have them readily available when writing.

Figure 10–1 Legal writing ground rules.

Legal Citations

It doesn't take much legal reading to realize the importance of citing legal materials in legal writing. At times it seems that every sentence is "punctuated" (i.e. supported) by a **citation.** Consider the following passage:

> Our workers' compensation act, Mass. Gen. L. ch. 152, §§ 1-86, as amended through St.1991, c. 398 (Act), is a "humanitarian measure" which the Legislature first enacted in 1911 . . . in response to strong public dissatisfaction with the remedies provided by traditional tort actions. L. Locke, Workmen's Compensation § 1, at 2 (2d ed. 1981) (hereinafter "Locke"). See *Young v. Duncan,* 218 Mass. 346, 349, 106 N.E. 1 (1914). The Act is based on the legislative judgment that "human loss directly arising out of commercial and industrial enterprises" is part of the operating cost of a business. *Zerofski's Case,* 385 Mass. 590, 592, 433 N.E.2d 869 (1982), quoting *Madden's Case,* 222 Mass. 487, 496, 111 N.E. 379 (1916). See *Ahmed's Case,* 278 Mass. 180,

183, 179 N.E. 684 (1932). Locke, *supra*. The Act applies only to employees who come within its ambit. See Mass. Gen. L. ch. 152, § 24 (1996). The Act requires that participating employees waive their right to sue in tort for work-related injuries. *Id.* In return, the Act gives these employees the possibility of obtaining compensation for loss of wages or earning capacity caused by a work-related injury, regardless of the fault of their employers or the foreseeability of harm. See *Zerofski's Case*, 385 Mass. at 592, 433 N.E.2d at 870; *Akins's Case*, 302 Mass. 562, 20 N.E.2d 453 (1939); *Ahmed's Case*, 278 Mass. at 183, 179 N.E. at 686. See also Mass. Gen. L. ch. 152, §§ 13, 30, 31, 34, 34A, 35 (1996).

The reason for all of this citation is clear. Because much American law is based on precedent — earlier rules and decisions —the reader must be able to verify that those earlier materials say what the writer claims. Unlike citation in literary or scientific material, which usually appears in footnotes or endnotes, legal citation is most often in-line. Just like literary and scientific citation, however, there is a specific form for legal citation. It is important to always follow that form and check legal citations for accuracy. Few things are more irritating to a reader of legal documents than to have to hunt for supporting materials incorrectly or inadequately cited. Citation form and substance are one part of legal writing.

The Bluebook. The **bluebook,** Harvard Law Review's *Uniform System of Citation,* is the legal professional's bible of legal citation.[1] Currently in its seventeenth edition, the *Bluebook* is a comprehensive guide to correct legal citation. The *Bluebook* covers contain citation forms for commonly cited legal materials. The book itself is divided into three parts. The first quarter of the book (rules 1 through 9) consists of standards of citation and style. These include Rules 10–20, which set out specific citation forms for cases, statutes, books, periodicals, and foreign materials. The third part, the *Bluebook*'s tables (printed on blue paper) are rules of citation and abbreviations for specific jurisdictions (i.e., the Michigan statutes) and documents. The book is indexed topically. Figure 10–2 shows a typical bluebook page.

The Bluebook pages shown cite Georgia Appeals Court cases as follows:

Heard v. Neighbor Newspapers, 190 Ga. App. 756, 380 S.E.2d 279 (1989).

Citation Rules: A Primer

In general, legal citations include the following four bits of information:

1. author of the material
2. title of the material
3. where the material can be found
4. publication date

The form those bits of information take depends on the type of materials being cited.

District Court of Appeal (Fla. Dist. Ct. App.): Cite to So. 2d., if therein; otherwise, cite to Fla. L. Weekly.

Southern Reporter	1957-date	So. 2d
FLorida Law Weekly		Fla. L. Weekly

Circuit Court (Fla. Cir. Ct.), **County Court** (e.g., Fla. Orange County Ct.), **Public Service Commission** (Fla. P.S.C.), and other lower courts of record: Cite to Fla. Supp. or Fla. Supp. 2d., if therein; otherwise, cite to Fla. L. Weekly Supp.

Florida Supplement	1948-1992	Fla. Supp., Fla. Supp. 2d
Florida Law Weekly Supplement		Fla. L. Weekly Supp.

Statutory compilations: Cite to Fla. STAT. if therein.

Florida Statutes	FLA. STAT. ch. x.xxx (year)
Florida Statutes Annotated (West)	FLA. STAT. ANN. § x (West year)
Florida Statutes Annotated (Harrison)	FLA. STAT. ANN. ch. x.xxx (Harrison year)

Session laws: Cite to Fla. Laws if therein.

Laws of Florida	year Fla. Laws ch. xxx
Florida Session Law Service (West)	year Fla. Sess: Law Serv. xxx (West)

Administrative compilation

Florida Administrative Cote Annotated	FLA. ADMIN. CODE ANN. r. x (year)

Administrative register

Florida Administrative Weekly	Fla. Admin. Weekly

Georgia (GA)
http://www.doas.state.ga.us/courts/supreme

Supreme Court (Ga.): Cite to S.E. or S.E.2d, if therein; otherwise, cite to Ga.

South Eastern Reporter	1887-date	S.E., S.E.2d
Georgia Reports	1846-date	Ga.

Court of Appeals (Ga. Ct. App.): Cite to S.E. or S.E.2d, if therein; otherwise, cite to Ga. App.

South Eastern Reporter	1907-date	S.E., S.E.2d
Georgia Appeals Reports	1907-date	Ga. App.

Statutory compilations: Cite to the official version of GA. CODE ANN. (published by Michie) if therein.

Official Code of Georgia Annotated (Michie)	GA. CODE ANN. § x (year)
Code of Georgia Annotated (Harrison)	GA. CODE ANN. § x (Harrison year)

Session laws

Georgia Laws	year Ga. Laws xxx

Administrative compilation

Official Compilation Rules and Regulations of the State of Georgia	GA. COMP. R. & REGS. r. x (year)

Hawaii (HI)
http://www.hawaii.gov/jud

Supreme Court (Haw.): Cite to P.2d or P.3d, if therein; otherwise, cite to Haw.

Pacific Reporter	1959-date	P.2d, P.3d
West's Hawaii Reports (begins with vol. 76)	1994-date	Haw.
Hawaii Reports (ends with vol. 75)	1847-1994	Haw.

Intermediate Court of Appeals (Haw. Ct. App.): Cite to P.2d or P.3d, if therein; otherwise, cite to Haw. App. or Haw.

Pacific Reporter	1980-date	P.2d, P.3d
West's Hawaii Reports (begins with vol. 76)	1994-date	Haw.
Hawaii Appellate Reports	1980-1994	Haw. App.

Statutory compilations: Cite to HAW. REV. STAT. if therein.

Hawaii Revised Statutes	HAW. REV. STAT. § x (year)

Figure 10–2 *Bluebook* rules of citation and abbreviations for the specific jurisdiction of the state of Georgia. Copyright © 2000 by The Columbia Law Review Association, The Harvard Law Review Association, *The University of Pennsylvania Law Review*, and *The Yale Law Journal*.

Case Citation. Appellate cases are the most regularly cited of all legal research materials, inevitably following the case name-volume-reporter-page number-date pattern of citation.

State Cases. The following is an example of the citation of a state court decision:

> *Young v. Duncan*, 218 Mass. 346, 349, 106 N.E. 1 (1914).

1. *Author:* The author of a case is the court deciding the case. In state court decisions, the identity of the court deciding the case can usually be found in the case reporter name. For instance, the *Young* case was decided by Massachusetts' highest court, the Supreme Judicial Court; only Massachusetts Supreme Judicial Court decisions are reported in the Massachusetts Reports (abbreviated "Mass.")

2. *Title:* A case title consists of the name of the plaintiff, a lower case "v.", and the name of the defendant, all underlined or italicized. In writing the title of a case, follow these rules:
   a. Use only the last names of individuals, for example,
      Young, Duncan
   b. Use the complete names of companies, for example
      Westinghouse Electric Co.
   c. If the case involves multiple plaintiffs or defendants, name only the first in the case title, for example, Adam Young, Julie Cash, and Jeremy Socha appear as "Young" in the case title.
   d. The first word in a multi-word name must be completely spelled out. For instance, Washington Apple Growers, Inc. (not WA Apple Growers, Inc.)

3. *Where the material may be found.* As you may recall from chapter 3, appellate courts decisions may be published in one, or several, reporters. A reporter published by the government is called the court's "official" reporter. If a court has an official reporter, the official reporter usually bears the name of the state or the state court. For instance, the *Young* case appears in the Massachusetts Reports at page 364 of volume 218.

   In addition, West Group publishes state appellate court decisions in regional reporters, which include decisions from several (often adjoining) states. The West regional reporter series is an "unofficial" reporter of state appellate court decisions.[2] The West Group publishes decisions of the Massachusetts Supreme Judicial Court in its North Eastern Reporter®. The *Young* case can be found in that unofficial reporter in volume 106 of the N.E.[3] series reporter beginning at page 1. When material (usually cases) can be found in two or more locations, those locations are called **parallel citations**. In parallel citing, always list the official citation first.

4. *Publication Date.* The date, 1914, in parenthesis following the case citation is the year the case was decided.[4]

Federal Cases. Federal district court decisions are published in West's *Federal Supplement®* (*F. Supp.*) only; Federal appellate decisions (except United States Supreme Court decisions) are published in West's *Federal Reporter®* (*F.*, *F.2d*, *F.3d*). Thus, a typical federal district court decision might be cited as follows:

> *Frizzle v. Department of Transportation*, 894 F. Supp. 912 (D. Ma. 1991).

> 1. *Author.* Because the specific federal district court deciding the case is not apparent from the reporter name (i.e., all federal district court decisions are published in *F. Supp*), it is necessary to more specifically identify the district court author in the parenthetical following the citation (as in *D. Mass*, district court for the District of Massachusetts).
> 2. *Title.* Case titles in federal cases follow the rules of state court case titles.
> 3. *Where the material may be found.* Federal case citations follow normal rules of legal material citation, as follows:

> VOLUME #, REPORTER NAME, FIRST PAGE #

> 894, F. Supp., 912

> With the exception of United States Supreme court cases, federal cases do not have parallel citations.
> 4. *Publication date.* 1991.

United States Supreme Court decisions are published in four publications. Chronologically, Supreme Court decisions appear first in *United States Law Week*, a weekly newspaper of federal court events, arguments, and decisions. A typical *United States Law Week* citation is as follows:

> *Charlesworth v. Mack*, 60 U.S.L.W. 4420 (U.S. Feb. 4, 1992).

Next, Supreme Court decisions are published by West Group and Lawyers Cooperative Publishing (now also part of the West Group) in unofficial reporters: *Supreme Court Reporter®* (*S. Ct*) and *Supreme Court Reporter, Lawyer's Edition (L. Ed.)*, respectively. For instance,

> *Charlesworth v. Mack*, 97 S. Ct. 1492 (1992)

> *Charlesworth v. Mack*, 108 L. Ed. 2d 948 (1992)

Finally, Supreme Court Cases are officially published in the *United States Reports* and are cited as follows:

> *Charlesworth v. Mack*, 410 U.S. 892 (1992)

Where the official citation is known, only that citation should be given. Otherwise, the unofficial citation should be used when available in preference to the *United States Law Week* citation.

Statutes and Constitutions. Statutes are cited in various ways, depending on the jurisdiction's codification process. Statutes most often are cited either by title or by chapter, number, a section number, and the copyright date of the volume in which it appears.

Federal Statutes.   Consider the following citation to a federal statute:

20 U.S.C.® § 8001 (1996)

1. *Author.* Because statutes are written by the Congress, the jurisdiction abbreviation (U.S.C. in this case) identifies the statute's author.
2. *Title.* Most statutes are codified in numbered (or named) titles or chapters. In the above example, "20" tells the reader that this statute is part of title 20 of the United States Code.
3. *Where the statute can be found.* 20 U.S.C. § 8001. The statute title, section number, jurisdiction, and, if available, publisher together define the location of the statute.
4. *Date.* The date (in this case, 1996) is the copyright date of the book containing the statute. If the version of the cited statute appears in a pocket part or supplement, the parenthetical will indicate so, as follows:

20 U.S.C.A.® § 8001 (West. 1996)

State Statutes.   Consider the following citation to a Massachusetts statute:

Mass. Gen. Law ch. 152, § 24 (1996)

1. *Author.* Because statutes are written by the jurisdiction's legislature, the jurisdiction abbreviation ("Mass." in this case) identifies the statute's author.
2. *Title.* Most statutes are codified in numbered (or named) titles or chapters. In the above example, the "ch. 152" tells the reader that this statute is part of chapter 152 of the Massachusetts General Laws.
3. *Where the statute can be found.* Mass. Gen. Laws ch. 152, § 24; The statute title, section number, jurisdiction, and, if available, publisher together define the volume and location of the statute.
4. *Date.* The date (in this case, 1996) is the copyright date of the book containing the statue. If the version of the cited statute appears in a pocket part or supplement, the parenthetical will indicate so, as follows:

Mass. Gen. Laws Ann. ch. 152, § 24 (West Supp. 1998)

Books.   Consider the following citation to section 1 at page 2 of Laurence Locke's workmen's compensation treatise:

L. Locke, *Workmen's Compensation* § 1, at 2 (2d ed. 1981)

1. *Author (s):* L. Locke; full first name or initial, middle initial, full last name of first two (if more than one) authors.

2. *Title*: Workmen's Compensation; full book title.
3. *Where the material can be found*: § 1 at p. 2; if a series of books, the book volume will precede the book title; if sectioned, the relevant section and/or page number where the supporting material can be found.
4. *Date*: (2d ed. 1981); book edition and copyright date.

Scholarly Articles. Consider the following law review article:

Lon L. Fuller, *The Case of the Speluncian Explorers*, 62 Harv. L. Rev. 616 (1949)

1. *Author*: Lon L. Fuller; article author's full first name, middle initial and full last name.
2. *Title*: The Case of the Speluncian Explorers; article title, underlined or italicized.
3. *Where the article can be found*: 62 Harv. L. Rev. 616; volume 62 of the Harvard Law Review beginning at page 616.
4. *Date*: 1949; copyright date of law review volume.

As well, general rules for citing legal authorities appear in Figure 10–3.

---

1. *Periods, commas, and spaces count.* If part of a citation abbreviation is a single letter, it is followed directly by a period and no space, e.g., N.E., N.Y. Supp., N.E.2d, but multi-letter abbreviations like Cal. 2d and So. 2d are surrounded by spaces.

2. *Spelling counts.* Including spelling of abbreviations!

3. *If support for an idea appears on a particular page in the cited material, specify that page (or pages) after the title and starting page number.* For instance, when citing the *McBoyle* case as an example of the rule that criminal statutes should be interpreted narrowly, which appears on the second page of that decision in the *U.S. Reports*, cite *McBoyle* thusly:

   McBoyle v. United States, 283 U.S. 25, 26 (1931)

4. *Citations should most often be used in sentence form.* They stand alone at the end of a sentence as a separate sentence beginning with a capital letter and ending with a period, like the following citation sentences from the Massachusetts statutes:

   Our workers' compensation act . . . is a "humanitarian measure" which the Legislature first enacted in 1911 . . . in response to strong public dissatisfaction with the remedies provided by traditional tort actions. L. Locke, *Workmen's Compensation* § 1, at 2 (2d ed. 1981) (hereinafter "Locke"). See *Young v. Duncan*, 218 Mass. 346, 349, 106 N.E. 1 (1914).

Figure 10–3 General rules for citing legal authorities.

Citation clauses (i.e., citations embedded in sentences) should be used sparingly. They are always set off by commas like the following citation sentences from the previous example:

Our workers' compensation act, Mass. Gen. L. ch. 152, §§ 1-86, as amended through St. 1991, c. 398 (Act), is a "humanitarian measure" which the Legislature first enacted in 1911 . . . .

5. *Use introductory signals to clue the reader into the use of the material.* Common introductory signals and their meanings include the following:

No signal: Cited authority clearly states the principle, identifies the source of a quotation or identifies an authority referred to in text. For example,

Our workers' compensation act . . . is a "humanitarian measure" which the Legislature first enacted in 1911 . . . in response to strong public dissatisfaction with the remedies provided by traditional tort actions. L. Locke, *Workmen's Compensation* § 1, at 2 (2d ed. 1981).

Accord: Two or more cases state or clearly support the principle but text quotes or refers to only one; accord introduces other cases.

E.g.: "For example;" cited authority is among authorities clearly stating the principle.

See (See, e.g. or See also): Cited authority clearly supports the principle, as in the following example:

In return, the Act gives these employees the possibility of obtaining compensation for loss of wages or earning capacity caused by a work-related injury, regardless of the fault of their employers or the foreseeability of harm. See *Zerofski's Case*, 385 Mass. at 592, 433 N.E.2d at 870; *Akins's Case*, 302 Mass. 562, 20 N.E.2d 453 (1939); *Ahmed's Case*, 278 Mass. at 183, 179 N.E. at 686. See also Mass. Gen. L. ch. 152, §§ 13, 30, 31, 34, 34A, 35 (1996).

Compare: Compares listed authorities supporting or exemplifying the principle; requires explanatory parenthetical.

Cf.: Cited authority supports a different, though analogous, principle requires explanatory parenthetical

Contra; but see; but cf.: Signals authority contrary to stated principle.

See generally: Cited material is background for the principle.

6. *Use explanatory parentheticals where necessary to clarify a citation.* For instance, in the following citation, the parenthetical clarifies the author's reason for citing the material:

Our workers' compensation act, Mass. Gen. L. ch. 152, §§ 1-86, as amended through St. 1991, c. 398 (Act), is a "humanitarian mea-

Figure 10–3 (continued)

sure" which the Legislature first enacted in 1911 . . . in response to strong public dissatisfaction with the remedies provided by traditional tort actions. L. Locke, *Workmen's Compensation* § 1, at 2 (2d ed. 1981) (hereinafter "Locke"). See *Young v. Duncan*, 218 Mass. 346, 349, 106 N.E. 1 (1914).

7. *Short citing.* Once material has been fully cited, the author may shorten later cites to the same material.

"Id." and "Id. at [page #]" refer to the immediately preceding citation, as in the following example:

The Act applies only to employees who come within its ambit. See Mass. Gen. L. ch. 152, § 24 (1996). The Act requires that participating employees waive their right to sue in tort for work-related injuries. *Id.*

Supra and *hereinafter* refer to previously cited material; hereinafter designates short name to be used in short cited material; *supra* "above," refers to previously cited material (supra and hereinafter may not be used to short cite cases), as in the following example:

Our workers' compensation act, Mass. Gen. L. ch. 152, §§ 1-86, as amended through St. 1991, c. 398 (Act), is a "humanitarian measure" which the Legislature first enacted in 1911 . . . in response to strong public dissatisfaction with the remedies provided by traditional tort actions. L. Locke, *Workmen's Compensation* § 1, at 2 (2d ed. 1981) (hereinafter "Locke"). . . . The Act is based on the legislative judgment that "human loss directly arising out of commercial and industrial enterprises" is part of the operating cost of a business. *Zerofski's Case*, 385 Mass. 590, 592, 433 N.E.2d 869 871 (1982), quoting *Madden's Case*, 222 Mass. 487, 496, 111 N.E. 379 (1916). See *Ahmed's Case*, 278 Mass. 180, 183, 179 N.E. 684 (1932). Locke, *supra*.

Short citing cases. Use *id.* if immediately subsequent to fully cited case. If citations appear between fully cited case and short cite, short cite by giving the identifying party name, volume number and reporter name *at* page number of reference. For example:

In return, the Act gives these employees the possibility of obtaining compensation for loss of wages or earning capacity caused by a work-related injury, regardless of the fault of their employers or the forseeability of harm. See *Zerofski's Case*, 385 Mass. 592, 433 N.E.2d at 870.

Figure 10–3 (continued)

Legal Writing is Organized

Clarity of writing reflects clarity of thought. Appellate judges know, and often advise legal professionals that, if a legal document won't "write," that is, cannot be written clearly and persuasively, it may be the fault of the analysis. Beyond that bit of wisdom, the following suggestions may aid writing clarity.

Macro-Organization: Organizing Your Document

A legal document must be logically organized from beginning to end. Document outlines aid in this process and help the writer (and the reader) follow the analysis through logical steps from a definition of the problem, to analysis of the problem, to the problem's logical conclusion.

Outlines. When I was in fourth grade in Virginia, my social studies teacher made me outline every chapter in our textbook. It took me thirty-one years to recover from that experience and realize that it still had not taught me the real value of **outlines:** to plan and test analysis before putting pen to paper. Once over that hurdle, I happily returned to outlining my planned writing and discovered other useful freedoms, the following: (1) each outline topic and subtopic didn't have to be stated as a complete sentence; (2) topics and subtopics didn't have to be labeled with capital Roman numerals, capital letters, and Arabic numerals; and (3) nobody was going to read or grade my outline, so I could change the outline as many times as I wanted. Freed of the fourth-grade rigor, I learned that outlines were quite useful:

- ✳ to provide sense and structure to writing
- ✳ to provide an overview of a topic
- ✳ to permit reorganization, to avoid duplication, enhance clarity, and generally "sharpen-up" writing
- ✳ to banish "writer's block" (if you don't know where or what to begin writing, start with an outline heading and follow the outline for a while)

Outlines can be very formal or (as mine tend to be) very informal. They may be handwritten or word processed (most current **word processors** have outlining capability). And, although Roman numeral/capital letter/Arabic numeral labels are unnecessary, the indentation of sub-points within main points and topics provides a useful overview or "map" of a legal analysis.

Overall Document Organization. Early wisdom suggests that a writer should (1) tell the reader where she is going; (2) take her there; and (3) tell the reader how she got there. Although to recite that rule suggests redundancy (and boredom) in writing and reading, it is not altogether a bad idea to let the reader know early on where she is going and how she will get there. Remember that in legal writing the end should not be a surprise. The informed reader is the most attentive and receptive. Later chapters of this book describe many different types of legal writing (including legal letter writing, interoffice and trial court legal memoranda, and appellate briefs). Most of those writing forms require formal introductory and concluding sections which render nearly mechanical the task of telling the reader where she's going and where she's been. Even in less formal legal writing (like legal correspondence), it is a good idea to let the reader know at the beginning where she is headed and, at the end, remind her where she's been.

The Beginning. In fiction and literary nonfiction, the beginning is the "attention grabber." It is the author's first and best opportunity to whet the reader's appetite. In legal writing, the reader comes to her task ready to learn. It is thus most important that the legal writer first describe her task and result. Hence, much legal writing begins with a summary of facts, the legal issues presented, and brief answers to those issues. In addition, it is useful to set out important steps or elements in the analysis so that the reader can easily follow that analysis.

The End. The end is likewise straightforward — it is the writer's conclusion and recommendation for further action, or in the case of legal writing to a court, a request for future action by the court.

Consider the introductory and concluding portions of a written closing argument in a special education case as shown in Figure 10–4.

The Middle. The middle of legal writing logically guides the reader from its beginning to its end. In informal legal writing — like informational and demand letters — the "middle" may be merely a description of a process, statement of facts and law, a summary of actions or steps taken or to be taken. In more formal legal writing — like intraoffice legal memoranda, trial and appellate court briefs — the "middle" will be the writer's legal analysis, her explanation and description of relevant legal rules and how those rules apply to the facts of the client's case. The IRAC method of legal analysis discussed in Chapter 8 is a convenient and common method of written legal analysis. In legal analysis of multiple issues, discuss each issue fully at once — do not skip from one issue to the next, one rule to the next, or one conclusion to the next. Be sure to conclude each issue before moving to the next. If issues have common elements, put those elements first to avoid later repetition.

Road Signs. Headings and subheadings in written legal documents help guide the reader through the analysis (and when writing to a court, offer a golden opportunity for informal "advocacy.") Notice how the **road signs** in Figure 10–5 ease the reader's understanding of the analysis of Brenda's special education problem.

COMMONWEALTH OF MASSACHUSETTS
BUREAU OF SPECIAL EDUCATION APPEALS

****

IN RE: *

                          *   NO. 92-1234

     BRENDA B   *

****

MEMORANDUM IN LIEU OF CLOSING ARGUMENT

In September of 1990, Brenda B (then 12 years old) entered the Abba public schools in fifth grade, having just completed her second year of fourth grade in Arizona. In sixth grade at the middle school, Brenda began skipping school. As the school year continued, Brenda's truancy and behavioral problems increased; as a result, she was increasingly suspended and given detentions. Her truancy continued in seventh grade, as did her aggressiveness. Even though Mrs. B drove Brenda to school daily, Brenda continued to skip classes and leave school early. The middle school nevertheless reported they could handle Brenda.

By October 5, 1992, Brenda ran amok. When required to attend gym, Brenda kicked the principal in the shins, threatened him with a pencil, and threw papers off his desk. Three days later, the Abba consulting psychiatrist recommended Brenda be committed to a psychiatric hospital. Later, Brenda entered a residential diagnostic center for an eight-week assessment. On December 7, 1992, the diagnostic team recommended Brenda be placed in a long term therapeutic residential treatment facility.

On December 16, 1992, Brenda's special education team recommended that while Brenda's educational needs might be met in a self-contained middle school classroom she not start that program until mid-January when a new special education teacher took over the self contained classroom.

On February 24, 1993, Brenda entered the Youth Center, a therapeutic residential school, which Mrs. B believes is the least restrictive, appropriate environment necessary to meet Brenda's unique constellation of educational deficits. At issue in this case is the public school's responsibility to provide such a therapeutic residential school placement to meet Brenda's educational needs.

* * *

Therefore, Mrs. B asks that the hearing officer rule that the Youth Center is the least restrictive, appropriate placement to meet Brenda's special needs.

Figure 10–4 Beginning and end of written legal argument.

LAW

Under the Education for All Handicapped Children Act, residential school placement is justifiable only when made for educational purposes. 20 U.S.C. § 1401 (16), 1413 (9) (4) (B), 34 C.F.R. § 300.347. Court decisions interpreting that act have interpreted "educational purposes" broadly. The source of the child's handicapping condition does not determine whether a placement is educational. Rather, the question is whether the placement is required to render the child educable. *Papacoda* v. *Connecticut,* 528 F. Supp. 68 (D. C. 1981). In *Abrahamson* v. *Hershman,* 701 F.2d 223 (1st Cir. 1983), the court ruled that where a child required residential placement to meet her unique needs, placement must be made at no cost to the child's parents. Additionally, certain non-educational services (e.g., psychotherapy) must be provided if those services are "required to assist [the child] to benefit from . . . special education." *Tatro* v. *Texas,* 516 F. Supp. 968, 974-975 (N. D. Tex. 1981).

ANALYSIS

Brenda is currently a 14 1/2 year old seventh grader of low average intellectual ability. Brenda's standardized tests reveal:

	12/90	10/92	4/9
Intelligence			
IQ (FS)	84	85	102
(V)	92	87	
(P)	77	86	
Achievement			
Math	4.2	4.5	5.1
Reading	5.8	6.8	6.6
Wd Att	12.9	high	
Wd Comp	4.1		low
Ltr Id	6.2		
Recog	5.5		7.9
Comp	6.0		6.0
Spelling			9.0
Gen Info			6.5

Brenda's diagnoses include: conduct disorder, identity disorder, immaturity, depression, and impulsivity, she is "a child in turmoil." Her turmoil has impeded her ability to perform in school. Brenda harbors a very poor self image; she sees herself as all bad and stupid. In his report, Brenda's psychologist said, "[Brenda's] intellectual prowess is of deep concern to Brenda, and it appears to influence her almost every move."

Figure 10–5 Road signs in a legal argument.

Brenda's image of herself depends on how she perceives others perceive her. Brenda craves attention and acceptance by her peers, indeed, she will readily sacrifice good judgment for that acceptance. When threatened, Brenda explodes aggressively or runs, impulsively, to any situation she perceives as a less threatening.

Any educational program, in addition to remediating Brenda's academics, must control Brenda's truancy.

A. The Self-Contained Abba Program Will Not Meet Brenda's Educational Needs.

Abba's plan fails to provide Brenda with consistent, full time, year-round programming. Brenda's truancy is well refined. She knows the places to run and has friends to run with. Mainstreaming provides Brenda many avenues of escape — before and after school, during class changes, at lunch.

While Abba has offered a taxi to carry Brenda to and from school, the evidence is that a ride will not stop Brenda's truancy: Mrs. B drove Brenda to school daily in 1992, yet Brenda missed 15 out of 31 school days and was suspended 5 times for truancy. The Abba plan condones Brenda's truancy: children in the self-contained classroom subject to normal suspension and expulsion; Brenda's truancy will rewarded by sending her home!

B. The Proposed Residential Educational Program Will Meet Brenda's Needs

Brenda's program at the Youth Center suffers none of the infirmities of Abba's program. At the Youth Center, Brenda is involved in a full time consistent, highly structured, integrated program. Most importantly, Brenda accepts the Youth Center program; Brenda has demonstrated, through her improved behavior, that she accepts the program and limits of the Youth Center.

At the Youth Center, truancy is not an option. All students must attend school, are monitored during transitions, breaks, lunch. Any girl not where she belongs within specific time limits is found and returned. The Youth Center does not condone missing school for any reason. While Brenda may leave class briefly for counseling, she is supervised during those periods and is reintegrated into class as soon as possible. Even when Brenda is restricted to her living unit, she attends school. Finally, as Abba so ably pointed out, when Brenda runs, she runs to known places. The Youth Center environs are unfamiliar to Brenda; her pattern of running behavior will therefore be broken and therapy can begin.

Ultimately, proof of the adequacy and appropriateness of any educational plan is its success. In two months at the Youth Center, Brenda has leapt in intellectual ability, increasing her math test score by six months, beginning to get good grades and teacher praise, adjusting to her peer group, responding to therapy.

Figure 10–5 (continued)

Micro-Organization: Organizing Sentences and Paragraphs

Just as the document as a whole must be logically organized, the document components, its sentences and paragraphs must follow some logical organization.

Sentences.

Word Order. Standard English word order in a sentence is subject-verb-direct object. It is the order the reader expects and is a good standard for legal writing. The writer need not slavishly write every sentence in standard word order, but it is important to understand that word order variation causes the reader to pause and attend to a differently structured sentence. Use that pause, that attention, in your legal writing. Don't use it foolishly, for simple variety; use word order variation to demand the reader's undivided attention: for emphasis, to introduce a new idea, or for the final conclusion.

Sentences should be short and simple. Each sentence should express a single thought in fifteen to thirty words. As in all things, moderation is best. Rewrite too-long sentences by dividing them in half, thirds, quarters, or by removing excess sentence "baggage" as outlined in the next section. Do not, however, shorten sentences to the point of choppiness; reading an entire document of short, choppy sentences is as (or more) tedious than parsing paragraph- or page-long sentences. Vary sentence length to keep the reader's attention.

Parallel Structure. Just as "road signs" help the reader follow the analysis, **parallel structure** helps the reader follow lengthy and complicated sentences. The rule of parallel structure requires the writer to express similar thoughts, sentences, and phrases similarly (e.g., begin each with a verb, a prepositional phrase, etc.) Read the following rewriting of Lincoln's second inaugural address:

> *Having malice toward none, having charity for all, firmness in the right, we strive on to finish our work, effect a binding up of the nation's wounds, caring for him who fought, to do all which may achieve and cherish a just and lasting peace.*

Now compare it with its melodic and parallel original:

> *With malice toward none, with charity for all, with firmness in the right as God gives us to see the right, let us strive on to finish the work we are in; to bind up the nation's wounds, to care for him who shall have borne the battle and for his widow and orphan, to do all which may achieve and cherish a just and lasting peace among ourselves and with all nations.*

Another way to achieve parallel structure is by using lists. When referring to a number of similar things in a single sentence, help the reader follow the items by listing them. Lists can be structured many ways; elements of the list may be set apart from the sentence remainder by a colon or dash, list elements may be numbered or lettered, set off with bullets or other markers, or set off on separate lines.

Follow each element in a list (except the last) with a comma (if the elements are words or phrases) or a semicolon (if the elements are clauses or sentences) and follow the second to last item with a conjunction (usually "and" or "or"). Read the following narrative:

> *Upon completing this course, the student should be able to explain the sources and types of law, read and understand the law, analyze the law, perform legal research, identify common research materials, write letters, memoranda, and appellate briefs, explain the steps in litigation, keyboard, word process, use CALRs, Shepardize, and advocate.*

Now compare it with the following list:

> *Upon completing this course, the student should be able to*
>
> *(a) explain the sources and types of law*
> *(b) read and understand the law*
> *(c) analyze the law*
> *(d) identify and use common research materials (including computer-assisted legal research materials)*
> *(e) explain the steps in litigation;*
> *(f) use a word processor to prepare letters, memoranda, and appellate briefs; and*
> *(g) present legal analysis orally*

Notice that each list element looks the same: it begins with a verb; is a clause; and is consistent in number, voice, subject, and structure.

Paragraphs.   **Paragraphs** break a lengthy discussion into easily digestible parts. A paragraph is a unit of writing developing a single idea. The reader expects, in beginning a paragraph, some indication of what the paragraph is about. Therefore, the first sentence of a paragraph should be an introductory topic sentence. Following sentences support and develop the topic. Paragraphs should not be too long — no more than half a page; any longer will weary and lose the reader. In addition, paragraphs should be limited to the development of a single idea, usually three to eight sentences. In most cases documents should be more than one paragraph, but multiple one-sentence paragraphs[5] are tedious and confusing. Consider this passage from Thoreau's *Walden.*

> *I went to the woods because I wished to live deliberately, to front only the essential facts of life, and see if I could not learn what it had to teach, and not, when I came to die, discover that I had not lived. I did not wish to live what was not life, living is so dear, nor did I wish to practice resignation, unless it was quite necessary. I wanted to live deep and suck out all the marrow of life, to live so*

sturdily and Spartan-like as to put to rout all that was not life, to cut a broad swath and shave close, to drive life into a corner, and reduce it to its lowest terms, and, if it proved to be mean, why then to get the whole and genuine meanness of it, and publish its meanness to the world; or if it were sublime, to know it by experience, and be able to give a true account of it in my next excursion. For most men, it appears to me, are in a strange uncertainty about it, whether it is of the devil or of God, and have somewhat hastily concluded that it is the chief end of men here to "glorify God and enjoy him forever."

The Topic Sentence.   The topic of a paragraph is usually expressed first in the paragraph topic sentence, as in Thoreau's paragraph:

> *I went to the woods because I wished to live deliberately, to front only the essential facts of life, and see if I could not learn what it had to teach, and not, when I came to die, discover that I had not lived.*

That sentence prepares the reader for the rest of the paragraph by clearly expressing its paragraph's topic: life in its simplest form.

Transitions.   Transitions in writing are of many types. Important among transitions are transitioning words that tie one sentence to the next, and transition sentences that tie one paragraph to the next.

Tie sentences in a paragraph together with introductory words of transition such as those in Figure 10–6.

Sentences should build on the paragraph topic to a final transitioning sentence which prepares the reader for the next paragraph. Paragraph transitions may be as simple as the following:

> The next issue is equally clear.
> Whether [issue] is less clear.
> Next, consider the issue [issue].

generally	likewise	accordingly
to	similarly	therefore
although	and	finally
however	for example	In conclusion
nevertheless	namely	additionally
moreover		

Figure 10–6   Introductory words of transition.

Legal Writing is Brief

To avoid wasting the reader's time (and patience), a legal document should be as brief as possible without sacrificing necessary content. Redundancy, wordiness, adjectives, and adverbs are among the hob-goblins of brevity in legal writing.

Redundancy and Repetition

Redundancy in writing is of two varieties: word redundancy and organizational redundancy. Many commonly used legal phrases are redundant. Steven Stark, a legal writing professor, hypothesizes that many redundant legal phrases began during the brief period after the Norman Conquest when France ruled the British empire. During that three-hundred-year period, lawyers drafting documents and commencing law suits were understandably uncertain whether those documents and lawsuits would be used in French or British courts. To cover the possibilities, lawyers pleaded their cases using equivalent French and British words. Hence, complaints plead that defendants "cease and desist" their conduct; wills "bequeathed and devised" property to "heirs and assigns:" leases were "null and void," and process was served by a "constable or sheriff." Moreover, in an effort to keep a listener interested, speakers often use words and phrases that are repetitious. Figure 10–7 shows a list of redundancies often found in legal documents (one of each alternative is sufficient).

7 A.M. in the morning	past experience	safe and sound
absolutely complete	past history	same identical
advance planning	past records	separate entities
aiding and abetting	permeate throughout	specific example
ask the question	personal friendship	state's prosecutor
assembled together	plan ahead	still remains
attorney at law	postponed until later	suddenly exploded
consensus of opinion	preplanning	temporary reprieve
continue on	probed into	thorough investigation
each and every	protest against	underlying (or basic)
enclosed herewith	rate of speed	assumption
exactly identical	recur again	unexpected surprise
merged together	pardon and forgive	usual custom (or habit)
my own (or personal) opinion	part and parcel	
never at any (time or before)	reflect back	
off of	reiterate (or repeat) again	
over exaggerate	revert back	

Figure 10–7 Redundancies.

Wordiness

Speakers notify listeners to pay attention to their words by beginning with introductory **throat-clearing phrases**. In writing, the reader comes to her task with full attention and excessive **wordiness** is distracting. Hence, those throat-clearing phrases are both unnecessary and waste the reader's time and attention. Figure 10–8 shows examples of throat-clearing introductions that are unnecessary (or reducible) in writing.

Throat-Clearing Phrase	Substitution
as a result of	because
at such time	when
at that point in time	then or omit
at this point in [the present time]	now or omit
attention should be called to the fact that	
because of the fact that	because
being as	because
by means of; by virtue of	by
despite the fact that	despite
due to the fact that	because
during the time that	while
except for the fact that	except for
for the reason of	because
in a very real sense	
in addition to	additionally
in an intentional manner	Intentionally
in favor of	for
in order to	to
in reality	
in regard to; with regard to	about
in response to [compliance with] your request	as requested
in spite of the fact that	although
in terms of	
in the absence of	without
in the case of	in
in the event that	if
in the neighborhood of	about
in this regard it is important to remember that	remember
in view of the fact that	because
it is interesting to note that	note
on the basis of	from
owing to the fact that	because
the next issue to be considered is	omit

Figure 10–8 Throat-clearing introductions.

Consider the following passage from a hypothetical news article describing a copyright infringement case:

> *The court concluded that in view of the fact questions raised as to ProTech Labs' knowledge of and participation in the infringement, and the fact that ProTech Labs' use of the copyrighted material was neither permitted by plaintiffs nor entirely non-commercial, entry of summary judgment in favor of ProTech Labs was inappropriate. The court held that for essentially the same reasons, the defendant DGD operator could be held liable for contributory, but not direct or vicarious, infringement.*

Compare it with the following rewrite:

> *The court concluded that, because factual questions remained about ProTech Labs' knowledge of and participation in the infringement and about ProTech Labs' permissive use of the copyrighted material, summary judgment for ProTech Labs was inappropriate. The court held that for the same reasons, the defendant DGD operator could be held liable for contributory, but not direct or vicarious, infringement.*

Excising Adjectives and Adverbs

Most **adjectives** and **adverbs** are unnecessary in legal writing; indeed, they often duplicate the meaning of the words they modify. Hence, a yellow daffodil is redundant, as is a yellow canary. Other examples include:

> absolutely none
> green grass
> totally flabbergasted
> pure white

This does not mean that adjectives and adverbs are wrong and should always be eliminated. It does mean, however, that like every word in a sentence, adjectives and adverbs need be carefully considered: If they add nothing important to the sentence, remove them.

Legal Writing is Readable

Legal writing should be readable. Because much of the description of the law is difficult and dry, it is important that legal writing be "reader friendly" lest the reader's attention flag halfway through the analysis. Simplicity is the hallmark of readable legal writing; elegant variation, negatives, passive voice, and legalese are its antithesis.

Use Simple Words, Sentences, and Paragraphs

A friend of mine from my computer programming days, Jim Addis, correctly suggests that the ultimate "elegance" in computer programming was "simplicity." His words are equally applicable to writing: Simple writing is the most elegant.

In order to calculate the amount of excess subject to an offset against future workers' compensation payments, the $30,000 paid to the employee's children to satisfy their loss of consortium claims must first be deducted from the $216,000, leaving $186,000. . . . Because G.L. c. 152, §15, entitles CNA to receive complete reimbursement for benefits already paid to the employee at the time she settles her third-party claims, that amount ($149,000) would ordinarily be deducted from $186,000. CNA, however, agreed to compromise its statutory lien and accept $50,000; consequently, it is the sum of $50,000 and not $149,000 that the judge should have deducted from $186,000.

Applying the mathematical formula set forth in *Hunter*, the employee's attorney's fees ($65,000.00), and costs ($8,000), as well as the reimbursement to the insurer for compensation paid before the settlement of the third-party action ($50,000), must be deducted from the third-party recovery ($186,000), in order to determine the insurer's offset. The total of the employee's attorney's fees, costs, and the amount of the reimbursement to the insurer is $123,000. When the $123,000 is subtracted from the third-party recovery ($186,000), the amount of $63,000 is reached. Therefore, the excess subject to offset is $63,000, not the $29,000 found by the judge. To hold otherwise would mean that the employee would receive a double recovery for her injury, to the extent her future medical bills exceed $29,000 but are less than $63,000 A double recovery is forbidden by the Workers' Compensation Act. . . . Further, the practice of compromising liens is recognized as a means of encouraging settlements when the payment of the full amount of the compensation lien would make third-party settlements an unattractive option for an employee.

Figure 10–9 Excerpt from state court decision.

Consider in Figure 10–9 the passage from a Massachusetts Appeals Court decision that vastly simplifies calculation of the final disbursement of worker's compensation recovery where a third party is liable for the worker's injuries.

In all writing, simplify, simplify, simplify; shorten, shorten, shorten. Prefer short, simple words to complex ones, short sentences to long ones, short paragraphs to long ones.

Elegant Variation

Unfortunately, efforts by writers to sound eloquent, (and more knowledgeable than they are), often results in **elegant variation** — substituting more complicated words or phrases for simpler, shorter words. For example, Figure 10–10 shows some elegant terms and their preferred substitutes.

At times, in legal writing, elegant variation is more than aesthetically unpleasing; it can create unnecessary uncertainty. Consider, for instance, the confusion caused if, after referring repeatedly to the owner of leased property, a writer (in an effort to insert variety), switches from the word "owner" to the word "landlord." The reader becomes confused: Is the landlord someone other than the owner? Who is the landlord? What significance does the landlord have to the problem?

automobile (car)
motor vehicle (car)
cease (stop)
commence (begin)
originate (start, begin)
utilize (use)
finalize, terminate (finish, end)
promulgate (issue)
previous, subsequent (before, after)

Figure 10–10 Elegant variation.

Fog Index

In the 1950s, the federal government went about shortening and simplifying government statutes, regulations, and documents. Their method of determining which documents needed simplification was to compute each document's **fog index**, a number developed in 1952 by Robert Gunning to relate the number of words per sentence and number of polysyllabic words per 100 to average grade reading level. The fog index of a document is calculated by applying the following formula to a sample of at least 100 words:

$$0.4 \text{ x (average number of words/sentence)}^6 *$$
$$\text{(number of polysyllabic words/100)}^6$$

For instance, the following paragraph (one of my own unedited writings) has a fog index well over Gunning's maximum index of 17 (college graduate):

This recitation of the facts and procedure is taken from the reviewing board's decision in this case, which, with the exception of one phrase (underlined in the following quotation), "When the passenger motioned to him, the employee then followed the passenger to the front of the bus, <u>allegedly to resolve the dispute</u>" (reviewing board decision 2) faithfully tracks the undisputed case facts and background. As the underlined (though hotly contested) phrase bore neither on the reviewing board's decision (reviewing board decision at n. 7), nor on my decision, I do not consider it or Hartford's argument that the reviewing board impermissibly usurped the AJ's fact-finding authority based on that phrase. . . . To the extent that Hartford argues that the reviewing board engaged in fact-finding when it reversed the AJ's determination that the employee's injuries did not "arise out of and in the course of" his employment, I note that in a case like this, where the essential facts are undisputed, the employee's claim of error raised a question of law, a matter fully within the reviewing board's authority.

Rewritten, the passage becomes a more manageable eighth-grade level:

The board's statement of facts tracks the argued facts except that the board states that the employee followed the passenger to the front of the bus "to resolve the dispute." As this decision does not turn on that phrase, I do not consider Hartford's argument that the board intruded on the AJ's factfinding. Additionally, where essential facts are undisputed ultimate factfinding raises a legal issue for the board.

In calculating the number of words per sentence, count each independent clause (i.e., those set off by semicolons or dashes) as a separate sentence.

Negatives

The legislature must surely have been created as a special purgatory for lawyers who speak best backward. Statutes (and many government regulations) seem singularly unable to begin at the beginning and in a straightforward, direct manner proceed to the end. Consider the following:

No individual shall be prohibited from refusing to submit to a breathalyzer test.

Even sober, an accused driver would find it difficult to determine whether he could refuse a breathalyzer test. Rewritten by substituting positives for double negatives, the statute simply says

Individuals may refuse a breathalyzer test.

Prefer Active over Passive Voice

Many legal writing failures center around verbs. Verbs are the most important words in sentences. They are what give the sentence punch and color. Simple, "punchy," active English verbs are best, most effective, and most efficient. **Passive voice** is the great hiding place of insecure writers. Passive voice is identifiable by the appearance of a helping verb (some form of the word "to be" or "to have") and the disappearance (or distancing in a "by" prepositional phrase) of the sentence subject. Hence, the **active voice** sentence "Jim kicked the ball" becomes "The ball was kicked by Jim" in passive voice. Passive voice leaves the reader with questions: Why? By whom? (in the case of subject disappearance) Where? and most importantly, "Why is it a secret?" Passive voice is a device used by writers to distance themselves or their subject from the action — to attribute some deed to an amorphous "he" or "they" rather than squarely placing responsibility on a particular "deed-doer." It is thus not surprising to hear defense counsel speak of a "victim being raped" while prosecutors charge that "the defendant raped the victim." Passive voice is vastly overused and in most cases is used without good reason, and therefore inappropriately. A good writer strives always to write in active rather than passive voice. Why? Several reasons: First, passive voice invariably results in longer sentences and phrases which waste both the writer's and the reader's time. To convey the same amount of information as "Jim kicked the ball," the writer of passive voice must write (and the reader must read!) two additional words: "The ball was kicked by Jim." Not much, you say? You're right if only a sentence or two is passive. But an entire passage, chapter, or legal memorandum in passive voice is significantly longer than its active counterpart. Passages written in passive voice are tedious and marshmallow-like to read. Consider again the hypothetical infringement case news article:

> *The court concluded that in view of the fact questions raised as to Pro Tech Labs' knowledge of and participation in the infringement, and the fact that Pro Tech Labs' use of the copyrighted material was neither permitted by plaintiffs nor entirely non-commercial, entry of summary judgment in favor of Pro Tech Labs was inappropriate. The court held that for essentially the same reasons, the defendant DGD operator could be held liable for contributory, but not direct or vicarious, infringement.*

Compare it with its active voice counterpart:

> *The court concluded that because factual questions about Pro Tech Labs' knowledge of and participation in the infringement, and about Pro Tech Labs' permissive use of the copyrighted material, entry of summary judgment for Pro Tech Labs was inappropriate. The court held that for the same reasons, the defendant DGD operator could be held liable for contributory, but not direct or vicarious, infringement.*

Second, passive voice adds an element of confusion to the reader's task. At the very least, the reader must wait till the end of the sentence or clause to find out who did the deed; if a sentence written in passive voice is subjectless, the poor reader may forever wonder who did "it." In any event, while the reader ponders those questions, she is not concentrating on the writer's message.

Finally, and perhaps most importantly, the passive voice hoax doesn't work — no one is fooled by the writer's ruse — if the writer is wrong in what he says, the reader will know instantly who made the mistake and why. Isn't it better to be someone who is occasionally wrong than someone who is wrong and secretive? As in softball: If you're going to strike out, it is better to strike out swinging than cringing!

Judge Rudolph Kass, an associate justice of the Massachusetts Appeals Court and a lover of clear, crisp, "punchy" English, tells of his college English professor, who surprised the class by announcing that he loved the lilt and poetry of the passive voice and that he genuinely hoped every member of the class would use the passive voice at every available opportunity. He had only one request — because of his love of the flexibility and variability of passive voice, he would appreciate it if each time students used passive voice they would drop a footnote explaining why they used passive voice in that instance. Although Judge Kass and his cohorts quickly learned it was easier to write in active voice than to drop a footnote every time they lapsed into passive, the teacher imparted an important rule: Use crisp, clear, active, hard-working verbs unless you have a reason for using the passive voice.

Forget the Legalese

In large part because of the history and diversity of legal writing, certain legal words and phrases have continued well past their useful lives and should be eliminated. Consider the examples of unnecessary **legalese** given in Figure 10–11.

Moreover, many legal writers insist on using arcane Latin phrases that could be simply eliminated or replaced with simpler English words. Consider the examples in Figure 10–12.

Some legal (often Latin) words and phrases, however, have no common English equivalents. Although the legal writer may be "stuck" with those few Latin words and phrases, consider dropping an explanatory footnote when using them unless you are certain your reader is familiar with them. Necessary "legalese" includes the terms shown in Figure 10–13.

Finally, the everpresent "said," "such," and "same." Why do lawyers insist on prefacing nouns with "said," "such," and "same" rather than "this," "that," and calling them by their proper names? Consider the following passage:[6]

> *It was snowing and icy on January 9, 1991, when Mr. Smith, the plaintiff, was driving home from work along a deserted highway in his 1990 Honda Accord*

case on all fours	hereof	aforementioned
case at bar	therein	aforesaid
case in chief	hereinunder	Comes now the plaintiff
hereafter	thereof	foregoing
heretofore	thereon	forthwith
thereafter	thereto	henceforth
whereas	whereby	pursuant to
hereby	wherefore	thence
herein	whereupon	to wit
		whomsoever

Figure 10–11   Unnecessary legalese.

> res ipsa loquitur (the thing speaks for itself)
> nunc pro tunc (now for then)
> arguendo (for the sake of argument)
> infra (below)
> supra (above)
> inter alia (among others)
> seriatim (in turn)
> viz (namely)
> in personam (personal)

Figure 10–12   Unnecessary Latin phrases.

certiorari

amicus curia

ex parte

ex post facto

consortium

de facto

de jure

de novo

dictum

in liminae

mens reus

quid pro quo

per se

prima facie

res judicata

stare decisis

estoppel

laches

voir dire

Figure 10–13 Necessary Latin phrases.

with chains on said vehicle's tires. Suddenly said plaintiff felt said vehicle jerk violently, and then said plaintiff heard a loud clanging of metal. Such clanging continued until such time as said plaintiff was able to pull said vehicle over to the shoulder of said highway. Upon inspection of said vehicle, said plaintiff realized that such clanging was caused when said chains had broken and then wrapped around the axle of said plaintiff's said vehicle. "Oh, *!?*!*" said the plaintiff.

Rewritten without arcane, redundant, and complicated language, the passage is straightforward.

It was snowing and icy on January 9, 1991, when Mr. Smith, the plaintiff, drove his 1990 Honda Accord home from work on a deserted highway. Suddenly, the plaintiff felt his car jerk and heard a loud clanging of metal. The plaintiff pulled his car to the shoulder of the road. Upon inspection, the plaintiff realized his tire chains had broken and wrapped around his front axle. "Oh, *!?*!*" said the plaintiff.

Actually, the paragraph suggests another failing common in legal writing: referring to parties by their legal roles (i.e., plaintiff, defendant, witness) rather than their names. Not only does a role reference add confusion to the writing (if your reader is unfamiliar with legal roles, or there is more than one plaintiff, defendant, or witness), but role references depersonalize writing. Remember that behind every rule of law and every case is a real story. It is those stories that make the law interesting and ever-changing; don't lose track of them. Rewritten with this in mind, Mr. Smith's winter adventure becomes the following story:

> *It was snowing and icy on January 9, 1991, when Harry Smith drove his 1990 Honda Accord home from work on a deserted highway. Suddenly, Harry felt his car jerk and heard a loud clanging of metal. Harry pulled his car to the shoulder of the road. Upon inspection, Harry realized his tire chains had broken and wrapped around his front axle. "Oh, *!?*!*" said Harry.*

Can't you imagine the look on Harry's face on realizing what happened?

Legal Writing is Accurate

ALWAYS USE THE RIGHT WORD!

An easy rule to write, isn't it? A bit harder to follow, though. What is the "right word?" Well, it has several characteristics, as shown in Figure 10–14.

Vagueness

An important goal of legal writing is precision. It is therefore important to avoid **vague** or overstated references in legal writing. Indeed, vague references are the second great hiding place for timid writers — and as a hiding place, they are as transparent as passive voice. Many vague references stem from using pronouns without clear antecedents; the "they" who say and do things, the ever-famous, though nebulous, "it." Other vague words include:

> the government (or state)
> situation
> process
> above
> herein
> below
> the matter

Certain common phrases are intolerably vague. There is no "clearer" indication that a point is "unclear" than for the writer to say, "It is clear that..." If it is clear, the writer doesn't need to say so; if the writer has to say it, it must be unclear. Similar vague, "wake-up" phrases include the following:

> It is beyond doubt that . . .
> It is axiomatic that . . .
> The legal principle . . . needs no citation.

1. It means exactly what you mean to say. Buy and use a dictionary — it is one of the writer's two best friends (the other is, of course, the thesaurus). Be aware of the meaning of words. Don't use a "nearly right" word — hold out for the right one, you'll know it when you see it. If you can't think of it when you are writing, leave a space for it or write a close substitute and mark it for later revision.

2. It says exactly what you want it to. Words have implied meanings not distinguished in the dictionary. For instance, the dictionary lists "cheap" as a synonym for "inexpensive." But the reader gets a very different message when reading that "Hillary Clinton arrived at the emperor's palace in an inexpensive sarong" than when she reads that "Hillary Clinton arrived at the emperor's palace in a cheap sarong." What a difference a word makes! The fix for word connotation slips is the writer's other best friend: the thesaurus. Buy and use a good thesaurus. Use a thesaurus not for its common use — to substitute synonyms for often-used words — but rather, for its true purpose — to find the right word for each situation.

3. Finally, the word should fit the mood and tone of your document; it should "sound" right. If your writing is (as it should be) simple and concise, don't insert a pompous, multi-syllabic word where a short simple word will do. Good writing has rhythm and cadence. Try to match all of your words to that rhythm. Consider again Thoreau's passage from *Walden*.

I went to the woods because I wished to live deliberately, to front only the essential facts of life, and see if I could not learn what it had to teach, and not, when I came to die, discover that I had not lived. I did not wish to live what was not life, living is so dear, nor did I wish to practice resignation, unless it was quite necessary. I wanted to live deep and suck out all the marrow of life, to live so sturdily and Spartan-like as to put to rout all that was not life, to cut a broad swath and shave close, to drive life into a corner, and reduce it to its lowest terms, and, if it proved to be mean, why then to get the whole and genuine meanness of it, and publish its meanness to the world; or if it were sublime, to know it by experience, and be able to give a true account of it in my next excursion. For most men, it appears to me, are in a strange uncertainty about it, whether it is of the devil or of God, and have somewhat hastily concluded that it is the chief end of men here to "glorify God and enjoy him forever."

Figure 10–14 The right word.

Rid your writing (and your thinking) of vague words, references, and phrases. See Figure 10–15 for some tips on professionalizing your legal writing.

Writing, Rewriting, and Revising

At some point, usually about midway through the semester, I tell my students my terrible secret: I am not a good writer. What I am, however, is reasonably adept at editing, revising, and rewriting. In this matter, I am not alone. I have known

1. Change passive verbs to active.
2. Eliminate adverbs and adjectives.
3. Eliminate redundancies.
4. Prefer simple words, phrases, sentences, concepts to complex ones.
5. Be consistent in person, place, point of view, and time.
6. Shorten long sentences and paragraphs by cutting them in half, thirds, quarters, and so on.
7. Turn prepositional phrases ("of the," "by the," etc.) into possessives.
8. Remember that the quickest fix may be to eliminate the word, phrase, sentence or paragraph causing the problem.

Figure 10.15 A few quick ways to professionalize legal writing.

authors who think so clearly, whose minds are so uncluttered, that when they put pen to paper simple, direct, clear prose flows from their pens. I admire them (indeed, I envy them), but I am not one of them. That people wrote and published before the invention of word processing is nothing short of amazing to me. When I was in high school and college, typing papers was overwhelming; it is no wonder that the time-pressed student only reluctantly made changes to their papers: spelling errors and omitted words meant completely retyping a twenty-or-more page paper. Fortunately, technology has unburdened writing of its production obstacles. Why, then, do authors remain "sensitive" about any criticism of their work? In part it is because our words and thoughts seem private and personal to us. We bring them out only reluctantly and rarely — and then we resent any suggestion that other words or thoughts might better serve. To be a good writer (or rewriter) you must shed this false pride of authorship.[7] It may help to remember the writer's obligation: to get the message across to the reader. It is not up to my reader to "figure out" what I really mean. If anyone — a student, an editor, a spouse, a good friend, a naive little boy willing to tell the emperor that he is naked — has a suggestion to clarify, simplify, or improve on wording, welcome him. The words will, after all, go out over your name — make them the very best, clearest, simplest words possible.

Word processing makes both wholesale and minute revisions a comparative joy. It is not unusual for my final written product to be *completely* different from my original — indeed, my writing goes through a minimum of five to seven revisions, typically two to four of which are major revisions. The key to editing and revising your work to good writing is time — time to let your eyes and brain recover from writing and editing to give you a "fresh look" at the project. Ideally, begin a moderate legal writing project (15 – 25 pages) at least a week in advance. Spend about half that time (the first 3 – 4 days) researching the project. Plan about a sixth of your available time (1 – 2 days) in an uninterrupted period to outline and draft the project. The remaining third (2 – 3 days) is left for editing and revising.

Separate revision from editing by a minimum of 1 – 3 hours. Use that "in-between" time to work on another project. When you return to editing, you will be able to look at your words as if they were not yours (and everyone knows how much fun it is to edit and correct someone else's work!) Ask yourself early and often "what do I really mean here — what am I trying to say — how would I explain this to the reader if she were right here?" When you answer those questions write your words down — the words will not be perfect, but will almost always clear out the clutter of familiarity. At some point, apply the "Few Quick Ways to Professionalize Legal Writing" to your document. Then check spelling, word choice, citation form, sentence and paragraph structure, etc. A final edit and last minute changes will complete your work.

"Don't have seven days," you say. "Don't have three days" . . . "Don't have time to read books with words . . ." Take whatever time is available and divide it up into 1/2 – 1/6 – 1/3 segments and follow the plan. If the issue is familiar to you, you may be able to spend less time on research and more time on writing and revising, or otherwise divide your time appropriately. Always save an hour or so at the end to apply the "Few Quick Ways to Professionalize Legal Writing" — it will make you look like you know what you are writing about even if you don't really.

Review Questions

1. What are legal citations?
2. Why are legal citations important?
3. What are the four elements of most legal citations? Describe those components for cases, statutes, books, and scholarly articles.
4. List some rules of correct legal citation.
5. What is the Bluebook? Why is it important?
6. How is the Bluebook organized?
7. What is a citation sentence?
8. What is a citation clause?
9. Describe some introductory signals for legal citations.
10. Describe short citing and when it is used.
11. What is the goal of good legal writing?
12. List and describe the characteristics of good legal writing.
13. Describe common methods of organizing legal writing.
14. Why are outlines important?
15. Why is it important to use transitions in legal writing? List some transitions.
16. What are road signs in legal writing?
17. What is a paragraph?
18. List and describe some common paragraph introductory words?
19. What is common English word order?
20. Why is word order important?
21. What is parallel structure? Why is it important? Give an example of parallel structure.
22. List grammatical rules for lists.
23. What is redundancy in legal writing? Give some examples.
24. What is wordiness in legal writing? Give some examples.
25. What are throat-clearing introductions? Give some examples.
26. What are elegant variations? Give some examples.
27. What is a fog index? How is the fog index of a passage calculated?
28. How can you correct double negatives? Give some examples.
29. What is the active voice?
30. What is the passive voice? When should passive voice be used?
31. Why is it important to prefer active to passive voice?
32. What is "legalese?" Give some examples.

33. List some components of accurate legal writing.

34. List some vague words to avoid.

35. List some quick ways to professionalize legal writing.

36. Describe the legal research, writing, and revising processes. Why is it important to revise legal writing?

Exercises

1. Give the correct citation for the following legal materials:

    a. A 1988 Maryland Supreme Court decision. The appellant was James Madison; the appellee was William Monroe. The opinion begins on page 55 of volume 108 of Atlantic Reporter® Second, and on page 119 of volume 329 of the Maryland Reports.

    b. The same decision as in question number 1, but instead of citing to the opinion as a whole, you want to direct the reader to a specific page within the opinion, that is, page 57 in Atlantic Reporter Second and page 121 in the Maryland Reports. Still assume this is the first time you have cited this opinion.

    c. A 1989 Washington Appeals Court decision. The appellant was Mary Brown; the appellee was Cary Onn. The opinion begins on page 225 of volume 555 of the Washington Appeals Court Reports and page 1019 of volume 46 of Pacific Reporter® Second.

    d. A 1980 Rhode Island Federal District Court decision. The appellant was Janet Black; the appellee was Judy Teal. The opinion begins on page 448 of volume 509 of the Federal Supplement®.

    e. A 1979 Seventh Circuit decision. The appellant was Benjamin Franklin; the appellee was Ira Figment. The opinion begins on page 1058 of volume 559 of the Federal Reporter® Second.

    f. A 1960 United States Supreme Court decision. The petitioner was Shirley Johnson; the respondent was Ann Dobmeyer. The opinion begins on page 45 of volume 354 of the United States Reports®, on page 558 of volume 997 of the Supreme Court Reporter®, and on page 68 of volume 199 of the United States Supreme Court Reports®.

    g. A 1988 Minnesota Supreme Court decision. The appellant was Robert Reidy; the appellee was Elmore Filbert. The opinion begins on page 787 of volume 556 of the North Western Reporter® Second. Minnesota stopped publishing its official reports in 1977.

    h. The 1973 Massachusetts statute on comparative negligence. You have located it in the Lawyer's Cooperative Publishing Massachusetts Annotated Laws hardbound volume. The copyright date on the inside page of that hardbound volume's 1986. The statute is chapter 231, section 85 of the Massachusetts General Laws.

    i. The 1963 Pennsylvania statute on spousal immunity. It is chapter 209, section 6 of the Pennsylvania Consolidated Statutes. You have located it in the 1991 pocket part of volume 34 of the West Pennsylvania Consolidated Statutes Annotated, beginning on page 174.

    j. Assume that you have cited to the Maryland court decision in question "a." above. You have cited no other authority. You want to cite to the opinion as a whole again. What would be the easiest way to do that?

    k. Assume you next cite to the Washington Appeals Court decision in question "c." above. You now want to cite to the Maryland court decision in question "a." again, but referring specifically to material located on page 120 in the Maryland Reports and page 56 in Atlantic Reporter® Second. What would be the easiest way to do that?

2. Rewrite the following passages using Celeste's method of legal writing:

    a. No seller shall prepare, approve, fund, disseminate or cause the dissemination of any advertisement which, because of its form and/or content, cannot be easily understood as being designed to effect the sale of hearing aids, or to create interest in the purchase of hearing aids by the audience to whom such advertisement is directed.

    b. It is an unfair or deceptive act or practice for any funeral service industry member to fail to prove by telephone, upon consumer request, accurate information regarding the funeral service industry member's retail prices of funeral products and services.

    c. In the event of failure of Purchaser to pay any installment when due, whether such failure be voluntary or involuntary, the only right of Seller arising thereunder shall be that of termination of this Agreement and retention of all sums previously paid as liquidated damages and not as a penalty, because Seller has taken the property off the real estate market, incurred expenses in selling the property to Purchaser, turned away other prospective purchasers and incurred or will be incurring development and other expenses in connection with the property. Upon such termination, any and all rights Purchaser may have in the property shall immediately terminate and Seller may return the property to its inventory and resell it free and clear of any claims, liens, encumbrances, or defects arising out of this Agreement or Purchaser's rights in the property.

    d. Massachusetts Continuing Legal Education-New England Law Institute, Inc. (MCLE-NELI) was formed in 1976 as the successor to Massachusetts Continuing Legal Education and New England Law Institute, each of which served the bar of Massachusetts and New England since the 1950's. The occasion of the name change and merger was an agreement among the Massachusetts Bar Association, Boston Bar Association, and New England Bar Association to become joint sponsors of an effort to make continuing legal education of the highest quality available to all Massachusetts as well as New England lawyers.

3. Describe a hypothetical schedule for researching and writing an analysis of Kitty's response to Attorney Mal Braithwaite's motion to dismiss. Research and analyze that response. Compare times actually spent with those hypothesized. What does this tell you about your research and writing style?

Glossary

Active Voice: Form of verb used when the sentence subject is the doer of action.

Adjectives: Words that modify or describe nouns.

Adverbs: Words that modify or describe verbs, adjectives, or other adverbs.

Bluebook: *A Uniform System of Citation*, published by The Harvard Law Review Association.

Citation clauses: Clauses identifying the location of a legal document.

Citation sentences: Sentence identifying the location of a legal document.

Citation: A phrase or sentence identifying the location of a legal document.

Concise: Succinct.

Elegant Variation: Substituting more complicated words or phrases for simpler, shorter words and phrases.

Federal Reporter®: A reporter of United States Circuit Court decisions.

Federal Supplement®: A reporter of United States District Court decisions.

Fog Index: A numerical scale for judging the reading level of a piece of writing.

Legalese: Arcane Latin or legal words and phrases.

Outlines: Word diagrams for legal analysis.

Paragraphs: One or more sentences about a single topic.

Parallel citations: Two or more locations for a single research document.

Parallel structure: Words, phrases, or clauses of similar form and structure.

Passive Voice: Form of verb used when the sentence subject receives the action.

Redundancy: Repetition.

Road signs: Headings delineating different parts of a writing.

Supreme Court Reporter® (S. Ct.): An unofficial reporter of United States Supreme Court decisions, published by West Group.

Supreme Court Reporter, Lawyer's Edition (L. Ed.): An unofficial reporter of United States Supreme Court decisions, published by Lawyers Cooperative Publishing.

Throat-clearing phrases: Unnecessary words introducing a sentence or topic.

United States Law Week: Weekly newspaper of federal court activity.

United States Reports: Official publication of United States Supreme Court decisions

Vagueness: Unclear of meaning.

Word processors: Computer-aided typing and revising systems. Typical word processors include Microsoft Word and WordPerfect.

Wordiness: Using many or long words when fewer or shorter words will do.

Notes

[1]The Association of Legal Writing Directors (ALWD) has recently released an alternative method of legal citation, Darby Dickelson's *ALWD Citation Manual: A Professional System of Citation* (2000). A comparison of the *Bluebook* and *ALWD* methods of citation appear in Appendix C to this book. Many states, as well, have special citation rules for legal writing to the state courts and administrative agencies. Where such rules exist, they should be followed rather than the *Bluebook* rules. Be sure to check your state's citation rules for variance with the *Bluebook*.

[2]Alaska and the District of Columbia have adopted the West regional reporters as their official state appellate court reporters; other states are migrating to the West regional reporters for official reporting of their recent appellate decisions. In these states, the West regional reporter will be the case's only citation.

[3]Periodically publishers of case reporters will begin a new series of reporters. For instance, the North Eastern Reporter® is now into its third series. Therefore, the North Eastern reporters are respectively abbreviated (1) N.E., (2) N.E.2d, and (3) N.E. 3d.

[4]Citation of advance sheets and Lexis/W citations.

[5]One-sentence paragraphs are not, as your high school English teacher probably declared, WRONG — consider for instance concluding paragraphs in many legal documents.

[6]From Laurel Currie Oates, et. al., *The Legal Writing Handbook: Research, Analysis, and Writing* 676 (1993).

[7]I lost my last bit of false pride when I was on the law review at my law school — some how, when the fiftieth idiot gets through strangling the last bit of creativity out of my writing, I became (and remained) goal oriented. I can well remember saying to my editors — "Fine, fine, do whatever you want . . ."

CHAPTER 11

Writing Letters

Chapter Outline

Introduction
Know Your Audience
Know Your Purpose
Legal Correspondence Form and Elements
Form of Legal Correspondence
Organizing the body of legal correspondence
E-mail
Sample Legal Correspondence

Learning Objectives

Upon completing this chapter, the student should be able to

* Understand why legal professionals write letters
* List and describe common letter types
* List and describe the components of legal correspondence
* List and describe important considerations in legal letter writing
* Describe the contents of the introductory paragraph in legal correspondence
* Describe the contents of the concluding paragraph in legal correspondence
* Describe some ways to organize legal correspondence
* Describe common letter format

Introduction

Legal professionals write letters — lots and lots of letters. They write letters to confirm, to inform, to demand, and to advise. They even write letters to send documents to someone. Legal letter writing is less formal than much legal writing and therefore offers an opportunity to stretch creative writing muscles. Before stretching too much, though, consider some important preliminaries.

Know Your Audience

As in all legal writing, it is important to know your audience. Who is going to receive the letter? Is it opposing counsel, who is intimately familiar with the case? A court clerk who will file a motion? A trial court judge? A panel of appellate court judges? A business? An insurer? A client? If it is a client, is this a sophisticated businessman or a poorly educated person? Answers to these questions will determine much about the letter, including whether it is written at all (can the information be better conveyed in person or over the telephone?); its language (simple or complex); and its length, tone, and mailing (do I need proof of receipt?). Be very careful in writing letters to maintain the tone you wish to convey. Choose words carefully; a less-than-ideal word will undo much hard work.

Know Your Purpose

Equally important as knowing who is receiving the letter is knowing the reason for the letter. Is it written to inform? To demand? To advise? To confirm? To transmit documents? Knowing the purpose of the letter will also help set its tone and impact. For instance, **cover letters** (or **transmittal letters**) inform the reader of the enclosure of other documents, **informational letters** (or **confirmation letters**) convey factual and legal information or confirm earlier discussions, **advice letters** offer legal advice to clients, and **demand letters** require action or response. Each different letter type has unique characteristics.

Legal Correspondence Form and Elements

Despite differences in tone, purpose, and audience, all legal correspondence shares certain common characteristics. Consider the parts of the edited informational letter shown in Figure 11–1.

Form of Legal Correspondence

Most often, legal correspondence is typed single-spaced, **left justified** or **fully justified**, with double spacing between letter parts (i.e., date, mailing notations, inside address, salutations, body, close, signature, copies and enclosures). Paragraphs may be indented or not, as long as they are consistent throughout the letter. The date, close, and signature are in line, roughly **centered**. Left and right margins are usually the same (1 to 1 1/2 inches) as are top and bottom margins (1 inch).

LETTERHEAD: The name, address, and telephone number of the sender.	*NEWPORT AND STEVENS* *ATTORNEYS AT LAW* *413-555-4355* 37 Main Street Amherst, OH 01002
DATE	February 1, 2001

MAILING NOTATIONS **INSIDE ADDRESS:** The address of the person receiving the letter. **REFERENCE:** Notation of the topic of the letter. **SALUTATION:** The greeting, usually "Dear," followed by the receiver's name. **BODY:** The information the letter writer wishes to convey to the receiver. **CLOSE:** This is the standard closing of a letter and the typed name and title of the signer. **COPIES AND ENCLOSURES**	**REGISTERED MAIL**
	
	Mr. and Mrs. McCall
	1234 Cushing Drive
	Arapahoe, OH 91123
	
	Re: Vincent's permanent exclusion from school
	
	Dear Mr. and Mrs. McCall:
	   It was nice meeting you yesterday and discussing your difficulties with the Cuyahoga school board. We have already begun looking into your case, have begun preliminary research, and have requested Vincent's school records. I thought I would take this opportunity to describe the expulsion language, law, and procedures.
	
	      * * *
	
	   I hope that this letter helps you understand a bit better the school exclusion law and process. As always, feel free to call me if you have any questions. As I receive Vincent's records, I will send them to you and we can further discuss legal and procedural issues as they arise.
	
	                 Sincerely yours,
	
	                 Anne M. Stevens
	                 Attorney
	
	cc: File

Figure 11–1 Sample letter.

Organizing the Body of Legal Correspondence

Although legal correspondence is usually less formal than other legal writing, it is nevertheless a good idea to plan legal correspondence, particularly if the letter concludes with instructions.

Begin with an introductory paragraph, identifying yourself, the law firm, and, if necessary or unclear, your role. Set out background facts and issues to be addressed. If the letter is lengthy or the issues are complicated, preview your conclusions. Discuss each issue separately in IRAC or another appropriate format. Use headings where appropriate and yes, although not preferred, use footnotes where necessary. Include a concluding paragraph explaining your overall conclusion, and if necessary, instructions required of the reader and writer, the dates for completing those steps, and the consequences for failing to complete required steps. Following this chapter are samples of various types of legal correspondence.

E-Mail

Electronic mail, or e-mail as it is called, is a more and more widely used form of communication. E-mail can be internal, in that one person in a business, firm, or office can only e-mail another person in that same business, firm, or office; or it may be external between e-mail users around the world (on the Internet or World Wide Web). Although generally a much less formal means of communication than "snail-mail" or ordinary formal letter writing, care nevertheless must be taken in sending e-mail. Figure 11–2 sets out some of the most common rules of *netiquette* that Internet and e-mail users have agreed upon.

- Unless you have your own Internet access through an Internet provider, be sure to check with your employer about ownership of electronic mail. Laws about the ownership of electronic mail vary from place to place.
- Unless you are using an encryption device (hardware or software), you should assume that mail on the Internet is not secure. Never put in a mail message anything you would not put on a postcard.
- Respect the copyright on material that you reproduce. Almost every country has copyright laws.
- If you are forwarding or re-posting a message you've received, do not change the wording. If the message was a personal message to you and you are re-posting to a group, you should ask permission first. You may shorten the message and quote only relevant parts, but be sure you give proper attribution.
- Never send chain letters via electronic mail. Chain letters are forbidden on the Internet. Your network privileges will be revoked. Notify your local system administrator if you ever receive one.
- A good rule of thumb: Be conservative in what you send and liberal in what you receive. You should not send heated messages (we call these "flames") even if you are provoked. On the other hand, you shouldn't be surprised if you get flamed and it's prudent not to respond to flames.
- In general, it's a good idea to at least check all your mail subjects before responding to a message. Sometimes a person who asks you for help (or clarification) will send another message which effectively says "Never Mind." Also make sure that any message you respond to was directed to you. You might be cc:ed rather than the primary recipient.

Figure 11–2 Netiquette. Sally Hambridge, *RFC 1855: Netiquette Guidelines*, IETF. Responsible Use of the Network Working Group (1995), *at* http://ftp.isi.edu/in=notes/rfcl855.txt.

- Make things easy for the recipient. Many mailers strip header information which includes your return address. In order to ensure that people know who you are, be sure to include a line or two at the end of your message with contact information. You can create this file ahead of time and add it to the end of your messages. (Some mailers do this automatically.) In Internet parlance, this is known as a ".sig" or "signature" file. Your .sig file takes the place of your business card. (And you can have more than one to apply in different circumstances.)
- Be careful when addressing mail. There are addresses which may go to a group but the address looks like it is just one person. Know to whom you are sending.
- Watch cc's when replying. Don't continue to include people if the messages have become a 2-way conversation.
- In general, most people who use the Internet don't have time to answer general questions about the Internet and its workings. Don't send unsolicited mail asking for information to people whose names you might have seen in RFCs or on mailing lists.
- Remember that people with whom you communicate are located across the globe. If you send a message to which you want an immediate response, the person receiving it might be at home asleep when it arrives. Give them a chance to wake up, come to work, and login before assuming the mail didn't arrive or that they don't care.
- Verify all addresses before initiating long or personal discourse. It's also a good practice to include the word "Long" in the subject header so the recipient knows the message will take time to read and respond to. Over 100 lines is considered "long."
- Know whom to contact for help. Usually you will have resources close at hand. Check locally for people who can help you with software and system problems. Also, know whom to go to if you receive anything questionable or illegal. Most sites also have "Postmaster" aliased to a knowledgeable user, so you can send mail to this address to get help with mail.
- Remember that the recipient is a human being whose culture, language, and humor have different points of reference from your own. Remember that date formats, measurements, and idioms may not travel well. Be especially careful with sarcasm.
- Use mixed case. UPPER CASE LOOKS AS IF YOU'RE SHOUTING.
- Use symbols for emphasis. That *is* what I meant. Use underscores for underlining. War and Peace is my favorite book.
- Use smileys to indicate tone of voice, but use them sparingly. :-) is an example of a smiley (Look sideways). Don't assume that the inclusion of a smiley will make the recipient happy with what you say or wipe out an otherwise insulting comment.
- Wait overnight to send emotional responses to messages. If you have really strong feelings about a subject, indicate it via FLAME ON/OFF enclosures. For example: FLAME ON: This type of argument is not worth the bandwidth it takes to send it. It's illogical and poorly reasoned. The rest of the world agrees with me. FLAME OFF
- Do not include control characters or non-ASCII attachments in messages unless they are MIME attachments or unless your mailer encodes these. If you send encoded messages make sure the recipient can decode them.
- Be brief without being overly terse. When replying to a message, include enough original material to be understood but no more. It is extremely bad form to simply reply to a message by including all the previous message: edit out all the irrelevant material.

Figure 11–2 (continued)

- Limit line length to fewer than 65 characters and end a line with a carriage return.
- Mail should have a subject heading which reflects the content of the message.
- If you include a signature, keep it short. Rule of thumb is no longer than 4 lines. Remember that many people pay for connectivity by the minute, and the longer your message is, the more they pay.
- Just as mail (today) may not be private, mail (and news) are (today) subject to forgery and spoofing of various degrees of detectability. Apply common sense "reality checks" before assuming a message is valid.
- If you think the importance of a message justifies it, immediately reply briefly to an e-mail message to let the sender know you got it, even if you will send a longer reply later.
- "Reasonable" expectations for conduct via e-mail depend on your relationship to a person and the context of the communication. Norms learned in a particular e-mail environment may not apply in general to your e-mail communication with people across the Internet. Be careful with slang or local acronyms.
- The cost of delivering an e-mail message is, on the average, paid about equally by the sender and the recipient (or their organizations). This is unlike other media such as physical mail, telephone, TV, or radio. Sending someone mail may also cost them in other specific ways like network bandwidth, disk space, or CPU usage. This is a fundamental economic reason why unsolicited e-mail advertising is unwelcome (and is forbidden in many contexts).
- Know how large a message you are sending. Including large files such as Postscript files or programs may make your message so large that it cannot be delivered or at least consumes excessive resources. A good rule of thumb would be to not send a file larger than 50 Kilobytes. Consider file transfer as an alternative, or cutting the file into smaller chunks and sending each as a separate message.
- Don't send large amounts of unsolicited information to people.
- If your mail system allows you to forward mail, beware the dreaded forwarding loop. Be sure you haven't set up forwarding on several hosts so that a message sent to you gets into an endless loop from one computer to the next to the next.

Figure 11–2 (continued)

Review Questions

1. Why do legal professionals write letters?
2. List and describe common letter types.
3. List and describe the components of legal correspondence.
4. List and describe important considerations in legal letter writing.
5. Describe the contents of the introductory paragraph in legal correspondence.
6. Describe the contents of the concluding paragraph in legal correspondence.
7. Describe some ways to organize legal correspondence.
8. Describe common letter format.

Exercises

1. Prepare a transmittal letter covering Kitty's response to Braithewaite's motion to dismiss.

2. Prepare a letter confirming the interview with Kitty and detailing the firm's next actions.

3. Prepare a letter describing the results of your preliminary research into Kitty's situation and accepting her case.

4. Prepare a letter to Kitty describing the firm's fee policy and estimating fees in her case. Include an appropriate fee agreement for her signature.

5. Find an advertisement for a job you would be interested in having. Write a letter applying for that job. Include a copy of your current resume.

Glossary

Advice letters: Letters offering a client legal advice on a problem.

Body: The information the writer wishes to convey.

Centered: Having the center of the lines of the document aligned with the document's vertical center.

Close: Letter closing words and typed name and title of signer.

Confirmation letters: Letters confirming appointments or conversations.

Copies and enclosures: Indicates where copies, if any, are being sent.

Cover letters: Letters transmitting material to the receiver.

Demand letters: Letters demanding response of the receiver.

Fully justified: All lines in the document lined up with both left and right margins.

Informational letters: Letters conveying information to receiver.

Inside address: Address of the person to whom the letter is sent.

Left justified: All lines in the document lined up with the left margin.

Letterhead: Name and address of the sender.

Mailing notations: Notations of special handling the letter received.

Reference: The letter's topic.

Salutation: The letter's greeting.

Transmittal letters: Letters transmitting material to the receiver.

Sample Correspondence

Figure 11–3, Figure 11–4, Figure 11–5, Figure 11–6, Figure 11–7, and Figure 11–8 are examples of various legal correspondence.

NEWPORT AND STEVENS
ATTORNEYS AT LAW
413-555-4355

37 Main Street   *Amherst, OH 01002*

February 1, 2001

Mr. and Mrs. McCall
1234 Cushing Drive
Arapahoe, OH 91123

Dear Mr. and Mrs McCall:

  Enclosed please find a copy of Judge Felman's recent decision in your son's expulsion case. Once you have had a chance to read and understand the decision, please call me so we can discuss the decision and any future action.

Sincerely,

Anne Stevens
Attorney

Enclosure

Figure 11–3 Cover Letter.

NEWPORT AND STEVENS
ATTORNEYS AT LAW
413-555-4355

37 Main Street   *Amherst, OH 01002*

May 31, 2001

Mr. and Mrs. McCall
1234 Cushing Drive
Arapahoe, OH 91123

Dear Mr. and Mrs. McCall:

   Enclosed please find the request for hearing before the
Cuyahoga school board that we discussed at our last meeting.
Once you have had a chance to read and understand the
request, please sign it and return it in the enclosed stamped
envelope.

                                    Sincerely,

                                    Anne Stevens
                                    Attorney

Enclosure

Figure 11–4 Transmittal letter.

NEWPORT AND STEVENS
ATTORNEYS AT LAW
413-555-4355

37 Main Street   *Amherst, OH 01002*

February 5, 2001

Mr. and Mrs. McCall
1234 Cushing Drive
Arapahoe, OH 91123

Dear Mr. and Mrs. McCall:

This letter will confirm our appointment next week on
Thursday, at 1:00 p.m., to review your testimony in the
upcoming Cuyahoga school board hearing.

If you are unable to meet with me then, please let me know
as soon as possible.

Sincerely,

Anne Stevens
Attorney

Figure 11–5 Confirmation letter.

NEWPORT AND STEVENS
ATTORNEYS AT LAW
413-555-4355

37 Main Street   *Amherst, OH 01002*

February 5, 2001

Leah A.
1234 Cushing Drive
Arapahoe, OH 91123

Dear Ms. A:

It was nice meeting you yesterday and discussing your difficulties with the Social Security Administration (SSA). We have already begun preliminary research, and have requested your social security file, and recent medical reports. I thought I would take this opportunity to describe the social security disability law and process, so you'll be more familiar with the SSA language, law, and procedures.

In general, the SSA determines your eligibility for benefits by answering the following five questions in sequence:

1. Are you working?
2. Is your condition severe (does your condition interfere with basic work activities)?
3. Does your condition meet (or equal) a listed SSA disability?
4. Can you do the work you did previously?
5. Can you do any other type of work?

We are responsible to show that you are not working, that your condition (agoraphobia) is severe, that your condition meets or equals a disability listed in SSA regulations, and that you cannot do the work you did previously; if we are successful, to deny benefits, the SSA may then show that there are other suitable jobs in the economy that you can perform.

From what you've told us, we should have no difficulty proving that you are not working, that your condition is severe, and that you can no longer perform the duties of teaching or soft drink delivery and repair. Our task will thus most likely center on the third question: Does your condition meet or equal a disability listed in the SSA regulations? We enclose with this letter the pertinent disability listing regulations, though regulation 12.06 Anxiety Related Disorders seems most relevant to your situation based on the information we have so far.

Since that regulation does not specifically mention "agoraphobia," we will have to demonstrate by medical reports and expert testimony that your condition is as severe as conditions defined by that regulation. In requesting information from your doctors and therapists, we will ask them to address the regulation's specific conditions, as well as reporting other relevant findings.

Figure 11–6 Informational letter.

I'd like as well to describe for you the social security disability application process. As you are aware (since you initiated that process), the process began with your application for benefits. When SSA denied your application initially, you correctly (and in a timely manner) requested that they reconsider your application. Now that SSA has reconsidered and denied your application a second time, we need to consider whether to appeal that decision to an administrative law judge ("ALJ") for an informal hearing. We have 60 days from when you received the reconsideration decision to make that decision.

To have a hearing before an ALJ and receive his decision can be quite lengthy; currently, an ALJ hearing and decision take up to 18 months to complete. We will use that pre-hearing period to find out what information the SSA has about your medical and work history, to update medical and therapeutic reports, and to explore alternative work situations for you. The ALJ will then allow us to present evidence, including your testimony, any updated medical reports, and any expert testimony we have. Although an ALJ's hearing resembles a trial in some ways, the hearing is less formal than a trial and is usually held in a conference room. Nevertheless, witnesses are sworn in and testimony is recorded. We will be with you for the hearing, calling witnesses, asking questions, and making legal arguments. SSA hearings are "non-adversarial," which means that the SSA will not be present to cross-examine our witnesses, and will not present evidence not in your SSA file. The ALJ, however, may have some questions to ask you or other witnesses. Once the hearing is complete, the ALJ will render a written decision, usually within six months.

If the ALJ's decision is unfavorable, we can appeal that decision to the SSA review council, a body within the SSA. The review council will not take any new evidence, and will review the ALJ's decision for legal errors based only on the hearing record (transcript, documents, etc.).

If the review council turns us down, we can bring legal action against the SSA in federal district court. The federal district court's review is again limited to the hearing record, though it is not uncommon for the court to overturn SSA decisions. From the district court, we can appeal to a local circuit court of appeal, and then, if warranted, to the U.S. Supreme Court.

As we discussed yesterday, I will immediately request a hearing. Whether we actually go to hearing or not, of course, will be determined by the information we gather during the pre-hearing period.

I hope that this letter helps you understand a bit better the SSA disability application law and process. As always, feel free to call me if you have any questions. As I receive medical and background information, I will send it to you and we can further discuss legal and procedural issues as they arise.

Sincerely yours,

Anne M. Stevens
Attorney

cc: File

Figure 11–6 (continued)

NEWPORT AND STEVENS
ATTORNEYS AT LAW
413-555-4355

37 Main Street   *Amherst, OH 01002*

May 31, 1996

REGISTERED, RETURN RECEIPT REQUESTED

Steve Freiday
Silverscape Jewelry
Main Street
Northampton, OH 0l060

Re: Tupper Stevens

Dear Mr. Freiday:

   I represent Tupper Stevens in her on-going request for a refund from your jewelry store. This is a demand letter under the state's consumer protection act, General Laws, ch. 93A, § 9. As you are no doubt aware, that law provides for triple damages, attorney's fees, and costs to consumers successfully prosecuting complaints against merchants engaging in unfair or deceptive acts or practices, or refusing, unreasonably, to settle or to offer to settle claims of unfair or deceptive acts or practices.

   Six weeks ago, Ms. Stevens came into your store looking for a Mother's Day gift. Earlier, Ms. Stevens' mother had admired a silver safari bracelet in your shop. Although you had none of those bracelets remaining when Ms. Stevens came in, you assured her that you could get one from your distributor in 1-2 week's time. Ms. Stevens placed her order. On Mother's Day, May 5, Ms. Stevens gave the bracelet to her mother only to discover that her father had purchased a similar bracelet the previous week.

   When Ms. Stevens tried to return the bracelet to your shop, she was told that: (1) she could not return the item because it was a "special order" item; and (2) in any event, store policy (which was printed on a small card behind and below the counter) precluded refunds on purchased items. Despite many attempts by Ms. Stevens to discuss this matter with you and your store personnel, and despite Ms. Stevens returning the bracelet to you, you have steadfastly refused to discuss the matter, or in any way modify your post-sale position.

   Ms. Stevens believes that your actions in: (1) misrepresenting the sale as a "special order," (2) failing to inform her before the sale of your "no returns" policy, (3) retaining the bracelet without issuing a refund, and/or (4) refusing to discuss or otherwise adjust this matter are unfair and deceptive acts and practices prohibited by the state consumer protection law. She demands you refund the bracelet's $260 purchase price or otherwise offer to adjust this matter within thirty days. If this matter is not adjusted within that time period, Ms. Stevens will bring suit under General Laws ch. 93A, § 9.

   Ms. Stevens and I look forward to your prompt response and adjustment of this unfortunate matter.

Sincerely,

Anne Stevens
Attorney

Figure 11–7 Demand letter.

NEWPORT AND STEVENS
ATTORNEYS AT LAW
413-555-4355

37 Main Street   *Amherst, OH 01002*

May 31, 1996

Mr. and Mrs. McCall
1234 Cushing Drive
Arapahoe, OH 91123

Dear Mr. and Mrs. McCall:

As you know, Judge Felman has denied Vincent's request to be reinstated to school. As I indicated to you yesterday, I have carefully reviewed the documents, transcript of evidence, and Judge Felman's decision in your case, along with relevant laws, regulations, and agency and court decisions. As well, I have considered the facts of your case, which follow:

Vincent's difficulties began when he was a 14-year-old student at the Cuyahoga Public Middle School. On January 24, 2001, a friend called Vincent over to his locker where he and two other boys showed Vincent a number of metal "tubes" that the friend explained were some really fine fireworks. The friend asked if Vincent was interested in buying a couple. Vincent asked their price and agreed to buy three later that afternoon. In the meantime, the boys selling these "super fireworks" sawed the lock off a nearby locker and stowed their "fireworks" in the other locker — and re-locked the "fireworks" locker with one of the boys' lock. When the owner of the storage locker came by to get the books he needed for class, he couldn't open the lock. He went to the school administrative office to ask for help. Help came in the form of a janitor who "snipped" the lock off with wire-cutters. When the janitor saw what looked like (and indeed, were) pipe bombs, he called the local bomb squad, who quietly removed the devices for testing and re-locked the locker with yet a third lock. The police then staked out the locker corridor until a number of youngsters (including Vincent) gathered around the locker. When they were unable to unlock the lock, the police moved in and took the boys, including Vincent, into custody. They were later released to their parents' custody pending the initiation of criminal charges. The school was evacuated for the remainder of the day so that the bomb specialists could ensure that there were no similar devices on the premises — there were not. An emergency school board meeting was held that night, at which the school board summarily expelled the boys indefinitely.

As the story unraveled, it seems that three boys had learned to make pipe bombs over the Internet and as a lark had made up about ten of the bombs and had taken them to school intending to sell them to some of their friends. As it turned out, of course, no sales were completed and all the bombs were confiscated.

An appeal to the Cuyahoga Court of Common Pleas resulted in Judge Felman's order denying Vincent's reinstatement. As I discussed with you yesterday, we just last week received Judge Felman's decision denying Vincent's request to be reinstated to school.

As I indicated to you yesterday, I believe that there are substantial grounds for appealing Judge Felman's decision. Moreover, I believe, based on the case law and the due process requirements mandated by Ohio's expulsion statutes, which were not followed by the Cuyahoga school system in Vincent's case, that there is a good likelihood that Vincent's expulsion will be reversed on appeal. Therefore and despite the potential cost of an appeal, which I estimate at $2000-$5000, I recommend that we appeal Judge Felman's decision. Let me know what you wish us to do. As always, if we can be of any assistance, or if you have any questions, please call.

Sincerely,

Anne Stevens

Figure 11–8 Advice letter.

The Legal Research Memoranda

Chapter Outline

Learning Objectives

Upon completing this chapter, the student should be able to

* Explain why legal professionals write legal memos
* List and distinguish common legal memo types
* List and describe the components of a research memo
* List and describe important considerations in legal memo writing
* Describe some ways to organize legal memos
* Describe a common research memo format

Introduction

Another kind of legal writing legal professionals do is preparing legal memoranda. Legal memoranda are of two types: the impartial informational or **legal research memorandum**, which organizes and communicates the results of legal research to another person(s) in the law firm, and the **persuasive** or **advocacy memorandum** (also called a trial court memo or an appellate brief), which communicates the results of legal research and analysis from a party's point of view. The legal research memo is intended to present a balanced view of the law and its application to the facts of a case — by contrast, the advocacy memo is an argument in favor of an outcome. As a result of these differences, legal memoranda differ greatly in tone, style, and even format. This chapter describes the informational or legal research memo. Later chapters will describe advocacy memos to trial court and appellate courts.

Know Your Audience

Just as it was important to know who would read the legal letter, it is also important to know who will read the research memo. Is the reader a paralegal or attorney familiar with the case or the head of litigation who has asked for a memo on each associate's active cases? Is the reader well-versed in the issues and the law involved, or is the reader an associate who is taking over but has never before handled a similar case? Determining the memo's audience will determine much about the depth and breadth of a legal memo, as well as its language, length, and tone.

Know Your Purpose

Equally important to knowing who is receiving the memo is understanding its purpose. All legal research memos are informational. However, memos may be written about a single troubling legal issue, or they may summarize case background, set out relevant law, and analyze how that law applies to the case. They may update co-workers who are already involved in the case or ensure that all members of the legal team stay current on the case.

Legal Research Memos: Form and Elements

Like legal correspondence, legal research memoranda can have many forms. Nevertheless, most legal research memos share common characteristics. Figure 12–1 shows one common format that includes all necessary information (i.e., the facts of the case, the issue presented, the law, the analysis, and a conclusion) in a logical and cohesive manner.[1]

The Body of a Legal Research Memorandum

Much of the body of the research memorandum is dictated by its form. Hence, the usual introductory information, the facts of the case, the question presented, and the applicable law are set out early to prepare the reader for the writer's legal analysis.

DATE	February 9, 2001
HEADING: To whom the memo is addressed.	To: Anne Stevens From: Peter Jones
REFERENCE: Memo topic **QUESTION(S)** **PRESENTED:** A short statement of the questions addressed in the memo. This and the brief answer(s) will be the last sec- tions written.	Re: Vincent McCall's exclusion from school **QUESTIONS PRESENTED** Whether the Cuyahoga Middle School properly perma- nently excluded Vincent McCall. Whether the Cuyahoga Middle School properly expelled or suspended Vincent McCall. Whether Vincent McCall is entitled to alternative school- ing during his period of suspension.
BRIEF **ANSWER(S):** Brief answers to the question pre- sented.	**BRIEF ANSWER** 1. No, the Cuyahoga Middle School did not properly per- manently exclude Vincent McCall from school. 2. No, the Cuyahoga Middle School did not properly expel or suspend Vincent McCall from school. 3. Yes, the Cuyahoga Middle School should provide Vincent with alternative schooling during any period he is excluded from school.

FACTS:
The factual back-
ground of the
case.
	STATEMENT OF FACTS AND PROCEDURE
	
	    Procedural Facts: On January 24, 2001, the Cuyahoga
	Middle School Principal suspended Vincent McCall and
	several other fourteen-year-olds from school for an inci-
	dent earlier that day involving the attempted sale of pipe
	bombs. Later that night, the Cuyahoga school board
	voted to permanently exclude McCall and the other
	youngsters from school. Although they were at the meet-
	ing, neither Vincent nor his parents, Mr. and Mrs.
	McCall, were allowed to speak.
	
	    Substantive Facts: Vincent's difficulties began when he
	was a 14-year-old student at the Cuyahoga Public

Figure 12-1 Sample legal research memorandum.

Middle School. On January 24, 2001, a friend called Vincent over . . . .

APPLICABLE STATUTE(S):
If the question discussed involves a statute or agency regulation, include the statute or regulation early in the memo.

APPLICABLE STATUTES

OHIO REVISED CODE § 3313.66 SUSPENSION, EXPULSION, AND REMOVAL FROM PREMISES

. . . .

(B)(1) Except as provided under division (B)(2), (3), or (4) of this section, the superintendent of schools of a city, exempted village, or local school district may expel a pupil from school for a period not to exceed the greater of eighty school days or the number of school days remaining in the semester or term in which the incident that gives rise to the expulsion takes place, unless the expulsion is extended pursuant . . .

ANALYSIS:
This is the "substance" of the legal research memo. It is here that the writer takes the reader through an application of existing law to the facts presented. In a research memo, this section should present a balanced view of the issue, omittting no valid arguments on either side.

ANALYSIS

I. The Cuyahoga school board could not properly permanently exclude Vincent McCall from school.

Ohio Revised Code, § 3313.662 governs permanent exclusion of studens from Ohio's public schools. In pertinent part, that statute provides as follows (emphasis added):

The superintendent of public instruction, pursuant to this section and the adjudication process of § 3301.121 of the Revised Code, may issue an adjudication order that permanently excludes a pupil from attending any of the public schools of this state if the pupil is convicted of, or adjudicated a delinquent child for, committing, <u>when the pupil was sixteen years of age or older</u>, an act that would be a criminal offense if committed by an adult . . . . [or] involved the pupil's bringing a firearm to a school operated by the board of education of any school district or on to any other property owned or operated by such board . . .

(I) As used in this section:

(1) "Permanently exclude" means to forever prohibit an individual from attending any public school in this state that is operated by a city, local, exempted village, or joint vocational school district . . .

Figure 12-1 (continued)

---

(6) "Firearm" has the same meaning as provided pursuant to the "Gun-Free Schools Act of 1994", 108 Stat. 270, 20 U.S.C. § 8001(a)(2) . . .

On January 24, 2001, the date of the pipe bomb incident, Vincent McCall (d.o.b. 6/1/86) was fourteen years old, too young to be permanently excluded from public school under § 3313.662. . . .

CONCLUSION:
What the memo writer concludes and why.

CONCLUSION

For the reasons set forth above, the McCalls should prevail in their efforts to have Vincent reinstated in school.

Figure 12-1 (continued)

In addition, the writer's conclusion is separately set out. Let's consider each section in some detail.

Heading and Reference

The **heading** of the legal research memorandum identifies the reader of the memo, its author, the date it was written, and the relevant topic. Often, in memos, the subject **reference** is the file name or number to which it applies. Identifying more substantively the memo's subject, however, makes it simpler to index memoranda based on subject matter, rather than merely by file reference. Thus, including in the subject section of the memo relevant topics (like "social security," "agoraphobia," or "expulsion") alerts the reader early on about the subject matter of the memo, as well as making it possible for the author or office manager to cross-reference memos by subject matter, so that later research can begin where earlier research stopped.

Question(s) Presented

The "Question(s) Presented" section of a legal memorandum alerts the reader to the precise legal question researched and answered by the memo. The question(s) presented should be specific, considering the facts of the case and some of the legal principles involved. Thus, while the question presented in the sample memo could be phrased very generally, for instance, "May public schools permanently exclude students from school?" an improved statement of a question incorporates the facts of the case and the legal principles involved, i.e.,

1. Whether the Cuyahoga Middle School properly permanently excluded Vincent McCall.
2. Whether the Cuyahoga Middle School properly expelled or suspended Vincent McCall.
3. Whether Vincent McCall is entitled to alternative schooling during his period of suspension.

It is best to limit the number of questions presented to no more than three in order to avoid confusion. If more than one question is presented, number the questions and brief answers correspondingly. The order of the questions presented should as well follow the organization of the analysis.

Brief Answer(s)

The "Brief Answer(s)" (one for each question presented) will be the last section written in the memo. These answers sum up, in a sentence or two, the writer's conclusion on each question presented. The brief answer is not the time to develop legal analysis, or even necessarily to cite supporting legal materials. The brief answer merely summarizes the writer's conclusions on each question presented; this section guides the reader through the analysis which follows. The brief answer(s) should, of course, follow the order of the question(s) presented. The following shows the brief answers in the Vincent McCall legal research memorandum:

1. No, the Cuyahoga Middle School did not properly permanently exclude Vincent McCall from school.
2. No, the Cuyahoga Middle School did not properly expel or suspend Vincent McCall from school.
3. Yes, the Cuyahoga Middle School should provide Vincent with alternative schooling during any period he is excluded from school.

Facts

This is the memo section that summarizes relevant substantive and procedural facts in the case. In writing the facts of a case, present a balanced picture of the case background. Do not omit "damaging" substantive or procedural facts. Because the legal research memo will form some or all of the basis for legal advice, it is important to present all relevant facts. Although this section might be drafted early in the writing process, it is a section to revise after the memo's analysis section is completed. Weed out facts unnecessary to the legal analysis — remember, that while the attempt is to provide a balanced picture of the case, it is unnecessary to include in the memo facts unnecessary or irrelevant to the legal analysis. Try to make the fact summary fair, yet pointed toward the analysis. Figure 12–2 is an example of a statement of facts in a legal research memorandum.

Procedural Facts: On January 24, 2001, the Cuyahoga Middle School Principal suspended Vincent McCall and several other fourteen-year-olds from school for an incident earlier that day involving the attempted sale of pipe bombs. Later that night, the Cuyahoga school board voted to permanently exclude McCall and the other youngsters from school. Although they were at the meeting, neither Vincent nor his parents, Mr. and Mrs. McCall, were allowed to speak.

Substantive Facts: Vincent's difficulties began when he was a 14-year-old student at the Cuyahoga Public Middle School. On January 24, 2001, a friend called Vincent over to his locker where he and two other boys showed Vincent a number of metal "tubes" that the friend explained were some really fine fireworks. The friend asked if Vincent was interested in buying a couple. Vincent asked their price and agreed to buy three later that afternoon. In the meantime, the boys selling these "super fireworks" sawed the lock off a nearby locker and stowed their "fireworks" in the other locker — and re-locked the "fireworks" locker with one of the boys' lock. When the owner of the storage locker came by to get the books he needed for class, he couldn't open the lock. He went to the school administrative office to ask for help. Help came in the form of a janitor who "snipped" the lock off with wire-cutters. When the janitor saw what looked like (and indeed, were) pipe bombs, he called the local bomb squad, who quietly removed the devices for testing and re-locked the locker with yet a third lock. The police then staked out the locker corridor until a number of youngsters (including Vincent) gathered around the locker. When they were unable to unlock the lock, the police moved in and took the boys, including Vincent, into custody. They were later released to their parents' custody pending the initiation of criminal charges. The school was evacuated for the remainder of the day so that the bomb specialists could ensure that there were no similar devices on the premises (there were not). An emergency school board meeting was held that night at which the school board summarily expelled the boys indefinitely. As the story unraveled, it seems that three boys had learned to make pipe bombs over the Internet, as a lark had made up about ten of the bombs, and had taken them to school intending to sell them to some of their friends. As it turned out, of course, no sales were completed and all the bombs were confiscated. Although Vincent was not one of the original three boys manufacturing the pipe bombs, the McCalls (all of them, including Vincent) agree that Vincent's involvement in the deal was at least stupid. Nevertheless, given Vincent's relatively minor involvement in the deal, they are horrified at the effect the expulsion will have on his chances for college.

Figure 12–2 Facts.

Applicable Statute(s)

Set out relevant portions of constitutional, statutory, and regulatory provisions in this section. If the specific words of the provisions are important, quote them; if only the nature or general thrust of the provisions are at issue, paraphrase them; do not, however, simply cite relevant statutes. The purpose of this section is to provide the reader a self-contained document that includes all information relevant to understanding the writer's analysis.

Analysis

The only hard part of writing a legal memo is writing the analysis. Since the memo writer has earlier listed the question(s) presented, it is usually unnecessary to begin a legal IRAC analysis with a statement of the issue, although if the memo discusses two or more questions, it may be helpful to the reader to head each analysis section with the issue analyzed. Follow with a statement of the rule applying to the issue: if a statute applies, quote relevant statutory provisions; if cases govern the result, set out case facts and holdings. Include some historical background if it will help the reader understand an emerging area of law. And, although brevity is a desirable goal, remember that the reader is human; sometimes a little "story-telling" keeps the reader interested and attentive.

Follow the summary of the applicable rule(s) with its application to the facts presented. Here is where a balanced approach is essential. As the basis for legal advice, the analysis must point out case weaknesses as well as strengths. This is where it is important to think carefully about and include possible arguments the opponent may have. It serves a client ill to take her through fruitless and expensive litigation when the case might more profitably be settled. Moreover, lawyers are ill-served by angry clients whose money and time has been wasted.

Figure 12–3 shows the analysis section of the Vincent McCall legal research memorandum.

Conclusion

This is the writer's overall conclusion regarding the questions presented in the memo. The conclusion is not the section for argument, analysis, or gathering supporting materials. That information belongs in the analysis section of the memo. Rather, the conclusion should summarize the results of the writer's analysis of the questions presented and the writer's recommendation based on those conclusion(s).

I. The Cuyahoga school board could not properly permanently exclude Vincent McCall from school.

Ohio Revised Code, § 3313.662 governs permanent exclusion of students from Ohio's public schools. In pertinent part, that statute provides as follows (emphasis added):

The superintendent of public instruction, pursuant to this section and the adjudication process of § 3301.121 of the Revised Code, may issue an adjudication order that permanently excludes a pupil from attending any of the public schools of this state if the pupil is convicted of, or adjudicated a delinquent child for, committing, *when the pupil was sixteen years of age or older*, an act that would be a criminal offense if committed by an adult . . . . [or] involved the pupil's bringing a firearm to a school operated by the board of education of any school district or on to any other property owned or operated by such board . . .As used in this section:

(2) "Permanently exclude" means to forever prohibit an individual from attending any public school in this state that is operated by a city, local, exempted village, or joint vocational school district . . .

(6) "Firearm" has the same meaning as provided pursuant to the "Gun-Free Schools Act of 1994", 108 Stat. 270, 20 U.S.C. § 8001(a)(2) . . .

On January 24, 2001, the date of the pipe bomb incident, Vincent McCall (d.o.b. 6/1/86) was fourteen years old, too young to be permanently excluded from public school under § 3313.662. . . .

Figure 12–3 Analysis.

Review Questions

1. Why do legal professionals write legal memos?
2. List and distinguish common legal memo types.
3. List and describe the components of a research memo.
4. List and describe important considerations in legal memo writing.
5. Describe some ways to organize legal memos.
6. Describe a common research memo format.

Exercise

Prepare a research memo on Attorney Braithwaite's motion to dismiss in the Kitty Barbour case.

Glossary

Advocacy or persuasive memorandum: A legal memorandum arguing for a particular result.

Analysis: The application of existing law to the facts of the case.

Applicable Statute(s): Copy of relevant parts of any constitutional, statutory, or regulatory provisions necessary to the analysis.

Brief Answer(s): Summary of the answer to the question presented in a research memorandum.

Conclusion: The research memo writer's conclusion and recommendation for further action in the case.

Facts: Summary of the factual and procedural background of the case.

Heading and **Reference:** Identify the sender, receiver, and subject matter of a legal research memorandum.

Legal research memorandum: Balanced, informative legal memorandum.

Question(s) Presented: A short statement of the legal question addressed in a legal research memorandum.

Notes

[1]Research memo adapted from *Zeitz v. Secretary of Health and Human Services*, 726 F. Supp. 343 (D. Mass. 1989).

Sample Legal Research Memoranda

Figure 12–4 and Figure 12–5 are examples of research memoranda.

February 9, 2001

To: Anne Stevens

From: Peter Paralegal

Re: Vincent McCall exclusion from school; research memorandum

QUESTIONS PRESENTED

1. Whether the Cuyahoga Middle School properly permanently excluded Vincent McCall.
2. Whether the Cuyahoga Middle School properly expelled or suspended Vincent McCall.
3. Whether Vincent McCall is entitled to alternative schooling during his period of suspension

BRIEF ANSWER

1. No, the Cuyahoga Middle School did not properly permanently exclude Vincent McCall from school.
2. No, the Cuyahoga Middle School did not properly expel or suspend Vincent McCall from school.
3. Yes, the Cuyahoga public school system should provide Vincent with alternative schooling during any period he is excluded from school.

FACTS

Procedural Facts: On January 24, 2001, the Cuyahoga Middle School Principal suspended Vincent McCall and several other fourteen-year-olds from school for an incident earlier that day involving the attempted sale of pipe bombs. Later that night, the Cuyahoga school board voted to permanently exclude McCall and the other youngsters from school. Although they were at the meeting, neither Vincent nor his parents, Mr. and Mrs. McCall, were allowed to speak.

Substantive Facts: Vincent's difficulties began when he was a 14-year-old student at the Cuyahoga Public Middle School. On January 24, 2001, a friend called Vincent over to his locker where he and two other boys showed Vincent a number of metal "tubes" that the friend explained were some really fine fireworks. The friend asked if Vincent was interested in buying a couple. Vincent asked their price and agreed to buy three later that afternoon. In the meantime, the boys selling these "super fireworks" sawed the lock off a nearby locker and stowed their "fireworks" in the other locker — and re-locked the "fireworks" locker with one of the boys' lock. When the owner of the storage locker came by to get the books he needed for class, he couldn't open the lock. He went to the school administrative office to ask for help. Help came in the form of a janitor who "snipped" the lock off with wire-cutters. When the janitor saw what looked like (and indeed, were) pipe bombs, he called the local bomb squad, who quietly removed the devices for testing and re-locked the locker with yet a third lock. The police then staked out the locker corridor until a number of youngsters (including Vincent) gath-

Figure 12–4 Vincent McCall research memo

ered around the locker. When they were unable to unlock the lock, the police moved in and took the boys, including Vincent, into custody. They were later released to their parents' custody pending the initiation of criminal charges. The school was evacuated for the remainder of the day so that the bomb specialists could ensure that there were no similar on the premises (there were not). An emergency school board meeting was held that night at which the school board summarily expelled the boys indefinitely. As the story unraveled, it seems that three boys had learned to make pipe bombs over the Internet, as a lark had made up about ten of the bombs, and had taken them to school intending to sell them to some of their friends. As it turned out, of course, no sales were completed and all the bombs were confiscated.

Although Vincent was not one of the original three boys manufacturing the pipe bombs, the McCalls (all of them, including Vincent) agree that Vincent's involvement in the deal was at least stupid. Nevertheless, given Vincent's relatively minor involvement in the deal, they are horrified at the effect the expulsion will have on his chances for college.

APPLICABLE STATUTES

OHIO REVISED CODE § 3313.66 SUSPENSION, EXPULSION, AND REMOVAL FROM PREMISES

. . . .

(B)(1) Except as provided under division (B)(2), (3), or (4) of this section, the superintendent of schools of a city, exempted village, or local school district may expel a pupil from school for a period not to exceed the greater of eighty school days or the number of school days remaining in the semester or term in which the incident that gives rise to the expulsion takes place, unless the expulsion is extended pursuant to division (F) of this section. If at the time an expulsion is imposed there are fewer than eighty school days remaining in the school year in which the incident that gives rise to the expulsion takes place, the superintendent may apply any remaining part or all of the period of the expulsion to the following school year.

    (2)(a) Unless a pupil is permanently excluded pursuant to section 3313.662 of the Revised Code, the superintendent of schools of a city, exempted village, or local school district shall expel a pupil from school for a period of one year for bringing a firearm to a school operated by the board of education of the district or onto any other property owned or controlled by the board, except that the superintendent may reduce this requirement on a case-by-case basis in accordance with the policy adopted by the board under section 3313.661 of the Revised Code.

    (b) The superintendent of schools of a city, exempted village, or local school district may expel a pupil from school for a period of one year for bringing a firearm to an interscholastic competition, an extracurricular event, or any other school program or activity that is not located in a school or on property that is owned or controlled by the district. The superintendent may reduce this disciplinary action on a case-by-case basis in accordance with the policy adopted by the board under section 3313.661 of the Revised Code.

    (c) Any expulsion pursuant to division (B)(2) of this section shall extend, as necessary, into the school year following the school year in which the incident that gives rise to the expulsion takes place. As used in this division, "firearm" has the same meaning as provided pursuant to the "Gun-Free Schools Act of 1994," 108 Stat. 270, 20 U.S.C. 8001(a)(2).

Figure 12–4 (continued)

(3) The board of education of a city, exempted village, or local school district may adopt a resolution authorizing the superintendent of schools to expel a pupil from school for a period not to exceed one year for bringing a knife to a school operated by the board, onto any other property owned or controlled by the board, or to an interscholastic competition, an extracurricular event, or any other program or activity sponsored by the school district or in which the district is a participant, or for possessing a firearm or knife at a school, on any other property owned or controlled by the board, or at an interscholastic competition, an extracurricular event, or any other school program or activity, which firearm or knife was initially brought onto school board property by another person. The resolution may authorize the superintendent to extend such an expulsion, as necessary, into the school year following the school year in which the incident that gives rise to the expulsion takes place.

(4) The board of education of a city, exempted village, or local school district may adopt a resolution establishing a policy under section 3313.661 of the Revised Code that authorizes the superintendent of schools to expel a pupil from school for a period not to exceed one year for committing an act that is a criminal offense when committed by an adult and that results in serious physical harm to persons as defined in division (A)(5) of section 2901.01 of the Revised Code or serious physical harm to property as defined in division (A)(6) of section 2901.01 of the Revised Code while the pupil is at school, on any other property owned or controlled by the board, or at an interscholastic competition, an extracurricular event, or any other school program or activity. Any expulsion under this division shall extend, as necessary, into the school year following the school year in which the incident that gives rise to the expulsion takes place.

(5) No pupil shall be expelled under division (B)(1), (2), (3), or (4) of this section unless, prior to the pupil's expulsion, the superintendent does both of the following:
   (a) Gives the pupil and the pupil's parent, guardian, or custodian written notice of the intention to expel the pupil;
   (b) Provides the pupil and the pupil's parent, guardian, custodian, or representative an opportunity to appear in person before the superintendent or the superintendent's designee to challenge the reasons for the intended expulsion or otherwise to explain the pupil's actions. The notice required in this division shall include the reasons for the intended expulsion, notification of the opportunity of the pupil and the pupil's parent, guardian, custodian, or representative to appear before the superintendent or the superintendent's designee to challenge the reasons for the intended expulsion or otherwise to explain the pupil's action, and notification of the time and place to appear. The time to appear shall not be earlier than three nor later than five school days after the notice is given, unless the superintendent grants an extension of time at the request of the pupil or the pupil's parent, guardian, custodian, or representative. If an extension is granted after giving the original notice, the superintendent shall notify the pupil and the pupil's parent, guardian, custodian, or representative of the new time and place to appear. If the proposed expulsion is based on a violation listed in division (A) of section 3313.662 of the Revised Code and if the pupil is sixteen years of age or older, the notice shall include a statement that the superintendent may seek to permanently exclude the pupil if the pupil is convicted of or adjudicated a delinquent child for that violation.

(6) A superintendent of schools of a city, exempted village, or local school district shall initiate expulsion proceedings pursuant to this section with respect to any pupil who has committed an act warranting expulsion under the district's policy regarding

Figure 12–4 (continued)

expulsion even if the pupil has withdrawn from school for any reason after the incident that gives rise to the hearing but prior to the hearing or decision to impose the expulsion. If, following the hearing, the pupil would have been expelled for a period of time had the pupil still been enrolled in the school, the expulsion shall be imposed for the same length of time as on a pupil who has not withdrawn from the school.

3313.662 PERMANENT EXCLUSION OF PUPILS; REVOCATION; PROBATIONARY ADMISSION

(A) The superintendent of public instruction, pursuant to this section and the adjudication procedures of section 3301.121 of the Revised Code, may issue an adjudication order that permanently excludes a pupil from attending any of the public schools of this state if the pupil is convicted of, or adjudicated a delinquent child for, committing, *when the pupil was sixteen years of age or older*, an act that would be a criminal offense if committed by an adult and if the act is any of the following:

(1) A violation of section 2923.122 of the Revised Code;

(2) A violation of section 2923.12 of the Revised Code, of a substantially similar municipal ordinance, or of section 2925.03 of the Revised Code that was committed on property owned or controlled by, or at an activity held under the auspices of, a board of education of a city, local, exempted village, or joint vocational school district;

(3) A violation of section 2925.11 of the Revised Code, other than a violation of that section that would be a minor drug possession offense, that was committed on property owned or controlled by, or at an activity held under the auspices of, the board of education of a city, local, exempted village, or joint vocational school district;

(4) A violation of section 2903.01, 2903.02, 2903.03, 2903.04, 2903.11, 2903.12, 2907.02, or 2907.05 or of former section 2907.12 of the Revised Code that was committed on property owned or controlled by, or at an activity held under the auspices of, a board of education of a city, local, exempted village, or joint vocational school district, if the victim at the time of the commission of the act was an employee of that board of education;

(5) Complicity in any violation described in division (A)(1), (2), (3), or (4) of this section that was alleged to have been committed in the manner described in division(A)(1), (2), (3), or (4) of this section, regardless of whether the act of complicity was committed on property owned or controlled by, or at an activity held under the auspices of, a board of education of a city, local, exempted village, or joint vocational school district.

FEDERAL GUN-FREE SCHOOLS ACT, 20 U.S.C. § 8001

Except as provided in paragraph (3), each State receiving Federal funds under this chapter shall have in effect a State law requiring local educational agencies to expel from school for a period of not less than one year a student who is *determined to have brought a* weapon *to a school* under the jurisdiction of local educational agencies in that State, except that such State law shall allow the chief administering officer of such local educational agency to modify such expulsion requirement for a student on a case-by-case basis.

(4) Definition

Figure 12–4 (continued)

For the purpose of this section, the term "weapon" means a firearm as such term is defined in section 921 of Title 18.

OHIO REVISED CODE §§ 3313.66, 3313.662, AND THE FEDERAL GUN-FREE SCHOOLS ACT

Both acts define "firearm" as follows:

(A) any weapon (including a starter gun) which will or is designed to or may readily be converted to expel a projectile by the action of an explosive; (B) the frame or receiver of any such weapon; (C) any firearm muffler or firearm silencer; or (D) any destructive device. Such term does not include an antique firearm. . . .

(4) The term "destructive device" means—
    (a) any explosive, incendiary, or poison gas—
        (i)   bomb,
        (ii) grenade,
        (iii) rocket having a propellant charge of more than four ounces,
        (iv) missile having an explosive or incendiary charge of more than one-quarter ounce,
        (v)   mine, or
        (vi) device similar to any of the devices described in the preceding clauses;
    (b) any type of weapon (other than a shotgun or a shotgun shell which the Secretary finds is generally recognized as particularly suitable for sporting purposes) by whatever name known which will, or which may be readily converted to, expel a projectile by the action of an explosive or other propellant, and which has any barrel with a bore of more than one-half inch in diameter; and
    (c) any combination of parts either designed or intended for use in converting any device into any destructive device described in subparagraph (A) or (B) and from which a destructive device may be readily assembled.

The term "destructive device" shall not include any device which is neither designed nor redesigned for use as a weapon; any device, although originally designed for use as a weapon, which is redesigned for use as a signaling, pyrotechnic, line throwing, safety, or similar device; surplus ordnance sold, loaned, or given by the Secretary of the Army pursuant to the provisions of section 4684(2), 4685, or 4686 of title 10; or any other device which the Secretary of the Treasury finds is not likely to be used as a weapon, is an antique, or is a rifle which the owner intends to use solely for sporting, recreational or cultural purposes.

ANALYSIS

I. The Cuyahoga school board could not properly permanently exclude Vincent McCall from school.

Ohio Revised Code, § 3313.662 governs permanent exclusion of students from Ohio's public schools. In pertinent part, that statute provides as follows (emphasis added):

Figure 12–4 (continued)

The superintendent of public instruction, pursuant to this section and the adjudication process of section 3301.121 of the Revised Code, may issue an adjudication order that permanently excludes a pupil from attending any of the public schools of this state if the pupil is convicted of, or adjudicated a delinquent child for, committing, *when the pupil was sixteen years of age or older*, an act that would be a criminal offense if committed by an adult . . . . [or] involved the pupil's bringing a firearm to a school operated by the board of education of any school district or on to any other property owned or operated by such board . . .

(II) As used in this section:

    (3) "Permanently exclude" means to forever prohibit an individual from attending any public school in this state that is operated by a city, local, exempted village, or joint vocational school district . . .

    (6) "Firearm" has the same meaning as provided pursuant to the "Gun-Free Schools Act of 1994", 108 Stat. 270, 20 U.S.C. § 8001(a)(2) . . .

On January 24, 2001, the date of the pipe bomb incident, Vincent McCall (d.o.b. 6/1/86) was fourteen years old, too young to be permanently excluded from public school under § 3313.662.

II. The Cuyahoga school board could not properly expel or suspend Vincent McCall.

To temporary exclude a child from public school, the school superintendent must complete the following two tasks:

"(a) Give[ ] the pupil and the pupil's parent, guardian, or custodian written notice of the intention to [exclude] the pupil; [and]

"(b) Provide[ ] the pupil and the pupil's parent, guardian, custodian, or representative an opportunity to appear in person before the superintendent or the superintendent's designee to challenge the reasons for the intended [exclusion]or otherwise to explain the pupil's actions.

The notice required in this division shall include the reasons for the intended [exclusion], notification of the opportunity of the pupil and the pupil's parent, guardian, custodian, or representative to appear before the superintendent or the superintendent's designee to challenge the reasons for the intended expulsion or otherwise to explain the pupil's action, and notification of the time and place to appear. The time to appear shall not be earlier than three nor later than five school days after the notice is given, unless the superintendent grants an extension of time at the request of the pupil or the pupil's parent, guardian, custodian, or representative."

Ohio Rev. Code § 3313.66 (B) (5) (Baldwin 1999).

A. The Cuyahoga school board gave insufficient notice of the suspension and expulsion.

The parties agree that the "hearing" afforded Vincent and his parents took place not before the school superintendent, but before the school board and that that "hearing" took place the same evening of the pipe-bomb incident. That hearing, then did not comply with § 3313.66 (B) (5). Moreover, there is no indication whether the school officials gave notice of that hearing to Vincent and/or his parents, nor whether that notice

Figure 12–4 (continued)

was oral or in writing. Although one Ohio appellate court has applied a "substantial compliance" test in determining whether or not a student received due process protection during exclusion proceedings, see *Stuble v. Cuyahoga Valley Joint Vocational School Dist. Bd. Of Educ.* 1982 WL 5953 (1982) (unpublished decision), the "substantial compliance" test has been uniformly rejected by other state appellate courts. Recently, the Ohio Supreme Court has admonished the courts to give effect to a statute's express wording and plain meaning when construing a statute and its legislative interest. *State ex rel. Richard v. Bd. Of Trustees of Police & Firemen's Disability & Pension Fund*, 69 Ohio St. 3d 409, 412, 632 N.E.2d 1292, 1295 (1994). Section 3313.66 (B) permits variance from exclusion hearing timelines only at the request of the student, his parents, or his representative. The plain language of the statute imposes a mandatory minimum three-day notice period before an expulsion hearing can be held. Therefore, this exclusion order must be vacated. *Id.*

B. The "hearing" held by the Cuyahoga School board was insufficient to suspend or expel McCall.

Moreover, the hearing provided the McCalls was insufficient to exclude Vincent from public school. Even temporary exclusion from public school impacts on liberty and property interests. *Goss v. Lopez*, 419 U.S. 565, 581 (1975) addressed the process due children suspended from public school for ten days or less. In case of a short suspension, the Supreme Court held that a "student [should] be given oral or written notice of the charges against him and, if he denies them, an explanation of the evidence the authorities have and an opportunity to present his side of the story." *Id.* Where a child is to be expelled from school, a punishment more severe than a temporary suspension, the Sixth Circuit has required that a "student faced with expulsion has the right to a pre-expulsion hearing before an impartial trier-of-fact, although does not have the right to a full-blown administrative appellate process." *Newsome v. Batavia Local Sch. Dist.*, 842 F.2d 920, 921 (6th Cir. 1988). See also *Turner v. South-Western City Sch. Dist.*, 82 F.3d 757 (6th Cir. 1999). Indeed, § 3313.66(B)(5) of the Ohio Revised Code establishes the procedures to be used in student exclusions, which are (emphasis added):

> No pupil shall be expelled under division (B)(1), (2), (3), or (4) of this section unless, prior to the pupil's expulsion, the superintendent does both of the following:
>
> (a) Gives the pupil and the pupil's parent, guardian, or custodian written notice of the intention to expel the pupil;
> (b) *Provides the pupil and the pupil's parent, guardian, custodian, or representative an opportunity to appear in person before the superintendent or the superintendent's designee to challenge the reasons for the intended expulsion or otherwise to explain the pupil's actions.* The notice required in this division shall include the reasons for the intended expulsion, notification of the opportunity of the pupil and the pupil's parent, guardian, custodian, or representative to appear before the superintendent or the superintendent's designee to challenge the reasons for the intended expulsion or otherwise to explain the pupil's action, and notification of the time and place to appear.

In this case, although the McCalls appeared for the pre-exclusion hearing, neither they nor Vincent were permitted to ask questions of the investigator of the incident or

Figure 12–4 (continued)

to offer any explanation for Vincent's behavior or involvement in the incident. The exclusion can not therefore stand. See, e.g., *State ex rel. Richard*, 69 Ohio St.3d at 412 632 N.E.2d at 1295.

C. Even were the "notice" and "hearing" offered by the Cuyahoga school board sufficient under Ohio Revised Code § 3313.66 or waived by the McCalls' appearance at the hearing, Vincent McCall did not commit nor was he party to an action warranting expulsion.

To expel a child from public school, the child must have committed an offense prohibited by a known school rule or policy. See, e.g., *Riley v. St. Ann Catholic School*, 2000 WL 1902430 (Ohio Ct. App. 8th Dist. 2000) (unpublished decision involving expulsion from a private school) and *Steinway v. Chillicothe City Schools*, 1999 WL 1604, *3 (Ohio Ct. App. 4th Dist. 1998) (unpublished decision, code of conduct; school disciplinary rules need not be as detailed as the criminal code).

The Cuyahoga Middle School's student handbook, which is annually distributed to all middle school students, provides in pertinent part as follows:

> School law provides the principal with the authority to recommend the expulsion of any student from school . . . who is found bringing on school premises or at a school-sponsored or school-related events . . .a firearm

That rule was promulgated in accordance with Ohio Revised Code § 3313.66, which provides, in pertinent part as follows:

> (B) (2)(a) Unless a pupil is permanently excluded pursuant to section 3313.662 of the Revised Code, the superintendent of schools of a city, exempted village, or local school district shall expel a pupil from school for a period of one year for bringing a firearm to a school operated by the board of education of the district or onto any other property owned or controlled by the board, except that the superintendent may reduce this requirement on a case-by-case basis in accordance with the policy adopted by the board under section 3313.661 of the Revised Code. . . .
>
> (c) Any expulsion pursuant to division (B)(2) of this section shall extend, as necessary, into the school year following the school year in which the incident that gives rise to the expulsion takes place. As used in this division, "firearm" has the same meaning as provided pursuant to the "Gun-Free Schools Act of 1994," 108 Stat. 270, 20 U.S.C. 8001(a)(2).

The Ohio exclusion statute, § 3313.66, in turn, was passed to comply with the Federal Gun-Free School Act, 20 U.S.C. § 8001, which provides in pertinent part as follows:

> Except as provided in paragraph (3), each State receiving Federal funds under this chapter shall have in effect a State law requiring local educational agencies to expel from school for a period of not less than one year a student who is determined to have brought a weapon to a school under the jurisdiction of local educational agencies in that State, except that such State law shall allow the chief administering officer of such local educational agency to modify such expulsion requirement for a student on a case-by-case basis.
>
> (4) Definition

Figure 12–4 (continued)

For the purpose of this section, the term "weapon" means a firearm as such term is defined in section 921 of Title 18.

Thus, to be validly excluded from school under these laws, Vincent must have *brought* a *firearm* to school.

The American Heritage Dictionary (2d college ed. 1982) defines "bring" as "To take with oneself to a place; convey or carry along." As it is undisputed that Vincent was not one of the youngsters to bring the pipe bombs to school, indeed, Vincent neither knew of the pipe bombs nor saw the pipe bombs before the morning the other youngsters brought them to school, Vincent did not "bring" a firearm to school.

Moreover, a pipe bomb is not a "firearm" as that term is used in Ohio Revised Code §§ 3313.66, 3313.662, or the Federal Gun-Free School Act.

As used in both federal and state statutes, the term "firearm" means as follows:

(A) any weapon (including a starter gun) which will or is designed to or may readily be converted to expel a projectile by the action of an explosive; (B) the frame or receiver of any such weapon; (C) any firearm muffler or firearm silencer; or (D) any destructive device. Such term does not include an antique firearm. . . .

(4) The term "destructive device" means—
  (A) any explosive, incendiary, or poison gas—
    (i) bomb,
    (ii) grenade,
    (iii) rocket having a propellant charge of more than four ounces,
    (iv) missile having an explosive or incendiary charge of more than one-quarter ounce,
    (v) mine, or
    (vi) device similar to any of the devices described in the preceding clauses;
  (B) any type of weapon (other than a shotgun or a shotgun shell which the Secretary finds is generally recognized as particularly suitable for sporting purposes) by whatever name known which will, or which may be readily converted to, expel a projectile by the action of an explosive or other propellant, and which has any barrel with a bore of more than one-half inch in diameter; and
  (C) any combination of parts either designed or intended for use in converting any device into any destructive device described in subparagraph (A) or (B) and from which a destructive device may be readily assembled.

The term "destructive device" shall not include any device which is neither designed nor redesigned for use as a weapon; any device, although originally designed for use as a weapon, which is redesigned for use as a signaling, pyrotechnic, line throwing, safety, or similar device; surplus ordnance sold, loaned, or given by the Secretary of the Army pursuant to the provisions of section 4684(2), 4685, or 4686 of title 10; or any other device which the Secretary of the Treasury finds is not likely to be used as a weapon, is an antique, or is a rifle which the owner intends to use solely for sporting, recreational or cultural purposes.

18 U.S.C. § 921 (1988). Notably, although pipe bombs were well known when 18 U.S.C. § 921 was latest amended in 1998, see, e.g., *Pipe bombs: Easy weapons you can whip up at home*, available at http://www.business-server.com/newsroom/nt/728easy.html, Congress did not include pipe bombs among "firearms" in enacting the statute. And while it may be argued that the category of "bombs" was intended to include pipe bombs, a careful look at the definition of firearms belies that intent. Common to all categories included

Figure 12–4 (continued)

in the Federal definition of "firearms" under 18 U.S.C. § 921, is the notion that a firearm is a device "designed to or may readily be converted to expel a projectile by the action of an explosive." Although the pipe bombs involved in this case were intended to emit a loud sound when ignited, the one-eighth ounce of explosive used in creating the pipe bombs was such that the pipe bombs' iron casing, i.e., the "pipe," prevented any expulsion of projectiles when ignited.

And, while certainly the school disciplinary rules are non-criminal in nature, but cf. *Steinway*, 1999 WL 1604 at 3, "it is reasonable that a fair warning should be given to the world in language that the common world will understand, of what the law intends to do if a certain line is passed. To make the warning fair, so far as possible the line should be clear. When a rule of conduct is laid down in words that evoke in the common mind only the picture of [propulsive devices], the statute should not be extended to [non-propulsive devices] simply because it may seem to us that a similar policy applies, or upon the speculation that if the legislature had thought of it, very likely broader words would have been used." *McBoyle v. U.S.*, 283 U.S. 25, 27 (1931). See also *Adrovet v. Brunswick City School District Board of Education*, 106 Ohio Misc. 2d 81, 86, 735 N.E.2d 995, 999 (1999).

III. Vincent McCall is entitled to alternative schooling during the period of his suspension.

For all the reasons given above, the McCalls believe that Cuyahoga school district's action in excluding Vincent from school was improper. In the unlikely event, however, that this court finds that the district acted properly in excluding Vincent from school for ANY amount of time, the McCalls argue that during the period of Vincent's exclusion, he be offered alternative education.

The Federal Gun-Free School Act of 1994, 20 U.S.C. § 8001, provides in pertinent part as follows:

> Nothing in this subchapter shall be construed to prevent a State from allowing a local educational agency that has expelled a student from such a student's regular school setting from providing educational services to such student in an alternative setting.

While that statement is not a requirement that public school districts provide alternative education to suspended or expelled students, an increasing number of states are recognizing the value in providing alternative education.

Indeed, although the U.S. Constitution does not recognize a fundamental right to public education, several states have proclaimed that the right to public education is a fundamental right. See Laura Beresh-Taylor, *Preventing Violence in Ohio's Schools*, 33 Akron L. Rev. 311, 334-335 (2000) and cases therein cited. In those states, students who are expelled or suspended have an enforceable right to alternative education during their period of exclusion. *Id. at* 335.

More importantly, though, studies done comparing school districts providing alternative education with those that do not, found that "[d]iversion and treatment programs provide some of the most promising examples of violence prevention techniques that work with youth involved in gun violence." That study found that alternative schools prevent violence in schools and communities because these programs prevent offenders from roaming the streets, that alternative school programs focus on rehabilitating troubled youth, and finally, that providing juveniles with alternative education deters future criminal activity.

Figure 12-4 (continued)

Section 3313.533 of the Ohio Revised Code empowers a board of education to create and maintain alternative schools "to meet the needs of students who are on suspension, who are having truancy problems, who are experiencing academic failure, who have a history of class disruption, or who are exhibiting other academic or behavioral problems." Indeed, section 3313.66(I) of the Ohio revised code provides that "during the period of the expulsion, the board of education . . . may provide educational services to the student in an alternative setting." Section 3313.534 of the Code mandates that the "big eight" school districts (of which the Cuyahoga School District is one) establish no later than July 1, 1999 at least one alternative school to serve students with "severe discipline problems."

Vincent's involvement in the Middle School pipe bomb incident was minimal – he neither manufactured the bombs, brought them to school, or sold them. At worst, Vincent's involvement in the incident might be described as at attempt to purchase three "super fireworks." Under these circumstances, should his expulsion be upheld, Vincent should be offered alternative schooling during his period of exclusion. Let's not turn an otherwise good boy into a violent criminal by releasing him for any length of time to the dangers of the streets.

CONCLUSION

For the reasons set forth above, this Court should vacate the judgment upholding the Cuyahoga board of education decision to exclude Vincent McCall from public school and order that the board of education expunge from McCall's school records his expulsion from school on January 24, 2001 and permit McCall to attend school effective immediately in the Cuyahoga school district.

In the alternative, the Court should order the Cuyahoga school district to provide alternative education to Vincent during any period that he is excluded from school.

Figure 12–4 (continued)

October 9, 1996

To: Anne Stevens

From: Peter Paralegal

Re: Leah A. Social Security disability case

QUESTION PRESENTED

Whether our client, Leah A., whose unique constellation of medical impairments, which include: inability to leave her apartment for any reason, including doctors' appointments, and short trips to a neighborhood store, inability to have any contact with strangers, whether in person or over the telephone, inability to interview for a job or interact on any regular basis, and inability to handle financial dealings, which has lasted for over seven years, is eligible for disability benefits under the Federal Social Security Act, 42 U.S.C. § 401, et. seq.

BRIEF ANSWER

Yes, under relevant social security regulations and decisions, Leah is entitled to Social Security disability benefits as a result of her agoraphobia.

FACTS

Procedural Facts: Leah A. originally filed for these benefits in June 1982, at the age of thirty-five, claiming she was disabled by agoraphobia since 1978. In June 1983, an Administrative Law Judge ("ALJ") who conducted a hearing and reviewed the evidence found no severe mental or physical impairment which would prevent Leah A. from engaging in substantial gainful activity. The ALJ's denial of benefits became the final decision of the Secretary in 1984 when the Social Security Administration's Appeals Council denied review of the decision. Leah filed claim for Supplemental Security Income ("SSI") benefits in 1985 and was held to be entitled to receive those benefits as of February 1985. Leah A. is now forty-two years old and remains confined to her apartment, "with virtually no face to face interactions with anyone other than her roommate." In May 1986, this Court remanded the case to the Secretary pursuant to the district court's invalidation of step two of the Secretary's evaluation process in *McDonnell v. Heckler*, 624 F. Supp. 375 (D. Mass. 1985). Upon remand, the ALJ conducted another hearing, reviewed some additional evidence, and again found that "there was no valid medical evidence of any disease process which would render the claimant 'disabled' as defined by the Social Security Act." A.R. at 255. The ALJ concluded that Leah A. suffered from no "severe medically determinable impairment, either physical or mental in nature." The ALJ acknowledged the possibility that the "claimant is suffering from psychiatric ilness [sic] which leads her to a life style which does not include employment commenserate [sic] with her education." The Appeals Council adopted the ALJ's findings, and again denied benefits for the period leading up to February 1985.

Substantive Facts: Leah A. is a college graduate who worked as a school teacher before taking a traveling sales job with the Coca-Cola Company in 1977. The first physical signs of Leah A.'s agoraphobia were palpitations, tingling and numbness in the arms, and lightheadedness manifested while driving home from a sales call in 1977. Leah A. became fearful of driving to visit the stores which stocked Coca-Cola, so

Figure 12–5 Leah A. research memo.

her roommate began to accompany her on sales calls. She began experiencing backaches and headaches during a business trip to Atlanta, prompting fear which caused Leah A. to walk out on a dinner appointment. By 1978, Leah A. had left Coca-Cola and was feeling "tired, shaky [and] disconnected."

In searching for the cause of her agoraphobia, Leah A. stated that in 1977 she was treated by a physician who prescribed tranquilizers, consulted a chiropractor for treatment of backache and numbness, and was examined by an internist who diagnosed sinus trouble and other maladies. In 1979, a psychiatrist interviewed Leah A. and reported that she had stopped a long-running practice of daily marijuana smoking, and that she was not willing to take tranquilizing drugs prescribed by other doctors for fear of becoming drug dependent. The psychiatrist recommended further psychotherapy and found "no [mental] abnormalities except by history" and "normal blood pressure and pulse." In February 1980, a neurologist reporting on Leah A.'s workers' compensation claim stated that she was given acupuncture treatments for "80% relief" of a "symptom complex" which was "entirely psychosomatic in origin." In May 1980, a psychologist stated that Leah A. would be "more than willing to return to work but not in [the] highly stressed job" she held with Coca-Cola, and he recommended relaxation therapy, meditative techniques, and alternative career planning in order to "re-enter the mainstream of life and gainful employment." Letter of Martin Markey, A.R. at 166-67. In June 1980, a neuro-psychiatric evaluation of Leah A. revealed complaints about her former job with Coca-Cola, and no physical symptoms other than "slightly elevated heart rate" and "possible weakness on forward movement of head and neck." Leah A. was advised to attend "group psychotherapy" in order to speed her recovery.

By 1981, Leah A. was doing "moderate" yoga exercises and "stained glass as a hobby." She came under the care of a psychiatrist who diagnosed agoraphobia and performed "behavior modification with the ancillary use of hypnosis" and recommended that "she not work at this time." Leah A. also visited a nutritional-biochemical consultant who prepared computer printouts of Leah A.'s "Nutrient Mineral Levels," "Mineral Rations" and "Toxic Metal Levels" and who diagnosed a "biochemical imbalance" as the cause of depression. Leah A. came under the belief that her agoraphobia was the result of birth control pills, junk food and "large amounts of Tab" consumed during the time she worked for Coca-Cola. In June 1982, Leah A. consulted a "wholistic [sic] physician" who advertised "nutritional analysis, hair analysis, kinesiology, reflexology, and dream analysis," and determined that Leah A.'s employment at the Coca-Cola Company set off a "stress-related condition" which included "pre-diabetes" and a "generalized biochemical disorder [affecting] all organs of the body, some more than others." Leah A. was advised to begin a "full-time" therapy program. Dr. Williams recommended acupuncture and chiropractic care, and Leah A. went to a nearby chiropractor who commended the holistic physician's findings and advised frequent treatments for spine problems diagnosed by x- ray.

In March 1982, "a hypnotist specializing in the treatment of agoraphobia" treated Leah A. and recommended more behavioral treatment. In June 1982, another chiropractor tested Leah A. and discovered "severe copper toxicity" and "a very strong pre-diabetic trend" which could be cured by "nutritional therapy to accomplish an excretion of the toxic tissue accumulations of Copper and Mercury." At the close of 1982, Leah A. opened her own retail store, a "Seasonal Christmas Shop," but "[t]he effort was a disaster. The store was closed and the business folded." During 1983, Leah A. stated that she was working at home with a series of cassette audio tapes produced by the Chaange [sic] Center for Help for Agoraphobia/Anxiety through New Growth Experiences. Leah A. stated that she only left her apartment for brief periods, mainly to attend doctor's appointments, and that she had an $11,000.00 credit card debt.

Figure 12–5 (continued)

ANALYSIS

The Social Security Administration regulations require the ALJ to follow a five-step analysis to determine whether an individual is disabled. This analysis is set out in *Goodermote v. Secretary of Health and Human Services*, 690 F.2d 5, 6–7 (1st Cir. 1982). The first step is to determine whether the claimant is working or engaged in substantial gainful activity. In the instant case, Leah A. was not working when she filed her claim although she worked briefly at her own small business in 1982.

The second step requires Leah A. to prove a severe impairment. In the instant case, the issue is whether Leah A.'s agoraphobia is a severe mental impairment. By 1981 a psychiatrist, Dr. Leff, had diagnosed Leah A.'s agoraphobia. Dr. Leff was graduated from the Middlesex University School of Medicine in Waltham, Massachusetts and became licensed in 1942. A.R. at 192. The regulations governing medical evidence of an impairment, 20 C.F.R. § 404.1513(a), state that licensed or certified physicians, osteopaths or psychologists are acceptable medical sources for information concerning a claimant's impairment. Therefore, while the ALJ may properly give little or no weight to the findings of hypnotists, herbalists, nutritionists, naturalists and chiropractors who do not meet this requirement, Dr. Leff qualifies as an acceptable source. There is likewise no doubt that Leah is severely impaired. As well, because Leah and the SSA agree that Leah is unable to perform her past relevant work as a salesperson or teacher, determining whether she is eligible for social security disability benefits will turn on the question of whether in step 3, Leah's condition meets or equals a listed Social Security impairment, specifically, the listed impairment.

Proceeding to the third step of inquiry, the Secretary must determine whether the claimant has an impairment which meets or exceeds the criteria in the Listing of Impairments. 20 C.F.R. § 404.1511. "If the claimant has an impairment of so serious a degree of severity, the claimant is automatically found disabled." *Goodermote*, 690 F.2d at 6. The "Listing" is set out at 20 C.F.R. § 404 Subpart P, App. 1, and includes "Anxiety Related Disorders." Id. at § 12.06. It is the opinion of this Court that the ALJ's finding of a complete absence of anxiety-related disorders during the entire period in question, as recorded in the Psychiatric Review Technique Form ("PRTF"), does not comport with the Administrative Record as applied to section 12.06. Leah A.'s statements regarding her symptoms, as confirmed by some of the medical evidence, indicate that anxiety disorders which meet the section 12.06 listing criteria may have arisen at some point before 1985.

By 1981 a psychiatrist, Dr. Leff, had diagnosed Leah A.'s agoraphobia. A.R. at 171. Dr. Leff was graduated from the Middlesex University School of Medicine in Waltham, Massachusetts and became licensed in 1942. A.R. at 192. The regulations governing medical evidence of an impairment, 20 C.F.R. § 404.1513(a), state that licensed or certified physicians, osteopaths or psychologists are acceptable medical sources for information concerning a claimant's impairment. Therefore, while the ALJ may properly give little or no weight to the findings of hypnotists, herbalists, nutritionists, naturalists and chiropractors who do not meet this requirement, Dr. Leff qualifies as an acceptable source. "If the claimant has an impairment of so serious a degree of severity, the claimant is automatically found disabled." *Goodermote*, 690 F.2d at 6. The "Listing" is set out at 20 C.F.R. § 404 Subpart P, App. 1, and includes "Anxiety Related Disorders." Id. at § 12.06. It is the opinion of this Court that the ALJ's finding of a complete absence of anxiety-related disorders during the entire period in question, as recorded in the PRTF, does not comport with the Administrative Record as applied to section 12.06. Leah A.'s statements regarding her symptoms, as confirmed by some of the medical evidence, indicate that anxiety disorders which meet the section 12.06 list-

Figure 12–5 (continued)

ing criteria may have arisen at some point before 1985. In any event, there is no substantial evidence to support the ALJ's finding of only slight functional limitations, as stated on the Psychiatric Review Technique Form ("PRTF"). If, it is determined that at no point did Leah A.'s agoraphobia rise to the level of an automatic disability, then the inquiry will proceed beyond the "threshold" to step five and determine whether "the claimant's impairment [prevents her] from performing other work of the sort found in the economy." *Goodermote*, 690 F.2d at 7.

CONCLUSION

Leah's unique constellation of impairments both equals the SSA listed impairment for anxiety related disorders and prevents her from any gainful employment. In particular, she is unable to leave her apartment for any reason, including doctors' appointments, and short trips to a neighborhood store. As well, any contact with strangers, whether in person or over the telephone is highly stressful. She is unable to interview for a job or interact on any regular basis. As well, as she demonstrated in the failed Christmas shop experience, she cannot handle the stress of financial dealings.

Based on the purpose of the social security disability act — to provide support for those who are without means, are permanently disabled, and are therefore unable to perform any substantial gainful activity — and Leah's demonstrated, long-standing, and severe inability to deal with any interpersonal contact or stress, a judge will likely find the SSA has not shown that jobs exist in substantial numbers in the national economy that Leah can perform.

APPLICABLE STATUTES

20 C.F.R. § 404 Subpart P, App. 1, 12.06. *Anxiety Disorders*. In these disorders anxiety is either the predominant disturbance or it is experienced if the individual attempts to master symptoms; for example confronting the dreaded object or situation in a phobic disorder or resisting the obsessions or compulsions in obsessive compulsive disorders.

The required level of severity for these disorders is met when the requirement in both A and B are satisfied, or when the requirements in both A and C are satisfied.

A. Medically documented findings of at least one of the following:
   1. Generalized persistent anxiety accompanied by three out of four of the following signs or symptoms:
      a. Motor tension; or
      b. Autonomic hyperactivity; or
      c. Apprehensive expectation; or
      d. Vigilance and scanning; or
   2. A persistent irrational fear of a specific object, activity, or situation which results in a compelling desire to avoid the dreaded object, activity, or situation; or
   3. Recurrent severe panic attacks manifested by a sudden unpredictable onset of intense apprehension, fear, terror and sense of impending doom occurring on the average of at least once a week; or
   4. Recurrent obsessions or compulsions which are a source of marked distress; or
   5. Recurrent and intrusive recollections of a traumatic experience, which are the source of marked distress;

Figure 12–5 (continued)

AND
B. Resulting in at least two of the following:
1. Marked restriction of activities of daily living; or
2. Marked difficulties in maintaining social functioning; or
3. Deficiencies of concentration, persistence of pace resulting in frequent failure to complete tasks in a timely manner (in work settings or elsewhere); or
4. Repeated episodes of deterioration or decompensation in work or work-liked settings which cause the individual to withdraw from that situations or to experience exacerbation of signs and symptoms (which may include deterioration of adaptive behaviors);
OR
C. Resulting in complete inability to function independently outside the area of one's home.

20 C.F.R. § 404.1511(a). *Disabled workers, persons disabled since childhood and, for months after December 1990, disabled widows, widowers, and surviving divorced spouses.* If you are entitled to disability cash benefits as a disabled worker, or to child's insurance benefits, or, for monthly benefits payable after December 1990, to widow's, widower's, or surviving divorced spouse's monthly benefits, a disabling impairment is an impairment (or combination of impairments) which, of itself, is so severe that it meets or equals a set of criteria in the Listing of Impairments in appendix 1 of this subpart or which, when considered with your age, education, and work experience, would result in a finding that you are disabled under § 404.1594. In determining whether you have a disabling impairment, earnings are not considered.

(b) Disabled widows, widowers, and surviving divorced spouses, for monthly benefits for months prior to January 1991. If you have been entitled to disability benefits as a disabled widow, widower, or surviving divorced spouse and we must decide whether you had a disabling impairment for any time prior to January 1991, a disabling impairment is an impairment (or combination of impairments) which, of itself, was so severe that it met or equaled a set of criteria in the Listing of Impairments in appendix 1 of this subpart, or results in a finding that you were disabled under § 404.1579. In determining whether you had a disabling impairment, earnings are not considered.

20 C.F.R. § 404.151 (a) *Acceptable sources.* We need reports about your impairments from acceptable medical sources. Acceptable medical sources are
(1) Licensed physicians;
(2) Licensed osteopaths;
(3) Licensed or certified psychologists;
(4) Licensed optometrists for the measurement of visual acuity and visual fields (we may need a report from a physician to determine other aspects of eye diseases); and
(5) Persons authorized to send us a copy or summary of the medical records of a hospital, clinic, sanitarium, medical institution, or health care facility. Generally, the copy or summary should be certified as accurate by the custodian or by any authorized employee of the Social Security Administration, Veterans' Administration, or State agency. However, we will not return an uncertified copy or summary for certification unless there is some question about the document.
(b) Medical reports. Medical reports should include
(1) Medical history;
(2) Clinical findings (such as the results of physical or mental status examinations);

Figure 12–5 (continued)

(3) Laboratory findings (such as blood pressure, x-rays);

(4) Diagnosis (statement of disease or injury based on its signs and symptoms);

(5) Treatment prescribed with response, and prognosis; and

(6) A statement about what you can still do despite your impairment(s) based on the medical source's findings on the factors under paragraphs (b)(1) through (b)(5) of this section (except in statutory blindness claims). Although we will request a medical source statement about what you can still do despite your impairment(s), the lack of the medical source statement will not make the report incomplete. See § 404.1527.

(c) Statements about what you can still do. Statements about what you can still do (based on the medical source's findings on the factors under paragraphs (b)(1) through (b)(5) of this section) should describe, but are not limited to, the kinds of physical and mental capabilities listed below. See §§ 404.1527 and 404.1545(c).

    (1) The medical source's opinion about your ability, despite your impairment(s), to do work-related activities such as sitting, standing, walking, lifting, carrying, handling objects, hearing, speaking, and traveling; and

    (2) In cases of mental impairment(s), the medical source's opinion about your ability to understand, to carry out and remember instructions, and to respond appropriately to supervision, coworkers, and work pressures in a work setting.

(d) Completeness. The medical evidence, including the clinical and laboratory findings, must be complete and detailed enough to allow us to make a determination about whether you are disabled or blind. It must allow us to determine

(1) The nature and limiting effects of your impairment(s) for any period in question;

(2) The probable duration of your impairment; and

(3) Your residual functional capacity to do work-related physical and mental activities.

(e) Information from other sources. Information from other sources may also help us to understand how your impairment affects your ability to work. Other sources include

(1) Public and private social welfare agencies;

(2) Observations by non-medical sources; and

(3) Other practitioners (for example, naturopaths, chiropractors, audiologists, etc.).

Figure 12–5 (continued)

Sample Student Briefs in the Vincent McCall Case

Figure 12–6, Figure 12–7, Figure 12–8, and Figure 12–9 are examples of briefs written by students.

MEMORANDUM

TO: Anne Stevens

FROM: Kathryn Ring

DATE: January 28, 2001

RE: Vincent McCall

    This memo discusses whether Vincent McCall, a 14-year-old student at the Cuyahoga Public Middle School, can be permanently expelled from school due to his involvement with explosive devices.

BACKGROUND SUMMARY

    Three students at Cuyahoga Public Middle School manufactured ten pipe bombs and tried to sell them as "fireworks" to friends. Our client's son, Vincent McCall, was approached by one the students and asked Vincent if he would be interested in purchasing some "fireworks." Vincent looked at the metal "tubes" and told his friend that he would purchase three of the "fireworks" in the afternoon. The three students then moved the bombs to a different locker and changed the lock.

    When a student was unable to open his locker, the janitor had to snip the lock off with a wire cutter. The janitor noticed the metal tubes and informed the proper authorities. The bomb squad then quietly removed the metal devices for testing, re-locked the locker and waited for someone to open the locker. Three students, along with Vincent McCall, were subsequently arrested and taken into custody after trying to open the locker that contained the pipe bombs.

RULES AND REGULATIONS

    Under the provisions of the Cuyahoga Public Middle School, a bomb threat is considered an extremely serious and dangerous situation. The policy in the handbook states that any students who make or cause to be made a bomb threat will be immediately suspended and referred for criminal prosecution and will be considered for expulsion from school, pursuant to state statute 120.13(1)(c). Anyone violating this policy will be immediately suspended from school and referred to local police department. Students found to have violated this policy may be considered for expulsion. (See Wis. Stat. §§ 948.60 and 948.61 [Date]).

    Based upon the Wisconsin state statutes, students are prohibited from possessing a weapon or objects that may be used as a weapon on school premises. "Dangerous

---

Figure 12–6 Student brief. Courtesy of Kathryn Ring.

weapon" is defined as any device designed as a weapon and capable of producing death or great bodily harm. (See Wis. Stat. § 939.22(10)). The school board may expel from school a pupil who is at least 16 years old if there is an alleged attempt made to destroy any school property by means of explosives. (See Wis. Stat. § 948.605(c)1 and 2).

In accordance with Wisconsin State Statute 120.13(1) (b) and (c), students whose behavior threatens the health, safety and welfare of others may be suspended out-of-school for up to three days. The School Board may expel a pupil from school whenever it finds the pupil engages in conduct which endangers the property, health, or safety of others while under the supervision of school authority. Expulsion proceedings will be conducted in accordance with Wis. Stat. § 120.13(1)(c).

In *Goss v. Lopez*, 419 U.S. 565 (1975), the Supreme Court held that students must be afforded some due process before their suspension from school, even for short periods of time. The Court sought to reduce the likelihood of faulty suspensions by ensuring that the right party was expelled. The Supreme Court held that the principal shall provide the student with written or oral notice of the charges, the basis or evidence for the charges, and a minimum of an opportunity to deny them.

DISCUSSION

The issue in this case is whether the School Board can expel Vincent McCall from school.

Wisconsin state law permits disciplinary action such as detention, suspension and expulsion. However, if a student is expelled or suspended for more than three days, Wisconsin law requires an optional hearing in front of the school board where the student can be represented by a lawyer. At this hearing, they will have the opportunity to question and present witnesses of their own. In addition, they are entitled to a full copy of the transcript should they wish to appeal the decision of the School Board.

Vincent McCall saw the metal "tubes" in a locker and believed they were fireworks. Vincent told his friend that he might be interested in purchasing these "fireworks." The facts show that Vincent had an intent to purchase in what he believed were fireworks – not a pipe bomb. Vincent was neither responsible for making the pipe bombs nor did he bring them into school. A person might argue that fireworks could also be considered a dangerous device. A dangerous weapon is described as being capable of producing death or great bodily harm. (See Wis. Stat. § 939.22(10)). Fireworks are less of a threat than a pipe bomb but fireworks can still cause damage to people and property.

CONCLUSION

According to the school handbook and state law, Vincent is entitled to a hearing before the School Board to determine whether or not his actions justify expulsion from school. It is likely that he will not be expelled. Wisconsin statute § 948.609(c)1 and 2 states the school board is allowed to expel from school a pupil who is at least 16 years old if the board determines the pupil guilty of endangering the property, health or safety of others. Vincent McCall should not be expelled based upon the minor role he played in this incident and that he is only 14 years old.

Figure 12–6 (continued)

MEMORANDUM

TO: Attorney Handling Case

FROM: Sarah Merlau

DATE: January 28, 2000

RE: Expulsion of Vincent McCall from Cuyahoga Public Middle School

This memo is in response to your request to determine if, under the facts given, Vincent McCall can be permanently excluded from school.

FACTS

A friend of Vincent's showed him a number of metal "tubes" that the friend explained were some really fine fireworks, when in actuality they were pipe bombs.

Vincent asked their price and agreed to buy 3 "fireworks" later that afternoon.

The police staked out the location of the fireworks/pipe bombs until a number of youngsters (including Vincent) gathered around the locker, at which time the police took the youngsters into custody.

The youngsters were released to their parents' custody pending the initiation of criminal charges.

There were no other bombs or incendiary devices on the premises.

Three of the boys had learned to make pipe bombs over the Internet.

Vincent was not one of the original three boys manufacturing the pipe bombs.

No sales were completed and all the bombs were confiscated.

ISSUES:

1. Can Cuyahoga Public Middle School permanently exclude Vincent McCall from school?
2. Considering that no sales were completed, was Vincent McCall in possession of the fireworks/pipe bombs?

SHORT ANSWER:

THE CONSTITUTION OF THE STATE OF NEW YORK, ARTICLE XI. EDUCATION. NY CLS Const Art XI, § 1 (2000) states that:

A child's right to free public education is paramount.

A student residing in the district administered by a board of education has a constitutionally guaranteed right to an education.

Figure 12–7 Student brief. Courtesy of Sarah Merlau.

The Education Article of the State Constitution imposes a duty on the legislature to ensure availability of sound basic education to all children of state, and courts are responsible for adjudicating the nature of such duty.

The Education Article of the State Constitution (NY Const, art XI, § 1) requires the State to offer all children the opportunity of a sound basic education consisting of the basic literacy, calculating, and verbal skills necessary to enable children to eventually function productively as civic participants capable of voting and serving on a jury.

NY CLS Educ § 3205 (2000) states that:

§ 3205. Attendance of minors upon full time day instruction

1. a. In each school district of the state, each minor from six to sixteen years of age shall attend full time instruction.

Compulsory features of the Education Law requiring that minors attend public school or be provided with appropriate equivalent education.

Education Law §§ 3204(1) and 3205(1)(a) require all children from 6 to 16 years of age attend full-time instruction at public school or elsewhere. If instruction is given other than at public school, it must be "substantially equivalent" to the instruction given to minors of similar age and attainment at the public schools of the district where the minor resides and must be given by a "competent" teacher.

A strong argument can be made that because there was no exchange of monies or merchandise between Vincent McCall and the owners of the pipe bombs that Vincent McCall was technically not in possession of any type of explosive device.

The school handbook states the following policies:

No Student is Left Without an Alternative. No student is left without a way to address the problems which may have necessitated a disciplinary action. School counselors, social workers, psychologists, youth outreach counselors, special education teachers, tutors in an Alternative Learning Center and a GED program are in place and parents/guardians are contacted every step of the way.

Security Presence in the High School. It is a time of zero tolerance for criminal and illegal behavior at high schools: no smoking anywhere in the building or on campus; zero tolerance for weapons. There are 10 security guards on staff at Hilton High School, three or four of whom work during the school day, 7 a.m. to 2:30 p.m. They monitor the parking areas, assist teachers in monitoring the halls, assist in the removal of a student from a classroom if necessary, conduct residency checks of students, and respond to any kind of building safety and security need.

Youth Asset Development. To further link parents and the community with the safety and security of students, the Hilton School District has received a grant to fund a

Figure 12–7 (continued)

Community Youth Assets Coordinator position which has been filled by Parma resident and parent Jodi Lysiak who spearheaded neighborhood watch programs in the mid-1990s in the village of Hilton. Supported by national research on youth, the Youth Asset Survey, the program works to make real the principles upon which it was based. In addition, the human resource of counselors, social workers and others in the district are there for students, teachers and staff. By merely reading this web page, parents and community members are helping to ensure that the learning environments safe, but also begin to see how important it is to support our young people and give them the internal strength they need to cope with emergency situations.

CONCLUSION:

Vincent McCall has otherwise been an exemplary student. His grades, attendance, and class participation have been excellent. Vincent's only crime was to attempt to participate in some mischievous fun (purchasing fireworks). Vincent did not intend to purchase a pipe bomb which would hurt, maim and possibly kill people. Vincent is being condemned to the same consequence as the boys who made and intended to sell the pipe bombs.

The law requires the district to provide Vincent with adequate schooling. If the school should choose to expel Vincent, the school would have to supply another form of education. This "alternative" form of education would burden the school with unnecessary costs, which would in turn cut into their budget.

The school handbook states that "no student is left without a way to address the problems which may have necessitated a disciplinary action." Expelling Vincent leaves him without the ability to address the situation. He is left with no supports (school counselors, social workers, psychologists, youth outreach counselors, etc.).

In essence, being that this is Vincent's first offense, I feel it would benefit all parties if the school chose an alternative form of consequence.

Figure 12–7 (continued)

MEMORANDUM

From: Holiday Mosher-Chiffy

Date: January 28, 2001

Re: Vincent McCall's involvement with a pipe bomb incident. Does it warrant expulsion?

This memorandum responds to your request as to whether Vincent McCall's involvement in the pipe bomb incident warrants his expulsion from school.

Facts

Vincent McCall is a 14-year-old student who attends Cuyahoga Public Middle School. On the day in question a friend of Vincent's showed him a locker that contained metal tubes, described as fireworks. Vincent was asked if he wanted to purchase any fireworks, and he agreed to purchase three later that afternoon. The boys who were selling the fireworks then placed them in another locker and placed a lock that belongs to them on the locker. The student whose locker the fireworks were placed in came back and couldn't open the locker. He went for help and the school janitor snipped off the lock with wire cutters. The janitor discovered the pipe bombs and notified a local bomb squad to remove the devices. The police staked out the locker, and when the boys returned the police took them into custody. The boys were released to their parents' custody. The three boys had taken the bombs to school with the intention of selling them. No sales were made and all the bombs were confiscated. At an emergency school committee meeting the committee instantly expelled the boys indefinitely.

Issues

Did Vincent have a weapon in his possession on school property?

Were the devices in question weapons?

What is the school's policy regarding the possession of a weapon?

What facts are there that prove Vincent's involvement?

Discussion

What needs to be determined is whether Vincent brought or had in his possession a weapon on school property. If Vincent did have a weapon in his possession then he would be in violation of 24 Pa. Cons. Stat. § 13-1317.2(a) ([date]) that states:

Except as otherwise provided in this section, a school district or area vocational-technical school shall expel, for a period of not less than one year, any student who is determined to have brought onto or is in possession of a weapon on any school property, to any school-sponsored activity or onto any public conveyance providing transportation to a school or school-sponsored activity.

Figure 12–8 Student brief. Courtesy of Holiday Mosher-Chiffy

Although Vincent had agreed to purchase three of the devices, the transaction was never completed. It has been determined that the original three boys had manufactured the devices, and it was their intent to sell the devices in school. It was one of the three, a friend of Vincent's, that had approached Vincent and tried to sell them. Since Vincent didn't bring the devices onto school property or have them in his actual possession there should be a modification of the expulsion as stated in 24 Pa. Cons. Stat. § 13-1317.2 (c).

Pennsylvania Statute, 24 Pa. Cons. Stat. § 13-1317.2 (c)

(c) The superintendent of the school district or an administrative director of an area vocational-technical school may recommend modifications of such expulsion requirements for a student on a case-by-case basis. The superintendent or other chief administrative officer of a school entity shall, in the case of an exceptional student, take all steps necessary to comply with the Individuals with Disabilities Education Act (Public Law 91-230. 20 U.S.C. section 1400 et seq.).

What now need to be determined are the devices considered weapons. Weapons are defined by 18 Pa. Cons. Stat. § 908, which states:

(a) OFFENSE DEFINED. A person commits a misdemeanor of the first degree if, except as authorized by law, he makes repairs, sells, or otherwise deals in, uses, or possesses any offensive weapon.

"OFFENSIVE WEAPONS" Any bomb, grenade, machine gun, sawed-off shotgun with a barrel less than 18 inches, firearm specially made or specially adapted for concealment or silent discharge, any blackjack, sandbag, metal knuckles, dagger, knife, razor or cutting instrument, the blade of which is exposed in an automatic way by switch, push button, spring mechanism, or otherwise, or other implement for the infliction of serious bodily injury which serves no common lawful purpose would be classified as "Offensive Weapons".

Under 24 Pa. Cons. Stat. § 1317 (g) "Weapon." As used in this section, the term "weapon" shall include, but not be limited to, any knife, cutting instrument, cutting tool, nunchaku, firearm, shotgun, rifle and any other tool, instrument or implement capable of inflicting serious bodily injury.

The construction of the devices were capable of inflicting serious injury if set off. Therefore, they are considered weapons.

What is the school's policy regarding the possession of a weapon?

Pennsylvania Statute 24 Pa. Cons. Stat. § 1317.2 (b) and (c) clearly explains the school's policies regarding the possession of weapons.

Pennsylvania Statute, 24 Pa. Cons. Stat. § 13-1317.2 (b) and (c) states:

(b) Every school district and area vocational-technical school shall develop a written policy regarding expulsions for the possession of a weapon as required under this section. Expulsions shall be conducted pursuant to all applicable regulations.

Pennsylvania Statute, 24 Pa. Cons. Stat. § 13-1317.2 (c) states:

(c) The superintendent of the school district or an administrative director of an area vocational-technical school may recommend modifications of such expulsion requirements for a student on a case-by-case basis. The superintendent or other chief admin-

Figure 12–8 (continued)

istrative officer of a school entity shall, in the case of an exceptional student, take all steps necessary to comply with the Individuals with Disabilities Education Act (Public Law 91–230. 20 U.S.C. § 1400 *et seq.*).

Conclusion

Although Vincent McCall did not bring any devices known as pipe bombs to school, his involvement would be a question whether the agreement to purchase the pipe bombs would place them in his possession. Since he did not have actual possession of the pipe bombs and there was no transaction completed then it can be assumed that he was not in possession. If the bombs had been in his possession than he would be in violation of 24 Pa. Cons. Stat. § 1317.2 (a) and there would be grounds for expulsion.

It has been determined that the three students that approached Vincent were the ones to manufacture the pipe bombs. It was one of the three students that had showed Vincent the pipe bombs and asked him if he was interested in purchasing them.

The fact remains that Vincent did agree to purchase three of the bombs, and the fact that he did not report to anyone the presence of these devices implicates his involvement. Vincent should be held accountable for these facts.

Under Pennsylvania Statute, 24 Pa. Cons. Stat. § 13-1317.2 (c) it states:

(c) The superintendent of the school district or an administrative director of an area vocational-technical school may recommend modifications of such expulsion requirements for a student on a case-by-case basis.

In Vincent's case modifications should be taken into consideration.

The Juvenile Act, 42 Pa. Cons. Stat. Ann. § 6301(b)(2), suggests the following recommendations:

Each individual, when apprehended, should be quickly but thoroughly evaluated by responsible police investigators, mental health professionals and juvenile correctional experts to determine the appropriate cause of action, determine its potential for success, and evaluate any previous deviance, violent behavior, suicidal thoughts or tendencies and potential for future similar behavior.

Although Vincent McCall's involvement seems relatively minor there needs to be further investigation as to what his intent was regarding the pipe bombs after he had purchased them.

Vincent McCall also needs to be evaluated to see if he has a history of violent or deviant behavior and if there is any potential for future behavior.

It is recommended that Vincent be placed on probation until after evaluations have been accessed and counseling has been obtained.

Figure 12–8 (continued)

MEMORANDUM

TO: MR. AND MRS. McCALL

FROM: DINA NEWTON

DATE: JANUARY 27, 2001

RE: VINCENT McCALL

Background:

Vincent, along with three other students, was expelled indefinitely from school after a janitor found ten pipe bombs in a locker.

A student approached Vincent to see if he was interested in purchasing some "fireworks." Vincent agreed to purchase three of the "fireworks." After Vincent left, the boys transferred the "fireworks" to another student's locker. The other student could not get his lock open and went for help. The janitor snipped off the lock and discovered the pipe bombs, called the police and when Vincent and the other boys showed up, the police took them into custody. At an emergency school committee meeting held that evening the committee expelled the boys.

Issue:

Can the school committee indefinitely expel students for possession of pipe bombs?

Answer:

Yes.

School District Policy:

According to the Murray School District Policy No. PS 416:   Grounds for suspension/change in placement from school/expulsion include:

    c. Behavior or threatened behavior which poses an immediate and significant threat to the welfare, safety, or morals of other students or school personnel or to the operation of the school;

    g. The *possession or control* of a weapon or facsimile, *explosive*, or flammable material or other serious violation affecting another student, staff member or patron. (Emphasis added.)

        The consequences of section (g) are:

        1. Law enforcement or juvenile court referral;
        2. Immediate notification of parent(s)/guardian(s). The student and/or parent(s)/guardian(s) will be given the opportunity to respond to the allegation;

Figure 12–9 Student brief. Courtesy of Dina Newton.

3. Student will be placed on alternative study or expelled from school for 180 school days;
4. Exclusion from extracurricular activities and elected or appointed office activities during the suspension;
5. A student suspended or placed on alternative study for 180 school days may have his/her suspension or alternative study program reviewed after 90 school days.

Discussion and Recommendation:

There is no doubt that the possession of pipe bombs requires expulsion from school. However, we can argue that Vincent never did have possession or control of the pipe bombs. Vincent was not involved in making the pipe bombs, was not involved in selling the pipe bombs, did not bring the pipe bombs to school, did not move the pipe bombs to the other student's locker and, in fact, did not even know that the "fireworks" were instead pipe bombs. Given these facts, we should be able to effectively appeal Vincent's expulsion and get him reinstated to school.

As school policy provides all students an opportunity for due process, I suggest that we request an immediate hearing based on the above facts and appeal to the school committee to reinstate Vincent to school. Unfortunately, as with all expulsions, there is a mandatory 10-day suspension from school prior to conducting an administrative hearing on the issue. And, until the hearing, Vincent should keep up his studies through alternative or private schooling.

Finally, Vincent is fortunate that he's only 14 and in the 8th grade. Had Vincent been in the 9th grade, this would have been on his permanent school record and reported on his school transcript when applying to colleges and universities.

Figure 12–9 (continued)

Trial Court Legal Memoranda

Chapter Outline

Learning Objectives

Upon completing this chapter, the student should be able to

* Explain why legal professionals write trial court memos
* List and distinguish common advocacy memos
* List and describe the components of a trial court memo
* List and describe important considerations in trial court memo writing
* Describe some ways to organize legal memos
* Describe a common trial court memo format

Introduction

The **advocacy memorandum**, whether written to a trial or appellate court, is another kind of memorandum prepared by lawyers. Unlike the legal research memorandum, the advocacy memo is intended to persuade a decision-maker to act on a particular point of view. This chapter describes the first of two advocacy memoranda: the **trial court legal memorandum**. Chapter 14 describes advocacy memos written to an appellate court: appellate briefs.

Know Your Audience and Purpose

Just as it was important to know who would read the legal letter, it is also important to know who will be reading the trial court memo. Usually, the only people reading an advocacy memo will be lawyers, including the judge's law clerk and the judge himself. Those readers should come to the memo with a fair understanding of the facts of the case, its issues, and the legal principles involved. Nevertheless, particularly if the memo will be filed early in the case, it remains important to include all relevant information.

Equally important to knowing who is receiving the memo is understanding its purpose. Advocacy memos are written legal arguments. They may involve one or many legal issues, or may, in the case of a "pre-trial memo," summarize the case background, set out the relevant law, and include some preliminary analysis.

Trial Court Memoranda: Form and Elements

The form and content of a trial court memorandum is dictated by **court rules** (both written and sometimes unwritten) of the courts hearing the case. Nevertheless, most trial court memos share certain common parts. The following example is one form of trial court memorandum that presents all information (i.e., the facts of the case, the issue presented, the law, the **argument**, and a **conclusion**) necessary to the judge's understanding. Consider the parts of the excerpted trial court legal memorandum in Figure 13–1.

Body of a Trial Court Memorandum

Much of the body of a trial court memorandum is dictated by its form. Hence, the usual introductory information, the facts of the case, the questions presented, and the applicable statutes are set out early to prepare the judge for the writer's legal analysis and conclusion. Let's consider each section in some detail.

Caption

Because a trial court memorandum is filed in ongoing litigation, the first section of the memorandum is the case caption. Typically, the case caption includes the name of the trial court, the parties' names, and the case number. The form of the case caption is dictated by the rules of the court hearing the case.

CAPTION: Court, case, and litigation in which the memo is filed. In this case, the memo is filed in support of a motion for summary judgment in the Ohio trial court.	CUYAHOGA COURT OF COMMON PLEAS Vincent McCall,) Plaintiff)) v.) C.A. 01-1234) Coyahoga Board of Education,) Defendant.))
INTRODUCTION: Purpose of the legal memo. **STATEMENT OF FACTS:** The factual and procedural background of the case.	**MEMORANDUM IN SUPPORT OF VINCENT McCALL'S MOTION FOR SUMMARY JUDGMENT** Vincent's difficulties began when he was a 14-year-old student at the Cuyahoga Public Middle School. On January 24, 2001, a friend called Vincent over to his locker where he and two other boys showed Vincent a number of metal "tubes" that the friend explained were some really fine fireworks. The friend asked if Vincent was interested in buying a couple. Vincent asked their price and agreed to buy three later that afternoon. In the meantime, the boys selling these "super fireworks" sawed the lock off a nearby locker and stowed their "fireworks" in the other locker — and re-locked the "fireworks" locker with one of the boys' lock. When the owner of the storage locker came by to get the books he needed for class, he couldn't open the lock. He went to the school administrative office to ask for help. Help came in the form of a janitor who "snipped" the lock off with wire-cutters. When the janitor saw what looked like (and indeed, were) pipe bombs, he called the local bomb squad, who quietly removed the devices for testing and re-locked the locker with yet a third lock. The police then staked out the locker corridor until a number of youngsters (including Vincent) gathered around the locker. When they were unable to unlock the lock, the police moved in and took the boys, including Vincent, into custody. They were later released to their parents' custody pending the initiation of criminal charges. The school was evacuated for the remainder of the day so that the bomb specialists could ensure that there were no similar devices on the premises (there were not). An emergency school board meeting was held that night at which the school board summarily

Figure 13–1 Sample trial court memorandum.

expelled the boys indefinitely. As the story unraveled, it seems that three boys had learned to make pipe bombs over the Internet and as a lark had made up about ten of the bombs and had taken them to school, intending to sell them to some of their friends. As it turned out, of course, no sales were completed and all the bombs were confiscated.

Although Vincent was not one of the original three boys manufacturing the pipe bombs, the McCalls (all of them, including Vincent) agree that Vincent's involvement in the deal was at least stupid. Nevertheless, given Vincent's relatively minor involvement in the deal, they are horrified at the effect the expulsion will have on his chances for college.

ARGUMENT:
This is the substance of the trial court memo. It is here that the memo writer presents her argument based on the law and its application to the facts presented.

ARGUMENT

I. The Cuyahoga school board could not properly permanently exclude Vincent McCall from school.

Ohio Revised Code, § 3313.662 governs permanent exclusion of students from Ohio's public schools. In pertinent part, that statute provides as follows (emphasis added):

> The superintendent of public instruction, pursuant to this section and the adjudication process of section 3301.121 of the Revised Code, may issue an adjudication order that permanently excludes a pupil from attending any of the public schools of this state if the pupil is convicted of, or adjudicated a delinquent child for, committing, when the pupil was sixteen years of age or older, an act that would be a criminal offense if committed by an adult . . . . [or] involved the pupil's bringing a firearm to a school operated by the board of education of any school district or on to any other property owned or operated by such board . . .
>
> (I) As used in this section:
>
> (1) "Permanently exclude" means to forever prohibit an individual from attending any public school in this state that is operated by a city,

Figure 13–1 (continued)

local, exempted village, or joint vocational school district . . .

(6) "Firearm" has the same meaning as provided pursuant to the "Gun-Free Schools Act of 1994", 108 Stat. 270, 20 U.S.C. § 8001(a)(2) . . .

On January 24, 2001, the date of the pipe bomb incident, Vincent McCall (d.o.b. 6/1/86) was fourteen years old, too young to be permanently excluded from public school under § 3313.662. . . . .

CONCLUSION:
What the memo writer concludes and why.

CONCLUSION

For the reasons set forth above, this Court should vacate the Cuyahoga board of education decision to exclude Vincent McCall from public school and order that the board of education expunge from McCall's school records his expulsion from school on January 24, 2001 and permit McCall to attend school effective immediately in the Cuyahoga school district.

SIGNATURE AND DATE:
"Respectfully submitted" and the party's name and signature, or if represented by counsel, the name and address of counsel for the party.

Respectfully submitted,

Dated: _____

_____

Anne M. Stevens
Newport & Stevens
37 Main St.
Amherst, OH 01002
Attorneys for Vincent McCall

CERTIFICATE OF SERVICE:
Attorney's sworn certification that document was provided to the opponent in a timely fashion.

CERTIFICATE OF SERVICE

On this twenty-second day of February, 2001, I declare, under the pains and penalties of perjury, that I served the foregoing document on all interested parties to this action by first class mail, postage prepaid.

_____

Anne M. Stevens

Figure 13–1 (continued)

Introduction

This is a statement of the purpose of the memorandum in litigation. Thus, the introduction may alert the court that it is a memorandum in support of or in opposition to a motion to dismiss or for summary judgment. It may be written in lieu of oral closing argument in a trial presided over by a judge. The introduction serves two important purposes: first, the introduction identifies the overall purpose of the memorandum, and second, it identifies where it belongs in the procedings (e.g., this memo accompanies an earlier filed motion for summary judgment, etc.)

Statement of Facts

This is the memo section that contains relevant substantive and procedural facts in the case. The facts of a case offer the advocate her first chance to persuade the decision-maker. Although it is important to not misrepresent the case facts, or to overlook damaging facts, damaging facts can be explained or reduced in importance. Like the research memo, after the trial court memo is complete, revise the fact statement to eliminate facts unnecessary to the legal argument.

Argument

As usual, the hard part of writing a trial court memo is writing the argument. Again, the IRAC method of written analysis is a useful argumentation method. Begin with a statement of the relevant legal issue. If the memo discusses two or more issues, it may be helpful to begin each analysis with a heading identifying the issue analyzed. Follow with a statement of the rule applicable to the issue. If a statute applies, quote relevant statutory language. If cases govern the result, set out the facts and holding of the relevant cases. Historical background may help the reader understand the context of an emerging area of law. And, while brevity is desirable, remember that the reader is human and sometimes a little "story-telling" keeps the reader interested and attentive.

Follow the summary of the applicable rule(s) with their application to the case facts. Trial court memos are persuasive memos. Thus, the memo argument section is the advocate's opportunity to argue for her client's point of view. Realistically appraise all possible arguments. Except in extremely complicated cases, limit your arguments to two or three; eliminate weak or doubtful arguments — those arguments only detract from stronger arguments. Begin with your strongest arguments, follow with lesser arguments. Remember that legal arguments are stronger than factual arguments; factual arguments are stronger than policy arguments.

Remember the rules of good writing. Analyze each word, each sentence, each paragraph for necessity and desirability. Eliminate the unnecessary and undesirable. Distinguish damaging facts and cases; do not ignore them.

Conclusion

This is the writer's overall conclusion regarding the memo issues. The conclusion is not the section for argument, analysis, or reproducing supporting materials. That information belongs in the argument section of the memo. Rather, the conclusion should include a summary of the advocate's argument and her recommendations.

Review Questions

1. Why do legal professionals write trial court memos?
2. List and distinguish common advocacy memos.
3. List and describe the components of a trial court memo.
4. List and describe important considerations in trial court memo writing.
5. Describe some ways to organize legal memos.
6. Describe a common trial court memo format.

Exercise

Prepare a trial court memo in opposition to Braithwaite's motion to dismiss Kitty Barbour's complaint.

Glossary

Advocacy memorandum: Legal memorandum arguing for a specific outcome or result.

Argument: Application of legal principles to the facts of the case.

Caption: Court, case, and litigation in which the memo is filed.

Certificate of service: Attorney's sworn statement that the memorandum was provided to the opponent in a timely fashion.

Conclusion: Author's conclusion from her argument and request for relief.

Court rules: Rules governing court procedure.

Introduction: Statement of the purpose of the advocacy memo.

Signature and date: "Respectfully submitted," the advocate identity (including any attorney number, if required by the court), address, and represented party.

Statement of Facts: A summary of the case factual and procedural background.

Trial court legal memorandum: A form of advocacy memo filed in the trial court.

Sample "Trial Court" Memoranda

UNITED STATES DISTRICT COURT
DISTRICT OF MASSACHUSETTS

Leah A.,	)	
Plaintiff	)	
	)	
v.	)	C.A. 96-1234
	)	
U.S. Department of Health and Human Services	)	
Social Security Administration, Defendant.	)	
	)	

**MEMORANDUM IN OPPOSITION TO THE SOCIAL SECURITY
ADMINISTRATION'S MOTION FOR SUMMARY JUDGMENT**

STATEMENT OF THE FACTS

<u>Procedural Facts</u>: Leah A. originally filed for these benefits in June 1982, at the age of thirty-five, claiming she was disabled by agoraphobia since 1978. In June 1983, an Administrative Law Judge ("ALJ") who conducted a hearing and reviewed the evidence found no severe mental or physical impairment which would prevent Leah A. from engaging in substantial gainful activity. The ALJ's denial of benefits became the final decision of the Secretary in 1984 when the Social Security Administration's Appeals Council denied review of the decision. Leah filed claim for Supplemental Security Income ("SSI") benefits in 1985 and was held to be entitled to receive those benefits as of February 1985. Leah A. is now forty-two years old and remains confined to her apartment, "with virtually no face to face interactions with anyone other than her roommate." In May 1986, this Court remanded the case to the Secretary pursuant to the district court's invalidation of step two of the Secretary's evaluation process in *McDonnell v. Heckler*, 624 F.Supp. 375 (D. Mass.1985). Upon remand, the ALJ conducted another hearing, reviewed some additional evidence, and again found that "there was no valid medical evidence of any disease process which would render the claimant 'disabled' as defined by the Social Security Act." A.R. at 255. The ALJ concluded that Leah A. suffered from no "severe medically determinable impairment, either physical or mental in nature." The ALJ acknowledged the possibility that the "claimant is suffering from psychiatric ilness [sic] which leads her to a life style which does not include employment commensurate [sic] with her education." The Appeals Council adopted the ALJ's findings, and again denied benefits for the period leading up to February 1985.

<u>Substantive Facts</u>: Leah A. is a college graduate who worked as a school teacher before taking a traveling sales job with the Coca-Cola Company in 1977. The first physical signs of Leah A.'s agoraphobia were palpitations, tingling and numbness in the arms, and lightheadedness manifested while driving home from a sales call in 1977. Leah A. became fearful of driving to visit the stores which stocked Coca-Cola, so her roommate began to accompany her on sales calls. She began experiencing back-

Figure 13–2 Leah A. summary judgment memo.

aches and headaches during a business trip to Atlanta, prompting fear which caused Leah A. to walk out on a dinner appointment. By 1978, Leah A. had left Coca-Cola and was feeling "tired, shaky [and] disconnected."

In searching for the cause of her agoraphobia, Leah A. stated that in 1977 she was treated by a physician who prescribed tranquilizers, consulted a chiropractor for treatment of backache and numbness, and was examined by an internist who diagnosed sinus trouble and other maladies. In 1979, a psychiatrist interviewed Leah A. and reported that she had stopped a long-running practice of daily marijuana smoking, and that she was not willing to take tranquilizing drugs prescribed by other doctors for fear of becoming drug dependent. The psychiatrist recommended further psychotherapy and found "no [mental] abnormalities except by history" and "normal blood pressure and pulse." In February 1980, a neurologist reporting on Leah A.'s workers' compensation claim stated that she was given acupuncture treatments for "80% relief" of a "symptom complex" which was "entirely psychosomatic in origin." In May 1980, a psychologist stated that Leah A. would be "more than willing to return to work but not in [the] highly stressed job" she held with Coca-Cola, and he recommended relaxation therapy, meditative techniques, and alternative career planning in order to "re-enter the mainstream of life and gainful employment." Letter of Martin Markey, A.R. at 166-67. In June 1980, a neuro-psychiatric evaluation of Leah A. revealed complaints about her former job with Coca-Cola, and no physical symptoms other than "slightly elevated heart rate" and "possible weakness on forward movement of head and neck." Leah A. was advised to attend "group psychotherapy" in order to speed her recovery.

By 1981, Leah A. was doing "moderate" yoga exercises and "stained glass as a hobby." She came under the care of a psychiatrist who diagnosed agoraphobia and performed "behavior modification with the ancillary use of hypnosis" and recommended that "she not work at this time." Leah A. also visited a nutritional-biochemical consultant who prepared computer printouts of Leah A.'s "Nutrient Mineral Levels," "Mineral Rations" and "Toxic Metal Levels" and who diagnosed a "biochemical imbalance" as the cause of depression. Leah A. came under the belief that her agoraphobia was the result of birth control pills, junk food and "large amounts of Tab" consumed during the time she worked for Coca-Cola. In June 1982, Leah A. consulted a "wholistic [sic] physician" who advertised "nutritional analysis, hair analysis, kinesiology, reflexology, and dream analysis," and determined that Leah A.'s employment at the Coca-Cola Company set off a "stress-related condition" which included "pre-diabetes" and a "generalized biochemical disorder [affecting] all organs of the body, some more than others." Leah A. was advised to begin a "full-time" therapy program. Report of Dr. William, A.R. at 174 (emphasis in original). Dr. Williams recommended acupuncture and chiropractic care, and Leah A. went to a nearby chiropractor who commended the holistic physician's findings and advised frequent treatments for spine problems diagnosed by x- ray.

In March 1982, "a hypnotist specializing in the treatment of agoraphobia" treated Leah A. and recommended more behavioral treatment. In June 1982, another chiropractor tested Leah A. and discovered "severe copper toxicity" and "a very strong pre-diabetic trend" which could be cured by "nutritional therapy to accomplish an excretion of the toxic tissue accumulations of Copper and Mercury." Letter of Dr. Miller, A.R. at 185-86. At the close of 1982, Leah A. opened her own retail store, a "Seasonal Christmas Shop," but "[t]he effort was a disaster. The store was closed and the business folded." During 1983, Leah A. stated that she was working at home with

Figure 13–2 (continued)

a series of cassette audio tapes produced by the Chaange [sic] Center for Help for Agoraphobia/Anxiety through New Growth Experiences. Leah A. stated that she only left her apartment for brief periods, mainly to attend doctor's appointments, and that she had an $11,000.00 credit card debt.

ARGUMENT

1. *Introduction.* The Social Security Administration regulations require the ALJ to follow a five-step analysis to determine whether an individual is disabled. This analysis is set out in *Goodermote v. Secretary of Health and Human Services*, 690 F.2d 5, 6-7 (1st Cir. 1982). The first step is to determine whether the claimant is working or engaged in substantial gainful activity. In the instant case, Leah A. was not working when she filed her claim although she worked briefly at her own small business in 1982.

The second step requires Leah A. to prove a severe impairment. In the instant case, the issue is whether Leah A.'s agoraphobia is a severe mental impairment. By 1981 a psychiatrist, Dr. Leff, had diagnosed Leah A.'s agoraphobia. Dr. Leff graduated from the Middlesex University School of Medicine in Waltham, Massachusetts and became licensed in 1942. A.R. at 192. The regulations governing medical evidence of an impairment, 20 C.F.R. § 404.1513(a), state that licensed or certified physicians, osteopaths or psychologists are acceptable medical sources for information concerning a claimant's impairment. Therefore, while the ALJ may properly give little or no weight to the findings of hypnotists, herbalists, nutritionists, naturalists and chiropractors who do not meet this requirement, Dr. Leff qualifies as an acceptable source. There is likewise no doubt that Leah is severely impaired. As well, because Leah and the SSA agree that Leah is unable to perform her past relevant work as a salesperson or teacher, determining whether she is eligible for social security disability benefits will turn on the question of whether in step 3, Leah's condition meets or equals a listed Social Security impairment, specifically, the listed impairment for "Anxiety Related Disorders," and, perhaps, whether under step 5, there is other relevant gainful employment Leah can perform.

2. *Meet or Equal Listed Impairment.* Proceeding to the third step of inquiry, the Secretary must determine whether the claimant has an impairment which meets or exceeds the criteria in the Listing of Impairments. 20 C.F.R. § 404.1511. "If the claimant has an impairment of so serious a degree of severity, the claimant is automatically found disabled." *Goodermote*, 690 F.2d at 6. The "Listing" is set out at 20 C.F.R. § 404 Subpart P, App. 1, and includes "Anxiety Related Disorders." *Id.* at § 12.06. It is the opinion of this Court that the ALJ's finding of a complete absence of anxiety-related disorders during the entire period in question, as recorded in the PRTF, does not comport with the Administrative Record as applied to section 12.06. Leah A.'s statements regarding her symptoms, as confirmed by some of the medical evidence, indicate that anxiety disorders which meet the section 12.06 listing criteria may have arisen at some point before 1985.

By 1981 a psychiatrist, Dr. Leff, had diagnosed Leah A.'s agoraphobia. Dr. Leff graduated from the Middlesex University School of Medicine in Waltham, Massachusetts and became licensed in 1942. The regulations governing medical evidence of an

Figure 13–2 (continued)

impairment, 20 C.F.R. § 404.1513(a), state that licensed or certified physicians, osteopaths or psychologists are acceptable medical sources for information concerning a claimant's impairment. Therefore, while the ALJ may properly give little or no weight to the findings of hypnotists, herbalists, nutritionists, naturalists and chiropractors who do not meet this requirement, Dr. Leff qualifies as an acceptable source. "If the claimant has an impairment of so serious a degree of severity, the claimant is automatically found disabled." *Goodermote*, 690 F.2d at 6. The "Listing" is set out at 20 C.F.R. § 404 Subpart P, App. 1, and includes "Anxiety Related Disorders." *Id.* at § 12.06. It is the opinion of this Court that the ALJ's finding of a complete absence of anxiety-related disorders during the entire period in question, as recorded in the PRTF, does not comport with the Administrative Record as applied to section 12.06. Leah A.'s statements regarding her symptoms, as confirmed by some of the medical evidence, indicate that anxiety disorders which meet the section 12.06 listing criteria may have arisen at some point before 1985. In any event, there is no substantial evidence to support the ALJ's finding of only slight functional limitations, as stated on the Psychiatric Review Technique Form ("PRTF"). If, it is determined that at no point did Leah A.'s agoraphobia rise to the level of an automatic disability, then the inquiry will proceed beyond the "threshold" to step five and determine whether "the claimant's impairment [prevents her] from performing other work of the sort found in the economy." *Goodermote*, 690 F.2d at 7.

To satisfy this fifth step, a vocational expert would be needed to determine whether Leah A.'s agoraphobia prevented her from working at any job available in the economy, thereby making her disabled. While Leah A. was unable to operate her own retail store, which would require frequent interaction with the public and expose Leah A. to other stresses of running a small business, she may have retained the functional capacity to work at a more sheltered occupation involving less stress and interaction. An expert opinion will be valuable in making a determination of Leah A.'s specific vocational abilities. See *Lancellotta v. Secretary of Health and Human Services*, 806 F.2d 284, 285-86 (1st Cir. 1986) (remanding case of claimant suffering from agoraphobia and other physical and mental impairments); *Bianchi v. Secretary of Health and Human Services*, 764 F.2d 44, 45-46 (1st Cir. 1985) (remanding case of claimant who was unable to hold factory and hairdressing positions because of agoraphobia and panic attacks); *Soba v. Department of Health and Human Services*, 724 F. Supp. 228 (S.D.N.Y. 1989) (agoraphobia did not preclude plaintiff from returning to past relevant work); *Carbonara v. Bowen*, C.A. No. 88-1961, slip op., 1989 WL 30932 (E.D. Pa. 1989) (ALJ's hypothetical to vocational expert took agoraphobic claimant's limitations into account and decision to deny benefits was supported by substantial evidence).

3. *Policy.* Finally, the Secretary has estimated that 24.1% of disabled persons collecting SSI benefits are suffering from mental disorders other than retardation. Social Security Bulletin, Annual Statistical Supplement 331 (1988). While agoraphobia is a mental disorder which may be overcome by the individual, the record of impairment in the instant case does illustrate some parallels with persons suffering from more severe and chronic mental disorders, in which:

> the routine demands of work and social relations are major stresses. So much effort goes into their struggle with illness that they have little energy left to deal with a work situation. Handling interpersonal relationships with supervisors and co-workers is a major stress. The very thought of work is frightening, for it carries the risk of yet another failure. A therapeutic or, at least, protective work setting and

Figure 13–2 (continued)

an adequate preparatory period of vocational rehabilitation should be made available for many of these precariously compensated people [who are supported by SSI].

W. Richard Lamb, M.D., "Incentives and Disincentives of Disability Insurance for the Chronically Mentally Ill," in *Psychiatric Disability: Clinical, Legal, and Administration Dimensions*, 343, 346 (1987) (emphasis added). One problem inherent in the SSI system's handling of persons disabled by mental impairment is a tendency to promote "regression and dependency." *Id.* at 347. Solutions for this tendency include encouraging individual and group therapy, and employment in sheltered work settings. *Id.* at 349. Unfortunately, middle class mental health professionals have been found to contribute to the problem since they "are frequently reluctant to see [their] patients take low-status, minimum-wage jobs even though this is the present limit of [the Social Security claimants'] capabilities." *Id.* at 348.

Encouraging the individual to seek some type of low stress work may promote progress by the individual, since there is a heightened self-esteem from:

> experiencing oneself as productive, making a contribution to society, and achieving at least partial self-support and independence. Work therapy is recognized as being fully as important as talking therapy. Having no reason to get up in the morning and no structured day to look forward to causes profound feelings of emptiness.... A combination of work and play is both normative and restorative.

Leah has repeatedly expressed her wish to return to work. Indeed, in 1986, Leah A. stated that she would be eager to do any type of work, but would be unable to sustain "more than perhaps an hour or two of low-stress work of some sort several days a week, and certainly nothing that would require any extended talking or face-to-face contact with people. In 1986, the naturopathic doctor stated that "endocrinological studies" had uncovered "markedly elevated uroporphyrin, serum catecholamine and an unusual thyroid reading."

He diagnosed Leah A.'s condition as "porphyria" and concluded that this was the cause of Leah A.'s "panic syndrome with secondary agoraphobia."

Indeed, federal courts have recognized that the effect of confinement and isolation from the outside world "is to rot away the health of [a person's] body, mind and spirit." *Inmates of the Boys' Training School v. Affleck*, 346 F. Supp. 1354, 1365-66 (D.R.I. 1972). The *Affleck* court's findings were made in the context of prison confinement and "were based on the affidavits of experts which stated that 'isolation can never constitute rehabilitation' and can produce sensory deprivation, withdrawal, or perhaps psychotic or autistic behavior." *Morgan v. Sproat*, 432 F. Supp. 1130, 1139 n. 13 (S.D. Miss. 1977). Likewise, continued confinement of an agoraphobic person may possibly lead to increased dependence and difficulties. It is hoped that the court will act on these observations lest Leah spend another ten years confined to her apartment by agoraphobia.

CONCLUSION

Leah's unique constellation of impairments both equals the SSA listed impairment for anxiety related disorders and prevents her from any gainful employment. In par-

Figure 13–2 (continued)

ticular, she is unable to leave her apartment for any reason, including doctors' appointments, and short trips to a neighborhood store. As well, any contact with strangers, whether in person or over the telephone is highly stressful. She is unable to interview for a job or interact on any regular basis. As well, as she demonstrated in the failed Christmas shop experience, she cannot handle the stress of financial dealings.

Based on the purpose of the social security disability act — to provide support for those who are without means, are permanently disabled, and are therefore unable to perform any substantial gainful activity — and Leah's demonstrated, long-standing, and severe inability to deal with any interpersonal contact or stress, a judge will likely find the SSA has not shown that jobs exist in substantial numbers in the national economy that Leah can perform.

Respectfully submitted,

Dated: _____   _____

Anne M. Cohen
Newport & Cohen
37 Main St.
Amherst, MA 01002
Attorneys for Leah A.

CERTIFICATE OF SERVICE

On this twenty-second day of October, 1996, I declare, under the pains and penalties of perjury, that I served the foregoing document on all interested parties to this action by first class mail, postage prepaid.

_____

Anne M. Cohen

Figure 13–2 (continued)

COMMONWEALTH OF MASSACHUSETTS
BUREAU OF SPECIAL EDUCATION APPEALS

****
IN RE: *
                                        *
                                        *   NO. 92-1234
                                        *
BRENDA B   *
****

MEMORANDUM IN LIEU OF CLOSING ARGUMENT

BACKGROUND

In September of 1990, Brenda B (then 12 years old) entered the Abba public schools in fifth grade, having just completed her second year of fourth grade in Arizona. In sixth grade at the middle school, Brenda began skipping school. As the school year continued, Brenda's truancy and behavioral problems increased: she was increasingly suspended and detentions. Her truancy continued in seventh grade, as did her aggressiveness. Even though Mrs. B drove Brenda to school daily, Brenda continued to skip classes and leave school early. The middle school nevertheless reported they could handle Brenda.

By October 5, 1992, Brenda ran amok. When required to attend gym, Brenda kicked the principal in the shins, threatened him with a pencil, and threw papers off his desk. Three days later, the Abba consulting psychiatrist recommended Brenda be committed to a psychiatric hospital. Later, Brenda entered a residential diagnostic center for an eight-week assessment. On December 7, 1992, the diagnostic team recommended Brenda be placed in a long-term therapeutic residential treatment facility.

On December 16, 1992, Brenda's special education team recommended that although Brenda's educational needs might be met in a self-contained middle school classroom, she should not start that program until mid-January when a new special education teacher took over the self-contained classroom.

On February 24, 1993, Brenda entered the Youth Center, a therapeutic residential school.

LAW

Under the Education for All Handicapped Children Act, residential school placement is justifiable only when made for educational purposes. 20 U.S.C. § 1401 (16), 1413 (9) (4) (B), 34 C.F.R. § 300.347. Court decisions interpreting that act have interpreted "educational purposes" broadly. The source of the child's handicapping condition does not determine whether a placement is educational. Rather, the question is whether the placement is required to render the child educable. *Papacoda v. Connecticut*, 528 F. Supp. 68 (D. C. 1981). In *Abrahamson v. Hershman*, 701 F.2d 223 (1st Cir. 1983), the court ruled that where a child required residential placement to meet her unique

Figure 13–3 Sample "trial court" memorandum: memorandum in lieu of closing argument in Brenda B. special education case.

needs, placement must be made at no cost to the child's parents. Additionally, certain non-educational services (e.g., psychotherapy) must be provided if those services are "required to assist [the child] to benefit from . . . special education." *Tatro v. Texas*, 516 F. Supp. 968, 974-975 (N. D. Tex. 1981).

ANALYSIS

Brenda is currently a 14 1/2-year-old seventh-grader of low average intellectual ability. Brenda's standardized tests reveal:

	12/90	10/92	4/93
Intelligence			
IQ (FS)	84	85	107
(V)	92	87	
(P)	77	86	
Achievement			
Math	4.2	4.5	5.1
Reading	5.8	6.8	6.6
Wd Att	12.9	high	
Wd Comp	4.1	low	
Ltr Id	6.2		
Recog	5.5		7.9
Comp	6.0		6.0
Spelling			9.0
Gen Info			6.5

Brenda's diagnoses include: conduct disorder, identity disorder, immaturity, depression, and impulsivity; she is "a child in turmoil." Her turmoil has impeded her ability to perform in school. Brenda harbors a very poor self-image; she sees herself as all bad and stupid. In his report, Brenda's psychologist said, "[Brenda's] intellectual prowess is of deep concern to Brenda, and it appears to influence her almost every move." Brenda's image of herself depends on how she perceives others perceive her. Brenda craves attention and acceptance by her peers; indeed, she will readily sacrifice good judgment for that acceptance. When threatened, Brenda explodes aggressively or runs, impulsively, to any situation she perceives as less threatening.

Any educational program, in addition to remediating Brenda's academics, must control Brenda's truancy.

A. <u>The Self-Contained Abba Program will not meet Brenda's Educational Needs</u>.

Abba's plan fails to provide Brenda with consistent, full time, year-round programming. Brenda's truancy is well refined. She knows the places to run and has friends

Figure 13–3 (continued)

to run with. Mainstreaming provides Brenda many avenues of escape — before and after school, during class changes, at lunch.

While Abba has offered a taxi to carry Brenda to and from school, the evidence is that a ride will not stop Brenda's truancy: Mrs. B drove Brenda to school daily in 1992, yet Brenda missed 15 out of 31 school days and was suspended 5 times for truancy. The Abba plan condones Brenda's truancy: children in the self-contained classroom subject to normal suspension and expulsion; Brenda's truancy will rewarded by sending her home!

B. The Proposed Residential Educational Program will meet Brenda's Needs

Brenda's program at the Youth Center suffers none of the infirmities of Abba's program. At the Youth Center, Brenda is involved in a full time consistent, highly structured, integrated program. Most importantly, Brenda accepts the Youth Center program; Brenda has demonstrated, through her improved behavior, that she accepts the program and limits of the Youth Center.

At the Youth Center, truancy is not an option. All students must attend school and are monitored during transitions, breaks, and lunch. Any girl not where she belongs within specific time limits is found and returned. The Youth Center does not condone missing school for any reason. While Brenda may leave class briefly for counseling, she is supervised during those periods and is reintegrated into class as soon as possible. Even when Brenda is restricted to her living unit, she attends school. Finally, as Abba so ably pointed out, when Brenda runs, she runs to known places. The Youth Center environs are unfamiliar to Brenda; her pattern of running behavior will therefore be broken and therapy can begin.

Ultimately, proof of the adequacy and appropriateness of any educational plan is its success. In two months at the Youth Center, Brenda has leapt in intellectual ability, increasing her math test score by six months, beginning to get good grades and teacher praise, adjusting to her peer group, and responding to therapy.

CONCLUSION

Abba's initial assessment of Brenda in October of 1992 was correct — Brenda cannot attend a public school. Brenda is on the fence — capable of developing a severe pathology if not properly treated. Brenda needs to be contained. Even if Brenda lived in a most highly structured setting, she could not progress if she also attended public school. Yet, even while contained, Brenda's poor self esteem demands she be educated in what feels to Brenda like a "normal" educational setting. Brenda's program at the Youth Center provides support within the appearance of normality. The Abba middle school does not. The Youth Center has demonstrated its ability to deal with Brenda's emotional and educational needs. While the most that Abba's program offers is containment, the Youth Center offers Brenda a normal future.

Therefore, Mrs. B asks that the hearing officer rule that the Youth Center is the least restrictive, appropriate placement to meet Brenda's special needs.

Figure 13–3 (continued)

Respectfully submitted,

Dated: _____   _____

Anne M. Stevens
Newport & Stevens
37 Main St.
Amherst, OH 01002
Attorneys for Mrs. B

CERTIFICATE OF SERVICE

On this twenty-second day of October, 1996, I declare, under the pains and penalties of perjury, that I served the foregoing document on all interested parties to this action by first class mail, postage prepaid.

_____
Anne M. Stevens

Figure 13–3 (continued)

Writing Appellate Briefs

Chapter Outline

Learning Objectives

Upon completing this chapter, the student should be able to

* Explain the appellate process and deadlines
* Explain court rules bearing on appeals
* Describe the parts of an appellate brief, their contents, and purpose
* Describe the purpose and contents of an appellate appendix
* Describe the purpose and contents of an appellate brief addendum

Introduction

The most formal of legal writings are the appellate brief and law review or journal articles. And while many legal professionals never have occasion to publish articles in law reviews and journals, many legal professionals do write appellate briefs.

Appellate Process, Rules, and Deadlines

An appellate brief is a much more formal and involved advocacy memo than that written for a trial court. In addition, an appellate brief must take into account the position of the appellate court relative to the trial court, particularly with regard to the level of review (i.e., standard of review) it applies to the lower court decision. An appellate court does not retry a case. This would be a waste of judicial time and would essentially render the trial court's task meaningless. Rather, based on the record of the trial court, including the transcript of testimony, the exhibits, and the arguments of counsel, the appellate court "reviews" the trial court action for procedural and legal errors.

To understand appellate brief writing, it is necessary to understand the **appellate process**. That process is governed by **court rules**; different appellate courts have different appellate rules. Many states, however, have adopted a form of the **Federal Rules of Appellate Procedure (FRAP)**. This description of the appellate process is based on those federal rules, some of which are shown later in this chapter.

The appellate process begins with the entry of a **judgment** on the trial court docket. Once a judgment enters, the loser in the trial court has thirty days[1] (unless extended by the trial court for an additional thirty days, or by an appellate court for up to one year) to file a **notice of appeal** in the trial court. If other parties to the case also wish to appeal, they have an additional fourteen days to file their appeal. Figure 14–1 is an example of a federal notice of appeal. Notice the information required on the form.

Once the notice of appeal is filed in the trial court, the **appellant** — the person appealing the trial court judgment — must request a **transcript** of any trial court proceedings and that the trial court clerk's office assemble the trial record — gather the papers, exhibits, and real evidence — for appeal. While the trial court assembles the record, the parties decide on the **issues on appeal** and on the contents of the **appellate appendix**. Once the court notifies the parties that the trial court record has been assembled, all appellants must **docket the appeal** — that is, enter the case on the appellate docket and pay a fee. Following docketing, the appellant(s) have forty days to file the appellate brief and record appendix. The **appellee**(s) — the winner in the trial court — may file response briefs within thirty days after the appellant's brief is filed. **Reply briefs**, appellant's briefs responding to new arguments made by the appellee, must be filed within ten days after the appellee's brief is filed. Briefing schedules may, however, be extended by permission of the appellate court. Once the case is completely briefed, the court may request a **pre-hearing conference** with the appellate attorneys or may schedule **oral argument**.

United States District Court for the _____
District of _____

_____

_____

_____

Plaintiff,

vs.   CASE NO. _____

_____

_____

_____

Defendant.

NOTICE OF APPEAL

Notice is hereby given that _____, hereby appeal to the

(here name all parties taking the appeal)

United States Court of Appeals for the Sixth Circuit from _____

(the final judgment)

_____ entered in this action on the _____

(from an order (describing it)

day of _____, _____.

(s) _____

Address: _____

_____

_____

Attorney for _____

cc: Opposing Counsel _____
    Court of Appeals _____

Figure 14–1 Notice of appeal.

Oral argument is also well-governed by appellate rules. In intermediate appellate courts, oral argument may be scheduled before three justices of the court; before the highest appellate court, if a certiorari court, oral argument is scheduled before the entire body. Appellate courts usually limit the time for oral argument to fifteen or thirty minutes per side, although those limits can be extended by the court.

DAY	EVENT	FRAP
1	Entry of judgment in trial court	3
30	Notice of appeal in trial court; 60 days if government is a party	4
40	Appellant orders transcript	10(b)
44	Notice of appeal by others	3
	Trial court record assembled	11
1	Record transferred to appellate court/appeal docketed	12
40	Appellant's brief and appellate appendix filed	28
70	Appellee's brief filed	28
	Prehearing conference	
	Oral argument	34
1	Decision	
15	Petition for rehearing	27

Figure 14–2 Appeal timeline.

Once oral argument is complete, the case is ready for decision. Appellate court decisions are rendered by a majority of the judges hearing the case. The court may issue its decision within a few days or, in complicated cases, a month or longer. Once a decision is issued, the parties have fourteen days to **petition for rehearing** if the court has overlooked or misapprehended points of law or fact.

The chart in Figure 14–2 summarizes common appellate process deadlines.

Know Your Audience and Purpose

The audience of an appellate brief is, of course, the justices deciding the appeal. Often, the parties will know before oral argument which justices will be hearing their case. Remember, in an appellate argument, the task is not to convince all of the justices (although that is a desirable goal); to win an appeal, it is necessary only that a majority of the judges on the panel agree with your position. Therefore, it is often possible to "slant" an appellate argument toward the politics and interests of some specific majority of the appellate panel. In all cases, the professional must take care in her choice of arguments, her use of factual and legal citation, and her presentation of those elements. Begin with a statement of facts, and weave the facts into the legal argument.

Appellate Briefs: Form and Elements

The contents and form of an appellate brief are detailed in the appellate court's rules of appellate procedure. For instance, FRAP 28 requires that any appellate brief filed in the federal circuit courts or in the United States Supreme Court contain the following:

> Cover/Title Page
> Table of Contents
> Table of Authorities

Statement of Jurisdiction
Statement of Issues
Statement of the Case
Summary of the Argument
Argument
Conclusion
Closing/Signature and Date
Certificate of Service
Addendum of Constitutional and Statutory Provisions
Appendix

Consider the parts of the abbreviated appellate brief in Figure 14–3.[2]

The Body of the Appellate Brief

As with much of legal writing, the body of the appellate brief is dictated by its form and by court rules like FRAP Rule 28, shown in Figure 14–4 on page 378.

Thus, introductory information, the facts of the case, the questions presented, and applicable law are set out early to prepare the appellate judges for the writer's legal analysis. In brief writing, it is most important that the rules of good writing are followed precisely and that every word, citation, sentence, and paragraph be carefully spell-checked and grammar-checked. An appellate judge reading an error-filled brief may conclude that the author does not care about the argument or believes her argument to be a "loser." Let's consider each appellate brief section in some detail.

Cover/Title Page

The cover, or title, page identifies the court hearing the case, relevant docket numbers, and names and roles of parties and their attorneys.

Table of Contents

The table of contents lists brief sections, including argument headings and subheadings and their page numbers. Table of contents headings are usually the first opportunity for advocacy. Include in a good heading the applicable law and enough facts so that the judges are ready to accept the professional's point of view. Make sure the headings tell a whole, logical story, and move smoothly from beginning to end. Complicated concepts deserve subheadings that the judges can understand and follow. Use the table of contents to summarize the argument. Follow court rules for typeface, design, and layout in the table of contents as well as elsewhere in the brief.

Table of Authorities

Set out relevant cases, statutes (or portions of statutes), and other authorities in this section. List authorities in alphabetical order, within categories of authority, listing

(Text continues on page 377.)

COVER/TITLE PAGE: Brief cover or initial page identifying the trial court hearing the case, relevant docket number, names and roles of parties and their attorneys, and the hearing date.	**Ohio Appeals Court No. 01-1234.** CUYAHOGA COUNTY. _____ VINCENT McCALL APPELLANT v. SCHOOL BOARD OF CUYAHOGA APPELLEE _____ ON APPEAL FROM A JUDGMENT BY THE CUYA-HOGA COURT OF COMMON PLEAS _____ **Brief for Vincent McCall** _____ ANNE M. STEVENS, Attorney for Vincent McCall 264 Richmond Road Richmond Heights, OH 44143 (216) 555-1212 January, 2001

Figure 14–3 An abbreviated sample appellate brief in the Vincent McCall case.

TABLE OF CONTENTS: Major brief headings and the brief pages on which they appear.	**TABLE OF CONTENTS**

Figure 14–3 (continued)

TABLE OF AUTHORITIES: List of legal authorities and the brief pages on which they appear.	**TABLE OF AUTHORITIES**

Cases

Adrovet v. Brunswick City School District Board of Education, 106 Ohio Misc. 2d 81, 735 N.E.2d 995 (1999).

Goss v. Lopez, 419 U.S. 565 (1975) . . . |

. . .

STATEMENT OF JURISDICTION: Statutes governing the court's substantive and procedural power to act.	Because Vincent McCall's appeal is in the Ohio state courts, courts of general jurisdiction, it is not necessary to include a Statement of Jurisdiction in his appellate brief.
STATEMENT OF ISSUES: A short statement of the questions that will be addressed in the memo. This and the brief answer(s) section of the memo will be the last sections written.	**STATEMENT OF ISSUES**

Whether the Cuyahoga Middle School properly permanently excluded Vincent McCall.

Whether the Cuyahoga Middle School properly expelled or suspended Vincent McCall.

Whether Vincent McCall is entitled to alternative schooling during his period of suspension. |

Figure 14–3 (continued)

STATEMENT OF THE CASE: Procedural and factual background of the case.	**STATEMENT OF THE CASE**

STATEMENT OF THE CASE

Procedural Facts. On January 24, 2001, the Cuyahoga Middle School Principal suspended Vincent McCall and several other fourteen-year-olds from school for an incident earlier that day involving the attempted sale of pipe. Later that night, the Cuyahoga school board voted to permanently exclude McCall and the other youngsters from school. Although they were at the meeting, neither Vincent nor his parents, Mr. and Mrs. McCall, were allowed to speak.

Following a January 29, 2001 emergency hearing on Vincent's appeal, the Cuyahoga County Court of Common Pleas upheld the school board's action.

McCall timely appealed.

Substantive Facts. Vincent's difficulties began when he was a 14-year-old student at the Cuyahoga Public Middle School. On January 24, 2001, a friend called Vincent over to his locker where he and two other boys showed Vincent a number of metal "tubes" that the friend explained were some really fine fireworks. The friend asked if Vincent was interested in buying a couple. Vincent asked their price and agreed to buy three later that afternoon. In the meantime, the boys selling these "super fireworks" sawed the lock off a nearby locker and stowed their "fireworks" in the other locker — and re-locked the "fireworks" locker with one of the boys' lock. When the owner of the storage locker came by to get the books he needed for class, he couldn't open the lock. He went to the school administrative office to ask for help. Help came in the form of a janitor who "snipped" the lock off with wire-cutters. . . . .

SUMMARY OF ARGUMENT: A short summary of the argument to guide the judges' reading.

Because Vincent McCall's argument is relatively short, it is not necessary to include a Summary of his Argument in the appellate brief.

ARGUMENT: This is the substance of the appellate brief. It is here that the memo writer presents her argument based on the law and its application to the facts presented.

ARGUMENT

Standard of Review

Upon review of an order of the Court of Common Pleas in a public school expulsion case, the appellate court is limited to determining only if the trial court has abused its discretion. *Kressler v. Sandusky Board of Educ.*, 2001 WL 27544 (Ohio App. 6th Dist. 2001). An abuse of discretion implies that the trial court's attitude is unreasonable, arbitrary, or unconscionable. *Id.*

Figure 14–3 (continued)

Absent an abuse of discretion, an appellate court must affirm the trial court's judgment. *Id.*

I. The Cuyahoga school board could not properly permanently exclude Vincent McCall from school.

Ohio Revised Code, § 3313.662 governs permanent exclusion of students from Ohio's public schools. . . .

CONCLUSION:
Brief conclusion and request for relief.

CONCLUSION.

For the reasons set forth above, this Court should vacate the judgment upholding the Cuyahoga board of education decision to exclude Vincent McCall from public school and order that the board of education expunge from McCall's school records his expulsion from school on January 24, 2001 and permit McCall to attend school effective immediately in the Cuyahoga school district.

In the alternative, the Court should order the Cuyahoga school district to provide alternative education to Vincent during any period that he is excluded from school.

SIGNATURE AND DATE:
"Respectfully submitted" and the party's name and signature, or if represented by counsel, counsel for the party.

Respectfully submitted,

ANNE M. STEVENS,
Attorney for Vincent McCall
264 Richmond Road
Richmond Heights, OH 44143
(216) 555-1212

CERTIFICATE OF SERVICE:
Attorney's sworn certificate that brief has been provided to opponent in timely fashion.

CERTIFICATE OF SERVICE

On this twenty-second day of February, 2001, I declare, under the pains and penalties of perjury, that I served the foregoing document on all interested parties to this action by first class mail, postage prepaid.

_____
Anne M. Stevens

Figure 14–3 (continued)

| ADDENDUM OF CONSTITUTIONAL AND STATUTORY PROVISIONS: Relevant constitutional, statutory, and regulatory provisions set out in full.

APPENDIX: The appellate appendix includes information and documents necessary to resolution of the appeal. | **ADDENDUM OF CONSTITUTIONAL AND STATUTORY PROVISIONS**

Vincent McCall's appellate appendix might include the following:

    relevant statutory provisions
    student handbook provisions

APPENDIX

Vincent McCall's appellate appendix might include the following documents:

Court of Common Pleas' docket
Vincent's complaint
Court of Common Pleas record
any motions or exhibits filed in the Court of
    Common Pleas
any court orders
Court of Common Pleas' decision
Notice of Appeal |

Figure 14–3 (continued)

cases first, constitutions, statutes, and regulations second, then all other authorities. Always cite authorities in *Bluebook* form unless specifically directed to cite otherwise (check the rules for that specific court). List the page numbers where each authority appears in the brief in the Table of Authorities. If particular authorities appear throughout the brief, list those authorities as appearing **passim**.

Statement of Jurisdiction

Certain courts (most notably the federal courts) require parties appealing a trial court decision to set out the jurisdiction of the appellate court hearing the appeal. The statement of jurisdiction may consist simply of the statutes giving the appellate court substantive and appellate jurisdiction. As Vincent's case is in state court, a court of general jurisdiction, no statement of jurisdiction is required.

Statement of Issues

The Issues section of an appellate brief tells the appellate judges of the precise legal question(s) being raised on appeal. While the Statement of Issues may be phrased very generally, as in "May public schools permanently exclude students?" a better statement incorporates the facts of the case and the legal principles involved, as in "May a public school permanently exclude a student seeking to buy a pipe bomb from another student?" Limit the number of issues presented to no more than three central, dispositive issues.

(1) A table of contents, with page references, and a table of cases (alphabetically arranged), statutes and other authorities cited, with references to the pages of the brief where they are cited.

(2) A statement of subject matter and appellate jurisdiction. . . .

(3) A statement of the issues presented for review.

(4) A statement of the case. The statement shall first indicate briefly the nature of the case, the course of proceedings, and its disposition in the court below. There shall follow a statement of the facts relevant to the issues presented for review, with appropriate references to the record (see subdivision (e)).

(5) A summary of argument. The summary should contain a succinct, clear, and accurate statement of the arguments made in the body of the brief. It should not be a mere repetition of the argument headings.

(6) An argument. The argument must contain the contentions of the appellant on the issues presented, and the reasons therefor, with citations to the authorities, statutes, and parts of the record relied on. The argument must also include for each issue a concise statement of the applicable standard of review; this statement may appear in the discussion of each issue or under a separate heading placed before the discussion of the issues.

(7) A short conclusion stating the precise relief sought.

. . . .

(f) <u>Reproduction of Statutes, Rules, Regulations, Etc.</u> If determination of the issues presented requires the study of statutes, rules, regulations, etc. or relevant parts thereof, they shall be reproduced in the brief or in an addendum at the end, or they may be supplied to the court in pamphlet form.

(g) <u>Length of Briefs.</u> Except by permission of the court, or as specified by local rule of the court of appeals, principal briefs must not exceed 50 pages, and reply briefs must not exceed 25 pages, exclusive of pages containing the corporate disclosure statement, table of contents, tables of citations, proof of service, and any addendum containing statutes, rules, regulations, etc.

Figure 14–4 Federal Rule Of Appellate Procedure 28.

Statement of the Case

In this section should appear a statement of the procedural and factual background of the case. The statement of the case tells the court how the case got to the appellate court: it details the events leading up to filing the complaint, procedural events in the lower court, the course of trial, the decision, any post-trial motions and events, notice of appeal, and relevant pre-appeal events. It also summarizes the relevant facts of the case. Use factual statements to further the argument. Be honest; do not try to bury "bad" or "negative" facts, but downplay those facts or consider a case theory that incorporates and uses negative as well as positive facts. An argument incorporating "not-so-good" facts is far stronger than one that ignores or buries those facts.

Summary of the Argument

Without extensive citation of legal materials, summarize your legal argument. Clearly indicate your conclusion at the end of each legal argument. This section may well be the last section of the brief to be written, even though it appears physically early in the brief. It appears early in the brief to prepare the judges for your legal argument; it is prepared late in the brief writing so it is an accurate summary of the brief's argument. Because the McCall brief is relatively short, it is not necessary to include a Summary of the Argument.

Argument

The only hard part of writing a legal memo is, as usual, writing its analysis. Because the brief writer has previously set out the question presented, it is usually unnecessary to begin the legal IRAC analysis with a statement of the issue; where the memo discusses two or more questions, it may be helpful to the reader to begin each analysis with a heading identifying the issue analyzed. Follow with a statement of the rule applying to the issue. If a statute applies, quote relevant statutory provisions. If cases interpret the statute or if cases govern the result, it is not enough to simply set out the case holding. Remember that the brief is persuasive and should be complete. The reader does not want to have to interrupt her reading to look up cited statutes and cases. Set out the facts, along with the holdings of relevant cases. Include some historical background if it will help the reader understand the context of an emerging area of law. For the sake of brevity, the writer should not include unnecessary information, but remember that the reader is human; a little "story-telling" helps the reader remain interested. Follow the summary of the applicable rule(s) with its application to the facts presented. It is important to think carefully about possible arguments the opponent may raise and either counter those arguments (if already made) or anticipate them (if not yet made). Remember to conclude and explain that conclusion for each legal argument.

Conclusion

This is the writer's overall conclusion regarding the issues presented on appeal. The conclusion section is not the section for argument, analysis, or gathering of supporting materials. That information belongs earlier in the brief. Rather, the conclusion should simply summarize the writer's overall conclusion on the outcome of the appeal.

Certificate of Service

This is the attorney's sworn statement that the document was provided to the opponent in timely fashion.

Addendum of Constitutional and Statutory Provisions

Include copies of all constitutional, statutory, regulatory, and local laws relevant to the brief in an Addendum to the brief. Do not assume that the court has those materials directly at hand. At times local (municipal) laws, including local zoning by-laws and regulations, are available only from the locality. In addition, federal and state regulations (particularly newly issued or outdated regulations) may be difficult to track down. It is often far easier for the parties (who have long lived with the case and its legal principles) to provide those materials than for the judges to track them down. In any event, it is better if the judges spend their time deciding cases rather than ferreting out obscure laws.

Appendix

Despite the appellate rules' discussion of the trial court's "assembling the trial court record" and "transferring the trial court record" to the appellate court, only rarely is the complete trial court record actually transmitted to the court hearing an appeal. More often, once the trial court record has been "assembled," that record is transferred to a storage area for safekeeping. Additionally, an assembled trial court record is rarely well-organized for appeal — that record was, after all, created during and for a trial, not an appeal. Moreover, the trial court record is almost always over-inclusive for an appeal. It is rare that the parties to a case really want to appeal "everything." Rather, only portions of the record are relevant to an appeal. As a result, rules of appellate procedure typically require the parties to jointly prepare an appellate appendix of trial court materials relevant to the issues on appeal. Consider FRAP Rule 30 regarding creation and contents of an appellate appendix in federal appeals, shown in Figure 14–5.

Form of an Appellate Brief

In addition to rules governing the content of appellate brief elements, rules of appellate procedure set out in excruciating detail (including type font size, spacing, paper weight, binding, and even cover color) the form of appellate briefs. Consider FRAP Rule 32, shown in Figure 14–6.

These rules are not merely "helpful hints;" a misstep in brief form or content will result in its rejection by the Appellate Court clerk's office.

(a) <u>Duty of Appellant to Prepare and File; Content of Appendix; Time for Filing; Number of Copies</u>. The appellant must prepare and file an appendix to the briefs which must contain: (1) the relevant docket entries in the proceeding below; (2) any relevant portions of the pleadings, charge, findings, or opinion; (3) the judgment, order, or decision in question; and (4) any other parts of the record to which the parties wish to direct the particular attention of the court. Except where they have independent relevance, memoranda of law in the district court should not be included in the appendix. The fact that parts of the record are not included in the appendix shall not prevent the parties or the court from relying on such parts.

Unless filing is to be deferred pursuant to the provisions of subdivision (c) of this rule, the appellant must serve and file the appendix with the brief. Ten copies of the appendix must be filed with the clerk, and one copy must be served on counsel for each party separately represented, unless the court requires the filing or service of a different number by local rule or by order in a particular case.

(b) <u>Determination of Contents of Appendix; Cost of Producing</u>. The parties are encouraged to agree as to the contents of the appendix. In the absence of agreement, the appellant shall, not later than 10 days after the date on which the record is filed, serve on the appellee a designation of the parts of the record which the appellant intends to include in the appendix and a statement of the issues which the appellant intends to present for review. If the appellee deems it necessary to direct the particular attention of the court to parts of the record not designated by the appellant, the appellee shall, within 10 days after receipt of the designation, serve upon the appellant a designation of those parts. The appellant shall include in the appendix the parts thus designated with respect to the appeal and any cross appeal. In designating parts of the record for inclusion in the appendix, the parties shall have regard for the fact that the entire record is always available to the court for reference and examination and shall not engage in unnecessary designation. The provisions of this paragraph shall apply to cross appellants and cross appellees.

Unless the parties otherwise agree, the cost of producing the appendix shall initially be paid by the appellant . . . .

(d) <u>Arrangement of the Appendix</u>. At the beginning of the appendix there shall be inserted a list of the parts of the record which it contains, in the order in which the parts are set out therein, with references to the pages of the appendix at which each part begins. The relevant docket entries shall be set out following the list of contents. Thereafter, other parts of the record shall be set out in chronological order. When matter contained in the reporter's transcript of proceedings is set out in the appendix, the page of the transcript at which such matter may be found shall be indicated in brackets immediately before the matter which is set out. Omissions in the text of papers or of the transcript must be indicated by asterisks. Immaterial formal matters (captions, subscriptions, acknowledgments, etc.) shall be omitted. A question and its answer may be contained in a single paragraph.

(e) <u>Reproduction of Exhibits</u>. Exhibits designated for inclusion in the appendix may be contained in a separate volume, or volumes, suitably indexed. Four copies thereof shall be filed with the appendix and one copy shall be served on counsel for each party separately represented. The transcript of a proceeding before an administrative agency, board, commission or officer used in an action in the district court shall be regarded as an exhibit for the purpose of this subdivision.

. . . .

Figure 14–5 Federal Rule Of Appellate Procedure 30.

(a) <u>Form of Briefs and the Appendix</u>. Briefs and appendices may be produced by standard typographic printing or by any duplicating or copying process which produces a clear black image on white paper. Carbon copies of briefs and appendices may not be submitted without permission of the court, except in behalf of parties allowed to proceed in forma pauperis. All printed matter must appear in at least 11 point type on opaque, unglazed paper. Briefs and appendices produced by the standard typographic process shall be bound in volumes having pages 6 1/8 by 9 1/4 inches and type matter 4 1/6 by 7 1/6 inches. Those produced by any other process shall be bound in volumes having pages not exceeding 8 1/2 by 11 inches and type matter not exceeding 6 1/2 by 9 1/2 inches, with double spacing between each line of text. . . .

If briefs are produced by commercial printing or duplicating firms, or, if produced otherwise and the covers to be described are available, the cover of the brief of the appellant should be blue; that of the appellee, red; that of an intervenor or amicus curiae, green; that of any reply brief, gray. The cover of the appendix, if separately printed, should be white. The front covers of the briefs and of appendices, if separately printed, shall contain: (1) the name of the court and the number of the case; (2) the title of the case . . . ; (3) the nature of the proceeding in the court (e.g., Appeal; Petition for Review) and the name of the court, agency, or board below; (4) the title of the document (e.g., Brief for Appellant, Appendix); and (5) the names and addresses of counsel representing the party on whose behalf the document is filed.

. . . .

Figure 14–6 Federal Rule Of Appellate Procedure 32.

Review Questions

1. Explain the appellate process and deadlines.

2. Explain court rules bearing on appeals.

3. Describe the parts of an appellate brief, their contents, and their purpose.

4. Describe the purpose and contents of an appellate appendix.

5. Describe the purpose and contents of an appellate brief addendum.

Exercise

Assume that Kitty has lost her trial court case against her attorney because the trial court has determined that the statute of limitations has run out on her malpractice claim. Prepare an appellate brief on her behalf to the appeals court of your state.

Glossary

Appellant: The party appealing a lower court decision.

Appellate appendix: Compilation of lower court documents, transcript, and decisions required to decide the appeal.

Appellate process: The process by which a losing litigant seeks review of an adverse court decision.

Appellee: The party supporting a lower court decision.

Assembling the record: Compiling the lower court record.

Court rules: Rules governing the procedure of a court.

Docket the appeal: Enter an appeal in the appellate court.

Federal Rules of Appellate Procedure (FRAP): Rules governing appeals in the federal appellate courts.

Issues on appeal: Claims of legal error in the lower court.

Judgment: Final decision of a trial court.

Notice of appeal: Document filed in trial court notifying the trial court and adverse parties that a litigant plans to seek review of a court decision by an appellate court.

Oral argument: Oral presentation to appellate court of litigants' arguments in favor of or against the decision of the lower court.

Passim: Throughout.

Petition for rehearing: Request that the appellate court re-hear the case.

Pre-hearing conference: Conference held by a court to prepare a case for trial or appeal.

Reply briefs: Appellant's answers to appellee's briefs.

Transcript: Written record of what occurred in a trial court.

Notes

[1]Sixty days if the government is a party to the case.

[2]Brief adapted from *Zeitz* v. *Secretary of Health and Human Services*, 726 F. Supp. 343 (D. Mass. 1989).

[3]In this brief, "A." refers to the record appendix filed in the defendant's brief, "Supp. A." refers to the supplemental appendix filed with this brief, "Tr. I" refers to pages in the first transcript volume, "Tr. II" refers to pages in the second transcript volume, and "G.J.Min." refers to pages in the grand jury minutes.

Sample Appellate Briefs

Figure 14–7 is the sample appellate brief in the Vincent McCall case, including an excerpt from the *Cuyahoga Middle School Student Handbook*. Figure 14–8 and Figure 14–9 are additional sample appellate briefs.

**Ohio Appeals Court
No. 01-1234.**

CUYAHOGA COUNTY.

———————————

VINCENT McCALL
APPELLANT

v.

SCHOOL BOARD OF CUYAHOGA
APPELLEE

———————————

ON APPEAL FROM A JUDGMENT BY THE CUYAHOGA COURT OF COMMON
PLEAS

———————————

Brief for Vincent McCall

———————————

ANNE M. STEVENS,
Attorney for Vincent McCall
264 Richmond Road
Richmond Heights, OH 44143
(216) 555-1212

January, 2001

Figure 14–7 Sample appellate brief in the Vincent McCall case

Table of Contents

**Table of Authorities
Cases**

Figure 14–7 (continued)

Figure 14–7 (continued)

Ohio Appeals Court
No. 01-1234.

CUYAHOGA COUNTY.

_____

VINCENT McCALL,
APPELLANT

v.

SCHOOL BOARD OF CUYAHOGA,
APPELLEE

_____

ON APPEAL FROM A JUDGMENT BY THE CUYAHOGA COURT OF COMMON
PLEAS

_____

Brief for Vincent McCall

_____

Statement of the Issues

Whether the Cuyahoga Middle School properly permanently excluded Vincent McCall.

Whether the Cuyahoga Middle School properly expelled or suspended Vincent McCall.

Whether Vincent McCall is entitled to alternative schooling during his period of suspension.

Prior Proceedings

On January 24, 2001, the Cuyahoga Middle School Principal suspended Vincent McCall and several other 14-year-olds from school for an incident earlier that day involving the attempted sale of pipe bombs. Later that night, the Cuyahoga school board voted to permanently exclude McCall and the other youngsters from school. Although they were at the meeting, neither Vincent nor his parents, Mr. and Mrs. McCall, were allowed to speak.

Figure 14–7 (continued)

Following a January 29, 2001 emergency hearing on Vincent's appeal, the Cuyahoga County Court of Common Pleas upheld the school board's action.

McCall timely appealed.

Statement of the Facts

Vincent's difficulties began when he was a 14-year-old student at the Cuyahoga Public Middle School. On January 24, 2001, a friend called Vincent over to his locker where he and two other boys showed Vincent a number of metal "tubes" that the friend explained were some really fine fireworks. The friend asked if Vincent was interested in buying a couple. Vincent asked their price and agreed to buy three later that afternoon. In the meantime, the boys selling these "super fireworks" sawed the lock off a nearby locker and stowed their "fireworks" in the other locker — and re-locked the "fireworks" locker with one of the boys' lock. When the owner of the storage locker came by to get the books he needed for class, he couldn't open the lock. He went to the school administrative office to ask for help. Help came in the form of a janitor who "snipped" the lock off with wire-cutters. When the janitor saw what looked like (and indeed, were) pipe bombs, he called the local bomb squad, who quietly removed the devices for testing and re-locked the locker with yet a third lock. The police then staked out the locker corridor until a number of youngsters (including Vincent) gathered around the locker. When they were unable to unlock the lock, the police moved in and took the boys, including Vincent, into custody. They were later released to their parents' custody pending the initiation of criminal charges. The school was evacuated for the remainder of the day so that the bomb specialists could ensure that there were no similar on the premises (there were not). An emergency school board meeting was held that night at which the school board summarily expelled the boys indefinitely. As the story unraveled, it seems that three boys had learned to make pipe bombs over the Internet, as a lark had made up about ten of the bombs, and had taken them to school intending to sell them to some of their friends. As it turned out, of course, no sales were completed and all the bombs were confiscated.

Although Vincent was not one of the original three boys manufacturing the pipe bombs, the McCalls (all of them, including Vincent) agree that Vincent's involvement in the deal was at least stupid. Nevertheless, given Vincent's relatively minor involvement in the deal, they are horrified at the effect the expulsion will have on his chances for college.

Argument

Standard of Review

Upon review of an order of the Court of Common Pleas in a public school expulsion case, the appellate court is limited to determining only if the trial court has abused its discretion. *Kressler v. Sandusky Board of Educ.*, 2001 WL 27544 (Ohio App. 6th Dist. 2001). An abuse of discretion implies that the trial court's attitude is unreasonable, arbitrary, or unconscionable. *Id.* Absent an abuse of discretion, an appellate court must affirm the trial court's judgment. *Id.*

Figure 14–7 (continued)

I. The Cuyahoga school board could not properly permanently exclude Vincent McCall from school.

Ohio Revised Code, § 3313.662 governs permanent exclusion of students from Ohio's public schools. In pertinent part, that statute provides as follows (emphasis added):

> The superintendent of public instruction, pursuant to this section and the adjudication process of section 3301.121 of the Revised Code, may issue an adjudication order that permanently excludes a pupil from attending any of the public schools of this state if the pupil is convicted of, or adjudicated a delinquent child for, committing, *when the pupil was sixteen years of age or older*, an act that would be a criminal offense if committed by an adult . . . . [or] involved the pupil's bringing a firearm to a school operated by the board of education of any school district or onto any other property owned or operated by such board . . .

> (I) As used in this section:

> (1) "Permanently exclude" means to forever prohibit an individual from attending any public school in this state that is operated by a city, local, exempted village, or joint vocational school district . . .

> (6) "Firearm" has the same meaning as provided pursuant to the "Gun-Free Schools Act of 1994", 108 Stat. 270, 20 U.S.C. § 8001(a)(2) . . .

On January 24, 2001, the date of the pipe bomb incident, Vincent McCall (d.o.b. 6/1/86) was 14 years old, too young to be permanently excluded from public school under § 3313.662.

II. The Cuyahoga school board could not properly expel or suspend Vincent McCall.

To temporarily exclude a child from public school, the school superintendent must complete the following two tasks:

> "(a) Give the pupil and the pupil's parent, guardian, or custodian written notice of the intention to [exclude] the pupil; [and]

> "(b) Provide the pupil and the pupil's parent, guardian, custodian, or representative an opportunity to appear in person before the superintendent or the superintendent's designee to challenge the reasons for the intended [exclusion] or otherwise to explain the pupil's actions.

> "The notice required in this division shall include the reasons for the intended [exclusion], notification of the opportunity of the pupil and the pupil's parent, guardian, custodian, or representative to appear before the superintendent or the superintendent's designee to challenge the reasons for the intended expulsion or otherwise to explain the pupil's action, and notification of the time and place to appear. The time to appear shall not be earlier than three nor later than five school days after the notice is given, unless the superintendent grants an extension of time at the request of the pupil or the pupil's parent, guardian, custodian, or representative."

Ohio Rev. Code § 3313.66 (B) (5) (Baldwin 1999).

A. The Cuyahoga school board gave insufficient notice of the suspension and expulsion.

The parties agree that the "hearing" afforded Vincent and his parents took place not before the school superintendent, but before the school board and that that "hearing"

Figure 14–7 (continued)

took place the same evening of the pipe-bomb incident. That hearing, then, did not comply with § 3313.66 (B) (5). Moreover, there is no indication whether the school officials gave notice of that hearing to Vincent and/or his parents, nor whether that notice was oral or in writing. Although one Ohio appellate court has applied a "substantial compliance" test in determining whether or not a student received due process protection during exclusion proceedings, see *Stuble v. Cuyahoga Valley Joint Vocational Sch. Dist. Bd. Of Educ.* 1982 WL 5953 (1982) (unpublished decision), the "substantial compliance" test has been uniformly rejected by other state appellate courts. Recently, the Ohio Supreme Court has admonished the courts to give effect to a statute's express wording and plain meaning when construing a statute and its legislative interest. *State ex rel. Richard v. Bd. Of Trustees of Police & Firemen's Disability & Pension Fund*, 69 Ohio St. 3d 409, 412, 632 N.E.2d 1292, 1295 (1994). Section 3313.66(B) permits variance from exclusion hearing timelines only at the request of the student, his parents, or his representative. The plain language of the statute imposes a mandatory minimum three-day notice period before an expulsion hearing can be held. Therefore, this exclusion order must be vacated. *Id.*

B. The "hearing" held by the Cuyahoga School Board was insufficient to suspend or expel McCall.

Moreover, the hearing provided the McCalls was insufficient to exclude Vincent from public school. Even temporary exclusion from public school impacts on liberty and property interests. *Goss v. Lopez*, 419 U.S. 565, 581 (1975) addressed the process due children suspended from public school for ten days or less. In case of a short suspension, the Supreme Court held that a "student [should] be given oral or written notice of the charges against him and, if he denies them, an explanation of the evidence the authorities have and an opportunity to present his side of the story." *Id.* Where a child is to be expelled from school, a punishment more severe than a temporary suspension, the Sixth Circuit has required that a "student faced with expulsion has the right to a pre-expulsion hearing before an impartial trier-of-fact, although does not have the right to a full-blown administrative appellate process." *Newsome v. Batavia Local Sch. Dist.*, 842 F.2d 920, 921 (6th Cir. 1988). See also *Turner v. South-Western City Sch. Dist.*, 82 F.3d 757 (6th Cir. 1999). Indeed, § 3313.66(B)(5) of the Ohio Revised Code establishes the procedures to be used in student exclusions, which are (emphasis added):

> No pupil shall be expelled under division (B)(1), (2), (3), or (4) of this section unless, prior to the pupil's expulsion, the superintendent does both of the following:
>
> (a) Gives the pupil and the pupil's parent, guardian, or custodian written notice of the intention to expel the pupil;
>
> (b) *Provides the pupil and the pupil's parent, guardian, custodian, or representative an opportunity to appear in person before the superintendent or the superintendent's designee to challenge the reasons for the intended expulsion or otherwise to explain the pupil's actions.* The notice required in this division shall include the reasons for the intended expulsion, notification of the opportunity of the pupil and the pupil's parent, guardian, custodian, or representative to appear before the superintendent or the superintendent's designee to challenge the reasons for the intended expulsion or otherwise to explain the pupil's action, and notification of the time and place to appear.

Figure 14–7 (continued)

In this case, although the McCalls appeared for the pre-exclusion hearing, neither they nor Vincent were permitted to ask questions of the investigator of the incident or to offer any explanation for Vincent's behavior or involvement in the incident. The exclusion can not therefore stand. See, e.g., *State ex rel. Richard,* 69 Ohio St. 3d at 412, 632 N.E.2d at 1295.

C. Even were the "notice" and "hearing" offered by the Cuyahoga school board sufficient under Ohio Revised Code § 3313.66 or waived by the McCalls' appearance at the hearing, Vincent McCall did not commit nor was he party to an action warranting expulsion.

To expel a child from public school, the child must have committed an offense prohibited by a known school rule or policy. See, e.g., *Riley v. St. Ann Catholic School,* 2000 WL 1902430 (Ohio App. 8th Dist. 2000) (unpublished decision involving expulsion from a private school) and *Steinway v. Chillicothe City Schools,* 1999 WL 1604, *3 (Ohio App. 4th Dist. 1998) (unpublished decision, code of conduct; school disciplinary rules need not be as detailed as the criminal code).

The Cuyahoga Middle School's student handbook, which is annually distributed to all middle school students, provides in pertinent part as follows:

> School law provides the principal with the authority to recommend the expulsion of any student from school . . . who is found bringing on school premises or at a school-sponsored or school-related events . . . a firearm.

That rule was promulgated in accordance with Ohio Revised Code § 3313.66, which provides, in pertinent part as follows:

> (B)(2)(a) Unless a pupil is permanently excluded pursuant to section 3313.662 of the Revised Code, the superintendent of schools of a city, exempted village, or local school district shall expel a pupil from school for a period of one year for bringing a firearm to a school operated by the board of education of the district or onto any other property owned or controlled by the board, except that the superintendent may reduce this requirement on a case-by-case basis in accordance with the policy adopted by the board under section 3313.661 of the Revised Code. . . .

> (c) Any expulsion pursuant to division (B)(2) of this section shall extend, as necessary, into the school year following the school year in which the incident that gives rise to the expulsion takes place. As used in this division, "firearm" has the same meaning as provided pursuant to the "Gun-Free Schools Act of 1994," 108 Stat. 270, 20 U.S.C. 8001(a)(2).

The Ohio exclusion statute, § 3313.66, in turn, was passed to comply with the Federal Gun-Free School Act, 20 U.S.C. § 8001, which provides in pertinent part as follows:

> Except as provided in paragraph (3), each State receiving Federal funds under this chapter shall have in effect a State law requiring local educational agencies to expel from school for a period of not less than one year a student who is determined to have brought a weapon to a school under the jurisdiction of local educational agencies in that State, except that such State law shall allow the chief administering officer of such local educational agency to modify such expulsion requirement for a student on a case-by-case basis.

Figure 14–7 (continued)

(4) Definition

For the purpose of this section, the term "weapon" means a firearm as such term is defined in section 921 of Title 18.

Thus, to be validly excluded from school under these laws, Vincent must have *brought a firearm* to school.

The American Heritage Dictionary (2d college ed., 1982) defines "bring" as "To take with oneself to a place; convey or carry along." As it is undisputed that Vincent was not one of the youngsters to bring the pipe bombs to school, indeed, Vincent neither knew of the pipe bombs nor saw the pipe bombs before the morning the other youngsters brought them to school, Vincent did not "bring" a firearm to school.

Moreover, a pipe bomb is not a "firearm" as that term is used in Ohio Revised Code §§ 3313.66, 3313.662, or the Federal Gun-Free School Act.

As used in both federal and state statutes, the term "firearm" means as follows:

(A) any weapon (including a starter gun) which will or is designed to or may readily be converted to expel a projectile by the action of an explosive; (B) the frame or receiver of any such weapon; (C) any firearm muffler or firearm silencer; or (D) any destructive device. Such term does not include an antique firearm. . . .

(4) The term "destructive device" means

(a) any explosive, incendiary, or poison gas

(i) bomb,

(ii) grenade,

(iii) rocket having a propellant charge of more than four ounces,

(iv) missile having an explosive or incendiary charge of more than one-quarter ounce,

(v) mine, or

(vi) device similar to any of the devices described in the preceding clauses;

(B) any type of weapon (other than a shotgun or a shotgun shell which the Secretary finds is generally recognized as particularly suitable for sporting purposes) by whatever name known which will, or which may be readily converted to, expel a projectile by the action of an explosive or other propellant, and which has any barrel with a bore of more than one-half inch in diameter; and

(C) any combination of parts either designed or intended for use in converting any device into any destructive device described in subparagraph (A) or (B) and from which a destructive device may be readily assembled.

The term "destructive device" shall not include any device which is neither designed nor redesigned for use as a weapon; any device, although originally designed for use as a weapon, which is redesigned for use as a signaling, pyrotechnic, line throwing, safety, or similar device; surplus ordnance sold, loaned, or given by the Secretary of the Army pursuant to the provisions of section 4684(2), 4685, or 4686 of title 10; or any other device which the Secretary of the Treasury finds is not likely to be used as a weapon, is an antique, or is a rifle which the owner intends to use solely for sporting, recreational or cultural purposes.

18 U.S.C. § 921 (1988). Notably, although pipe bombs were well known when 18 U.S.C. § 921 was latest amended in 1998, see, e.g., *Pipe bombs: Easy weapons you can whip up at home* <http://www.business-server.com/newsroom/nt/728easy.html> (last visited

Figure 14–7 (continued)

1/28/01), Congress did not include pipe bombs among "firearms" in enacting the statute. And while it may be argued that the category of "bombs" was intended to include pipe bombs, a careful look at the definition of firearms belies that intent. Common to all categories included in the Federal definition of "firearms" under 18 U.S.C. § 921, is the notion that a firearm is a device "designed to or may readily be converted to expel a projectile by the action of an explosive." Although the pipe bombs involved in this case were intended to emit a loud sound when ignited, the one-eighth ounce of explosive used in creating the pipe bombs was such that the pipe bombs' iron casing, i.e., the "pipe," prevented any expulsion of projectiles when ignited.

And, while certainly the school disciplinary rules are non-criminal in nature, but cf. *Steinway, supra,* "it is reasonable that a fair warning should be given to the world in language that the common world will understand, of what the law intends to do if a certain line is passed. To make the warning fair, so far as possible the line should be clear. When a rule of conduct is laid down in words that evoke in the common mind only the picture of [propulsive devices], the statute should not be extended to [nonpropulsive devices] simply because it may seem to us that a similar policy applies, or upon the speculation that if the legislature had thought of it, very likely broader words would have been used." *McBoyle v. United States,* 283 U.S. 25, 27 (1931). See also *Adrovet v. Brunswick City Sch. Dist. Bd of Educ,* 106 Ohio Misc. 2d 81, 86, 735 N.E.2d 995, 999 (1999).

III. Vincent McCall is entitled to alternative schooling during the period of his suspension.

For all the reasons given above, the McCalls believe that the Cuyahoga school district's action in excluding Vincent from school was improper. In the unlikely event, however, that this court finds that the district acted properly in excluding Vincent from school for ANY amount of time, the McCalls argue that during the period of Vincent's exclusion, he be offered alternative education.

The Federal Gun-Free School Act of 1994, 20 U.S.C. § 8001, provides in pertinent part as follows:

> Nothing in this subchapter shall be construed to prevent a State from allowing a local educational agency that has expelled a student from such a student's regular school setting from providing educational services to such student in an alternative setting.

While that statement is not a requirement that public school districts provide alternative education to suspended or expelled students, an increasing number of states are recognizing the value in providing alternative education.

Indeed, although the U.S. Constitution does not recognize a fundamental right to public education, several states have proclaimed that the right to public education is a fundamental right. See Laura Beresh-Taylor, *Preventing Violence in Ohio's Schools,* 33 Akron L. Rev. 311, 334-335 (2000) and cases therein cited. In those states, students who are expelled or suspended have an enforceable right to alternative education during their period of exclusion. *Id. at 335.*

More importantly, though, studies done comparing school districts providing alternative education with those that do not, found that "[d]iversion and treatment programs provide some of the most promising examples of violence prevention techniques that work with youth involved in gun violence." That study found that alternative schools prevent violence in schools and communities because these programs prevent offenders from roaming the streets, that alternative school programs focus on rehabilitating

Figure 14–7 (continued)

troubled youth, and finally, that providing juveniles with alternative education deters future criminal activity.

Section 3313.533 of the Ohio Revised Code empowers a board of education to create and maintain alternative schools "to meet the needs of students who are on suspension, who are having truancy problems, who are experiencing academic failure, who have a history of class disruption, or who are exhibiting other academic or behavioral problems." Indeed, § 3313.66(I) of the Ohio revised code provides that "during the period of the expulsion, the board of education . . . may provide educational services to the student in an alternative setting." Section 3313.534 of the Code mandates that the "big eight" school districts (of which the Cuyahoga School District is one) establish no later than July 1, 1999 at least one alternative school to serve students with "severe discipline problems."

Vincent's involvement in the Middle School pipe bomb incident was minimal — he neither manufactured the bombs, brought them to school, or sold them. At worst, Vincent's involvement in the incident might be described as at attempt to purchase three "super fireworks." Under these circumstances, should his expulsion be upheld, Vincent should be offered alternative schooling during his period of exclusion. Let's not turn an otherwise good boy into a violent criminal by releasing him for any length of time to the dangers of the streets.

Conclusion

For the reasons set forth above, this Court should vacate the judgment upholding the Cuyahoga Board of Education decision to exclude Vincent McCall from public school and order that the Board of Education expunge from McCall's school records his expulsion from school on January 24, 2001 and permit Vincent McCall to attend school effective immediately in the Cuyahoga School District.

In the alternative, the Court should order the Cuyahoga School District to provide alternative education to Vincent during any period that he is excluded from school.

Respectfully submitted,

_____

ANNE M. STEVENS,
Attorney for Vincent McCall
264 Richmond Road
Richmond Heights, OH 44143
(216) 555-1212

CERTIFICATE OF SERVICE

On this twenty-second day of February, 2001, I declare, under the pains and penalties of perjury, that I served the foregoing document on all interested parties to this action by first class mail, postage prepaid.

_____

Anne M. Stevens

February, 2001

Figure 14–7 (continued)

Addendum

OHIO REVISED CODE § 3313.66 SUSPENSION, EXPULSION, AND REMOVAL FROM PREMISES

. . . .

(B)(1) Except as provided under division (B)(2), (3), or (4) of this section, the superintendent of schools of a city, exempted village, or local school district may expel a pupil from school for a period not to exceed the greater of eighty school days or the number of school days remaining in the semester or term in which the incident that gives rise to the expulsion takes place, unless the expulsion is extended pursuant to division (F) of this section. If at the time an expulsion is imposed there are fewer than eighty school days remaining in the school year in which the incident that gives rise to the expulsion takes place, the superintendent may apply any remaining part or all of the period of the expulsion to the following school year.

(2)(a) Unless a pupil is permanently excluded pursuant to section 3313.662 of the Revised Code, the superintendent of schools of a city, exempted village, or local school district shall expel a pupil from school for a period of one year for bringing a firearm to a school operated by the board of education of the district or onto any other property owned or controlled by the board, except that the superintendent may reduce this requirement on a case-by-case basis in accordance with the policy adopted by the board under section 3313.661 of the Revised Code.

(b) The superintendent of schools of a city, exempted village, or local school district may expel a pupil from school for a period of one year for bringing a firearm to an interscholastic competition, an extracurricular event, or any other school program or activity that is not located in a school or on property that is owned or controlled by the district. The superintendent may reduce this disciplinary action on a case-by-case basis in accordance with the policy adopted by the board under section 3313.661 of the Revised Code.

(c) Any expulsion pursuant to division (B)(2) of this section shall extend, as necessary, into the school year following the school year in which the incident that gives rise to the expulsion takes place. As used in this division, "firearm" has the same meaning as provided pursuant to the "Gun-Free Schools Act of 1994," 108 Stat. 270, 20 U.S.C. 8001(a)(2).

(3) The board of education of a city, exempted village, or local school district may adopt a resolution authorizing the superintendent of schools to expel a pupil from school for a period not to exceed one year for bringing a knife to a school operated by the board, onto any other property owned or controlled by the board, or to an interscholastic competition, an extracurricular event, or any other program or activity sponsored by the school district or in which the district is a participant, or for possessing a firearm or knife at a school, on any other property owned or controlled by the board, or at an interscholastic competition, an extracurricular event, or any other school program or activity, which firearm or knife was initially brought onto school board property by another person. The resolution may authorize the superintendent to extend such an expulsion, as necessary, into the school year following the school year in which the incident that gives rise to the expulsion takes place.

Figure 14–7 (continued)

(4) The board of education of a city, exempted village, or local school district may adopt a resolution establishing a policy under section 3313.661 of the Revised Code that authorizes the superintendent of schools to expel a pupil from school for a period not to exceed one year for committing an act that is a criminal offense when committed by an adult and that results in serious physical harm to persons as defined in division (A)(5) of section 2901.01 of the Revised Code or serious physical harm to property as defined in division (A)(6) of section 2901.01 of the Revised Code while the pupil is at school, on any other property owned or controlled by the board, or at an interscholastic competition, an extracurricular event, or any other school program or activity. Any expulsion under this division shall extend, as necessary, into the school year following the school year in which the incident that gives rise to the expulsion takes place.

(5) No pupil shall be expelled under division (B)(1), (2), (3), or (4) of this section unless, prior to the pupil's expulsion, the superintendent does both of the following:

    (a) Gives the pupil and the pupil's parent, guardian, or custodian written notice of the intention to expel the pupil;

    (b) Provides the pupil and the pupil's parent, guardian, custodian, or representative an opportunity to appear in person before the superintendent or the superintendent's designee to challenge the reasons for the intended expulsion or otherwise to explain the pupil's actions. The notice required in this division shall include the reasons for the intended expulsion, notification of the opportunity of the pupil and the pupil's parent, guardian, custodian, or representative to appear before the superintendent or the superintendent's designee to challenge the reasons for the intended expulsion or otherwise to explain the pupil's action, and notification of the time and place to appear. The time to appear shall not be earlier than three nor later than five school days after the notice is given, unless the superintendent grants an extension of time at the request of the pupil or the pupil's parent, guardian, custodian, or representative. If an extension is granted after giving the original notice, the superintendent shall notify the pupil and the pupil's parent, guardian, custodian, or representative of the new time and place to appear. If the proposed expulsion is based on a violation listed in division (A) of section 3313.662 of the Revised Code and if the pupil is sixteen years of age or older, the notice shall include a statement that the superintendent may seek to permanently exclude the pupil if the pupil is convicted of or adjudicated a delinquent child for that violation.

(6) A superintendent of schools of a city, exempted village, or local school district shall initiate expulsion proceedings pursuant to this section with respect to any pupil who has committed an act warranting expulsion under the district's policy regarding expulsion even if the pupil has withdrawn from school for any reason after the incident that gives rise to the hearing but prior to the hearing or decision to impose the expulsion. If, following the hearing, the pupil would have been expelled for a period of time had the pupil still been enrolled in the school, the expulsion shall be imposed for the same length of time as on a pupil who has not withdrawn from the school.

Figure 14–7 (continued)

3313.662 PERMANENT EXCLUSION OF PUPILS; REVOCATION; PRO-BATIONARY ADMISSION

(A) The superintendent of public instruction, pursuant to this section and the adjudication procedures of section 3301.121 of the Revised Code, may issue an adjudication order that permanently excludes a pupil from attending any of the public schools of this state if the pupil is convicted of, or adjudicated a delinquent child for, committing, *when the pupil was sixteen years of age or older*, an act that would be a criminal offense if committed by an adult and if the act is any of the following:

(1) A violation of section 2923.122 of the Revised Code;

(2) A violation of section 2923.12 of the Revised Code, of a substantially similar municipal ordinance, or of section 2925.03 of the Revised Code that was committed on property owned or controlled by, or at an activity held under the auspices of, a board of education of a city, local, exempted village, or joint vocational school district;

(3) A violation of section 2925.11 of the Revised Code, other than a violation of that section that would be a minor drug possession offense, that was committed on property owned or controlled by, or at an activity held under the auspices of, the board of education of a city, local, exempted village, or joint vocational school district;

(4) A violation of section 2903.01, 2903.02, 2903.03, 2903.04, 2903.11, 2903.12, 2907.02, or 2907.05 or of former section 2907.12 of the Revised Code that was committed on property owned or controlled by, or at an activity held under the auspices of, a board of education of a city, local, exempted village, or joint vocational school district, if the victim at the time of the commission of the act was an employee of that board of education;

(5) Complicity in any violation described in division (A)(1), (2), (3), or (4) of this section that was alleged to have been committed in the manner described in division(A)(1), (2), (3), or (4) of this section, regardless of whether the act of complicity was committed on property owned or controlled by, or at an activity held under the auspices of, a board of education of a city, local, exempted village, or joint vocational school district.

EXCERPT FROM THE CUYAHOGA MIDDLE SCHOOL STUDENT HANDBOOK

WHAT WE EXPECT OF YOU

Weapons
All weapons including but not limited to knives or any kind of guns are banned from school.

Expulsion from school
State law provides the principal with the authority to recommend the expulsion of any student from school under the conditions stated below.

- Any student who brings on school premises or at school-sponsored or school-related events, including athletic games, a dangerous weapon, including, but not limited to, a gun or knife; or a controlled substance as defined in Chapter

Figure 14–7 (continued)

94C, including but not limited to, marijuana, cocaine, and heroin, may be subject to expulsion from the school or school district by the principal.

- Any student who assaults a principal, assistant principal, teacher, teacher's aide or other educational staff on school premises or at school-sponsored or school-related events, including athletic games, may be subject to expulsion from the school or school district by the principal.

- Any student who is charged with a violation of either paragraph (1) or (2) shall be notified in writing of an opportunity for a hearing; provided, however, that the student may have representation, along with the opportunity to present evidence and witnesses at said hearing before the principal.

- After said hearing, a principal may, in his/her discretion, decide to suspend rather than expel a student who has been determined by the principal to have violated either paragraph (1) or (2); provided, however, that any principal who decides that said student should be suspended shall state in writing to the school committee his/her reasons for choosing the suspension instead of the expulsion as the most appropriate remedy. In this statement, the principal shall represent that, in his/her opinion, the continued presence of this student in the school will not pose a threat to the safety, security and welfare of the other students and staff in the school.

- Any student who has been expelled from a school district pursuant to these provisions shall have the right to appeal to the superintendent. The expelled student shall have ten days from the date of the expulsion in which to notify the superintendent of his appeal. The student has the right to counsel at a hearing before the superintendent. The subject matter of the appeal shall not be limited solely to a factual determination of whether the student has violated any provisions of this section.

- When a student is expelled under the provisions of this section and applies for admission to another school for acceptance, the superintendent of the sending school shall notify the superintendent of the receiving school of the reasons for the pupil's expulsion.

Behaviors that may result in suspension and/or recommendation for expulsion

...

- Possession of a weapon

Figure 14–7 (continued)

UNITED STATES CIRCUIT COURT
FOR THE FIRST CIRCUIT

Leah A.,   )
      Plaintiff   )
)
                        v.   )   C.A. 96-1234
)
U.S. Department of Health and Human   )
Services Social Security Administration, Defendant.)
)

APPELLANT'S BRIEF

On Appeal from the United States District Court
for the District of Massachusetts

Anne M. Stevens
Newport & Stevens
37 Main St.
Amherst, OH 01002
Attorney for the Appellant Leah A.

TABLE OF CONTENTS

Figure 14–8 Sample appellate brief in a Social Security disability case.

TABLE OF AUTHORITIES

CASES

Bianchi v. Secretary of Health and Human Services, 764 F.2d 44, 45-46 (1st Cir.1985)

Carbonara v. Bowen, C.A. No. 88-1961, slip op., 1989 WL 30932 (E.D. Pa. 1989)

Goodernote v. Secretary of Health & Human Servs., 690 F.2d 5, 6-7 (1st Cir. 1982)

Inmates of the Boys' Training School v. Affleck, 346 F. Supp. 1354, 1365-66 (D.R.I. 1972)

Lancellotta v. Secretary of Health and Human Services, 806 F.2d 284, 285-86 (1st Cir. 1986)

McDonnell v. Heckler, 624 F. Supp. 375 (D. Mass. 1985)

Morgan v. Sproat, 432 F. Supp. 1130, 1139 n. 13 (S.D. Miss. 1977)

Soba v. Department of Health and Human Services, 724 F. Supp. 228 (S.D.N.Y. 1989)

STATUTES

Social Security Act, 42 U.S.C. § 401, *et. seq.*

REGULATIONS

20 C.F.R. § 404.1513 (a)

20 C.F.R. § 404.1511

20 C.F.R. § 404 Subpart P, App. 1, 12.06.

OTHER

W. Richard Lamb, MD. "Incentives and Disincentives of Disability Insurance for the Chronically Mentally Ill," in *Psychiatric Disability: Clinical, Legal, and Administration Dimensions*, 343, 346 (1987)

STATEMENT OF JURISDICTION

This Federal district court for the district of Massachusetts has jurisdiction to hear this appeal under 42 U.S.C. §§ 401 and 405 (g).

ISSUES PRESENTED

Whether Leah A., whose unique constellation of medical impairments, which include: inability to leave her apartment for any reason, including doctors' appointments, and short trips to a neighborhood store, inability to have any contact with strangers, whether in person or over the telephone, inability to interview for a job or interact on any regular basis, and inability to handle financial dealings, which has lasted for over seven years, is eligible for disability benefits under the Federal Social Security Act, 42 U.S.C. § 401, *et. seq.*

Figure 14–8 (continued)

STATEMENT OF THE CASE

Procedural Facts. Leah A. originally filed for these benefits in June 1982, at the age of thirty-five, claiming she was disabled by agoraphobia since 1978. In June 1983, an Administrative Law Judge ("ALJ") who conducted a hearing and reviewed the evidence found no severe mental or physical impairment which would prevent Leah A. from engaging in substantial gainful activity. The ALJ's denial of benefits became the final decision of the Secretary in 1984 when the Social Security Administration's Appeals Council denied review of the decision. Leah filed claim for Supplemental Security Income ("SSI") benefits in 1985 and was held to be entitled to receive those benefits as of February 1985. Leah A. is now forty-two years old and remains confined to her apartment, "with virtually no face to face interactions with anyone other than her roommate." In May 1986, this Court remanded the case to the Secretary pursuant to the district court's invalidation of step two of the Secretary's evaluation process in *McDonnell v. Heckler*, 624 F. Supp. 375 (D. Mass. 1985). Upon remand, the ALJ conducted another hearing, reviewed some additional evidence, and again found that "there was no valid medical evidence of any disease process which would render the claimant 'disabled' as defined by the Social Security Act." (A. at 255) The ALJ concluded that Leah A. suffered from no "severe medically determinable impairment, either physical or mental in nature." The ALJ acknowledged the possibility that the "claimant is suffering from psychiatric ilness [sic] which leads her to a life style which does not include employment commensurate [sic] with her education." The Appeals Council adopted the ALJ's findings, and again denied benefits for the period leading up to February 1985.

Substantive Facts. Leah A. is a college graduate who worked as a school teacher before taking a traveling sales job with the Coca-Cola Company in 1977. The first physical signs of Leah A.'s agoraphobia were palpitations, tingling and numbness in the arms, and lightheadedness manifested while driving home from a sales call in 1977. Leah A. became fearful of driving to visit the stores which stocked Coca-Cola, so her roommate began to accompany her on sales calls. She began experiencing backaches and headaches during a business trip to Atlanta, prompting fear which caused Leah A. to walk out on a dinner appointment. By 1978, Leah A. had left Coca-Cola and was feeling "tired, shaky [and] disconnected."

In searching for the cause of her agoraphobia, Leah A. stated that in 1977 she was treated by a physician who prescribed tranquilizers, consulted a chiropractor for treatment of backache and numbness, and was examined by an internist who diagnosed sinus trouble and other maladies. In 1979, a psychiatrist interviewed Leah A. and reported that she had stopped a long-running practice of daily marijuana smoking, and that she was not willing to take tranquilizing drugs prescribed by other doctors for fear of becoming drug dependent. The psychiatrist recommended further psychotherapy and found "no [mental] abnormalities except by history" and "normal blood pressure and pulse." In February 1980, a neurologist reporting on Leah A.'s workers' compensation claim stated that she was given acupuncture treatments for "80% relief" of a "symptom complex" which was "entirely psychosomatic in origin." In May 1980, a psychologist stated that Leah A. would be "more than willing to return to work but not in [the] highly stressed job" she held with Coca-Cola, and he recommended relaxation therapy, meditative techniques, and alternative career planning in order to "re-enter the mainstream of life and gainful employment." Letter of Martin Markey, (A. at

Figure 14–8 (continued)

166-67. In June 1980, a neuro-psychiatric evaluation of Leah A. revealed complaints about her former job with Coca-Cola, and no physical symptoms other than "slightly elevated heart rate" and "possible weakness on forward movement of head and neck." Leah A. was advised to attend "group psychotherapy" in order to speed her recovery. By 1981, Leah A. was doing "moderate" yoga exercises and "stained glass as a hobby." She came under the care of a psychiatrist who diagnosed agoraphobia and performed "behavior modification with the ancillary use of hypnosis" and recommended that "she not work at this time." Leah A. also visited a nutritional-biochemical consultant who prepared computer printouts of Leah A.'s "Nutrient Mineral Levels," "Mineral Rations" and "Toxic Metal Levels" and who diagnosed a "biochemical imbalance" as the cause of depression. Leah A. came under the belief that her agoraphobia was the result of birth control pills, junk food and "large amounts of Tab" consumed during the time she worked for Coca-Cola. In June 1982, Leah A. consulted a "wholistic [sic] physician" who advertised "nutritional analysis, hair analysis, kinesiology, reflexology, and dream analysis," and determined that Leah A.'s employment at the Coca-Cola Company set off a "stress-related condition" which included "pre-diabetes" and a "generalized biochemical disorder [affecting] all organs of the body, some more than others." Leah A. was advised to begin a "full-time" therapy program. Report of Dr. William, (A. at 174) (emphasis in original). Dr. Williams recommended acupuncture and chiropractic care, and Leah A. went to a nearby chiropractor who commended the holistic physician's findings and advised frequent treatments for spine problems diagnosed by x-ray.

In March 1982, "a hypnotist specializing in the treatment of agoraphobia" treated Leah A. and recommended more behavioral treatment. In June 1982, another chiropractor tested Leah A. and discovered "severe copper toxicity" and "a very strong pre-diabetic trend" which could be cured by "nutritional therapy to accomplish an excretion of the toxic tissue accumulations of Copper and Mercury." Letter of Dr. Miller, (A. at 185-86). At the close of 1982, Leah A. opened her own retail store, a "Seasonal Christmas Shop," but "[t]he effort was a disaster. The store was closed and the business folded." During 1983, Leah A. stated that she was working at home with a series of cassette audio tapes produced by the Chaange [sic] Center for Help for Agoraphobia/Anxiety through New Growth Experiences. Leah A. stated that she only left her apartment for brief periods, mainly to attend doctor's appointments, and that she had an $11,000.00 credit card debt.

SUMMARY OF ARGUMENT

Leah believes that because medical documents demonstrate that she cannot: (1) leave home even briefly; (2) talk on the telephone; (3) talk to strangers; and (4) handle financial dealings, that her condition meets or equals the listed condition for Anxiety Disorders at 20 C.F.R. § 404 Subpart P, App. 1 at 12.06.

Moreover, given the severity of her disability and her past failed attempt to run a business out of her home, that there are no jobs existing in suitable numbers in the economy that she can perform.

ARGUMENT

1. *Introduction.* The Social Security Administration regulations require the ALJ to follow a five-step analysis to determine whether an individual is disabled. This analysis is set out in *Goodermote v. Secretary of Health and Human Services,* 690 F.2d 5, 6-7 (1st Cir. 1982). The first step is to determine whether the claimant is working or

Figure 14–8 (continued)

engaged in substantial gainful activity. In the instant case, Leah A. was not working when she filed her claim although she worked briefly at her own small business in 1982.

The second step requires Leah A. to prove a severe impairment. In the instant case, the issue is whether Leah A.'s agoraphobia is a severe mental impairment. By 1981 a psychiatrist, Dr. Leff, had diagnosed Leah A.'s agoraphobia. Dr. Leff was graduated from the Middlesex University School of Medicine in Waltham, Massachusetts and became licensed in 1942. (A. at 192). The regulations governing medical evidence of an impairment, 20 C.F.R. § 404.1513(a), state that licensed or certified physicians, osteopaths or psychologists are acceptable medical sources for information concerning a claimant's impairment. Therefore, while the ALJ may properly give little or no weight to the findings of hypnotists, herbalists, nutritionists, naturalists and chiropractors who do not meet this requirement, Dr. Leff qualifies as an acceptable source. There is likewise no doubt that Leah is severely impaired. As well, because Leah and the SSA agree that Leah is unable to perform her past relevant work as a salesperson or teacher, determining whether she is eligible for Social Security disability benefits will turn on the question of whether in step 3, Leah's condition meets or equals a listed Social Security impairment, specifically, the listed impairment for "Anxiety Related Disorders," and, perhaps, whether under step 5, there is other relevant gainful employment Leah can perform.

2. *Leah A.'s Condition Meets or Equals a Listed Impairment.* Proceeding to the third step of inquiry, the Secretary must determine whether the claimant has an impairment which meets or exceeds the criteria in the Listing of Impairments. 20 C.F.R. § 404.1511. "If the claimant has an impairment of so serious a degree of severity, the claimant is automatically found disabled." *Goodermote, supra* 6. The "Listing" is set out at 20 C.F.R. § 404 Subpart P, App. 1, and includes "Anxiety Related Disorders." *Id.* at § 12.06. It is the opinion of this Court that the ALJ's finding of a complete absence of anxiety-related disorders during the entire period in question, as recorded in the PRTF, does not comport with the Administrative Record as applied to section 12.06. Leah A.'s statements regarding her symptoms, as confirmed by some of the medical evidence, indicate that anxiety disorders which meet the section 12.06 listing criteria may have arisen at some point before 1985.

By 1981 a psychiatrist, Dr. Leff, had diagnosed Leah A.'s agoraphobia. Dr. Leff graduated from the Middlesex University School of Medicine in Waltham, Massachusetts and became licensed in 1942. The regulations governing medical evidence of an impairment, 20 C.F.R. § 404.1513(a), state that licensed or certified physicians, osteopaths or psychologists are acceptable medical sources for information concerning a claimant's impairment. Therefore, while the ALJ may properly give little or no weight to the findings of hypnotists, herbalists, nutritionists, naturalists and chiropractors who do not meet this requirement, Dr. Leff qualifies as an acceptable source. "If the claimant has an impairment of so serious a degree of severity, the claimant is automatically found disabled." *Goodermote,* 690 F.2d at 6. The "Listing" is set out at 20 C.F.R. § 404 Subpart P, App. 1, and includes "Anxiety Related Disorders." *Id.* at § 12.06. It is the opinion of this Court that the ALJ's finding of a complete absence of anxiety-related disorders during the entire period in question, as recorded in the PRTF, does not comport with the Administrative Record as applied to section 12.06. Leah A.'s statements regarding her symptoms, as confirmed by some of the medical evidence, indicate that anxiety disorders which meet the section 12.06 listing criteria may have arisen at some point before 1985. In any event, there is no substantial evidence to support the ALJ's finding of only slight functional limitations, as stated on the Psychiatric Review Technique Form (PRTF). If, it is determined that at no point did

Figure 14–8 (continued)

Leah A.'s agoraphobia rise to the level of an automatic disability, then the inquiry will proceed beyond the "threshold" to step five and determine whether "the claimant's impairment [prevents her] from performing other work of the sort found in the economy." *Goodermote, supra* 7.

To satisfy this fifth step, a vocational expert would be needed to determine whether Leah A.'s agoraphobia prevented her from working at any job available in the economy, thereby making her disabled. While Leah A. was unable to operate her own retail store, which would require frequent interaction with the public and expose Leah A. to other stresses of running a small business, she may have retained the functional capacity to work at a more sheltered occupation involving less stress and interaction. An expert opinion will be valuable in making a determination of Leah A.'s specific vocational abilities. See *Lancellotta v. Secretary of Health and Human Services*, 806 F.2d 284, 285-86 (1st Cir. 1986) (remanding case of claimant suffering from agoraphobia and other physical and mental impairments); *Bianchi v. Secretary of Health and Human Services*, 764 F.2d 44, 45-46 (1st Cir.1985) (remanding case of claimant who was unable to hold factory and hairdressing positions because of agoraphobia and panic attacks); *Soba v. Department of Health and Human Services*, 724 F.Supp. 228 (S.D.N.Y.1989) (agoraphobia did not preclude plaintiff from returning to past relevant work); *Carbonara v. Bowen*, C.A. No. 88-1961, slip op., 1989 WL 30932 (E.D.Pa. 1989) (ALJ's hypothetical to vocational expert took agoraphobic claimant's limitations into account and decision to deny benefits was supported by substantial evidence).

3. *Policy.* Finally, the Secretary has estimated that 24.1% of disabled persons collecting SSI benefits are suffering from mental disorders other than retardation. Social Security Bulletin, Annual Statistical Supplement 331 (1988). While agoraphobia is a mental disorder which may be overcome by the individual, the record of impairment in the instant case does illustrate some parallels with persons suffering from more severe and chronic mental disorders, in which:

> the routine demands of work and social relations are major stresses. So much effort goes into their struggle with illness that they have little energy left to deal with a work situation. Handling interpersonal relationships with supervisors and co-workers is a major stress. The very thought of work is frightening, for it carries the risk of yet another failure. A therapeutic or, at least, protective work setting and an adequate preparatory period of vocational rehabilitation should be made available for many of these precariously compensated people [who are supported by SSI].

W. Richard Lamb, MD, "Incentives and Disincentives of Disability Insurance for the Chronically Mentally Ill," in *Psychiatric Disability: Clinical, Legal, and Administration Dimensions,* 343, 346 (1987) (emphasis added). One problem inherent in the SSI system's handling of persons disabled by mental impairment is a tendency to promote "regression and dependency." *Id.* at 347. Solutions for this tendency include encouraging individual and group therapy, and employment in sheltered work settings. *Id.* at 349. Unfortunately, middle class mental health professionals have been found to contribute to the problem since they "are frequently reluctant to see [their] patients take low-status, minimum-wage jobs even though this is the present limit of [the Social Security claimants'] capabilities." *Id.* at 348.

Encouraging the individual to seek some type of low stress work may promote progress by the individual, since there is a heightened self-esteem from:

> experiencing oneself as productive, making a contribution to society, and achieving at least partial self-support and independence. Work therapy is recognized

Figure 14–8 (continued)

as being fully as important as talking therapy. Having no reason to get up in the morning and no structured day to look forward to causes profound feelings of emptiness . . . . A combination of work and play is both normative and restorative.

Leah has repeatedly expressed her wish to return to work. Indeed, in 1986, Leah A. stated that she would be eager to do any type of work, but would be unable to sustain "more than perhaps an hour or two of low-stress work of some sort several days a week, and certainly nothing that would require any extended talking or face-to-face contact with people.

Federal courts as well have recognized that the effect of confinement and isolation from the outside world "is to rot away the health of [a person's] body, mind and spirit." *Inmates of the Boys' Training School v. Affleck*, 346 F. Supp. 1354, 1365-66 (D.R.I. 1972). The *Affleck* court's findings were made in the context of prison confinement and "were based on the affidavits of experts which stated that 'isolation can never constitute rehabilitation' and can produce sensory deprivation, withdrawal, or perhaps psychotic or autistic behavior." *Morgan v. Sproat*, 432 F. Supp. 1130, 1139 n. 13 (S.D. Miss. 1977). Likewise, continued confinement of an agoraphobic person may possibly lead to increased dependence and difficulties. It is hoped that the court will act on these observations lest Leah spend another ten years confined to her apartment by agoraphobia.

CONCLUSION

Leah's unique constellation of impairments both equals the SSA listed impairment for anxiety related disorders and prevents her from any gainful employment. In particular, she is unable to leave her apartment for any reason, including doctors' appointments, and short trips to a neighborhood store. As well, any contact with strangers, whether in person or over the telephone, is highly stressful. She is unable to interview for a job or interact on any regular basis. As well, as she demonstrated in the failed Christmas shop experience, she cannot handle the stress of financial dealings.

Based on the purpose of the Social Security Disability Act — to provide support for those who are without means, are permanently disabled, and are therefore unable to perform any substantial gainful activity — and Leah's demonstrated, long-standing, and severe inability to deal with any interpersonal contact or stress, a judge will likely find the SSA has not shown that jobs exist in substantial numbers in the national economy that Leah can perform.

Respectfully submitted,

Dated: _____   _____

Anne M. Stevens
Newport & Stevens
37 Main St.
Amherst, OH 01002
Attorneys for Leah A.

Figure 14–8 (continued)

CERTIFICATE OF SERVICE

On this twenty-second day of October, 1996, I declare, under the pains and penalties of perjury, that I served the foregoing document on all interested parties to this action by first class mail, postage prepaid.

_____

Anne M. Stevens

ADDENDUM

42 U.S.C.A. § 405(g)

Judicial review. Any individual, after any final decision of the Commissioner of Social Security made after a hearing to which he was a party, irrespective of the amount in controversy, may obtain a review of such decision by a civil action commenced within sixty days after the mailing to him of notice of such decision or within such further time as the Commissioner of Social Security may allow. Such action shall be brought in the district court of the United States for the judicial district in which the plaintiff resides, or has his principal place of business, or, if he does not reside or have his principal place of business within any such judicial district, in the United States District Court for the District of Columbia. As part of the Commissioner's answer the Commissioner of Social Security shall file a certified copy of the transcript of the record including the evidence upon which the findings and decision complained of are based. The court shall have power to enter, upon the pleadings and transcript of the record, a judgment affirming, modifying, or reversing the decision of the Commissioner of Social Security, with or without remanding the cause for a rehearing. The findings of the Commissioner of Social Security as to any fact, if supported by substantial evidence, shall be conclusive, and where a claim has been denied by the Commissioner of Social Security or a decision is rendered under subsection (b) of this section which is adverse to an individual who was a party to the hearing before the Commissioner of Social Security, because of failure of the claimant or such individual to submit proof in conformity with any regulation prescribed under subsection (a) of this section, the court shall review only the question of conformity with such regulations and the validity of such regulations. The court may, on motion of the Commissioner of Social Security made for good cause shown before the Commissioner files the Commissioner's answer, remand the case to the Commissioner of Social Security for further action by the Commissioner of Social Security, and it may at any time order additional evidence to be taken before the Commissioner of Social Security, but only upon a showing that there is new evidence which is material and that there is good cause for the failure to incorporate such evidence into the record in a prior proceeding; and the Commissioner of Social Security shall, after the case is remanded, and after hearing such additional evidence if so ordered, modify or affirm the Commissioner's findings of fact or the Commissioner's decision, or both, and shall file with the court any such additional and modified findings of fact and decision, and a transcript of the additional record and testimony upon which the Commissioner's action in modifying or affirming was based. Such additional or modified findings of fact and decision shall be reviewable only to the extent provided for review of the original findings of fact and decision. The judgment of the court shall be final except that

Figure 14–8 (continued)

it shall be subject to review in the same manner as a judgment in other civil actions. Any action instituted in accordance with this subsection shall survive notwithstanding any change in the person occupying the office of Commissioner of Social Security or any vacancy in such office.

<u>20 C.F.R. § 404 Subpart P, App. 1, 12.06:</u>

In these disorders anxiety is either the predominant disturbance or it is experienced if the individual attempts to master symptoms; for example confronting the dreaded object or situation in a phobic disorder or resisting the obsessions or compulsions in obsessive compulsive disorders.

The required level of severity for these disorders is met when the requirement in both A and B are satisfied, or when the requirements in both A and C are satisfied.

A. Medically documented findings of at least one of the following:
  1. Generalized persistent anxiety accompanied by three out of four of the following signs or symptoms:
      a. Motor tension; or
      b. Autonomic hyperactivity; or
      c. Apprehensive expectation; or
      d. Vigilance and scanning; or
  2. A persistent irrational fear of a specific object, activity, or situation which results in a compelling desire to avoid the dreaded object, activity, or situation; or
  3. Recurrent severe panic attacks manifested by a sudden unpredictable onset of intense apprehension, fear, terror and sense of impending doom occurring on the average of at least once a week; or
  4. Recurrent obsessions or compulsions which are a source of marked distress; or
  5. Recurrent and intrusive recollections of a traumatic experience, which are the source of marked distress;
  AND
B. Resulting in at least two of the following:
  1. Marked restriction of activities of daily living; or
  2. Marked difficulties in maintaining social functioning; or
  3. Deficiencies of concentration, persistence of pace resulting in frequent failure to complete tasks in a timely manner (in work settings or elsewhere); or
  4. Repeated episodes of deterioration or decompensation in work or work-liked settings which cause the individual to withdraw from that situation or to experience exacerbation of signs and symptoms (which may include deterioration of adaptive behaviors);
  OR
C. Resulting in complete inability to function independently outside the area of one's home.
<u>20 C.F.R. § 404.1511(a).</u>

<u>Disabled workers, persons disabled since childhood and, for months after December 1990, disabled widows, widowers, and surviving divorced spouses.</u> If you are entitled to disability cash benefits as a disabled worker, or to child's insurance benefits, or, for monthly benefits payable after December 1990, to widow's, widower's, or surviving

Figure 14–8 (continued)

divorced spouse's monthly benefits, a disabling impairment is an impairment (or combination of impairments) which, of itself, is so severe that it meets or equals a set of criteria in the Listing of Impairments in appendix 1 of this subpart or which, when considered with your age, education, and work experience, would result in a finding that you are disabled under § 404.1594. In determining whether you have a disabling impairment, earnings are not considered.

(b) Disabled widows, widowers, and surviving divorced spouses, for monthly benefits for months prior to January 1991. If you have been entitled to disability benefits as a disabled widow, widower, or surviving divorced spouse and we must decide whether you had a disabling impairment for any time prior to January 1991, a disabling impairment is an impairment (or combination of impairments) which, of itself, was so severe that it met or equaled a set of criteria in the Listing of Impairments in appendix 1 of this subpart, or results in a finding that you were disabled under § 404.1579. In determining whether you had a disabling impairment, earnings are not considered.

<u>20 C.F.R. § 404.151</u>

(a) <u>Acceptable sources.</u> We need reports about your impairments from acceptable medical sources. Acceptable medical sources are

(1) Licensed physicians;

(2) Licensed osteopaths;

(3) Licensed or certified psychologists;

(4) Licensed optometrists for the measurement of visual acuity and visual fields (we may need a report from a physician to determine other aspects of eye diseases); and

(5) Persons authorized to send us a copy or summary of the medical records of a hospital, clinic, sanitorium, medical institution, or health care facility. Generally, the copy or summary should be certified as accurate by the custodian or by any authorized employee of the Social Security Administration, Veterans' Administration, or State agency. However, we will not return an uncertified copy or summary for certification unless there is some question about the document.

(b) Medical reports. Medical reports should include

(1) Medical history;

(2) Clinical findings (such as the results of physical or mental status examinations);

(3) Laboratory findings (such as blood pressure, x-rays);

(4) Diagnosis (statement of disease or injury based on its signs and symptoms);

(5) Treatment prescribed with response, and prognosis; and

(6) A statement about what you can still do despite your impairment(s) based on the medical source's findings on the factors under paragraphs (b)(1) through (b)(5) of this section (except in statutory blindness claims). Although we will request a medical source statement about what you can still do despite your impairment(s), the lack of the medical source statement will not make the report incomplete. See § 404.1527.

(c) Statements about what you can still do. Statements about what you can still do (based on the medical source's findings on the factors under paragraphs (b)(1) through (b)(5) of this section) should describe, but are not limited to,

Figure 14–8 (continued)

the kinds of physical and mental capabilities listed below. See §§ 404.1527 and 404.1545(c).

(1) The medical source's opinion about your ability, despite your impairment(s), to do work-related activities such as sitting, standing, walking, lifting, carrying, handling objects, hearing, speaking, and traveling; and

(2) In cases of mental impairment(s), the medical source's opinion about your ability to understand, to carry out and remember instructions, and to respond appropriately to supervision, coworkers, and work pressures in a work setting.

(d) Completeness. The medical evidence, including the clinical and laboratory findings, must be complete and detailed enough to allow us to make a determination about whether you are disabled or blind. It must allow us to determine—

(1) The nature and limiting effects of your impairment(s) for any period in question;

(2) The probable duration of your impairment; and

(3) Your residual functional capacity to do work-related physical and mental activities.

(e) Information from other sources. Information from other sources may also help us to understand how your impairment affects your ability to work. Other sources include

(1) Public and private social welfare agencies;

(2) Observations by non-medical sources; and

(3) Other practitioners (for example, naturopaths, chiropractors, audiologists, etc.).

Figure 14–8 (continued)

COMMONWEALTH OF MASSACHUSETTS
Appeals Court
No. 99-P-1177.

WORCESTER COUNTY.

COMMONWEALTH OF MASSACHUSETTS,
APPELLEE

v.

HAYDEE VILLANUEVA,
DEFENDANT/APPELLANT

ON APPEAL FROM A JUDGMENT BY THE WORCESTER DIVISION OF THE
SUPERIOR COURT DEPARTMENT

Brief for the Commonwealth of Massachusetts

ANNE M. STEVENS,
Special Assistant District Attorney for the Middle
District,
BBO # 088420
Courthouse, Room 220
Two Main Street
Worcester, MA 01670
(508) 757-2786

January, 2000

Figure 14–9 Sample appellate brief in a criminal case.

Table of Contents

I. Whether the indictments should have been dismissed.
  A. Defendant's argument on this issue does not rise to the level of appellate argument.
  B. There was sufficient evidence presented to the grand jury to support the indictments.
II. Whether the Superior Court judge properly denied the defendant's motion for a required finding of not guilty where the evidence was sufficient to prove beyond a reasonable doubt that the defendant possessed 28 to 100 grams of heroin with intent to distribute it within 1000 feet of a school.

Table of Authorities
Cases

Figure 14–9 (continued)

Figure 14–9 (continued)

COMMONWEALTH OF MASSACHUSETTS
APPEALS COURT

No. 99-P-1177

WORCESTER COUNTY.

COMMONWEALTH OF MASSACHUSETTS
APPELLEE

v.

HAYDEE VILLANUEVA
DEFENDANT/APPELLANT

ON APPEAL FROM A JUDGMENT BY THE WORCESTER DIVISION OF THE
SUPERIOR COURT DEPARTMENT

Brief for the Commonwealth

Questions Presented.

Whether the indictment should have been dismissed.

Whether the Superior Court judge properly denied the defendant's motion for a
required finding of not guilty.

Prior Proceedings

On July 18, 1997, indictments were returned against Haydee Villanueva (the "defendant") charging that on March 28, 1997, the defendant: (1) trafficked in twenty-eight

Figure 14–9 (continued)

to one hundred grams of heroin in violation of G. L. c. 94C, § 32E(c)(2), and (2) possessed that heroin within 1000 feet of a school in violation of G. L. c. 94C, § 32J. (Docket; A. 4-6)[3] On December 24, 1997, a Superior Court judge denied the defendant's motion to dismiss those indictments.

On March 27, 1998, the defendant filed motions for required finding of not guilty on both counts, Mass. R. Crim. P. 25(a), 378 Mass 896 (1979). The trial judge (Travers, J.) denied the motions. That same day, the jury returned guilty verdicts on both charges. (Docket) On March 31, 1998, the defendant was sentenced to seven years to seven years and 1 day at the Cedar Junction Correctional Institution to be served at the Framingham Correctional Institution on the possession with intent to traffick charge and two and a half to two and a half years and one day from and after her sentence on the trafficking charge at the Cedar Junction Correctional Institution also to be served at the Framingham Correctional Institution.

The defendant appeals.

Statement of the Facts

At approximately 10:00 a.m. on March 28, 1997, Worcester police officer Robert O. Rourke and fifteen to twenty other Worcester Police officers executed a warrant to search 86 Austin Street, Apartment 719 in Worcester, MA. (Tr. I 76-77). Apartment 719 was a one-bedroom apartment. (Tr. I 80). Rourke began his search in the kitchen. (Tr. I 81). There were six people in the apartment at the time of the search: the defendant, her daughter Yvette, her son, Edwin Carrion, Manual Tavares, Carmen Baretti, and someone named Hector. (Tr. I 76-77). The defendant was seated at a table in the kitchen. (Tr. I 109-110; Tr. II. 30). In the kitchen, Officer Rourke and another officer found a quantity of cocaine, ten packets of heroin hidden on the counter under the microwave and behind "jars and some things on the sink," and a mortar and pestle. (Tr. I 83-84; Tr. II 22-23). When searched, Manual Tavares had $1570.00, a key to the apartment, and "a small book" with numbers and names of unknown origin on his person (Tr. II 51); Edwin Carrion was possessed of a key to the apartment and $1,010.00 in cash. (Tr. I 99-101). In the bedroom, a police officers found a small quantity of marijuana on top of the bureau and the defendant's Social Security card, her Massachusetts driver's license, mail addressed to her at 86 Austin Street, Apartment 719, women's clothing, and the defendant's electric bill, cable bill, checkbook, and savings account deposit. (Tr. I 102, 108). Sergeant Michael Coakley also searched the bedroom where he found a pillow case located inside another pillow that contained 188 zip-lock bags of heroin. (Tr. I 130-133). The officers found no evidence of drug consumption — no needles, syringes, or cooking equipment — in the apartment. (Tr. I 155). Also found behind the bedroom door was a box of Captain Crunch Cereal containing 60 bundles (i.e., 600 separate packets) of heroin weighing a total of 28 grams. (Tr. I 114; Tr. II 5). In the living room, an officer found the defendant's car title. (Tr. II 29).

The distance from 86 Austin Street to the Chamber Elementary School was 587 feet. (Tr. II 54-56).

---

[1]In this brief, "A." refers to the record appendix filed in the defendant's brief, "Supp. A." refers to the supplemental appendix filed with this brief, "Tr. I" refers to pages in the first transcript volume, "Tr. II" refers to pages in the second transcript volume, and "C.J. Min." refers to pages in the grand jury minutes.

Figure 14–9 (continued)

Argument

I. Whether the indictments should have been dismissed.

A. Defendant's argument on this issue does not rise to the level of appellate argument.

As an initial matter, defendant devotes only two and a half pages to her argument that the indictments should have been dismissed because the grand jury heard no evidence that she was present during execution of the search warrant; one of those two and a half pages constitutes a recitation of the testimony before the grand jury. The defendant has neither included the motion to dismiss the indictment in her appellate appendix to this court, nor has she anywhere cited to the grand jury minutes to support either her statement of the evidence or her appellate argument on this issue. As such, her argument does not rise to the level of appellate argument and should be disregarded. See, e.g., *Commonwealth v. Montez*, 45 Mass. App. Ct. 802, 807 n. 2 (1998), and Mass. R.A.P. 16(a)(4), as amended, 367 Mass. 921 (1975).

B. There was sufficient evidence presented to the grand jury to support the indictments.

Moreover, the Superior Court properly denied the defendant's motion to dismiss the indictments. Generally, a "court will not inquire into the competency or sufficiency of the evidence before the grand jury." *Commonwealth v. McCarthy*, 385 Mass. 160, 162-163 (1982) quoting *Commonwealth v. Robinson*, 373 Mass. 591, 592 (1977). Additionally, indictments may be based solely on hearsay. *Id.* Nevertheless, to avoid dismissal of the indictment, the grand jury must hear "reasonably trustworthy information . . . sufficient to warrant a prudent man in believing that the defendant had committed or was committing an offense." *Id.* quoting *Commonwealth v. Stevens*, 362 Mass. 24, 26 (1972). "[A]t the very least the grand jury must hear sufficient evidence to establish the identity of the accused" and probable cause to arrest him. *Commonwealth v. Arias*, 29 Mass. App. Ct. 613, 616-617 (1990), *aff'd* 410 Mass. 1005 (1991). If, as here, the defendant's liability is based on her complicity as a joint venturer, there must be evidence that she "commanded, counseled, or encouraged" commission of the crime. *Commonwealth v. McCarthy*, 385 Mass. 160, 164 (1982). In this case, the grand jury heard Officer O'Rourke's evidence from identifying the defendant as the subject of the indictments, her date of birth (G.J. Min. 4), and that during execution of the warrant, the officers found heroin sufficient to support the charges against the defendant in the bedroom of this one-bedroom apartment along with mail, a Social Security card, an identification card, and a checkbook, identifying the defendant as living at the address being searched. (G.J.Min. 7-8). As well, Officer O'Rourke testified that the apartment searched, 86 Austin Street, Apartment 719, Worcester, MA was located less than a thousand feet from the Chandler Elementary School. (G.J.Min. 10) That evidence was sufficient to support the indictment. See, e.g., *Commonwealth v. Lawrence*, 404 Mass. 378, 384-385 (1989) (evidence that defendant's wallet containing the defendant's driver's license and credit cards in his name found near the bound victim and corroborating evidence found in a search of the defendant's apartment was sufficient to support the defendant's indictment for murder of the victim and manslaughter of the victim's viable fetus).

Figure 14–9 (continued)

II. Whether the Superior Court judge properly denied the defendant's motion for a required finding of not guilty where the evidence was sufficient to prove beyond a reasonable doubt that the defendant possessed 28 to 100 grams of heroin with intent to distribute it within 1000 feet of a school.

This case was tried on a theory of joint venture. Under that theory, the Commonwealth had to prove that the defendant was "(1) present at the scene of the crime, (2) with knowledge that [the others] intend[ed] to commit the crime, or with intent to commit [the] crime, and (3) by agreement, [was] willing and available to help . . . if necessary." *Commonwealth v. Stephens*, 44 Mass. App. Ct. 940, 945 (1998), quoting *Commonwealth v. Ortiz*, 424 Mass. 853, 86 (1997). On appeal, the defendant argues that because the evidence established only that she was present where the drugs were found (i.e., was an "innocent bystander"), the Commonwealth presented insufficient evidence connecting her to the crime.

Although mere presence at the scene of the crime is insufficient to support a conviction as a joint venturer, *id.*, proof of possession of a controlled substance may be established "by circumstantial evidence" and reasonable inferences that can be drawn therefrom. *Commonwealth v. Arias*, 29 Mass. App. Ct. 613, 617-618 (1990). There was no evidence that the defendant tried at any time to distance herself from the contents or events of the apartment. To the contrary, the quantity of drugs (packaged for distribution) supporting the indictment, see, e.g., *Commonwealth v. Arias*, 29 Mass. App. Ct. 613, 617 (1990), were found behind the door in the defendant's bedroom where women's clothes and many articles (including her social security card, her driver's license, and her mail) identifying the defendant as residing at the apartment were also found. (Tr. I 102-108). A quantity of marijuana was found in plain view on her dresser. (Tr. I 83-84; Tr. II 22-23). Heroin (also packaged for distribution) and cocaine were found on a counter in her kitchen, where the defendant sat as the warrant was executed. Men present in the apartment were possessed of large sums of cash and had keys to the defendant's apartment. (Tr. I 99-101; Tr. II 51) That evidence moves the defendant's actions beyond presence alone to a permissible finding that she had knowledge of the criminal activity and was willing and available to help if necessary, i.e., she was a participant in the joint venture. Indeed, nothing, save the defendant's own testimony, suggested that the defendant was uninvolved in the crimes charged. See, e.g., *Arias*, 29 Mass. App. Ct. at 617-620; *Commonwealth v. Rivera*, 31 Mass. App. Ct. 554, 556-557 (1991). See also *Commonwealth v. Gonzalez*, 42 Mass. App. Ct. 235, 238 (1997). Cf. *Commonwealth v. Amparo*, 43 Mass. App. Ct. 922, 923 (1997) (evidence of constructive possession of drugs insufficient where there was no evidence that the defendant rented or exercised control over apartment and its contents; neither the defendant's personal papers nor clothes were found in the apartment).

As the Commonwealth presented sufficient evidence that the defendant actively participated in possessing and trafficking in twenty-eight to one hundred grams of heroin within one thousand feet of a school, a rational trier of fact, taking the evidence and reasonable inferences therefrom in the light most favorable to the Commonwealth, "could have found the essential elements of the crime beyond a reasonable doubt." *Commonwealth v. Robicheau*, 421 Mass. 176, 181 (1995) citing *Commonwealth v. Latimore*, 378 Mass. 671, 677 (1979). That was all that was required to defeat the defendant's motion for required finding of not guilty. See, e.g., *Commonwealth v. Stephens*, 44 Mass. App. Ct. 940, 945 (1998).

Figure 14–9 (continued)

Conclusion

For the reasons set forth above, this Court should affirm the conviction of the defendant.

Respectfully submitted,

_____

ANNE M. STEVENS,
Special Assistant District Attorney
for the Middle District,
BBO # 088420
Courthouse, Room 220
Two Main Street
Worcester, MA 01608
(508) 757-2786

January, 2000

Addendum

MASSACHUSETTS GENERAL LAWS, c. 94C, §§ 32E(C)(2) and 32J

**MASSACHUSETTS GENERAL LAWS ANNOTATED
PART I. ADMINISTRATION OF THE GOVERNMENT
TITLE XV. REGULATION OF TRADE
CHAPTER 94C. CONTROLLED SUBSTANCES ACT**

§ 32E. Trafficking in marijuana, cocaine, heroin, morphine, opium, etc.

. . . .(c) Any person who traffics in heroin or any salt thereof, morphine or any salt thereof, opium or any derivative thereof by knowingly or intentionally manufacturing, distributing or dispensing or possessing with intent to manufacture, distribute, or dispense or by bringing into the commonwealth a net weight of fourteen grams or more of heroin or any salt thereof, morphine or any salt thereof, opium or any derivative thereof or a net weight of fourteen grams or more of any mixture containing heroin or any salt thereof, morphine or any salt thereof, opium or any derivative thereof shall, if the net weight of heroin or any salt thereof, morphine or any salt thereof, opium or any derivative thereof or any mixture thereof is:— . . . .

(2) Twenty-eight grams or more but less than one hundred grams, be punished by a term of imprisonment in the state prison for not less than seven nor more than twenty years. No sentence imposed under the provisions of this clause shall be for less than a mandatory minimum term of imprisonment of seven years and a fine of not less than five thousand nor more than fifty thousand dollars may be imposed, but not in lieu of the mandatory minimum term of imprisonment, as established herein.

Figure 14–9 (continued)

---

§ 32J. Controlled substances violations in, on, or near school property.

Any person who violates the provisions of section thirty-two, thirty-two A, thirty-two B, thirty-two C, thirty-two D, thirty-two E, thirty-two F or thirty- two I while in or on, or within one thousand feet of the real property comprising a public or private accredited preschool, accredited headstart facility, elementary, vocational, or secondary school whether or not in session, or within one hundred feet of a public park or playground shall be punished by a term of imprisonment in the state prison for not less than two and one-half nor more than fifteen years or by imprisonment in a jail or house of correction for not less than two nor more than two and one-half years. No sentence imposed under the provisions of this section shall be for less than a mandatory minimum term of imprisonment of two years. A fine of not less than one thousand nor more than ten thousand dollars may be imposed but not in lieu of the mandatory minimum two year term of imprisonment as established herein. In accordance with the provisions of section eight A of chapter two hundred and seventy-nine such sentence shall begin from and after the expiration of the sentence for violation of section thirty-two, thirty-two A, thirty-two B, thirty-two C, thirty-two D, thirty-two E, thirty-two F or thirty-two I.

Lack of knowledge of school boundaries shall not be a defense to any person who violates the provisions of this section.

Figure 14–9 (continued)

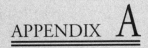

Selected Codes Governing Paralegal Ethics

NALA Code of Ethics and Professional Responsibility[1]

A legal assistant must adhere strictly to the accepted standards of legal ethics and to the general principles of proper conduct. The performance of the duties of the legal assistant shall be governed by specific canons as defined herein so that justice will be served and goals of the profession attained. (See Model Standards and Guidelines for Utilization of Legal Assistants, Section II.)

The canons of ethics set forth hereafter are adopted by the National Association of Legal Assistants, Inc., as a general guide intended to aid legal assistants and attorneys. The enumeration of these rules does not mean there are not others of equal importance although not specifically mentioned. Court rules, agency rules and statutes must be taken into consideration when interpreting the canons.

Definition: Legal assistants, also known as paralegals, are a distinguishable group of persons who assist attorneys in the delivery of legal services. Through formal education, training and experience, legal assistants have knowledge and expertise regarding the legal system and substantive and procedural law which qualify them to do work of a legal nature under the supervision of an attorney.

Canon 1.

A legal assistant must not perform any of the duties that attorneys only may perform nor take any actions that attorneys may not take.

Canon 2.

A legal assistant may perform any task which is properly delegated and supervised by an attorney, as long as the attorney is ultimately responsible to the client, maintains a direct relationship with the client, and assumes professional responsibility for the work product.

Canon 3.

A legal assistant must not: 9a) engage in, encourage, or contribute to any act which could constitute the unauthorized practice of law; and (b) establish attorney-client relationships, set fees, give legal opinions or advice or represent a client before a court or agency unless so authorized by that court or agency; and (c) engage in conduct or take any action which would assist or involve the attorney in a violation of professional ethics or give the appearance of professional impropriety.

Canon 4.

A legal assistant must use discretion and professional judgment commensurate with knowledge and experience but must not render independent legal judgment in

---

[1] Used by permission of the National Association of Legal Assistants.

place of an attorney. The services of an attorney are essential in the public interest whenever such legal judgment is required.

Canon 5.

A legal assistant must disclose his or her status as a legal assistant at the outset of any professional relationship with a client, attorney, a court or administrative agency or personnel thereof, or a member of the general public. A legal assistant must act prudently in determining the extent to which a client may be assisted without the presence of an attorney.

Canon 6.

A legal assistant must strive to maintain integrity and a high degree of competency through education and training with respect to professional responsibility, local rules and practice, and through continuing education in substantive areas of law to better assist the legal profession in fulfilling its duty to provide legal service.

Canon 7.

A legal assistant must protect the confidences of a client and must not violate any rule or statute now in effect or hereafter enacted controlling the doctrine of privileged communications between a client and an attorney.

Canon 8.

A legal assistant must do all other things incidental, necessary, or expedient for the attainment of the ethics and responsibilities as defined by statute or rule of court.

Canon 9.

A legal assistant's conduct is guided by bar associations' codes of professional responsibility and rules of professional conduct.

National Federation of Paralegal Associations, Inc. Model Code of Ethics and Professional Responsibility and Guidelines for Enforcement[2]

Preamble

The National Federation of Paralegal Associations, Inc. ("NFPA") is a professional organization comprised of paralegal associations and individual paralegals throughout the United States and Canada. Members of NFPA have varying backgrounds,

---

[2] Used by permission of the National Federation of Paralegal Associations

experiences, education and job responsibilities that reflect the diversity of the paralegal profession. NFPA promotes the growth, development and recognition of the paralegal profession as an integral partner in the delivery of legal services.

In May 1993 NFPA adopted its Model Code of Ethics and Professional Responsibility ("Model Code") to delineate the principles for ethics and conduct to which every paralegal should aspire.

Many paralegal associations throughout the United States have endorsed the concept and content of NFPA's Model Code through the adoption of their own ethical codes. In doing so, paralegals have confirmed the profession's commitment to increase the quality and efficiency of legal services, as well as recognized its responsibilities to the public, the legal community, and colleagues. Paralegals have recognized, and will continue to recognize, that the profession must continue to evolve to enhance their roles in the delivery of legal services. With increased levels of responsibility comes the need to define and enforce mandatory rules of professional conduct. Enforcement of codes of paralegal conduct is a logical and necessary step to enhance and ensure the confidence of the legal community and the public in the integrity and professional responsibility of paralegals.

In April 1997 NFPA adopted the Model Disciplinary Rules ("Model Rules") to make possible the enforcement of the Canons and Ethical Considerations contained in the NFPA Model Code. A concurrent determination was made that the Model code of Ethics and Professional Responsibility, formerly aspirational in nature, should be recognized as setting forth the enforceable obligations of all paralegals.

The Model Code and Model Rules offer a framework for professional discipline, either voluntarily or through formal regulatory programs.

NFPA Model Disciplinary Rules and Ethical Considerations

1.1
A PARALEGAL SHALL ACHIEVE AND MAINTAIN A HIGH LEVEL OF COMPETENCE.
    Ethical Considerations
EC-1.1(a)
    A paralegal shall achieve competency through education, training, and work experience.
EC-1.1(b)
    A paralegal shall participate in continuing education in order to keep informed of current legal, technical and general developments.
EC-1.1(c)
    A paralegal shall perform all assignments promptly and efficiently.

---

2 Used by permission of the National Federation of Paralegal Associations

1.2

A PARALEGAL SHALL MAINTAIN A HIGH LEVEL OF PERSONAL AND PROFESSIONAL INTEGRITY.

Ethical Considerations

EC-1.2(a)

A paralegal shall not engage in any ex parte communications involving the courts or any other adjudicatory body in an attempt to exert undue influence or to obtain advantage or the benefit of only one party.

EC-1.2(b)

A paralegal shall not communicate, or cause another to communicate, with a party the paralegal knows to be represented by a lawyer in a pending matter without the prior consent of the lawyer representing such other party.

EC-1.2(c)

A paralegal shall ensure that all timekeeping and billing records prepared by the paralegal are thorough, accurate, honest, and complete.

EC-1.2(d)

A paralegal shall not knowingly engage in fraudulent billing practices. Such practices may include, but are not limited to: inflation of hours billed to a client or employer; misrepresentation of the nature of tasks performed; and/or submission of fraudulent expense and disbursement documentation.

EC-1.2(e)

A paralegal shall be scrupulous, thorough and honest in the identification and maintenance of all funds, securities, and other assets of a client and shall provide accurate accounting as appropriate.

EC-1.2(f)

A paralegal shall advise the proper authority of non-confidential knowledge of any dishonest or fraudulent acts by any person pertaining to the handling of the funds, securities, or other assets of a client. The authority to whom the report is made shall depend on the nature and circumstances of the possible misconduct (e.g., ethics committees of law firms, corporations and/or paralegal associations, local or state bar associations, local prosecutors, administrative agencies, etc.). Failure to report such knowledge is in itself misconduct and shall be treated as such under these rules.

1.3

A PARALEGAL SHALL MAINTAIN A HIGH STANDARD OF PROFESSIONAL CONDUCT.

Ethical Considerations

EC-1.3(a)

A paralegal shall refrain from engaging in any conduct that offends the dignity and decorum of proceedings before a court or other adjudicatory body and shall be respectful of all rules and procedures.

EC-1.3(b)

    A paralegal shall avoid impropriety and the appearance of impropriety and shall not engage in any conduct that would adversely affect his/her fitness to practice. Such conduct may include, but is not limited to violence, dishonesty, interference with the administration of justice, and/or abuse of a professional position or public office.

EC-1.3(c)

    Should a paralegal's fitness to practice be compromised by physical or mental illness, causing that paralegal to commit an act that is in direct violation of the Model Code/Model Rules and/or the rules and/or laws governing the jurisdiction in which the paralegal practices, that paralegal may be protected from sanction upon review of the nature and circumstances of that illness.

EC-1.3(d)

    A paralegal shall advise the proper authority of non-confidential knowledge of any action of another legal professional that clearly demonstrates fraud, deceit, dishonesty, or misrepresentation. The authority to whom the report is made shall depend on the nature and circumstances of the possible misconduct (e.g., ethics committees of law firms, corporations and/or paralegal associations, local or state bar associations, local prosecutors, administrative agencies, etc.). Failure to report such knowledge is in itself misconduct and shall be treated as such under these rules.

EC-1.3(e)

    A paralegal shall not knowingly assist any individual with the commission of an act that is in direct violation of the Model Code/Model Rules and/or the rules and/or laws governing the jurisdiction in which the paralegal practices.

EC-1.3(f)

    If a paralegal possesses knowledge of future criminal activity, that knowledge must be reported to the appropriate authority immediately.

1.4

A PARALEGAL SHALL SERVE THE PUBLIC INTEREST BY CONTRIBUTING TO THE IMPROVEMENT OF THE LEGAL SYSTEM AND DELIVERY OF QUALITY LEGAL SERVICES, INCLUDING PRO BONO PUBLICO SERVICES.

    Ethical Considerations

EC-1.4(a)

    A paralegal shall be sensitive to the legal needs of the public and shall promote the development and implementation of programs that address those needs.

EC-1.4(b)

    A paralegal shall support efforts to improve the legal system and access thereto and shall assist in making changes.

EC-1.4(c)

> A paralegal shall support and participate in the delivery of Pro Bono Publico services directed toward implementing and improving access to justice, the law, the legal system or the paralegal and legal professions.

EC-1.4(d)

> A paralegal should aspire annually to contribute twenty-four (24) hours of Pro Bono Publico services under the supervision of an attorney or as authorized by administrative, statutory or court authority to:
> 1. persons of limited means; or
> 2. charitable, religious, civic, community, governmental and educational organizations in matters that are designed primarily to address the legal needs of persons with limited means; or
> 3. individuals, groups, or organizations seeking to secure or protect civil rights, civil liberties, or public rights.

1.5
A PARALEGAL SHALL PRESERVE ALL CONFIDENTIAL INFORMATION PROVIDED BY THE CLIENT OR ACQUIRED FROM OTHER SOURCES BEFORE, DURING, AND AFTER THE COURSE OF THE PROFESSIONAL RELATIONSHIP.

> Ethical Considerations

EC-1.5(a)

> A paralegal shall be aware of and abide by all legal authority governing confidential information in the jurisdiction in which the paralegal practices.

EC-1.5(b)

> A paralegal shall not use confidential information to the disadvantage of the client.

EC-1.5(c)

> A paralegal shall not use confidential information to the advantage of the paralegal or of a third person.

EC-1.5(d)

> A paralegal may reveal confidential information only after full disclosure and with the client's written consent; or, when required by law or court order; or, when necessary to prevent the client from committing an act that could result in death or serious bodily harm.

EC-1.5(e)

> A paralegal shall keep those individuals responsible for the legal representation of a client fully informed of any confidential information the paralegal may have pertaining to that client.

EC-1.5(f)

> A paralegal shall not engage in any indiscreet communications concerning clients.

1.6

A PARALEGAL SHALL AVOID CONFLICTS OF INTEREST AND SHALL DISCLOSE ANY POSSIBLE CONFLICT TO THE EMPLOYER OR CLIENT, AS WELL AS TO THE PROSPECTIVE EMPLOYERS OR CLIENTS.

Ethical Considerations

EC-1.6(a)

A paralegal shall act within the bounds of the law, solely for the benefit of the client, and shall be free of compromising influences and loyalties. Neither the paralegal's personal or business interest, nor those of other clients or third persons, should compromise the paralegal's professional judgment and loyalty to the client.

EC-1.6(b)

A paralegal shall avoid conflicts of interest that may arise from previous assignments, whether for a present or past employer or client.

EC-1.6(c)

A paralegal shall avoid conflicts of interest that may arise from family relationships and from personal and business interests.

EC-1.6(d)

In order to be able to determine whether an actual or potential conflict of interest exists a paralegal shall create and maintain an effective record-keeping system that identifies clients, matters, and parties with which the paralegal has worked.

EC-1.6(e)

A paralegal shall reveal sufficient non-confidential information about a client or former client to reasonably ascertain if an actual or potential conflict of interest exists.

EC-1.6(f)

A paralegal shall not participate in or conduct work on any matter where a conflict of interest has been identified.

EC-1.6(g)

In matters where a conflict of interest has been identified and the client consents to continued representation, a paralegal shall comply fully with the implementation and maintenance of an Ethical Wall.

1.7

A PARALEGAL'S TITLE SHALL BE FULLY DISCLOSED.

Ethical Considerations

EC-1.7(a)

A paralegal's title shall clearly indicate the individual's status and shall be disclosed in all business and professional communications to avoid misunderstanding and misconceptions about the paralegal's role and responsibilities.

EC-1.7(b)

A paralegal's title shall be included if the paralegal's name appears on business cards, letterhead, brochures, directories, and advertisements.

EC-1.7(c)

> A paralegal shall not use letterhead, business cards, or other promotional materials to create a fraudulent impression of his/her status or ability to practice in the jurisdiction in which the paralegal practices.

EC-1.7(d)

> A paralegal shall not practice under color of any record, diploma, or certificate that has been illegally or fraudulently obtained or issued or which is misrepresentative in any way.

EC-1.7(e)

> A paralegal shall not participate in the creation, issuance, or dissemination of fraudulent records, diplomas, or certificates.

1.8
A PARALEGAL SHALL NOT ENGAGE IN THE UNAUTHORIZED PRACTICE OF LAW.

Ethical Considerations

EC-1.8(a)

> A paralegal shall comply with the applicable legal authority governing the unauthorized practice of law in the jurisdiction in which the paralegal practices.

2
NFPA GUIDELINES FOR THE ENFORCEMENT OF THE MODEL CODE OF ETHICS AND PROFESSIONAL RESPONSIBILITY

2.1
BASIS FOR DISCIPLINE

2.1(a)

> Disciplinary investigations and proceedings brought under authority of the Rules shall be conducted in accord with obligations imposed on the paralegal professional by the Model Code of Ethics and Professional Responsibility.

2.2
STRUCTURE OF DISCIPLINARY COMMITTEE

2.2(a)

> The Disciplinary Committee ("Committee") shall be made up of nine (9) members including the Chair.

2.2(b)

> Each member of the Committee, including any temporary replacement members, shall have demonstrated working knowledge of ethics/professional responsibility-related issues and activities.

2.2(c)

The Committee shall represent a cross-section of practice areas and work experience. The following recommendations are made regarding the members of the Committee.

1) At least one paralegal with one to three years of law-related work experience.

2) At least one paralegal with five to seven years of law-related work experience.

3) At least one paralegal with over ten years of law-related work experience.

4) One paralegal educator with five to seven years of work experience; preferably in the area of ethics/professional responsibility.

5) One paralegal manager.

6) One lawyer with five to seven years of law-related work experience.

7) One lay member.

2.2(d)

The Chair of the Committee shall be appointed within thirty (30) days of its members' induction. The Chair shall have no fewer than ten (10) years of law-related work experience.

2.2(e)

The terms of all members of the Committee shall be staggered. Of those members initially appointed, a simple majority plus one shall be appointed to a term of one year, and the remaining members shall be appointed to a term of two years. Thereafter, all members of the Committee shall be appointed to terms of two years.

2.2(f)

If for any reason the terms of a majority of the Committee will expire at the same time, members may be appointed to terms of one year to maintain continuity of the Committee.

2.2(g)

The Committee shall organize from its members a three-tiered structure to investigate, prosecute, and/or adjudicate charges of misconduct. The members shall be rotated among the tiers.

2.3
OPERATION OF COMMITTEE

2.3(a)

The Committee shall meet on an as-needed basis to discuss, investigate, and/or adjudicate alleged violations of the Model Code/Model Rules.

2.3(b)

A majority of the members of the Committee present at a meeting shall constitute a quorum.

2.3(c)

A Recording Secretary shall be designated to maintain complete and accurate minutes of all Committee meetings. All such minutes shall be kept confidential until a decision has been made that the matter will be set for hearing as set forth in Section 6.1 below.

2.3(d)

If any member of the Committee has a conflict of interest with the Charging Party, the Responding Party, or the allegations of misconduct, that member shall not take part in any hearing or deliberations concerning those allegations. If the absence of that member creates a lack of a quorum for the Committee, then a temporary replacement for the member shall be appointed.

2.3(e)

Either the Charging Party of the Responding Party may request that, for good cause shown, any member of the Committee not participate in a hearing or deliberation. All such requests shall be honored. If the absence of a Committee member under those circumstances creates a lack of a quorum for the Committee, then a temporary replacement for the member shall be appointed.

2.3(f)

All discussions and correspondence of the Committee shall be kept confidential until a decision has been made that the matter will be set for hearing as set forth in Section 6.1 below.

2.3(g)

All correspondence from the Committee to the Responding Party regarding any charge of misconduct and any decisions made regarding the charge shall be mailed certified mail, return receipt requested, to the Responding Party's last known address and shall be clearly marked with a "Confidential" designation.

2.4
PROCEDURE FOR THE REPORTING OF ALLEGED VIOLATIONS OF THE MODEL CODE/DISCIPLINARY RULES

2.4(a)

An individual or entity in possession of non-confidential knowledge or information concerning possible instances of misconduct shall make a confidential written report to the Committee within thirty (30) days of obtaining same. This report shall include all details of the alleged misconduct.

2.4(b)

The Committee so notified shall inform the Responding Party of the allegation(s) of misconduct no later than ten (10) business days after receiving the confidential written report from the Charging Party.

2.4(c)

Notification to the Responding Party shall include the identity of the Charging Party, unless, for good cause shown, the Charging Party requests anonymity.

2.4(d)

> The Responding Party shall reply to the allegations within ten (10) business days of notification.

2.5
PROCEDURE FOR THE INVESTIGATION OF A CHARGE OF MISCONDUCT
2.5(a)

> Upon receipt of a Charge of Misconduct ("Charge"), or on its own initiative, the Committee shall initiate an investigation.

2.5(b)

> If, upon initial or preliminary review, the Committee makes a determination that the charges are either without basis in fact or, if proven, would not constitute professional misconduct, the Committee shall dismiss the allegations of misconduct. If such determination of dismissal cannot be made, a formal investigation shall be initiated.

2.5(c)

> Upon the decision to conduct a formal investigation, the committee shall:
> 1) mail to the Charging and Responding Parties within three (3) business days of that decision notice of the commencement of a formal investigation. That notification shall be in writing and shall contain a complete explanation of all Charge(s), as well as the reasons for a formal investigation and shall cite the applicable codes and rules;
> 2) allow the Responding Party thirty (30) days to prepare and submit a confidential response to the Committee, which response shall address each charge specifically and shall be in writing; and
> 3) upon receipt of the response to the notification, have thirty (30) days to investigate the Charge(s). If an extension of time is deemed necessary, that extension shall not exceed ninety (90) days.

2.5(d)

> Upon conclusion of the investigation, the Committee may:
> 1) dismiss the Charge upon the finding that it has no basis in fact;
> 2) dismiss the Charge upon the finding that, if proven, the Charge would not constitute Misconduct;
> 3) refer the matter for hearing by the Tribunal; or
> 4) in the case of criminal activity, refer the Charge(s) and all investigation results to the appropriate authority.

2.6
PROCEDURE FOR A MISCONDUCT HEARING BEFORE A TRIBUNAL
2.6(a)

> Upon the decision by the Committee that a matter should be heard, all parties shall be notified and a hearing date shall be set. The hearing shall take place no more than thirty (30) days from the conclusion of the formal investigation.

2.6(b)

The Responding Party shall have the right to counsel. The parties and the Tribunal shall have the right to call any witnesses and introduce any documentation that they believe will lead to the fair and reasonable resolution of the matter.

2.6(c)

Upon completion of the hearing, the Tribunal shall deliberate and present a written decision to the parties in accordance with procedures as set forth by the Tribunal.

2.6(d)

Notice of the decision of the Tribunal shall be appropriately published.

2.7

SANCTIONS

2.7(a)

Upon a finding of the Tribunal that misconduct has occurred, any of the following sanctions, or others as may be deemed appropriate, may be imposed upon the Responding Party, either singularly or in combination:
1) letter of reprimand to the Responding Party; counseling;
2) attendance at an ethics course approved by the Tribunal; probation;
3) suspension of license/authority to practice; revocation of license/authority to practice;
4) imposition of a fine; assessment of costs; or
5) in the instance of criminal activity, referral to the appropriate authority.

2.7(b)

Upon the expiration of any period of probation, suspension, or revocation, the Responding Party may make application for reinstatement. With the application for reinstatement, the Responding Party must show proof of having complied with all aspects of the sanctions imposed by the Tribunal.

2.8

APPELLATE PROCEDURES

2.8(a)

The parties shall have the right to appeal the decision of the Tribunal in accordance with the procedure as set forth by the Tribunal.

DEFINITIONS

"Appellate Body" means a body established to adjudicate an appeal to any decision made by a Tribunal or other decision-making body with respect to formally-heard Charges of Misconduct.

"Charge of Misconduct" means a written submission by any individual or entity to an ethics committee, paralegal association, bar association, law enforcement agency, judicial body, government agency, or other appropriate body or entity, that sets forth non-confidential information regarding any instance of alleged misconduct by an individual paralegal or paralegal entity.

"Charging Party" means any individual or entity who submits a Charge of Misconduct against an individual paralegal or paralegal entity.

"Competency" means the demonstration of: diligence, education, skill, and mental, emotional, and physical fitness reasonably necessary for the performance of paralegal services.

"Confidential Information" means information relating to a client, whatever its source, that is not public knowledge nor available to the public. ("Non-Confidential Information" would generally include the name of the client and the identity of the matter for which their paralegal provided services.)

"Disciplinary Hearing" means the confidential proceeding conducted by a committee or other designated body or entity concerning any instance of alleged misconduct by an individual paralegal or paralegal entity.

"Disciplinary Committee" means any committee that has been established by an entity such as a paralegal association, bar association, judicial body, or government agency to: (a) identify, define and investigate general ethical considerations and concerns with respect to paralegal practice; (b) administer and enforce the Model Code and Model Rules and; (c) discipline any individual paralegal or paralegal entity found to be in violation of same.

"Disclose" means communication of information reasonably sufficient to permit identification of the significance of the matter in question.

"Ethical Wall" means the screening method implemented in order to protect a client from a conflict of interest. An Ethical Wall generally includes, but is not limited to, the following elements: (1) prohibit the paralegal from having any connection with the matter; (2) ban discussions with or the transfer of documents to or from the paralegal; (3) restrict access to files; and (4) educate all members of the firm, corporation, or entity as to the separation of the paralegal (both organizationally and physically) from the pending matter. For more information regarding the Ethical Wall, see the NFPA publication entitled "The Ethical Wall — Its Application to Paralegals."

"Ex parte" means actions or communications conducted at the instance and for the benefit of one party only, and without notice to, or contestation by, any person adversely interested.

"Investigation" means the investigation of any charge(s) of misconduct filed against an individual paralegal or paralegal entity by a Committee.

"Letter of Reprimand" means a written notice of formal censure or severe reproof administered to an individual paralegal or paralegal entity for unethical or improper conduct.

"Misconduct" means the knowing or unknowing commission of an act that is in direct violation of those Canons and Ethical Considerations of any and all applicable codes and/or rules of conduct.

"Paralegal" is synonymous with "Legal Assistant" and is defined as a person qualified through education, training, or work experience to perform substantive legal work that requires knowledge of legal concepts and is customarily, but not exclusively, performed by a lawyer. This person may be retained or employed by a lawyer, law office, governmental agency, or other entity or may be authorized by administrative, statutory, or court authority to perform this work.

"Pro Bono Publico" means providing or assisting to provide quality legal services in order to enhance access to justice for persons of limited means; charitable, religious, civic, community, governmental and educational organizations in matters that are designed primarily to address the legal needs of persons with limited means; or individuals, groups, or organizations seeking to secure or protect civil rights, civil liberties or public rights.

"Proper Authority" means the local paralegal association, the local or state bar association, Committee(s) of the local paralegal or bar association(s), local prosecutor, administrative agency, or other tribunal empowered to investigate or act upon an instance of alleged misconduct.

"Responding Party" means an individual paralegal or paralegal entity against whom a Charge of Misconduct has been submitted.

"Revocation" means the recession of the license, certificate, or other authority to practice of an individual paralegal or paralegal entity found in violation of those Canons and Ethical Considerations of any and all applicable codes and/or rules of conduct.

"Suspension" means the suspension of the license, certificate or other authority to practice of an individual paralegal or paralegal entity found in violation of these Canons and Ethical Considerations of any and all applicable codes and/or rules of conduct.

"Tribunal" means the body designated to adjudicate allegations of misconduct.

ABA Model Standards and Guidelines for Utilization of Legal Assistants[3]

NALA's study of the professional responsibility and ethical considerations of legal assistants is ongoing. This research led to the development of the NALA Model Standards and Guidelines for Utilization of Legal Assistants. This guide summarizes case law, guidelines, and ethical opinions of the various states affecting legal assistants. It provides an outline of minimum qualifications and standards necessary for legal assistant professionals to assure the public and the legal profession that they are, indeed, qualified. The following is a listing of the standards and guidelines. The annotated version of the Model was revised extensively in 1997. It is on-line — NALA Model Standards and Guidelines — and may be ordered through NALA Headquarters.

Introduction

Proper utilization of the services of legal assistants affects the efficient delivery of legal services. Legal assistants and the legal profession should be assured that some measures exist for identifying legal assistants and their role in assisting attorneys in the delivery of legal services. Therefore, the National Association of Legal Assistants, Inc., hereby adopts these Model Standards and Guidelines as an educational document for the benefit of legal assistants and the legal profession.

Standards

A legal assistant should meet certain minimum qualifications. The following standards may be used to determine an individual's qualifications as a legal assistant:

1. Successful completion of the Certified Legal Assistant certifying (CLA) examination of the National Association of Legal Assistants;
2. Graduation from an ABA approved program of study for legal assistants;
3. Graduation from a course of study for legal assistants which is institutionally accredited but not ABA approved, and which requires not less than the equivalent of 60 semester hours of classroom study;
4. Graduation from a course of study for legal assistants, other than those set forth in (2) and (3) above, plus not less than six months of in-house training as a legal assistant;
5. A baccalaureate degree in any field, plus not less than six months in-house training as a legal assistant.
6. A minimum of three years of law-related experience under the supervision of an attorney, including at least six months of in-house training as a legal assistant; or
7. Two years of in-house training as a legal assistant.

---

[3] Used by permission of the American Bar Association.

For purposes of these Standards, "in-house training as a legal assistant" means attorney education of the employee concerning legal assistant duties and these Guidelines. In addition to review and analysis of assignments, the legal assistant should receive a reasonable amount of instruction directly related to the duties and obligations of the legal assistant.

Guidelines

These guidelines relating to standards of performance and professional responsibility are intended to aid legal assistants and attorneys. The responsibility rests with an attorney who employs legal assistants to educate them with respect to the duties they are assigned and to supervise the manner in which such duties are accomplished.

Guideline 1

Legal assistants should:
1. Disclose their status as legal assistants at the outset of any professional relationship with a client, other attorneys, a court or administrative agency or personnel thereof, or members of the general public;
2. Preserve the confidences and secrets of all clients; and
3. Understand the Attorney's Code of Professional Responsibility and these guidelines in order to avoid any action which would involve the attorney in a violation of that Code, or give the appearance of professional impropriety.

Guideline 2

Legal assistants should not:
1. Establish attorney-client relationships; set legal fees, give legal opinions or advice; or represent a client before a court; nor
2. Engage in, encourage, or contribute to any act which would constitute the unauthorized practice of law.

Guideline 3

Legal assistants may perform services for an attorney in the representation of a client, provided:
1. The services performed by the legal assistant do not require the exercise of independent professional legal judgment;
2. The attorney maintains a direct relationship with the client and maintains control of all client matters;
3. The attorney supervises the legal assistant;
4. The attorney remains professionally responsible for all work on behalf of the client, including any actions taken or not taken by the legal assistant in connection therewith; and
5. The services performed supplement, merge with, and become the attorney's work product.

Guideline 4

In the supervision of a legal assistant, consideration should be given to:

1. Designating work assignments that correspond to the legal assistant's abilities, knowledge, training, and experience.
2. Educating and training the legal assistant with respect to professional responsibility, local rules and practices, and firm policies;
3. Monitoring the work and professional conduct of the legal assistant to ensure that the work is substantively correct and timely performed;
4. Providing continuing education for the legal assistant in substantive matters through courses, institutes, workshops, seminars, and in-house training; and
5. Encouraging and supporting membership and active participation in professional organizations.

Guideline 5

Except as otherwise provided by statute, court rule or decision, administrative rule or regulation, or the Attorney's Code of Professional Responsibility, and within the preceding parameters and proscriptions, a legal assistant may perform any function delegated by an attorney, including but not limited to the following:

1. Conduct client interviews and maintain general contact with the client after the establishment of the attorney-client relationship, so long as the client is aware of the status and function of the legal assistant, and the client contact is under the supervision of the attorney.
2. Locate and interview witnesses, so long as the witnesses are aware of the status and function of the legal assistant.
3. Conduct investigations and statistical and documentary research for review by the attorney.
4. Conduct legal research for review by the attorney.
5. Draft legal documents for review by the attorney.
6. Draft correspondence and pleadings for review by and signature of the attorney.
7. Summarize depositions, interrogatories, and testimony for review by the attorney.
8. Attend executions of wills, real estate closings, depositions, and court or administrative hearings and trials with the attorney.
9. Author and sign letters provided the legal assistant's status is clearly indicated and the correspondence does not contain independent legal opinions or legal advice.

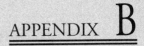
APPENDIX B

Comparison of Selected ALWD and Bluebook 17th Edition Rules

RULE	ALWD CITATION	BLUEBOOK CITATION	DIFFERENCES
Typeface (Rule 1)	Ordinary type and *italics* (or underlining). No distinctions based on type of document (law review v. court document) or place-ment of citation within the paper.	Ordinary type, *italics* (or underlining), and small caps. Different fonts required depending on type of document and where source is cited within the paper.	ALWD has one set of conventions, not two. ALWD eliminates small caps as a typeface.
Spacing (Rule 2)	F. Supp. F.3d	F. Supp. F.3d	No substantial differences.
Capitalization (Rule 3)	*Federal Civil Procedure before Trial*	*Federal Civil Procedure Before Trial*	ALWD eliminates the "and prepositions of four or fewer letters" part of the *Bluebook*, which brings legal citation closer to non-legal style.
Ordinal Numbers (Rule 4) Page spans (Rule 5)	1st, 2d, 3d, 4th 125-126 **or** 125-26	1st, 2d, 3d, 4th 125-26	No substantial differences. ALWD gives a choice on how to present a page span; you may retain all digits or drop repetitive digits and retain two digits on the right-hand side of the span, as in *Bluebook* 3.3(d).
Footnotes and endnotes (Rule 7)	n. 7 nn. 12-13	n.7 nn.12-13	ALWD requires a space after n. or nn. abbreviation.

From D. Dickerson, ANLD Citation Manual: A Professional System of Citation available at www.alwd.org. Used by permission of Aspen Law & Business.

RULE	ALWD CITATION	BLUEBOOK CITATION	DIFFERENCES
Supra and *infra* (Rule 10)	*Supra* n. 45.	*Supra* note 45.	Under ALWD, abbreviate note as "n." and place a space after the period.
Id. (Rule 11.3)	*Id.* at 500.	*Id.* at 500.	Basically similar rules. ALWD eliminates the "5 *id.* in a row" rule found in *Bluebook* 10.9.
Cases (Rule 12)	*Brown v. Bd. of Educ.*, 349 U.S. 294, 297 (1955). *MBNA Am. Bank, N.A. v. Cardoso*, 707 N.E.2d 189 (Ill. App. 1st Dist. 1998). [required inclusion of district court information]	*Brown v. Bd. of Educ.*, 349 U.S. 294, 297 (1955). *MBNA Am. Bank, N.A. v. Cardoso*, 707 N.E.2d 189 (Ill. App. 1st Dist. 1998). [permissive inclusion of district information] Under 10.3.3, the *Bluebook* provides for public domain citation. Under this rule, the official public domain citation must be given as well as the parallel citation to the regional reporter, if available. *Beck v. Beck*, 1999 ME 110, ¶ 6, 733 A. 2d 981, 983.	Case names are always italicized. Do not have to abbreviate words in case names. For those who want to abbreviate, Appendix 3 provides a longer list of words. ALWD eliminates the "multiple date" rule found in *Bluebook* 10.5. ALWD uses S. instead of So. for the regional reporter. ALWD requires division and district information for state appellate courts.

RULE	ALWD CITATION	BLUEBOOK CITATION	DIFFERENCES
		Rule 10 now allows abbreviation of the first word of a party's name when the name appears in Table 6.	"Ct." eliminated from most court abbreviations.
			For cases cited from Westlaw or LEXIS, ALWD does not require the docket number of the case. ALWD also requires two asterisks to iden-tify multiple pages of a pinpoint cite.
Constitutions (Rule 13)	U.S. Const. amend. V	U.S. Const. amend. V.	No substantial differences.
Statutes (Rule 14)	18 U.S.C. § 1965 (1994).	18 U.S.C. § 1965 (1994).	No substantial differences.
Legislative Materials (Rules 15 and 16)	Sen. Res. 35, 106th Cong. (1999).	S. Res. 35, 106th Cong. (1999).	ALWD abbreviates Senate as "Sen." instead of "S." to avoid confusion with other abbreviations. Most forms are relatively consistent.
Court Rules (Rule 17)	Fed. R. Civ. P. 11 (1999).	Fed. R. Civ. P. 11.	ALWD requires a date, even for current rules, to help avoid confu-sion.
Administrative Materials (Rules 19 and 20)	42 C.F.R. § 422.206(a) (1999).	42 C.F.R. § 422.206(a) (1999).	C.F.R. citation is the same.
	64 Fed. Reg. 12473 (Mar. 12, 1999).	64 Fed. Reg. 12473 (1999).	ALWD requires an exact date for Fed. Reg. citations.

RULE	ALWD CITATION	BLUEBOOK CITATION	DIFFERENCES
Books and Treatises (Rule 22)	Charles Alan Wright, Arthur R. Miller, & Mary Kay Kane, *Federal Practice and Procedure* vol. 6A, § 1497, 70–79 (2d ed., West 1990). OR Charles Alan Wright et al., *Federal Practice and Procedure* vol. 6A, § 1497, 70–79 (2d ed., West 1990).	6A Charles Alan Wright, Arthur R. Miller & Mary Kay Kane, *Federal Practice and Procedure* § 1497, at 70–79 (2d ed. 1990). OR 6A Charles Alan Wright et al., *Federal Practice and Procedure* § 1497, at 70–79 (2d ed. 1990).	ALWD places volume information after the title, just like any other subdivision. ALWD separates subdivisions separated with a comma, but no "at." ALWD requires that the publisher be included.
Legal Periodicals (Rule 23)	L. Ray Patterson, *Legal Ethics and the Lawyer's Duty of Loyalty*, 29 Emory L.J. 909, 915 (1980). Hope Viner Samborn, *Navigating Murky Waters*, 85 ABA J. 28 (July 1998). Tara Burns Koch, Student Author, *Betting on Brownfields—Does Florida's Brownfields Redevelopment Act Transform Liability into Opportunity?*, 28 Stetson L. Rev. 171 (1998).	L. Ray Patterson, *Legal Ethics and the Lawyer's Duty of Loyalty*, 29 Emory L.J. 909, 915 (1980). Hope Viner Samborn, *Navigating Murky Waters*, A.B.A. J., July 1998, at 28. Tara Burns Koch, Comment, *Betting on Brownfields—Does Florida's Brownfields Redevelopment Act Transform Liability into Opportunity?*, 28 Stetson L. Rev. 171 (1998).	ALWD eliminates most distinctions between consecutively and non-consecutively paginated articles. Include longer date for non-consecutively paginated journals, but do so within the parenthetical. ALWD uses the term "Student Author" to replace Note, Comment, etc.

RULE	ALWD CITATION	BLUEBOOK CITATION	DIFFERENCES
A.L.R. Annotations (Rule 24)	Marjorie A. Caner, *Validity, Construction, and Application of Stalking Statutes*, 29 A.L.R. 5th 487, 489 (1995).	Marjorie A. Caner, Annotation, *Validity, Construction, and Application of Stalking Statutes*, 29 A.L.R.5th 487, 489 (1995).	ALWD eliminates the "Annotation" reference.
Legal Dictionaries (Rule 25)	*Black's Law Dictionary* 101 (Bryan A. Garner ed., 7th ed., West 1999).	*Black's Law Dictionary* 101 (7th ed. 1999).	ALWD treats dictionaries like treatises.
Legal Encyclopedias (Rule 26)	11 C.J.S. *Bonds* § 21 (1995).

76 Am. Jur. 2d *Trusts* §§ 1–4 (1992 & Supp. 1999). | 11 C.J.S. *Bonds* § 21 (1995).

76 Am. Jur. 2d *Trusts* §§ 1–4 (1992 & Supp. 1999). | No substantial differences; however, ALWD provides expanded coverage and includes a list of many abbreviations for state encyclopedias. |
| Web Sites (Rule 40) | Federal Judicial Center, *Federal Judicial Center Publications* <http://www.fjc. gov/pubs.html> (accessed July 10, 1999). | Federal Judicial Center, *Federal Judicial Center Publications* (visited July 10, 1999) <http://www. fjc.gov/pubs.html>. | ALWD moved the date to end to be more consistent with other sources.

ALWD uses "accessed" instead of "visited" to give a more professional tone and be consistent with non-legal citation guides. |

RULE	ALWD CITATION	BLUEBOOK CITATION	DIFFERENCES
Neutral Citation (Rule 43)	ALWD indicates that neutral citation may be used (not limited to cases). ALWD also indicates that a parallel citation to a print source should also be used. ALWD permits use of the citation format used by the state whose case is being cited, the citation used on the source, or the form suggested by the AALL.	The *Bluebook* indicates that a public domain citation for cases must be used when available and requires a parallel citation.	
Signals (Rule 45)	Signals are *e.g., see, cf., contra, compare . . with, but see, but cf.,* and *see generally.*	Signals are *e.g., accord, see, see also, cf., contra, compare . . . with, but see, but cf.,* and *see generally.* In Rule 1.2, among other things, in the 17th edition, *e.g.* was restored to a separate signal, the definition of *see* changed, and **contra** was revived.	ALWD eliminates the *accord* and *see also* signals because they are too close to other signals. Under ALWD, all signals may be separated with semicolons. ALWD does not have a comma after *e.g.*
Order of Citations (Rule 46)	ALWD lists federal and state court cases first by jurisdiction, then in reverse chronological order.	Federal and state court cases are ordered in reverse chronological order.	
Quotations (Rule 48)	ALWD says to block indent passages if they contain at least fifty words OR if they exceed four lines of typed text.	The *Bluebook* says to block indent passages if they contain at least 50 words.	ALWD does not require you to count the exact number of words in long quotations.

Glossary

Act: Public law.

Active Voice: Form of verb used when the sentence subject is the doer of action.

Adjectives: Words that modify or describe nouns.

Advance sheets: A paperback pamphlet containing very recent decisions not yet officially (or unofficially) bound.

Adverbs: Words that modify or describe verbs, adjectives, or other adverbs.

Advice letters: Letters offering a client legal advice on a problem.

Advocacy or persuasive memorandum: A legal memorandum arguing for a particular result.

Affirm: To agree with or enforce a lower court decision.

ALWD citation system: Alternate (to the bluebook) citation guide.

Amended: Changed.

American Jurisprudence 2d (Am.Jur. 2d): Lawyer's Cooperative Publishing's national legal encyclopedia.

American Law Reports (A.L.R.): Reports of selected cases with accompanying annotations analyzing the law of the case nationally.

Analysis: The application of existing law to the facts of the case.

Appellant: The party appealing a lower court decision.

Appellate appendix: Compilation of lower court documents, transcript, and decisions required to decide the appeal.

Appellate brief: A written document setting out the case factual and procedural background and making legal arguments for reversing or affirming a lower court decision.

Appellate process: The process by which a losing litigant seeks review of an adverse court decision.

Appellee: The party supporting a lower court decision.

Applicable Statute(s): Copy of relevant parts of any constitutional, statutory, or regulatory provisions necessary to the analysis.

Argument: Application of legal principles to the facts of the case.

ARPANET: The original "Internet" created by the U.S. Department of Defense to protect research contracts and projects with various universities around the country.

Assembling the record: Compiling the lower court record.

AutoCite®: Reed's automated service for retrieving and validating cited material.

Beyond a reasonable doubt: The government's very high standard of proof in a criminal prosecution. The beyond a reasonable doubt standard reflects society's belief that it is better that ten criminals go free than that a single innocent person be jailed.

Bicameral: "Of two houses," as compared to unilateral, "of one house."

Bill number: A number issued proposed legislation.

Bill of Rights: First ten amendments to the United States Constitution.

Bill: Proposed legislation.

Bluebook: A Uniform System of Citation, published by The Harvard Law Review Association.

Body: The information the writer wishes to convey.

Boolean searching: CALR searching for documents based on key words.

Brief Answer(s): Summary of the answer to the question presented in a research memorandum.

Browsers: Internet programs that help locate information.

Browsing: Looking through retrieved documents.

Canons of statutory construction: Rules developed over the years to aid in statutory interpretation.

Caption: Court, case, and litigation in which the memo is filed.

Case brief: A structured summary of an appellate court decision.

Case Name Citator: Volumes listing cases alphabetically by plaintiff and defendant name.

CD-ROM: Compact disk, read-only memory; a storage device for legal research information.

Centered: Having the center of the lines of the document aligned with the document's vertical center.

Certificate of service: Attorney's sworn statement that the memorandum was provided to the opponent in a timely fashion.

Circuit: A geographical region covered by an appellate court.

Citation clauses: Clauses identifying the location of a legal document.

Citation field: Where a CALR document is located.

Citation: A phrase or sentence identifying the location of a legal document.

Cited material: Material whose validity and currentness the researcher wishes to check.

Citing material: More recent material citing and cited material.

Civil case: A case brought between individuals (plaintiff and defendant) for damages or other wrongs allegedly caused by the defendant.

Close: Letter closing words and typed name and title of signer.

Closing Table: Chart in digest supplements indicating the most current reporter volume available when supplement was published.

Code of Federal Regulations (C.F.R.): Official publication of federal agency regulations.

Codify: Include in topically arranged published laws.

Common law: Court-made law.

Computer Assisted Legal Research (CALR): Legal research accomplished through the use of a computer.

Concise: Succinct.

Conclusion: Author's conclusion from her argument and request for relief.

Confirmation letters: Letters confirming appointments or conversations.

Congress: The federal legislature.

Connectors: AND, OR, NEAR, WITHIN, BUT NOT; words that set the proximity of words in full-text searching.

Copies and enclosures: Indicates where copies, if any, are being sent.

Corpus Juris Secundum (CJS): West Group's national legal encyclopedia.

Court rule: Rule of procedure governing court actions.

Cover letters: Letters transmitting material to the receiver.

Criminal case: A case brought by the government to redress societal harms; a criminal case is always brought under an applicable criminal statute; the penalties are most often fines, jail, and/or community service.

Database: Collection of related CALR information.

Defendant-Plaintiff Table of Cases: An alphabetic listing of case citations by defendant's name.

Defendant: The party defending against or opposing a lawsuit.

Deliberative Process: A process by which a body makes decisions.

Demand letters: Letters demanding response of the receiver.

Descriptive word index: Digest topical index.

Digest: An alphabetically and topically organized collection of case headnotes.

Docket the appeal: Enter an appeal in the appellate court.

Documents: CALR research materials.

Download: Print or save CALR research off-line.

Editorial features: Publisher-created aids to legal research.

Educative Process: A process by which one is educated.

Ejusdem generis: Where a statute specifically enumerates items followed by a catchall phrase, the catchall phrase applies only to items in the same class.

Elegant Variation: Substituting more complicated words or phrases for simpler, shorter words and phrases.

Elements: Stated preconditions to operation of the statute.

Enjoining: Prohibition by a judicial order. See injunction.

Executive Agency, Department: An executive department or officer empowered to carry out the purposes of one or more statutes.

Executive Order: Statement of executive policy issued by the chief executive.

Executive Proclamations: Chief executive's statements commemorating a public event.

Expel: To force to leave (as a place or organization) by official action: take away rights or privileges of membership <expelled from college>.

Expressio unis est exclusio alternus: The expression of one context requires denial in other contexts;

Facts: Summary of the factual and procedural background of the case.

Federal Administrative Procedure Act: Statute governing procedure before federal agencies.

Federal depository library: Library storing federal government documents.

Federal law: Any case involving the United States Constitution, federal laws, or federal decisions.

Federal Register: A daily publication of agency activities, including proposed rules, final rules, notices, regulatory agenda, Presidential documents.

Federal Reporter®: A reporter of United States Circuit Court decisions.

Federal Rules of Appellate Procedure (FRAP): Rules governing appeals in the federal appellate courts.

Federal Supplement®: A reporter of United States District Court decisions.

Fields: Discrete sections of CALR-retrieved documents.

Finding aids: A remark, note, case summary, or commentary on some passage of a book, statute, or case directing the researcher to more materials.

Fog Index: A numerical scale for judging the reading level of a piece of writing.

Freestyle search: English-language searching capability offered on LEXIS.

Full-text Searching: Word-for-word searching of documents to determine their relevance to the issue researched.

Fully justified: All lines in the document lined up with both left and right margins.

Government Printing Office (GPO): Official publisher of federal government legal materials.

Hard-wired: Computers wired directly to each other.

Harmonizing: Resolving seemingly conflicting legal resources into a rule applicable to a broader class of cases.

Heading and Reference: Identify the sender, receiver, and subject matter of a legal research memorandum.

Headnote field: Summary of a legal point decided in a case.

Headnote number: One of a series of numbers identifying headnotes to a case.

Headnotes: Publisher's summary of a single point of law addressed in a case.

History: Treatment of the case on appeal and/or remand.

Hornbooks: Text or elementary books on a single legal subject.

House of Representatives: One of two houses in the federal legislature. Members of House of Representatives include varying numbers (based on district population) of state-elected representatives serving two-year terms.

HTTP: HyperText Transfer Protocol—the language of the Internet.

Hypertext: Words that link Web pages together.

In derogation of the common law: Statutes changing the common law.

In pari materia: Statutes related to the same subject should be read consistently.

Index to Legal Periodicals: Index of legal journals and law reviews.

Informational letters: Letters conveying information to receiver.

Injunction: Court order to do (or stop doing) a certain action.

Inside address: Address of the person to whom the letter is sent.

Internet service providers (ISPs): Organizations providing access to the Internet or a CALR on-line service.

Internet: A worldwide network of computers sharing information.

Introduction: Statement of the purpose of the advocacy memo.

Issue, rule, application, and conclusion (IRAC): A method of written analysis that consists of stating the *i*ssue involved, the applicable *r*ule, *a*pplying that rule to the client's factual situation, and *c*oncluding the likely result in the client's situation.

Issues on appeal: Claims of legal error in the lower court.

Judge or author field: The author of a computer document.

Judgment: A final decision in a case after trial.

Jurisdiction: The power of a court to act. Jurisdiction includes the power to act in certain geographical regions, subject areas, and over persons and things.

Key numbers: Numbered digest subtopics.

Law reviews and journals: Student written, edited, and produced journals of articles on current legal topics.

Left justified: All lines in the document lined up with the left margin.

Legal Analysis: The process of applying legal research (the law) to the facts of a client's situation.

Legal research memorandum: Balanced, informative legal memorandum.

Legal synthesis: Deriving (from a variety of legal sources) and applying a legal rule to a client's situation.

Legalese: Arcane Latin or legal words and phrases.

Letterhead: Name and address of the sender.

LexCite®: Reed's CALR tool for gathering the previous and subsequent history of cited material.

LEXIS: CALR service based on official publications.

List of C.F.R. Sections Affected (L.S.A.): Publication of Federal Register documents affecting the Code of Federal Regulations.

Local area networks: Networks of computers within offices, businesses, or homes.

Loose-leaf services: Easily updated three-ring binders of materials.

Mailing notations: Notations of special handling the letter received.

Meta-engines: Search engines that use other engines to do multiple searches of a single query.

Mini-digests: Short digests in case reporters digesting only decisions appearing in that volume.

Mode: Browsing method.

Modem: Device for transmitting data over a telephone line.

Natural language search: English-language searching capability offered on Westlaw.

Nodes: Computers on the Internet.

Notice of appeal: Document filed in trial court notifying the trial court and adverse parties that a litigant plans to seek review of a court decision by an appellate court.

Official publication: Legal materials published by the government.

Opinion field: The court's words in a CALR document.

Oral argument: Oral presentation to appellate court of litigants' arguments in favor of or against the decision of the lower court.

Outlines: Word diagrams for legal analysis.

Page: A computer screen of data.

Paragraphs: One or more sentences about a single topic.

Parallel citations: Two or more locations for a single research document.

Parallel structure: Words, phrases, or clauses of similar form and structure.

Parts Affected Tables: A section of the Federal Register which daily lists updates to federal regulations.

Passim: Throughout.

Passive Voice: Form of verb used when the sentence subject receives the action.

Password: Code necessary to access and pay for use of CALR service.

Personal computer: A small compact computer for personal use.

Petition for rehearing: Request that the appellate court re-hear the case.

Plaintiff: The complaining party or government (in a criminal case); the party bringing the lawsuit.

Pocket parts: Paperback supplements stored in the backs of legal research books.

Pocket veto: When an executive refuses to act on a bill and the legislature adjourns during the ten days for executive action, the bill is said to be "pocket vetoed."

Popular Names Table: A table cross-referencing statutes' common names to their official citation.

Pre-hearing conference: Conference held by a court to prepare a case for trial or appeal.

Preconditions: Necessary conditions that must be met before statute will operate.

Preponderance of evidence: The standard of proof in a civil case. To prove a case by the preponderance of evidence, a civil litigant need only prove that her version of events more likely occurred than her opponent's.

Prima facie case: The minimum case a plaintiff (or the state) must prove to sustain its burden of proof; the elements of a cause of action.

Primary sources: Research materials containing the law.

Procedural issues: An issue involving how the legal system operates: Did police violate the criminal defendant's constitutional right against unreasonable search and seizure? Has the plaintiff waited too long to bring her lawsuit?

Promulgating: Enacting agency rules and regulations.

Public Law: A bill passed by both congressional houses. Same as act.

Question(s) Presented: A short statement of the legal question addressed in a legal research memorandum.

QuickCite®: West's automated system for using Westlaw as a citator.

Rank: Number of documents retrieved.

Redundancy: Repetition.

Reference: The letter's topic.

Regional reporters: West published appellate court opinions grouped geographically.

Regulations: Rules promulgated by a government agency regulating rights and procedures before the agency.

Remand: Return a case for further action.

Reply briefs: Appellant's answers to appellee's briefs.

Research Verification: Checking the validity of documents relevant to an issue.

Retrieve: Find and return information.

Reverse: Overturn a lower court decision and either enter a proper decision, or if more evidence is necessary, remand the case for further action by the lower court.

Road signs: Headings delineating different parts of a writing.

Salutation: The letter's greeting.

Search engine: Software that searches Web pages for relevant query language.

Secondary materials: Research materials about the law.

Senate: One of two houses in the federal legislature. Members of Senate include two elected senators from each state serving six-year terms.

Separation of powers: The principle that each branch of government is independent and may not intrude on other branches' duties.

Shepard's Citations®: Listings of the citations of materials citing earlier legal materials.

Shepard's history codes: Code letters describing a cited document's history before and after its existence.

Shepard's supplements: Red softbound volumes updating bound Shepard's Citations.

Shepard's treatment codes: Code letters describing a document's treatment by other, more recent materials.

Shepardizing®: Checking the validity of research materials through Shepard's Citations.

Signature and date: "Respectfully submitted," the advocate identity (including any attorney number, if required by the court), address, and represented party.

Slip law: The pamphlet form of a law when first enacted.

State law: Laws of a state or ordinances of a city or town (compare to federal law).

Statement of Facts: A summary of the case factual and procedural background.

Statutory preamble: Legislature's statement of purpose in enacting a statute.

Statutory title: Title of legislation.

Substantive issues: An issue involving the merits of a law suit: Is the criminal defendant guilty? Did the defendant breach his contract with the plaintiff?

Sunshine Act: Open Meeting Law; requires that government meetings be open to the public.

Supreme Court Reporter®, Lawyer's Edition (L. Ed.): An unofficial reporter of United States Supreme Court decisions, published by Lawyers Cooperative Publishing.

Supreme Court Reporter® (S. Ct.): An unofficial reporter of United States Supreme Court decisions, published by West Group.

TCP/IP: Internet communication language or "protocol."

Terms-and-connectors searching: CALR searching for documents based on key words.

Thinking: That preliminary part of legal analysis that occurs in the legal professional's head before she puts pen to paper.

Throat-clearing phrases: Unnecessary words introducing a sentence or topic.

Title field: Document name.

Titled: Labeled according to the numbering system for federal statutes.

Topic Analysis: Outline of key numbers or sections in a digest topic.

Topic and key number: West's system of indexing and cross-referencing legal materials.

Transcript: Written record of what occurred in a trial court.

Transmittal letters: Letters transmitting material to the receiver.

Treatises: Scholarly books on a single legal subject.

Trial court legal memorandum: A form of advocacy memo filed in the trial court.

Uniform Resource Locators (URLs): Electronic "addresses" for information on the internet.

United States Circuit Courts of Appeal: Intermediate appellate courts for the federal government. Each of the thirteen circuit courts hears appeals from the federal district courts in its region.

United States Code Annotated® (U.S.C.A.): West publication of federal statutes.

United States Code Service (U.S.C.S.): Reed publication of federal statutes.

United States Code: Official publication of federal statutes.

United States District Courts: Federal trial courts. Numbering more than ninety, the federal district courts try cases involving federal questions or diversity of citizenship.

United States Law Week: Weekly newspaper of federal court activity.

United States Reports: Official publication of United States Supreme Court decisions

United States Statutes at Large: Compilation of slip laws.

United States Supreme Court: Highest federal court. Nine justices hear appeals from the thirteen national circuit courts of appeal in cases involving federal questions.

Unofficial publications: Legal materials published by a private publisher.

Update: Find the most recent references for a legal issue.

Using the CALR as a citator: Using a CALR to search for subsequent references to a cited document.

Vagueness: Unclear of meaning.

Verdict: The jury's decision.

Veto: Act of an executive officer declining to enact legislation passed by the legislature.

Web pages: Information documents on the Internet.

WestCheck®: West Group's automated service for retrieving and validating cited material.

Westlaw®: CALR service based on the West Group publications.

Word processors: Computer-aided typing and revising systems. Typical word processors include Microsoft Word and WordPerfect.

Wordiness: Using many or long words when fewer or shorter words will do.

World Wide Web: The Internet. Also, the Web or "www."

Writ of certiorari: A request to appeal to the highest court in a jurisdiction, usually the United States Supreme Court.

Written legal analysis: Rendering legal analysis to paper for the benefit of others.

Index